ANNUAL REVIEW OF
Global Peace Operations
2008

This volume is a product of the Center on International Cooperation's (CIC) Global Peace Operations program. The CIC is an independent institution housed at New York University.

Project Team

VOLUME EDITOR AND RESEARCH SCHOLAR
A. Sarjoh Bah

SERIES EDITOR
Bruce D. Jones

SERIES COORDINATOR
Benjamin C. Tortolani

RESEARCH OFFICER
Victoria DiDomenico

GUEST CONTRIBUTORS
Lakhdar Brahimi, Salman Ahmed

CONTRIBUTORS
Marcus E. Bouillon, Adam Day, Lansana Gberie,
Richard Gowan, Gordon Peake, Martin Rupiya,
Jake Sherman, Erin Weir

The project's advisory board is composed of Lakhdar Brahimi, Jayantha Dhanapala, Rosario Green, 'Funmi Olonisakin, John Ruggie, Sir Rupert Smith, and Stephen J. Stedman. CIC is grateful for their advice and support.

The Center on International Cooperation is solely responsible for the content of this publication. Any errors of fact or analysis, and any and all judgments and interpretations about missions and operations discussed herein, are those of the CIC alone.

This project was undertaken at the request of and with the support of the Best Practices Section of the UN Department of Peacekeeping Operations.

ANNUAL REVIEW OF
Global Peace Operations

2008

A PROJECT OF THE
Center on International Cooperation

LYNNE
RIENNER
PUBLISHERS

BOULDER
LONDON

Published in the United States of America in 2008 by
Lynne Rienner Publishers, Inc.
1800 30th Street, Boulder, Colorado 80301
www.rienner.com

and in the United Kingdom by
Lynne Rienner Publishers, Inc.
3 Henrietta Street, Covent Garden, London WC2E 8LU

ISBN: 978-1-58826-564-7
ISSN: 1932-5819

Printed and bound in Canada

The paper used in this publication meets the requirements
of the American National Standard for Permanence of
Paper for Printed Library Materials Z39.48-1992.

5 4 3 2 1

Contents

Preface, *Bruce D. Jones*   vii
List of Mission Acronyms   ix
Map of Global Peace Operations, 2007   xii

Strategic Summary 2007   1

1 In Pursuit of Sustainable Peace:
   The Seven Deadly Sins of Mediation   9
   Lakhdar Brahimi and Salman Ahmed

2 Peace Operation Partnerships: Lessons and Issues from
   Coordination to Hybrid Arrangements   21
   A. Sarjoh Bah and Bruce D. Jones

3 Mission Reviews   31
   Alphabetical order by location

   3.1 Afghanistan (ISAF, UNAMA)   32
   3.2 Democratic Republic of Congo
        (MONUC, EUSEC RD Congo, EUPOL RD Congo)   41
   3.3 Kosovo (UNMIK, KFOR, OMIK)   49
   3.4 Liberia (UNMIL)   57
   3.5 Middle East (UNIFIL, UNDOF, UNTSO, EUBAM Rafah,
        EUPOL COPPS, TIPH, MFO Sinai)   64
   3.6 Sudan (AMIS, UNAMID, UNMIS)   73
   3.7 Timor-Leste (UNMIT, International Security Forces)   82

4 Mission Notes   89
   Alphabetical order by location

   4.1 Abkhazia-Georgia (UNOMIG, CIS)   90
   4.2 Bosnia and Herzegovina (EUFOR Althea, EUPM,
        OSCE, NATO Headquarters Sarajevo)   93
   4.3 Burundi (BINUB)   96
   4.4 Central African Republic (FOMUC, BONUCA)   99
   4.5 Chad (MINURCAT, EUFOR TCHAD/RCA)   101
   4.6 Comoros (MAES)   103
   4.7 Côte d'Ivoire (UNOCI, Operation Licorne)   105
   4.8 Cyprus (UNFICYP)   108
   4.9 Ethiopia and Eritrea (UNMEE)   110

4.10   Haiti (MINUSTAH, OAS)   112
4.11   India and Pakistan (UNMOGIP)   116
4.12   Iraq (MNF-I, NTM-I, UNAMI)   117
4.13   Mindanao, Philippines (IMT)   119
4.14   Moldova-Transdniestria (CIS)   121
4.15   Nepal (UNMIN)   123
4.16   Sierra Leone (UNIOSIL)   125
4.17   Solomon Islands (RAMSI)   127
4.18   Somalia (AMISOM)   129
4.19   South Ossetia–Georgia (CIS, OSCE)   131
4.20   Sri Lanka (SLMM)   133
4.21   Western Sahara (MINURSO)   134

5   Global Statistics on UN Missions   137

6   Global Statistics on Non-UN Missions   167

7   UN Mission-by-Mission Statistics   195
    Alphabetical order by mission acronym

7.1   BINUB (UN Integrated Office in Burundi)   200
7.2   MINURSO (UN Mission for the Referendum in Western Sahara)   204
7.3   MINUSTAH (UN Stabilization Mission in Haiti)   211
7.4   MONUC (UN Organization Mission in the Democratic Republic of Congo)   220
7.5   UNAMA (UN Assistance Mission in Afghanistan)   230
7.6   UNAMI (UN Assistance Mission for Iraq)   238
7.7   UNDOF (UN Disengagement Observer Force)   246
7.8   UNFICYP (UN Peacekeeping Force in Cyprus)   254
7.9   UNIFIL (UN Interim Force in Lebanon)   263
7.10 UNIOSIL (UN Integrated Office for Sierra Leone)   273
7.11 UNMEE (UN Mission in Ethiopia and Eritrea)   279
7.12 UNMIK (UN Interim Administration Mission in Kosovo)   288
7.13 UNMIL (UN Mission in Liberia)   296
7.14 UNMIN (UN Mission in Nepal)   306
7.15 UNMIS (UN Mission in the Sudan)   311
7.16 UNMIT (UN Integrated Mission in Timor-Leste)   321
7.17 UNMOGIP (UN Military Observer Group in India and Pakistan)   328
7.18 UNOCI (UN Operation in Côte d'Ivoire)   333
7.19 UNOMIG (UN Observer Mission in Georgia)   343
7.20 UNTSO (UN Truce Supervision Organization)   351

8   Statistics on the African Union Mission in Sudan   357

Index   367
About the Book   375

Preface

The 2008 edition of the *Annual Review of Global Peace Operations* comes at a time when turbulence in some of the world's hotspots is creating rising demand for peacekeepers and simultaneously complicating their work. In this context, the *Annual Review*'s unique compilation of data and analysis on both UN and non-UN peace operations* continues to be recognized as a valuable resource to support policymaking and research on this increasingly important dimension of global security.

The *Annual Review* is editorially independent but produced with the support of the UN Department of Peacekeeping Operations (DPKO), Best Practices Section, and the African Union's Peace and Security Department. The Center on International Cooperation (CIC) remains grateful to the two institutions for their continued support. Special thanks to Jean-Marie Guèhenno, the UN Under-Secretary-General for Peacekeeping Operations, and to Said Djinnit, the AU Commissioner for Peace and Security.

The publication would not have been possible without the continuing financial support of the Global Conflict Prevention Pool of the UK government, the government of Norway, the government of Canada, the government of the Federal Republic of Germany, and the Compton Foundation. My thanks to all of them. I also wish to express my gratitude to all the individuals and institutions that made possible last year's outreach efforts, especially the staff of the AU Commission for Peace and Security, the Kofi Annan International Peacekeeping Training Center in Accra, the Berlin-based Center for International Peace Operations–ZIF, the Institute for Security Studies in Pretoria, the Henry L. Stimson Center in Washington, D.C., FRIDE in Madrid, and Canada House in London. I am particularly indebted to Martti Ahtisaari, former president of Finland and Special Envoy for the Future Status Process for Kosovo, Festus Aboagye, Ambassador Harro Adt, Mariano Aguirre, Kwesi Aning, General John Attipoe, Sara John de Sousa, Bill Durch, Belen Galindo, Amelie Gauthier, Victoria Holt, Ian Johnstone, Ambassador Class D. Knoop, Winrich Kühne, Chris Lynch, Ana Martiningui, and Heiko Nitzschke.

The *Annual Review* would not be realized without a dedicated editorial and research team. This year, that team was led by volume editor and research scholar A. Sarjoh Bah, who coauthored with me a thematic essay on the complex dynamics of peacekeeping partnerships. Benjamin Tortolani, the project's researcher and this year's series coordinator, contributed enormously to the drafting and editing phases, while liaising with our publisher and other partners in the publication process. Victoria DiDomenico, the CIC's research associate, took on the onerous but critical assignment of

---

*We define these as in-country operations that are authorized by a multilateral body, that are multinational in their composition, that have a substantial military component, and that are deployed principally in support of a peace process or conflict management objective.

generating and managing the UN data. The research team benefited from the support of Grace Gabala and Kelly Tek, for which I am grateful. We are indebted to Adam Day, who helped with the drafting and the early phase of the editing, which contributed to enhancing the quality of the text. Markus E. Bouillon, Tatianna Carayannis, Rahul Chandran, Lansana Gberie, Richard Gowan, Gordon Peake, Martin Rupiya, Jake Sherman, and Erin Weir made invaluable contributions to this year's volume. My thanks to all of them, and particularly to Sarjoh for effectively and efficiently steering the project to completion.

The project team is indebted to several CIC staff members, Andrew Frazer Hart, Yvonne Alonzo, Lynn Denesopolis, and Louise Andersen, for their support throughout the year. I am particularly grateful to Shepard Forman and Barnett Rubin for their support and guidance.

I am especially grateful to Lakdhar Brahimi and Salman Ahmed for agreeing to serve as guest contributors to this year's volume. Their chapter vividly illustrates the central theme of this year's *Annual Review*—that peace operations are embedded in and contribute to broader political processes, the management or mismanagement of which shape peacekeeping outcomes. Brahimi and Ahmed's elucidation of the "seven deadly sins" that can infect such processes is a sobering reminder of their complexity and of the need for modesty and caution when engaging with complex national dynamics.

Several people from the UN and its peace operations provided help along the way. We thank, in particular, General Anis Bajwa, Tania Belisle-Leclerc, Dalila Benmehdi, Johanne Brathwaite, Tonderai Chikuhwa, Jack Christofides, Edna Dela Cruz, Walter Dorn, Helle Falkman, Kelly Fleck, Megh Gurun, David Haeri, David Harland, Katja Hemmerich, Bela Kapur, Paul Keating, Corinna Kuhl, Elisabeth Lothe, Richard Ponzio, Ugo Solinas, and Fatemeh Ziai. Gratitude also goes to the many UN desk officers who reviewed drafts of the mission reviews and notes; the CIC of course remains responsible for the final content. We are also thankful for the cooperation of members of the DPKO's Military Division, Police Division, Office of Operations and Office of Mission Support, Logistics Division, Department of Management, Executive Office, Situation Center, UN Volunteers Programme, and Office of Programme Planning, Budget, and Accounts, and Peacebuilding Support Office including the Cartographic Section and especially Roy Doyon.

We benefited from the support of a number of officials from the African Union, the AU Mission in Sudan, the Darfur Integrated Task Force, and the Embassy of the Republic of Sierra Leone to Addis Ababa, and are grateful to Ambassador Ibrahim Baba Kamara, Ambassador Ibrahim Sorie Conteh, and Tamba E. Juana. We are particularly grateful to Geofrey Mugumya, El-Ghassim Wane, Bereng Mtimkulu, Ambassador Mahmoud Kane, Solomon Gomez, Biscut Tessema, Naison Ngoma, General Jaotody Jean de Matha, General Benon Biraro, Squadron Leader Frank Hanson, Colonel George Amamoo, and Lieutenant-Colonel Almustafar Umar.

The CIC continues to profit from its ongoing partnership with the Stockholm International Peace Research Institute on this project, and we thank Sharon Wiharta and Kirsten Soder for their support.

Finally, we remain grateful to the staff at Lynne Rienner Publishers, especially Steve Barr for his assistance, support, and patience.

Bruce D. Jones
Director and Senior Fellow
NYU Center on International Cooperation

Mission Acronyms

AMIS	AU Mission in Sudan
AMISOM	AU Mission in Somalia
BINUB	UN Integrated Office in Burundi
BONUCA	UN Peacebuilding Support Office in the Central African Republic
CISPKF	CIS Peacekeeping Force in Abkhazia-Georgia
EUBAM Rafah	EU Border Assistance Mission at Rafah Crossing Point
EUFOR Althea	EU Force in Bosnia and Herzegovina
EUFOR TCHAD/RCA	EU Force in the Republic of Chad and the Central African Republic
EUPM	EU Police Mission in Bosnia and Herzegovina
EUPOL Afghanistan	EU Police Mission in Afghanistan
EUPOL COPPS	EU Police Mission for the Palestinian Territories
EUPOL RD Congo	EU Police Mission in the Democratic Republic of Congo
EUSEC RD Congo	EU Security Reform Mission in the Democratic Republic of Congo
FOMUC	Force Multinational de la Communauté Économique et Monétaire de l'Afrique Centrale
IMT	International Monitoring Team
ISAF	International Security Assistance Force
ISF	International Security Forces
JPKF	CIS–South Ossetia Joint Peacekeeping Forces
KFOR	NATO Kosovo Force
MAES	AU Electoral and Security Assistance Mission in Comoros
MFO Sinai	Multinational Force and Observers in Sinai
MINURCAT	UN Mission in the Central African Republic and Chad
MINURSO	UN Mission for the Referendum in Western Sahara
MINUSTAH	UN Stabilization Mission in Haiti
MNF-I	Multinational Force in Iraq
MONUC	UN Organization Mission in the Democratic Republic of Congo
NTM-I	NATO Training Mission in Iraq
OMIK	OSCE Mission in Kosovo
RAMSI	Regional Assistance Mission in the Solomon Islands
SLMM	Sri Lanka Monitoring Mission
TIPH	Temporary International Presence in Hebron
UNAMA	UN Assistance Mission in Afghanistan
UNAMI	UN Assistance Mission in Iraq

UNAMID	UN-AU Mission in Darfur
UNDOF	UN Disengagement Force
UNFICYP	UN Peacekeeping Force in Cyprus
UNIFIL	UN Interim Force in Lebannon
UNIOSIL	UN Integrated Office in Sierra Leone
UNMEE	UN Mission in Ethiopia and Eritrea
UNMIK	UN Interim Administration Mission in Kosovo
UNMIL	UN Mission in Liberia
UNMIN	UN Mission in Nepal
UNMIS	UN Mission in Sudan
UNMIT	UN Integrated Mission in Timor-Leste
UNMOGIP	UN Military Observer Group in India and Pakistan
UNOCI	UN Operation in Côte d'Ivoire
UNOMIG	UN Observer Mission in Georgia
UNTSO	UN Truce Supervision Organization

ANNUAL REVIEW OF
Global Peace Operations
2008

PEACE OPERATIONS 2007

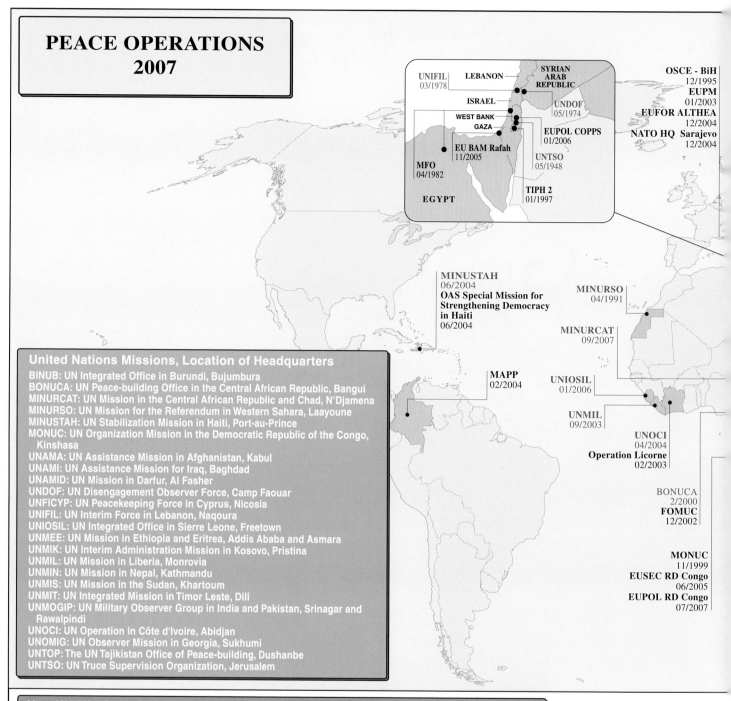

UNIFIL
03/1978

LEBANON

SYRIAN ARAB REPUBLIC

OSCE - BiH
12/1995
EUPM
01/2003
EUFOR ALTHEA
12/2004
NATO HQ Sarajevo
12/2004

ISRAEL

WEST BANK
GAZA

UNDOF
05/1974

EUPOL COPPS
01/2006

EU BAM Rafah
11/2005

UNTSO
05/1948

MFO
04/1982

EGYPT

TIPH 2
01/1997

MINUSTAH
06/2004
OAS Special Mission for Strengthening Democracy in Haiti
06/2004

MINURSO
04/1991

MINURCAT
09/2007

UNIOSIL
01/2006

MAPP
02/2004

UNMIL
09/2003

UNOCI
04/2004
Operation Licorne
02/2003

BONUCA
2/2000
FOMUC
12/2002

MONUC
11/1999
EUSEC RD Congo
06/2005
EUPOL RD Congo
07/2007

United Nations Missions, Location of Headquarters

BINUB: UN Integrated Office in Burundi, Bujumbura
BONUCA: UN Peace-building Office in the Central African Republic, Bangui
MINURCAT: UN Mission in the Central African Republic and Chad, N'Djamena
MINURSO: UN Mission for the Referendum in Western Sahara, Laayoune
MINUSTAH: UN Stabilization Mission in Haiti, Port-au-Prince
MONUC: UN Organization Mission in the Democratic Republic of the Congo, Kinshasa
UNAMA: UN Assistance Mission in Afghanistan, Kabul
UNAMI: UN Assistance Mission for Iraq, Baghdad
UNAMID: UN Mission in Darfur, Al Fasher
UNDOF: UN Disengagement Observer Force, Camp Faouar
UNFICYP: UN Peacekeeping Force in Cyprus, Nicosia
UNIFIL: UN Interim Force in Lebanon, Naqoura
UNIOSIL: UN Integrated Office in Sierra Leone, Freetown
UNMEE: UN Mission in Ethiopia and Eritrea, Addis Ababa and Asmara
UNMIK: UN Interim Administration Mission in Kosovo, Pristina
UNMIL: UN Mission in Liberia, Monrovia
UNMIN: UN Mission in Nepal, Kathmandu
UNMIS: UN Mission in the Sudan, Khartoum
UNMIT: UN Integrated Mission in Timor Leste, Dili
UNMOGIP: UN Military Observer Group in India and Pakistan, Srinagar and Rawalpindi
UNOCI: UN Operation in Côte d'Ivoire, Abidjan
UNOMIG: UN Observer Mission in Georgia, Sukhumi
UNTOP: The UN Tajikistan Office of Peace-building, Dushanbe
UNTSO: UN Truce Supervision Organization, Jerusalem

Non-UN Missions, Location of Headquarters

AMIS: African Union Mission in Sudan, Khartoum - AU
AMISOM: African Union Mission in Somalia, Mogadishu
CIS Peacekeeping Forces in Georgia, Sukhumi
EU BAM Rafah: EU Border Assistance Mission at Rafah, Rafah
EUFOR ALTHEA: EU Military Operation in Bosnia and Herzegovina, Sarajevo
EUFOR TCHAD/RCA: European Union Military Operations in Eastern Chad and Northeastern Central African Republic, Mont Valérien (France)
EUPM: EU Police Mission in Bosnia and Herzegovina, Sarajevo
EUPOL COPPS: EU Police Mission for the Palestinian Territories, Ramallah
EUPOL RD Congo: EU Police Mission in the Democratic Republic of the Congo, Kinshasa
EUSEC RD Congo: EU Security Reform Mission in the Democratic Republic of the Congo, Kinshasa
FOMUC: CEMAC (Central African Monetary and Economic Community) Multinational Force in the Central African Republic, Bangui
IMT: International Monitoring Team, Cotabato City
International Security Forces, Dili
ISAF: International Security Assistance Force, Kabul - NATO

Dates following the abbreviated mission names represent dates of effect (for UN missions), and start dates (for non-UN missions).

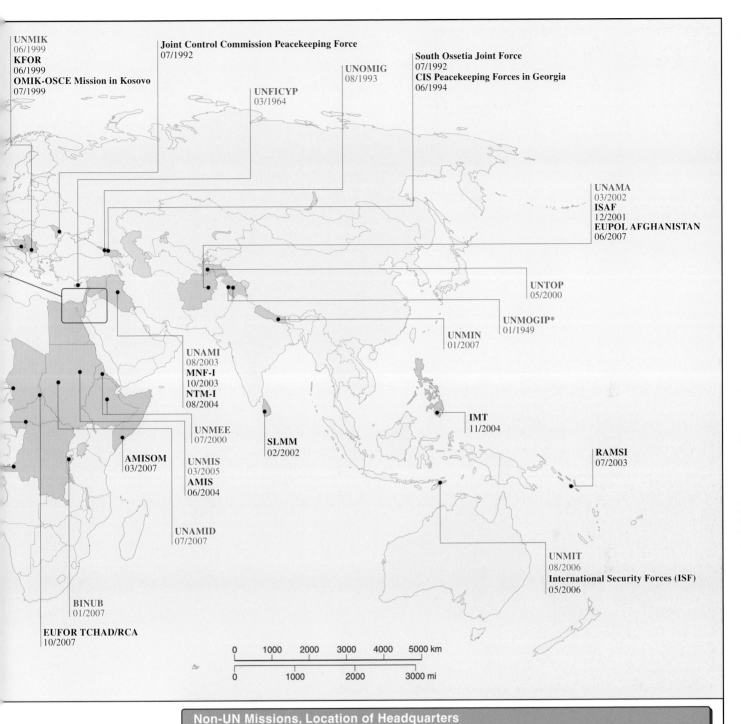

UNMIK
06/1999
KFOR
06/1999
OMIK-OSCE Mission in Kosovo
07/1999

Joint Control Commission Peacekeeping Force
07/1992

UNOMIG
08/1993

South Ossetia Joint Force
07/1992
CIS Peacekeeping Forces in Georgia
06/1994

UNFICYP
03/1964

UNAMA
03/2002
ISAF
12/2001
EUPOL AFGHANISTAN
06/2007

UNTOP
05/2000

UNMOGIP*
01/1949

UNMIN
01/2007

UNAMI
08/2003
MNF-I
10/2003
NTM-I
08/2004

IMT
11/2004

UNMEE
07/2000

SLMM
02/2002

RAMSI
07/2003

AMISOM
03/2007

UNMIS
03/2005
AMIS
06/2004

UNAMID
07/2007

UNMIT
08/2006
International Security Forces (ISF)
05/2006

BINUB
01/2007

EUFOR TCHAD/RCA
10/2007

0   1000   2000   3000   4000   5000 km

0   1000   2000   3000 mi

The boundaries and names shown and the designations used on this map do not imply official endorsement or acceptance by the United Nations.

*Dotted line represents approximately the Line of Control in Jammu and Kashmir agreed upon by India and Pakistan. The final status of Jammu and Kashmir has not yet been agreed upon by the parties.

Non-UN Missions, Location of Headquarters

Joint Control Commission Peacekeeping Force, Trans-Dniester - CIS
KFOR: Kosovo Force, Pristina - NATO
MAPP: Mission to Support the Peace Process in Colombia, Bogotá - OAS
MFO: Multinational Force and Observers, Rome
MNF-I: Multinational Force in Iraq, Baghdad
NATO Headquarters Sarajevo, Sarajevo
NTM-I: NATO Training Mission in Iraq, Baghdad
OAS Special Mission for Strengthening Democracy in Haiti, Port-au-Prince
OMIK-OSCE Mission in Kosovo, Pristina
Operation Licorne, Abidjan
OSCE - BiH: OSCE Mission to Bosnia and Herzegovina, Sarajevo
RAMSI: Regional Assistance Mission in the Solomon Islands, Honiara - Pacific Islands Forum
SLMM: Sri Lanka Monitoring Mission, Colombo
South Ossetia Joint Force, Tskhinvali - CIS
TIPH 2: Temporary International Presence in Hebron, Hebron

Strategic Summary 2007

The year 2007 was a troubled one for global peace operations. Following a successful 2005 and a surprisingly resilient 2006, in 2007 prominent peace operations in Europe, Africa, Asia, and the Middle East all encountered challenges that impeded their performance. These challenges arose primarily from failed or stalled political processes, though they were often manifested in insecurity or direct attacks on peacekeepers. In Africa, these issues were compounded by serious logistical challenges combined with weak commitments from troop contributors that slowed the pace of peacekeeping growth—indeed, despite authorization of new missions, the number of UN forces in Africa actually declined, by just over 2,000, in the period between October 2006 and October 2007. Political, security, and logistical challenges were all featured in one of the year's most contested operations, in Darfur, as the UN and the AU negotiated to define the arrangements for a "hybrid" mission.

Meanwhile, largely beyond the headlines, Latin America's sole large-scale peace operation, in Haiti, saw its most positive year to date, and was becoming a proving ground for a broader approach by the UN to issues of statebuilding and the rule of law. In several other mission contexts, also, the multidimensional, political, and civilian character of peacekeeping was on display as missions strove to help restore state capacity and foster broader peacebuilding processes, including with respect to economic development. By contrast, NATO in Afghanistan struggled with its lack of an integrated or comprehensive operational structure.

The UN tackled organizational issues of a different type, launching an extensive reform of its peacekeeping machinery at headquarters.

The Year 2007 in Numbers

These themes of the year in review were set against a backdrop of still-rising global numbers of peacekeepers. As it has for the past six years, the UN experienced substantial growth in the total number of peacekeepers deployed, though 2007 saw the rate of that growth slow to 10 percent, from 20 percent in each of the past six years. On 31 October, the UN had 82,701 uniformed personnel (troops, military observers, and police) in the field, plus approximately 20,000 civilian staff (international and local). The UN remained the largest peacekeeping provider in the world, deploying more personnel than all other peacekeeping organizations combined. NATO was second, with just under 57,000 troops deployed in the field. Simultaneously, non-UN operations involved over 78,000 personnel. While over half of these were NATO troops in Afghanistan and Kosovo, both the European Union and the African Union initiated new missions in 2007.

Rising overall numbers in 2007 masked a different reality, however, namely a number of missions in Africa that failed to materialize or for which deployments were agonizingly slow. Detailed plans to send over 10,000 UN personnel to Chad and the Central African Republic were scrapped in the face of Chadian opposition. A smaller contingent of EU troops and UN police were authorized to cover the same territory. During that period, tentative

Military Personnel Deployed in UN and Non-UN Missions: 31 October 2007

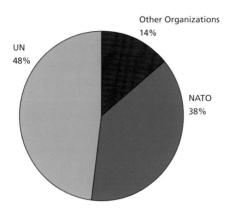

Other Organizations
14%

UN
48%

NATO
38%

Military Deployments (Troops and Military Observers) in Global Peace Operations: 1997–2007

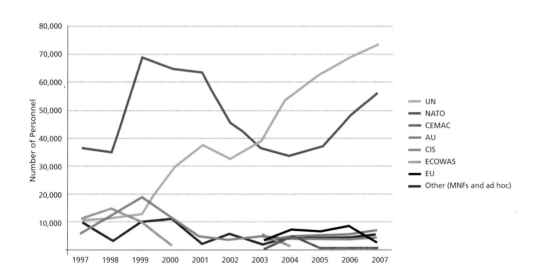

proposals for a UN force in Somalia remained on the drawing board. While the AU approved an interim deployment of 8,000 troops to Somalia, it could only muster little more than a quarter of this force in almost a year. And most visible, the Security Council's August 2006 resolution that authorized deployment of over 20,000 UN troops to Darfur went virtually entirely unfulfilled. In July 2007, the UN Security Council (acting jointly with the AU Peace and Security Council) approved a joint UN-AU operation in the region instead, but admitted that this would take at least a year to deploy in its entirety. Still, once these mandated UN, EU, and AU missions reach full deployment strengths, during 2008, the broader Horn of Africa region will become one of the most concentrated peacekeeping theaters in the world. However, African troop contributors faced their own version of overstretch, with merely twelve countries providing 86 percent of the total African contribution to UN and AU peacekeeping operations on the continent. On the other hand, 2007 saw an increase in capacity-building efforts for African peacekeeping, with the G8-supported Global Peace Operations Initiative undertaking programs, and the EU's African Peace Facility providing critical financing to AU operations.

The failures to mount large-scale responses to African conflicts in 2007 were in contrast to more decisive UN deployments elsewhere, most obviously its rapid intervention in Lebanon in late 2006. There it proved possible to put nearly 10,000 troops on the ground in four months. Indeed, the 10 percent growth in the UN's global presence in the year ending September 2007 largely reflects the expansion of the Lebanese operation.

Patterns of Deployment

The resulting patterns of deployment suggested the emergence of three clusters of global peace operations, defined by the combination of sources of troops, the location of their deployment, and the authorizing institutions:

• *Asian-African nexus.* Operations in Africa, where 62,000 military personnel were deployed, drew heavily on troops from the continent itself and from three primary external contributors: Bangladesh, India, and Pakistan. This nexus comprises three subregional clusters of operations: in West Africa (including Liberia and Côte d'Ivoire), Central Africa and the Democratic Republic of Congo (centering on the latter), and the broader Horn (including Sudan, the Central African Republic, Chad, Somalia, and Ethiopia/Eritrea). In this cluster of missions, the UN and the AU cooperated to respond through a range of inter-institutional deployments, with periodic EU support. The authorized EU deployment of 3,000 troops in Chad and the Central African Republic

will constitute the only major Western peace-keeping presence on the continent other than France's Operation Licorne in Côte d'Ivoire.

• *Euro–Middle Eastern nexus.* Operations in the broader Middle East and South Central Asia, where 57,661 troops were deployed, relied on European forces under UN command (mainly in Lebanon), EU deployments (Gaza, West Bank), or NATO (Afghanistan). European troops composed the bulk of UNIFIL's expansion during 2006, maintained more than 60 percent of the troops under UN helmets there, and composed over 50 percent of the more than 41,000 NATO troops under ISAF in Afghanistan. In most of these contexts, the UN provided the overall political framework for diverse institutional operations.

• *Regional specializations.* A variety of regionally specialized forces were deployed, including the largely Latin American–composed UN force in Haiti; the mainly Australian and New Zealand military presence in Timor-Leste and the Australian-led presence in the Solomon Islands; the largely Russian peacekeeping forces in the Commonwealth of Independent States; the ongoing European presence—nearly 20,000 peacekeepers (under the EU, NATO, and the OSCE)—across the Western Balkans; and the more than 7,000 African personnel operating in Darfur and Somalia under AU command. In each instance, regional organizations or regional actors led the deployment, though again usually within a UN-provided political framework.

These patterns were reflected in the composition of troops in various regions. For instance, 60 percent of UN troops in the Middle East in 2007 were European. By contrast, European contributors comprised 2 percent of UN forces in Africa. The rest of the UN's troops in Africa were from South Asia (53 percent), from Africa itself (33 percent), and other regions (14 percent). This divergence in composition in the various regions was an issue that continued to generate political tensions at the UN.

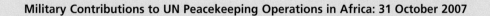

Military Contributions to UN Peacekeeping Operations in Africa: 31 October 2007

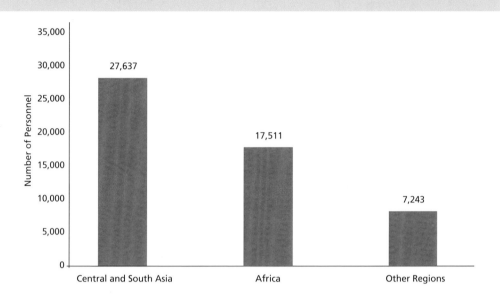

**Deployment of UN and Non-UN Military Personnel
in the Broader Middle East by Region of Origin: 31 October 2007**

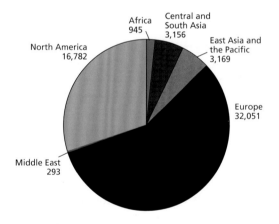

The Interplay of
Political and Security Issues

Across this enormous deployment of personnel, and for all its complexities, the issues that attracted the greatest attention in 2007 were neither military nor logistical, but political. Nowhere was this more evident than in Kosovo, where deep political uncertainty about the future status of the territory clouded both UN and NATO missions. Failure to achieve an agreed outcome during summer 2007 raised fears of renewed violence, and contributed to ratcheting up broader international tensions.

In Lebanon, too, the successful deployment in 2006 of a reinvigorated UNIFIL, with

Selected African Military and Police Contributions to Peace Operations: 30 September 2007			
	AU	UN	Total
Benin		1,208	1,208
Ethiopia		1,807	1,807
Ghana	423	1,940	2,363
Kenya	105	1,024	1,129
Morocco		1,537	1,537
Namibia	24	631	655
Niger		411	411
Nigeria	2,103	2,043	4,146
Rwanda	1,790	277	2,067
Senegal	574	1,463	2,037
South Africa	631	1,205	1,836
Uganda	1,600		1,600
Subtotal	**7,250**	**13,546**	**20,796**
Other African Country Contributions	519	2,685	3,204
Total	**7,769**	**16,231**	**24,000**

a larger, more robust troop complement and a broader mandate, was by the end of 2007 overshadowed by a deepening domestic political crisis. As highlighted in this volume's review of missions in the Middle East, that political crisis combined with continuing cross-border tensions significantly impeded the implementation of the two resolutions (1559 and 1701) that framed mission mandates as well as the broader UN political engagement in Lebanon.

The interwoven relationship between political process and peace operations was highlighted also in Sudan, on two fronts. In Darfur, two dimensions of political negotiations, with Khartoum over its efforts to stymie the deployment of a broader peacekeeping mission, and in revitalizing the Darfur peace talks, complicated efforts to deploy a larger and more robust operation throughout 2007. Meanwhile, overshadowed by negotiations over the deployment of UNAMID to Darfur, implementation of the Comprehensive Peace Agreement, governing north-south relations in Sudan, was stalled.

Another focus of concern in 2007 was the darkening prospects in Afghanistan. There, the main challenge to NATO's International Security Assistance Force was manifested in deteriorating security conditions in Afghanistan's southeastern provinces, and in a rise in direct attacks against the mission and against civilians in Kabul and elsewhere, all from a resurgent Taliban and associated forces. However, underlying this was a declining confidence in the central political institutions of the Afghan government under President Hamid Karzai, and a lagging process of building core institutions of the state, especially a credible and capable police force. Corruption and rampant drug production and trafficking also impeded the already delayed processes of institution building and economic development in the country.

In none of these missions was the relationship between politics and security either straightforward or unidirectional. Much was determined by the political ambitions and agenda of forces arrayed against the mission in question and the peace agreement that framed it. Where those forces had no national political ambitions or base, robust peacekeeping was able to hold sway. In Haiti, for example, a large-scale security crackdown by MINUSTAH against criminal gangs and drug lords in the slums of Cité Soleil breathed new momentum into the mission and into Haiti's previously stalled recovery. Still, there is little doubt that the election of René Préval in 2006, bringing to power a prime minister with the support of the population and the confidence of the international community, was a necessary condition for MINUSTAH to undertake its security crackdown.

Beyond the Headlines: The Multiple Dimensions of Peace Operations

Security and political activities were just one part of MINUSTAH's strategy in 2007. In addition, the mission worked in close collaboration with the government, the World Bank, the

International Monetary Fund, and the UN Development Programme to push forward the development of key state institutions, especially *judicial institutions.* The joined-up actions by the UN and the international financial institutions illustrated how far peace operations have come since Alvaro de Soto and Graciana del Castillo in 1994 likened the efforts of the UN and the IMF in El Salvador to two surgeons operating on the same patient with a curtain dividing them.[1]

Subsequently, the UN has paid ever-greater attention to what it refers to as "multidimensional" operations—a term that attests to the political, legal/judicial, institutional, and economic roles played by peace operations. Particularly UN operations and increasingly those of the EU have become a major vehicle for the allocation of civilian and economic support to states recovering from conflict.

The numerous forms this takes are evident in this volume's mission reviews and mission notes. In Liberia, for example, UNMIL supported a major program of *economic governance* and *natural resources management,* undertaken by the Liberian government, the World Bank, and donors. In Afghanistan, in addition to counterinsurgency battles, efforts focused on *economic reconstruction* and its interplay with security, including through the use of joint security/civilian provincial reconstruction teams. In Timor-Leste, UNMIT has focused its attention on elections and on *security sector reform,* especially as pertains to the development of *police institutions.* In other contexts such as Lebanon and Nepal, the issue of *elections,* and the broader political process that surrounds (or should surround) them, dominated mission activity.

This multidimensional facet of peace operations was reflected also in 2007 in rising numbers of police deployments. Through the UN alone, police deployments rose from 6,167 in 2005 to 9,414 in 2007. Additional police, roughly 2,123, were deployed through other organizations, primarily the EU and AU. These overall numbers were set to rise sharply with the authorization of 3,700 police to be deployed in Darfur and an additional 300 to Chad and the Central African Republic.

Meanwhile, the political/civilian aspects of peacekeeping face at least two core challenges. The first is highlighted by Lakhdar Brahimi and Salman Ahmed in Chapter 1, which raises important questions about the ambitiousness of UN operations and highlights the potential for mediators to commit a range of "sins" in relation to domestic political processes. Second, and more prosaic, the UN and other peacekeeping organizations faced serious challenges in providing an adequate supply of appropriate civilian staff to their multiple nonmilitary functions. At the UN, for example, average civilian vacancy rates during 2007 were about 30 percent, a number that actually underestimates the problem, since the bulk of those civilian vacancies were in critical functional areas such as the rule of law and judicial reform. The absence of a credible international mechanism for maintaining a ready supply of civilian personnel to such operations is a major gap, though far from the only one, in the organizational arrangements for peace operations.

Organizational Challenges

As noted in previous editions of our *Annual Review,* the slim scale and excess burden on the headquarter mechanisms for managing peace operations continued to pose serious challenges to the viability of peace operations in 2007. The AU struggled to maintain adequate support for its operations; its institutional limitations were among the factors that led to calls for a UN force to replace AMIS in Darfur. It should be noted, however, that the two mission environments the AU struggled to manage, in Sudan and Somalia, were among the most complex imaginable.

At the UN, the question of organizational arrangements for peacekeeping became a central issue in 2007. Specifically, incoming Secretary-General Ban Ki-Moon made a major overhaul of the UN's Department of Peacekeeping Operations a centerpiece of his early reform efforts (several other elements of which were blocked early by member states). Although the Secretary-General's reform proposals for the DPKO initially met with considerable resistance from troop contributors and major donors alike, a modified version of his proposal was endorsed by the UN's Committee on Peacekeeping (C-34) in March 2007. The associated budget, stripped of a few proposed new senior posts, was approved by the UN General Assembly's budget committee in June 2007.

That reform saw three significant changes. First, the DPKO's division for field support and logistics was established as the self-standing Department of Field Support, headed at the level of Under-Secretary-General. Second, a total of 287 posts were added to the total staff complement of the two departments. Third, the post of military advisor in DPKO was upgraded, and a new pillar was added to the department, comprising rule of law and police operations.

The split of DPKO raised concerns among both field commanders and member states about unity of command, one of the UN's core strengths. Two mechanisms were put in place to assuage these concerns. First, it was agreed that the head of the Department of Field Support, while normally reporting to the Deputy Secretary-General, would report to the head of the DPKO on all operational matters. Second, and perhaps more promising, new arrangements were put in place for staff from the various pillars of the DPKO and from the Department of Field Support to work together in unified teams (called "integrated" mission teams—confusingly so, given the use of that term also to refer to integration processes among peacekeeping, political, humanitarian, development, and other departments of the UN). The

effect of these arrangements, on paper, was to give the DPKO's Office of Operations, which oversees and directs field missions, a structured system for drawing together the resources of all parts of both departments, thus strengthening unity of command over *operations,* while simultaneously, at least in theory, reducing the management burden on the DPKO by giving oversight of logistics, financial management, and personnel systems to the newly formed Department of Field Support.

Conclusion

It is striking that as the year 2007 drew to a close, the two organizations that were experiencing the greatest management strain in terms of headquarter/field ratios, and had the slimmest intrinsic logistics capacity—the AU and the UN—were set to begin working together to tackle what is undoubtedly one of the most complex logistical operations ever undertaken, in Darfur. In addition to logistical challenges, the two organizations were working together—not always entirely smoothly—to tackle the entwined processes of peacekeeping and political negotiations.

Beyond Darfur, the challenge of managing the security, political, and broader civilian dimensions of peacekeeping was in some cases exacerbated, in others facilitated, by the increasingly common phenomenon of peace operations being undertaken in partnership between two or more peacekeeping organizations. Indeed, inter-institutional arrangements, ranging from sequential deployments to fully integrated "hybrid" operations, were a major feature of the peace operation landscape in 2007—an issue explored further in Chapter 2 by A. Sarjoh Bah and Bruce D. Jones. Most critically, though, stalled political processes and linked security challenges presented an even more testing situation for the year ahead.

Note

The information provided in the graphs and tables in this chapter, where not cited otherwise, has been aggregated from the data presented in Chapters 5 through 8 of this volume. For scaling purposes, the tables and graphs in this chapter do not take into account personnel deployed in the Multinational Force-Iraq.

1. Alvaro de Soto and Graciana del Castillo, "Obstacles to Peacebuilding," *Foreign Policy* 1994.

In Pursuit of Sustainable Peace: The Seven Deadly Sins of Mediation

Lakhdar Brahimi and Salman Ahmed

One of the most important roles played by the civilian leadership of a peace operation is to help the parties to a conflict resolve their fundamental political differences through dialogue and compromise, rather than through violence. This role can be described in various ways: diplomatic efforts, mediation, peace-making, political facilitation, political process management, or, simply, as the "political role" of the operation.[1] It is an extremely difficult undertaking by any name, where success is difficult to achieve but mistakes come easily. Some of these mistakes can have fatal consequences for the peace process in which the operation is embedded, and are referred to here as "the seven deadly sins." These are: ignorance, arrogance, partiality, impotence, haste, inflexibility, and false promises.

The Context

The opportunity to commit one of these seven deadly sins arises in a number of different contexts, from diplomatic efforts to prevent an initial outbreak of fighting to the negotiations that seek to stop a conflict that is under way. The need for effective mediation is also required after the conclusion of a peace agreement and the deployment of a peace operation.

It is easy to lose sight of the connection between mediation and peacekeeping once attention shifts to the deployment of military, police, and civilian personnel and the individual tasks they are expected to support. These include: restoration of security and basic services; disarmament, demobilization, and reintegration of soldiers; return of displaced persons and refugees; the holding of elections and adoption of constitutions; promotion of the rule of law and human rights; repair of infrastructure and rebuilding of institutions; and revitalization of the economy. These are all crucially important activities to be sure, but the manner in which they are conducted can threaten the core interests of any one of the parties. Skilled political process management is critical to keeping the parties engaged as they reconsider agreements they have made. Effective mediation is also needed to broker additional political agreements between the parties, as one agreement is seldom enough.

Most peace agreements that call for the deployment of peace operations to assist with their implementation only partially address the underlying political problems of the conflict. In some instances, agreements signed in bad faith unravel and have to be renegotiated (Sierra Leone, 1999). In other cases, those who have signed the agreement represent only a fraction of the actors whose consent and cooperation is required to bring peace to a war-torn area (Darfur, 2006). Unresolved political problems rather than technical difficulties can account for delays in the implementation of key provisions of an agreement, for example, the disarmament of soldiers or the registration of voters (Côte d'Ivoire, 2002). Constitutional or electoral processes can create a new set of political problems, especially if one or more of the parties are not willing to accept the result (Angola, 1992). Latent political tensions can surface even after the successful installation of a democratically elected government (Timor-Leste, 2006). In other cases still, the operation might have been deployed before a political agreement has even been reached (Kosovo, 1999).

The circumstances will vary, but one thing

remains constant across peace operations: the political role is vital. It manifests itself at many levels, from the high politics of formal agreements, to low-key engagement with those parties that might rethink the wisdom of the concessions they have made.

In the case of the United Nations (UN), the political role may be entrusted to the Special Representative of the Secretary-General (SRSG), who also serves as the civilian head of the peace operation on the ground. SRSGs in charge of the larger multidisciplinary operations are responsible for: mediating political disputes among the parties to the conflict; overseeing international military, humanitarian, human rights, and peacebuilding in a particular theater; and ensuring that all these and related international efforts contribute positively to the political process (DRC, Liberia, Haiti, and Timor-Leste).[2] But in many other cases, these responsibilities are divided among several individuals and organizations (Lebanon, Sudan, Afghanistan, and Kosovo), the consequences of which are highlighted in this *Review*'s thematic essay on inter-institutional arrangements.

The effective exercise of the political role of SRSGs and other international mediators is acutely needed now in several conflict areas where over 160,000 peacekeepers are already on the ground under the flag of the UN, the African Union (AU), the European Union (EU), and NATO. Fundamental political problems—be they disputes over power, territory, resources, or spheres of influence—in Lebanon, Sudan, the Democratic Republic of Congo (DRC), Eritrea/Ethiopia, Côte d'Ivoire, Georgia/Abkhazia, Somalia, Chad, Nepal, Afghanistan, and Kosovo have yet to be fully addressed. The parties concerned are not in a position to resolve these political differences without third-party mediation. The unresolved political problems in any of these countries may well present formidable challenges in the coming year. The various SRSGs and other international mediators concerned might not be able to effectively meet all of these challenges, however,

for reasons that are not entirely within their control.

Challenges to the Effective Exercise of the Mediator's Role

First, the SRSG's or other international mediator's political room for maneuver and leverage increases when he or she is acting on behalf of a united Security Council and with the backing of key regional players. In several of the conflict areas where peacekeepers are presently deployed, divisions within the Security Council and between the regional players remain, in some cases due to competing strategic national interests. Divisions are arguably growing. The current geopolitical landscape is far more fragmented than in the immediate post–Cold War "honeymoon" period, when the international community brokered political solutions to the problems that had plagued Namibia, Lebanon, South Africa, El Salvador, Cambodia, and Mozambique. The international consensus required for political solutions to several current crises is nowhere near as strong today. As a result, recent operations have deployed not only without the benefit of a comprehensive peace agreement in place, but also without the necessary leverage in hand to overcome political deadlock during the implementation phase.

Second, as implied above, the proliferation of "hybrid operations" has obscured responsibility for the political role in many situations, for example, in Afghanistan and Sudan. The increasing role played by regional organizations and high-level ad hoc arrangements in conflict management is a very positive development, not least because it has increased the level of attention and expertise certain crises receive. At the same time, having multiple high-level mediators and several international organizations with a large operational presence on the ground can create confusion about who is in charge of the political role.

Third, modern-day peace operations are remaining in theater longer than those created in the immediate aftermath of the Cold War. This is a positive development, insofar as more resources, time, and attention are now being afforded to help rebuild the institutions of war-damaged states. At the same time, there may well be an inverse relationship between the longevity of the peace operation and the room for it to play an effective political role. As the host government rebuilds its legitimacy and strength over time, it understandably and rightfully might see international mediation as undermining its authority. Ideally, the ground should be prepared with the host government long in advance to assure them that the objective remains for the peace operation to phase out, as quickly as possible, including on the political front, and that mediation assistance can be provided in more discreet ways that pose no threat to the government's authority. When that does not happen, however, the host government can seize the opportunity of a new SRSG's arrival to curtail the political space available to him or her at the outset.

Fourth, there is a tendency to change the profile of the leadership of operations from a politically oriented to a more developmentally oriented one over time, on the assumption that the conflict has moved beyond the political crisis phase. Key members of the international community, likewise, might downgrade the seniority or switch the profile of their "point persons" on the conflict, at capital and country level. This transformation can help to assure the host government that its authority is being respected. And it makes perfect sense when the fundamental political problems have, indeed, been solved. But, it can prematurely deplete political expertise and capital when that is not the case.

Fifth, today's peace operations continue to grow in breadth and complexity, placing enormous demands on their leadership. SRSGs ignore at their peril the administrative and logistics aspects of missions comprised of tens of thousands of military, police, and civilian personnel, with budgets of up to one billion dollars per year. SRSGs cannot shirk their leadership responsibilities to ensure good order and discipline of personnel, proper management of mission assets, and effective integration and unity of effort across components. Attention to

the managerial role, however, can come at the expense of the political role, and vice versa. A single Principal Deputy responsible for overseeing daily management of the mission, in all its aspects, can help an SRSG to do justice to both roles. But few UN peace operations are presently designed and staffed accordingly.

For these reasons, among others, the SRSG's political role is more difficult than ever. Meanwhile, the direction he or she receives in its performance remains scant. Security Council resolutions do not provide a road map on how the role is to be conducted, and there is still no official political doctrine upon which to rely.[3] General blueprints, in any event, can only go so far in navigating one through the treacherous waters of any specific conflict. SRSGs and other international mediators are thus left to define and conduct the political role as best they can. It is not surprising, therefore, that there is such variance in the manner in which different SRSGs approach the job.

The Seven Deadly Sins

Each conflict is unique but at the same time, based on bitter personal experience in the management of several political processes and close observation of the work of others, there do appear to be certain recurrent traps that materialize in many different situations, across the spectrum of crisis response, and regardless of whether the mediator is operating with a small team or heading an operation comprised of thousands of personnel. Seven of the traps can be fatal to the ability of an SRSG or other international mediators (terms used interchangeably here) to conduct the political role effectively. The "seven deadly sins" to which attention is now turned are: ignorance, arrogance, partiality, impotence, haste, inflexibility, and false promises.

1. Ignorance

In order to be in a position to help the parties identify and reach solutions to their political problems, the SRSG obviously must have a basic understanding of the country in all its facets, from the history and culture to the economy and social structure. They need to be aware of the different explanations for why the violence erupted in the first place, why the conflict has persisted for as long as it has, and what solutions have already been tried and discussed. And they need to understand the motivations, interests, and strengths of those with whom they must work. Namely, they must have what one might call "the political map" of the area.

A detailed political map requires answers to key critical questions, which among others include: Who are the national actors with the power to stop or restart the war and from where are they acquiring external support (e.g., arms, financing, and recognition)? Do they believe they can still prevail militarily, or have they accepted the need or desire to reach a negotiated solution? Which key constituencies can they legitimately claim to represent? Which key constituencies are unrepresented in the current political process? Which actors have opted out or been left out of the process, and what capacity or motivation do they have to disrupt or derail it? To what extent are the relevant members of the international community—neighbors, key regional players, big powers—united or working at cross-purposes with one another? Do they consider their strategic national interests to be at stake? Which of the participating domestic and international players are undecided about or actively opposed to the mediator's role?

It can be a daunting challenge for SRSGs and other international mediators to confront these questions when they are deploying to regions unfamiliar to them, with an insufficient complement of seasoned regional specialists on their political staff, inadequate knowledge of management systems in the field or at headquarters on which to rely, and interlocutors who have an obvious incentive to feed them with biased or deliberately misleading information. The odds are that it will take far longer than they might wish to alleviate their ignorance of the political map. They do not have the luxury

UN Special Envoy for Darfur Jan Eliasson and the African Union's Special Envoy for Darfur Salim Ahmed Salim during the Darfur Peace Talks in Libya, 27 October 2007

of waiting several months to take key decisions on the political process, however. As a result, they may end up in the position of making misinformed and misguided choices early on, only to then spend much of the remainder of their tenure trying to recover from them.

Arguably, this ignorance-based decision-making process is the norm rather than the exception in postconflict environments and is the original sin of mediation.

2. Arrogance

The first step in alleviating ignorance is for one to openly acknowledge that "I do not know enough" and to ask for help. Many SRSGs and other international mediators are keenly aware of their ignorance and the need to seek the views of others, particularly the people of the country themselves.

One challenge is to know which individuals to approach and what to ask them. An easy trap to fall into is to depend heavily on "the fifty people in the country who are most fluent in English" who readily say exactly what the mediator wants to hear. It is both naive and arrogant, and often a recipe for failure, to rely almost exclusively on the views of those who flatter us and appear to most resemble ourselves.

To compound matters further, the temptation is great to conclude that: "I have seen this all before"; the problems in this country are "just like X" (where one happened to have served previously); the views of the belligerents should not be taken too seriously, because "they caused the problems in the first place"; the particularities of the conflict in question are not that relevant, because "we already know what works and what doesn't" (which is certainly questionable); and/or "there is no point exploring all these options, because the donors and implementing agencies have other priorities."

Of course, an entirely custom-tailored approach is not always realistic, particularly when narrow windows for peace have to be capitalized on quickly. Certain dynamics and trends can be discerned across a variety of conflicts. General lessons learned in previous experiences should be taken into account. It is true that, in the aftermath of war, the parties to the conflict do not have all the answers themselves and require third-party assistance. And institutional and donor interests cannot be ignored, as discussed below.

Nonetheless, the people of the country concerned—the educated and the illiterate, the governors and the governed, the suspected perpetrators of the violence and the victims, the men and the women, alike—understand their own country far better than the foreign mediators who have just arrived on the scene. They will have to live with the consequences of the political process long after the mediator has departed. They also can help the mediator to identify where a potential course of action could lead to a dead end, fail to command domestic support, or worse, exacerbate political divisions in the country and potentially provoke violence. It is therefore not only a question of shrewd diplomacy, but good sense and basic respect to listen to a diverse range of views in the host country.

The combination of arrogance, which takes many forms, coupled with ignorance, can be a particularly deadly combination for a mediator's

credibility with the parties and for the viability of the political proposals he or she makes.

3. Partiality

One of the mediator's indispensable contributions to the political process is the ability to tell the parties when they do not appear to be 100-percent right or their adversaries 100-percent wrong; where their arguments are not supported by evidence or their previous commitments are not being honored; how their actions are inconsistent with the wishes of the vast majority of the population or violate international law; and why the time has come to contemplate politically sensitive compromises that had hitherto been declared off-limits or taboo.

Some mediators are listened to seriously when they deliver these most difficult messages, but many others are ignored, met with active hostility, or declared personae non grata not long after. Why? Much depends on whether the substance of the message is informed by a sophisticated understanding of the issues. The deftness of the diplomacy plays a part: how, where, and when something is said matters as much as what is being said. Perhaps most of all, the parties' perception of the messenger and his or her motivations can be decisive.

The mediator can say a great deal and be heard when he or she is accepted as an impartial and honest broker. An impartial and honest broker is seen to be—and is—able to work with everyone who can contribute to the peace, without creating the impression that he or she is doing so on behalf of or actively against any one of them, or in pursuit of any agenda other than to help all the people of the country concerned attain a sustainable peace.

The trap one quite easily falls into is to begin delivering the tough messages to the parties, even publicly, prior to having been accepted by them as an honest and impartial broker. What might otherwise be received as constructive criticism instead is perceived as evidence of partiality.

Before the mediator even arrives in theater, assumptions are made about his or her partiality on the basis of nationality, religion, prior public pronouncements, organizational affiliation, past associations, international reputation, and hearsay. These prejudices can work both for and against the mediator. Sometimes the negative prejudices can be assuaged, on the basis of assurances from trusted intermediaries, but not always or entirely.

The mediator does well to assume that one or more of the parties consider them to be partial and motivated by various personal and external agendas from the outset; they will have to work hard to prove otherwise through everything they say and do, throughout their tenure. The mediator commits a deadly sin when they take their status as an impartial and honest broker for granted.

4. Impotence

A well-informed, honest, and impartial broker plays an indispensable role in the political process, but within limits. Just because the parties are willing to listen to the mediator with an open mind does not mean that they will do what the mediator suggests or even what they themselves promise to do. Parties that believe they are 100-percent right do not opt for a negotiated solution because they are inclined to make painful concessions, but rather because circumstances might have left them no other choice. Their continued participation in the political process often depends on the negotiated option being the least unattractive option available to them.

The SRSG or other international mediator is entirely reliant on the relevant members of the international community to make the negotiated option more attractive to the parties relative to the alternatives. Thus, an honest broker can be an irrelevant broker as well if he or she does not carefully manage his or her relations with the relevant members of the international community. The parties need to see a tangible connection between the recommendations the mediator makes and the decisions and actions these members of the international community take, especially in the face of refusal to compromise or unwillingness to abide by commitments.

Naturally, key members of the international community will not back the mediator if they perceive that he or she is indifferent to, or working against, their legitimate concerns and interests. Security Council members need to be constantly consulted and assured that the courses of action the mediator proposes are faithful to the mandate that they have authorized (and carefully calibrated to reconcile points of disagreement among them). Countries in the region, neighbors in particular, have an understandable interest in the kind of government that will emerge in the postconflict period, particularly where there has been a legacy of hostile relations, the flow of illicit arms or drugs, or destabilizing refugee movements across porous borders. Troop-contributing countries have a legitimate interest not to be drawn into a role for which they did not sign up. Donor countries have a legitimate concern that their financial contributions be used as intended.

These various interests and concerns cannot be ignored. On the contrary, the mediator has to help satisfy the interests of these external stakeholders in a way that contributes positively to the political process, or at minimum, helps to avoid the stakeholders working at cross-purposes to it. If the mediator fails to take these interests into account, then he or she will quickly find himself or herself impotent to stave off the death of a political process in the face of impasse.

5. Haste

In order to obtain a clear picture of the political map, gain the confidence of the parties, build their sense of ownership of the process, and identify common ground among domestic and relevant external actors, the SRSG or other international mediator will need to consult with hundreds of actors, over and over again. Even if working at the pace normally demanded of mediators, and depending on the number of parties involved, this may require several months of effort.

No matter how sound the proposals of an SRSG or other international mediator might be, they risk being rejected if they have not emanated from a process that enjoys the confidence of all the parties to the conflict and is considered legitimate in the eyes of the population at large. The process matters, and it takes time. A particular peace conference itself might conclude an agreement in days or weeks, but rarely without the months or years of consultations prior to convening it. The failure to recognize this crucially important point can be deadly to a political process. A certain way to derail or kill a potentially viable political solution is to float it prematurely.

In the rush to conclude an agreement or implement its key political provisions—such as the demobilization of soldiers, the adoption of a constitution, or the conduct of an election—the mediator can simply forge ahead with only some of the parties on board. It is tempting to exclude the most difficult holdouts, especially if the leaders concerned are considered to be irrational. A small group of individuals should be not allowed to hijack a process, especially if they may be motivated more by personal gain than legitimate grievance.

The SRSG or other international mediator must resist the temptation to rush to judgment, however. Sometimes the individual leaders' unwillingness to compromise is motivated by a genuine belief—rightly or wrongly—in the justness of their cause. Even when it is not, it is one thing to sideline individuals and another to deny large key constituencies their rightful role in the political process. The peace will not be sustainable without these constituencies, especially if they remain well-armed and easily mobilized. It should not come as a surprise when these processes run aground or are actively attacked by those excluded from them.

Haste partially explains why the agreements referred to earlier failed to resolve crucial underlying political issues and subsequently unraveled. Sometimes such haste is unavoidable simply to stop the fighting and to prevent the slaughter of thousands or tens of thousands. This cannot be discounted by any means. The sin in such instances is to treat agreements born out of such haste as conclusive and comprehensive, rather than as what they are, namely elaborate cease-fire agreements or interim political arrangements.

6. Inflexibility

Once an SRSG or other international mediator has constructed the political map, has engaged in several months of consultation, and has carefully said and done all the right things vis-à-vis the internal and external players to establish himself or herself as an honest and serious broker, then he or she might be in a position to propose the contours of the political process and even secure agreement on it.

It is crucial to remember, however, that the situation on the ground has not been frozen during this time. Skirmishes or full-blown fighting might have been occurring in parts of the country all along, as the parties seek to bolster their hand at the negotiating table. Old alliances might have been broken and new ones forged. Old leaders might have departed the scene and new ones taken their place. The contest for power within particular constituencies can be as fierce as the one that occurs between them. Whether "moderates" or "hardliners" emerge from that struggle can transform the dynamics of the political process. The mediator must be aware of this at all times.

Meanwhile, developments elsewhere in the world could have altered external actors' perceptions, stakes, or positions on the conflict concerned. For example, changes of government in major troop or financial contributors also can mean a decrease or increase in resources and attention available to respond to that particular conflict. On a more profound level, the start of new wars can transform the context for international action entirely. The start of the Gulf War in 1991 understandably took attention away from addressing the regional implications of the Taif Agreement on Lebanon brokered one year earlier. The events of 9/11, on the other hand, led to renewed attention to the festering problems in Afghanistan, only to be partially diverted again by the onset of the Iraq War in 2003.

Constantly evolving developments can create new opportunities to be exploited or new formidable obstacles to be overcome. The SRSG or other international mediator does not have the luxury of being indifferent to the change in context, simply because he or she has invested too much time already in a process conceived in a different set of circumstances. Inflexibility to course adjustments in response to major changes in the political map or on the international scene can lead a peace process down a dead-end or away from new avenues to take it forward.

7. False Promises

The preceding discussion will hopefully make clear that the political role of the SRSGs and other international mediators is a perilous one. At a minimum, this should lead them to constantly reinforce a few basic messages: progress will be slow; mistakes will be made; setbacks will occur; periodic review and course correction will be required; technical problems can be resolved through technical solutions, but political problems need political solutions; painful compromises and concessions will be expected of everyone; there is no shortcut to sustainable peace in the aftermath of war; it will take several years if not decades to rebuild a war-torn state and achieve reconciliation; this is just the beginning of the process.

These messages should be repeated loudly when the peace operation arrives in theater and often throughout its presence. Unless expectations are managed, the peace operation's welcome can wear thin, and calls for its departure can grow surprisingly quickly. Tens of thousands of peacekeepers might be able to prevent poorly organized and ill-equipped "spoilers" or criminal gangs from hijacking a political process or threatening some population centers. Even if such peacekeepers are well-armed and well-trained, however, they will be no match for much larger and well-organized forces intent on destroying the peace or committing mass atrocities. It has to be said up-front that the military forces, civilian

police, human rights experts, and international aid workers will not provide security, protection, justice, social services, and jobs for all of the millions or tens of millions of inhabitants of the country. The peace operation can make only a modest contribution, at best, relative to the expectations and demands of the host population.

This modest contribution can provide the parties with the time, space, and assistance required to contemplate, discuss, and eventually put into effect the political compromises required for the peace to be sustainable. It cannot, however, obviate the need for these compromises to be made.

The SRSG commits the seventh and final deadly sin when he or she fails to counter false expectations or promises that a peaceful and prosperous democracy will emerge relatively quickly from the ashes of war, even where it never existed previously, simply because the peace operation has appeared on the scene.

Concluding Observations

The inherent caution underlying the foregoing analysis of the "seven deadly sins" is neither new nor revolutionary. It bears repeating nonetheless because the sins keep getting committed, especially in peacekeeping contexts.

Fundamental political problems are seldom fully addressed prior to the peacekeepers' arrival, despite expectations to the contrary. Given the unprecedented numbers of peacekeepers now deployed across the globe, in particularly volatile areas, the role of effective mediation in peacekeeping contexts urgently needs to be given more attention. It is becoming considerably more complicated to manage these political problems—before and after peacekeepers arrive—due to evolutions on the geopolitical landscape and in the practice of peacekeeping. Some of these complications limit from the outset how effectively the civilian leadership of peace operations can play the political role expected of them.

The year ahead promises to be a particularly challenging one for the UN and regional organizations engaged in peace operations. The unaddressed political problems are accumulating faster than they are being solved. This presents a number of policy dilemmas that will need to be confronted, sooner rather than later. Three dilemmas are alluded to in this chapter and warrant policy discussion in the coming year.

First, there is strong appeal for humility throughout this essay. The description of the sins concludes with a plea to diminish expectations as much as possible. In contrast, the mandate for each new operation appears to be even more ambitious than the last. Has the time come to declare a moratorium on new tasks until such time as capabilities and expertise are adequately built on the ones already assigned?

Second, it needs to be recognized that the SRSG's exercise of the political role while sitting atop a mission comprised of tens of thousands of personnel should not necessarily rely on exactly the same approaches and techniques employed by mediators operating with a small team prior to the mission's deployment. This chapter has focused on the similarities. What are the differences? Presumably, the SRSG has much greater leverage at his or her disposal when he or she can direct the mission's efforts in a way that informs, generates, and underpins political solutions to the underlying problems in the country concerned. Does the SRSG really have that authority, or is it in name only? What needs to be done to better synchronize the mediation efforts with all the other activities undertaken by a peace operation? Is such synchronization even realistic in those situations where there is no designated overall lead, such as in the "hybrid" arrangements, where responsibilities for the political process, military activities, and development efforts are divided among different organizations?

And finally, given the existing exposure to operational risk, it would be preferable if no new peace operations were deployed in circumstances where a durable and comprehensive political settlement has yet to be reached. Unfortunately, that is wishful thinking. If anything, recent precedent and prevailing geopolitical dynamics point to trends in the opposite direction. At least some peace operations will be called upon to deploy into situations where mediation efforts have not advanced the discussion very far on the core political issues, where there is only a partial peace to keep, and where consent of the parties is ambiguous. The lessons of the mid-1990s would suggest that the deployment of peacekeepers in such circumstances can be a recipe for failure. Where should the line be drawn?

There are many more difficult policy questions that need to be confronted. They will not have easy answers. Even if the mediator can avoid the deadly sins outlined here, there is no guarantee of success. Failure is inevitable, however, when we throw peacekeepers at conflicts or cast stones at the mediator, as a substitute for facing the painful political compromises necessary from all sides in order to achieve a sustainable peace.

————

Lakhdar Brahimi is former Foreign Minister of Algeria, a former UN SRSG, and international mediator in several conflict areas over the past two decades, including Lebanon, South Africa, the DRC, Haiti, Afghanistan, and Iraq. In 2000, he chaired a panel of eminent personalities, at the request of the UN Secretary-General, which produced a report ("The Brahimi Report") recommending sweeping reform of the UN's capacity to plan and mount peace operations. He is presently based at the Institute for Advanced Study in Princeton, New Jersey.

Salman Ahmed has been involved with the planning and conduct of UN Peace Operations over the past 15 years, at UN Headquarters and in several field assignments. He is presently a Visiting Professor at Princeton University's Woodrow Wilson School and the Lichtenstein Institute on Self-Determination (LISD).

Notes

The views expressed in this chapter are entirely those of the authors, and do not necessarily reflect those of the United Nations.

1. The role of a third party to help warring parties reach a negotiated political settlement to a deadly conflict is often described as one of "mediation" or "peacemaking." The management of the political aspects of that settlement, often with the assistance of peacekeepers (military, police, and civilian peacekeepers), can be referred to as "political process management," or the "political role" of the operation. Where political settlements are being negotiated and implemented concurrently, it is easy to get into a debate about terminology. The terms are used interchangeably in this chapter.

2. With the exception of life-saving humanitarian assistance, which should be delivered on the basis of need and not as reward for participation in the political process or punishment for lack thereof.

3. While no official UN political doctrine currently exists, the newly created Mediation Support Unit in the Department of Political Affairs has assembled a very useful online database of past political agreements and various lessons learned during their negotiation. The Best Practices Section of the Department of Peacekeeping Operations has developed online systems for collecting and disseminating lessons learned on all aspects of peace operations, including those related to political processes. The United Nations Institute for Training and Research (UNITAR) has developed some relevant training material on the role of SRSGs. Nongovernmental organizations (NGOs) have also produced some useful guidance material. For example, the Henri Dunant Centre has recently produced the useful publication *A Guide to Mediation: Enabling Peace Processes in Violent Conflicts*. And the Fafo research foundation's 1999 report, *Command from the Saddle: Managing United Nations Peace-Building Missions,* provides nuggets of insight that remain relevant today.

2 Peace Operation Partnerships: Lessons and Issues from Coordination to Hybrid Arrangements

A. Sarjoh Bah and Bruce D. Jones

If a central preoccupation for peace operations in 2007 was managing the interplay between political processes and security operations, that challenge was exacerbated when two or more institutions were jointly responsible for the overall peacekeeping response. The difficulties of inter-institutional arrangements were most visible in Darfur, where the United Nations and the African Union negotiated both over arrangements for a "hybrid" operation and over co-management of the Darfur peace process. But during 2007, inter-institutional arrangements complicated efforts in Kosovo and Afghanistan as well, and in a host of other settings.

While public debate over the UN-AU operation in Darfur proceeded as if it was the first time such arrangements had been used, the hybrid operation there should more correctly be understood as the latest development on a continuum, as a continuation of a trend that has increasingly characterized peace operations over the past decade. Indeed, of the more than fifty peace operations covered in this volume, nearly forty involved some form of inter-institutional partnership.

This trend has taken multiple forms of joint or joined-up action by the UN, regional organizations, the North Atlantic Treaty Organization (NATO), the Organization for Security Cooperation in Europe (OSCE), and UN-mandated multinational forces. A combination of the multidimensional mandates of contemporary peace operations, the resurgence of regional and subregional organizations, legitimacy and capacity considerations, and the exponential growth of peace operations precipitated this wave of institutional partnerships.

Despite their frequency, these partnerships continue to be primarily driven by operational exigencies, and have been managed through ad hoc mechanisms. Although there have been calls for more formalized partnerships, little progress in this direction has occurred.

This chapter explores the contours of these partnerships, and elucidates some of the associated problems, benefits, and lessons learned. While there was some evidence over the past two years of the emergence of a rational system for these partnerships based on comparative advantage or division of labor, the reality of international and regional politics is pushing global peacekeeping toward a different future, one in which several different organizations—principally, the UN, NATO, the EU, and the AU—each develop a fuller range of multifaceted capabilities, ranging from rapid, robust response to longer-term, civilian peacebuilding functions.

There are benefits to this model, but also costs. It will also take years to develop, even if trends continue on their present course. In the long interim, it looks likely that inter-institutional arrangements, in a variety of forms, will continue to dominate the peacekeeping landscape. The lessons learned suggest that these actors will have to overcome issues of politics, planning, personnel, and predictable funding.

Background: Evolving Partnerships

Inter-institutional partnerships have evolved dramatically over the past decade. Some of the earliest experiments occurred in West Africa, where the Economic Community of West African States (ECOWAS) and the UN were both involved in peacekeeping operations in Liberia (1993–1998) and Sierra Leone (1997–2005).[1] The relationship between the two organizations at the time was at best testy, sometimes downright antagonistic. ECOWAS claimed both a more immediate ability to respond, and a greater legitimacy that arose from the regional character of its operations. The UN, by contrast, claimed that the Charter gave it primacy of response, notwithstanding the recognition in Chapter VIII of the role that regional organizations can play in helping to maintain international peace and security.[2] These early partnerships were not limited to West Africa, as the UN entered into similar arrangements elsewhere, most notably in the Balkans.

Over time, however, the UN has come to see the value of regional action,[3] especially in immediate response to breaking crises, while regional and subregional organizations have increasingly recognized the merit—even the requirement—for Security Council authorization or at least support for their actions. Moreover, the simple reality of rising operational demands and the political requirements of different regions gave rise to a whole range of operational and political partnerships between organizations. Although each has been sui generis, they have broadly conformed to one of three types: sequential, parallel, or integrated operations.[4]

Sequential Operations

In the first type of partnership, different peacekeeping organizations undertook sequential operations at various stages of a response. For instance, in East Timor in 1999, Australia led the deployment of a mandated multinational force, the International Force for East Timor (INTERFET), which created the security framework for the subsequent deployment of the UN Transitional Administration in East Timor (UNTAET). Similarly in Liberia in 2003, ECOWAS deployed temporarily to create the conditions for the longer-term presence of the UN Mission in Liberia (UNMIL)—a far happier collaboration than in the first UN-ECOWAS experience in Liberia in the 1990s. Several sequential operations, dating back to

the early 1990s, have taken place—in Somalia, Kosovo, Côte d'Ivoire, Haiti, and Burundi.

Most of these sequential operations have been from a regional or multinational organization to the UN. However, we are now witnessing another generation of sequencing. The handover from NATO to the EU in Bosnia (and potentially from the UN to the EU in Kosovo), and the handover from the UN to an AU special task force in Burundi,[5] mark a new phenomenon of regional organizations mounting longer-term stabilization missions in the wake of robust international peacekeeping.

Parallel Operations

Increasingly common are parallel operations—where the UN and other entities operate in the same theater, under different command, but to achieve the same broad goals. In the 1990s there were several such parallel deployments—in Liberia, Bosnia, Georgia, Tajikistan, Ethiopia and Eritrea, Sierra Leone, and Côte d'Ivoire. There have been several variants.

One version is *short-term military support* from one organization to another. These operations are well illustrated by two different EU deployments to the Democratic Republic of Congo (DRC)—the International Emergency Multinational Force, codenamed Operation Artemis, and the EU Force Democratic Republic of Congo (EUFOR RD Congo), in 2003 and 2006 respectively.[6] National variants on this model include the UK deployment to Sierra Leone in 1999 in short-term support to the UN Assistance Mission in Sierra Leone (UNAMSIL), and France's (longer-term) deployment of Operation Licorne alongside the UN mission in Côte d'Ivoire.

A further variant is found in *linked military-observer operations*. The first such deployments were the joint UN and Commonwealth of Independent States (CIS) operations in Georgia and Tajikistan. Here we see one organization (the CIS) providing the military backbone of the operation, with a second (the UN) undertaking military observation, with the UN Mission of Observers to Tajikistan (UNMOT) and the UN Observer Mission in

Georgia (UNOMIG) mandated to ensure international oversight and add Security Council legitimacy to the CIS operations. Similarly, the UN-AU linked deployments along the Eritrea-Ethiopia border combined capability and legitimacy, though in that context the AU and the UN helped legitimate each other's presence.

A final variant is found in *parallel civilian-military operations*. Undertaken by NATO and the UN in Bosnia, this model has also been replicated in Kosovo (Kosovo Force [KFOR] and the UN Interim Administration Mission in Kosovo [UNMIK]) and Afghanistan (Operation Enduring Freedom, the International Security Assistance Force [ISAF], and the UN Assistance Mission in Afghanistan [UNAMA]). In all of these cases, the UN provides both a political framework for the military operation, bolstering its legitimacy, and the core political and civilian support to the national authorities. A quite different type of parallel civilian-military operation is found in Gaza, where the EU has a civilian operation (the EU Border Assistance Mission at Rafah [EU BAM Rafah]) that undertakes border monitoring on the Palestinian side of what is known as the Philadelphi corridor, while the US-led Multinational Force and Observers in Sinai (MFO Sinai) has a military presence on the Egyptian side, which in turn oversees Egyptian army deployments along the Rafah corridor.[7] The recently authorized EU-UN deployments to eastern Chad and the Central Africa Republic—whereby the EU will provide troops while the UN provides the police and civilian component—is the latest iteration of this model. EU police deployments in the DRC and Afghanistan are similar.[8]

Integrated Operations

Rarest are integrated operations—missions in which two organizations share command or where one organization subordinates its command to another. Indeed, so far there have been only three such operations. The first was the International Civilian Mission in Haiti (MICIVIH), which joined the operations of the UN and the Organization of American States (OAS) during 1993. There, the UN and the OAS operated under a dual-hatted Special Representative who had full command over both organizations' capabilities.

A second, partially integrated operation was in Kosovo. We have already noted the parallel military and civilian deployment of KFOR and UNMIK respectively. However, within UNMIK four different organizations—the UN Secretariat, the UN High Commissioner for Refugees (UNHCR), the European Union, and the Organization for Security and Cooperation in Europe—fused their civilian capabilities into a single operational structure under the command of a UN Special Representative. This arrangement was first mandated by UN Security Council Resolution 1244 (1999), and then negotiated and confirmed by the governing councils of the separate organizations.

Perhaps the financial and logistical support to the AU Mission in Sudan (AMIS) should be listed under this type of partnership as well. Although at no point did the UN, NATO, or the EU—all of which provided a range of financial and logistical support to AMIS—actually place their capabilities under direct AU command, nevertheless their capabilities were deployed for the sole purpose of enabling the AU operation and did not constitute co-deployed missions in their own right.[9]

The UN-AU Mission in Darfur (UNAMID) is of course the latest and the most developed of this rare breed of partnerships. Unlike the previous versions of this model, it establishes unified operational command over both the military and civilian components of the operation.[10]

The Darfur Operation

Capacity and legitimacy considerations played roles in the negotiation—"design" would be the wrong word—of UNAMID's structure. First, the experience of AMIS highlighted the financial and logistical shortcomings of the AU. Second, there was the need to resolve the government of Sudan's protracted refusal to accept a UN force, alongside Western troop contributors' inability to place their forces under non-UN command. The eventual compromise was for a force under joint UN and AU command.[11] (For further details, see the Sudan mission review in this volume, Chapter

3.6.) The agreement in its most basic form comprises the following elements: (1) joint decisionmaking by the UN Secretary-General and the AU chairperson about the appointment of the Special Representative and force commander, (2) operational command at the field level by the force commander, and (3) joint reporting to the AU Peace and Security Council and the UN Security Council.

Of the various issues confronting UN-AMID, by far the most controversial and the most likely to be challenging on the ground is the issue of integrated command and control. Joint reporting has been tested before—by the OAS and the UN in Haiti; by the UN and the ad hoc Office of the High Representative in Bosnia; and by the UN, the OSCE, the EU, and the UNHCR in Kosovo—but never over unified military action. While the appointment of a joint UN-AU head of UNAMID is a good first step, it remains to be seen how reporting to the UN and the AU will work in practice. The challenge is not with the command and control at the operational level per se, but with the strategic management of the mission. Although Resolution 1769 reiterates that command and control and backstopping will be provided by the UN, the issue of backstopping could be subject to different interpretations. Thus the success of UNAMID requires both institutions to be innovative and flexible to avoid serious risks to the missions.

Benefits and Costs

There have been important benefits to these various institutional partnerships. Sequential and coordinated military operations have enabled robust peacekeeping when the UN could not or would not meet that need. ECOWAS troops in Liberia were widely credited for stabilizing the situation in 2003, paving the way for the deployment of the larger UN force, as were Australian forces in Timor-Leste. Similarly, the EU's short-term military operations in DRC have been credited with critical backstopping of the UN in hostile environments. Parallel military-civilian operations have also allowed for institutions to build on each other's comparative advantages—for example, the UN and the EU

Secretary-General Ban Ki-Moon speaks with AMIS Force Commander General Martin Agwai during his visit to Darfur in advance of UNAMID deployment, 5 September 2007.

REUTERS/ Zohra Bensemra

have lent their respective civilian capabilities to NATO and AU military operations, as well as to each other; or put obversely, NATO in particular has added its muscle to UN political-civilian engagements in the Balkans and Afghanistan.

There have also been costs, however, and difficulties. In both sequential and short-term coordinated operations, the UN (and other institutions) faced significant handover challenges. This has been acute when the UN has taken over from poorly equipped or poorly supported regional organizations. In Liberia, for instance, the UN had to divert resources from other missions to meet the immediate logistical challenges of some of the rehatted troops.[12] Even with better-resourced organizations, however, handover problems occur. For example, according to a DPKO study, the UN Organization Mission in the Democratic Republic of Congo (MONUC) did not fully benefit from Operation Artemis's assets at handoff, since there was no residual presence of personnel or equipment, and since the EU did not consent to further requests for follow-up visits by its personnel.[13]

There have also been recurrent coordination problems between parallel operations.

Early experience of this in Bosnia (between the UN and NATO) shaped both US and UN thinking about peacekeeping in the following years—but in divergent ways, with the United States learning that military and civilian elements should be kept separate, and the UN learning that they should be integrated. The current operation in Afghanistan is reliving some of these tensions. In Kosovo the experience has by and large been smoother, but even there, at times, NATO and UNMIK have undertaken divergent strategies to deal with violence against or emanating from minority Serb populations (see the Kosovo mission review, Chapter 3.3).

Political issues also arise from the use of parallel or sequential operations. For example, the robust use of national assets, usually by Western countries (Australia, the United Kingdom, France, the United States), to prepare the ground for follow-on UN operations or bolster existing ones while providing clear benefits, raises the question of why these contributors are not willing to place their assets inside UN command structures (such are the politics of peacekeeping that this question is rarely raised vis-à-vis ECOWAS or AU actions). It is notable, of course, that this is precisely what occurred in the 2006 Lebanon operation, though European contributors to that mission did insist on special management arrangements (the Strategic Military Cell—see the Middle East mission review, Chapter 3.5).

Similarly, important questions of legitimacy and ownership are raised by inter-institutional arrangements. Strikingly, whereas the late 1990s and the early 2000s saw a trend of UN authorization creating legitimacy for regional and multinational forces, more recently we have seen the UN's legitimacy challenged (Sudan, Chad)—however cynically—and the use of regional peacekeeping as a legitimating mechanism for broader international engagement.

Lessons Learned

Many of these problems have been shared by several missions, even if the operations are themselves sui generis, and from some can be identified lessons that are applicable to contemporary operations:

• *Politics:* Whereas some early sequential and coordinated operations functioned without a shared political framework for action, over the past decade both regional and multinational forces have by and large come to accept the merits of Security Council authorization for their deployment and a UN political framework for their action. UN Security Council authorization of NATO's ISAF operation in Afghanistan, support to the Pacific Islands Forum–sanctioned operation in the Solomon Islands, authorization of AU missions in Africa, and UN requests for EU deployments clearly add a dimension of legal and/or political legitimacy to these institutions' operations.

• *Personnel:* Although the rehatting of troops in sequential or parallel operational contexts can create logistical burdens (as noted above), experiences from East Timor, Burundi, Liberia, and elsewhere suggest a high value to the remaining mission from retaining some of the troops who participated in previous or parallel operations—especially if those troops are from the lead nation.

• *Planning:* The use of joint planning mechanisms to overcome coordination problems was perhaps best developed in Kosovo, during the early phase of UNMIK, which created a joint planning cell that linked the operational heads of each of the composite organizations (EU, UN, UNHCR, and OSCE). A similar unit has belatedly been created in Afghanistan (the Policy Action Group—see the Afghanistan mission review, Chapter 3.1), in this instance also linked into the government.

• *Predictable funding mechanisms:* This further lesson is specific to cooperation with the AU. Support to AMIS clearly demonstrates that such a complex peace operation cannot function on ad hoc financial and logistical support systems. Rather, the experience emphasized the importance of predictable funding mechanisms to support peace operations undertaken by less well resourced regional organizations. The African Peace Facility provided a useful model for this, though the option of using UN-assessed contributions for authorized AU operations has gained support from previously reluctant donors—especially those who both found themselves financing AU operations through voluntary funds and now find themselves paying, at several times the rate, for the UN operations that were made necessary by the limits on the AU's capacity.[14]

Trends and Policy Options

Looking ahead, assessing the costs, benefits, and lessons learned from inter-institutional cooperation raises critical policy questions: whether arrangements will continue to be ad hoc; or whether we are heading toward a system of ever-more intricate and predictable partnerships between institutions, based on comparative advantage; or, alternatively, whether we will see each of the major peacekeeping institutions develop their own multidimensional capabilities, ranging from rapid, robust response to long-term civilian stabilization tools—thereby avoiding the need for inter-institutional collaboration.

On the face of it, a system of predictable partnerships based on comparative advantage would seem to be the most sensible and the most cost-effective approach. Such a system, presumably, would be based on the following institutional comparative advantages:

- Use of regional organizations, where they exist, for immediate response in peacekeeping contexts.
- Use of the UN as the mainstay provider of peacekeeping operations.
- Use of NATO or its assets as the core enforcement capacity for global peace operations.
- Use of the UN as the central coordinating entity, and as the core civilian and rule-of-law component for global operations.
- Supplemental support for civilian, rule-

of-law, and police functions from the EU.
- Additional capacities for civilian and military action as developed on a regional basis.

Logically, perhaps. But in reality, experience and politics appear to be forcing the alternative model—each of the main peacekeeping platforms developing the full range of capabilities. There is an advantage to this. Where one organization finds itself, perhaps unpredictably, barred from responding (e.g., NATO in Lebanon, the UN in Darfur and Chad), another will have the full capacity to take its place. But there are significant costs, too: in the need for multiple planning staffs, multiple civilian staffs, and most importantly, multiple standby forces—this in a context of sharply strained troop supply and rising peacekeeping budgets.

The rationale for the current approach differs from context to context. In both a European and an African context, a high premium on security independence appears to be the driving force of this model. The EU's aspiration for a security architecture independent of NATO is clearly articulated in the European Security and Defense Policy (ESDP) (though indications of a possible shift in French policy may presage a change in NATO-EU relations). In Africa, a history of instability and disappointing international response to conflict and crisis, notably the genocide in Rwanda in 1994 and the ongoing crisis in Darfur, is driving the AU's interest in developing robust response capabilities, as well as a civilian component. In NATO, the experience of Afghanistan is generating demand among some members at least for the organization to develop what it terms a "comprehensive" capacity—though EU-NATO politics may cut against this ambition. Finally at the UN, the recurrent experience of finding that putative partners are either unwilling to deploy or unacceptable to local counterparts drives a sense that the organization must have, intrinsic to itself, the full complement of response options, from robust enforcement to support for civilian governance, rule of law, and economic governance.

Conclusion

The complexities of the international political system militate against developing a predictable and reliable interlocking system. Given this, but given also that development of the full range of capacities at each of the major peacekeeping institutions is years away, inter-institutional arrangements—from sequencing to parallel operations to full-blown integration—will be the dominant mode of peacekeeping for the foreseeable future. These would benefit from standardization of the lessons discussed above: the use of joint planning mechanisms to overcome problems of strategic coordination; rehatting troops, especially from the lead nation, in the context of sequential or parallel operations; establishing appropriate and sustainable financing mechanisms for weaker institutions; and—perhaps most important, because it creates the context for the others—establishing a common political framework for action.

Notes

1. For more on operations undertaken by ECOWAS, the ECOWAS Cease-Fire Monitoring Group (ECOMOG), and the UN in the 1990s, see Alhaji M. S. Bah, "A Tale of Cooperation: ECOWAS, the United Nations, and Conflict Resolution in West Africa," *Queen's International Observer,* January–February 2006, http://www.qiaa.org/observer/bah.htm; Adekeye Adebajo, *Liberia's Civil War: Nigeria, ECOMOG, and Regional Security in West Africa* (Boulder: Lynne Rienner, 2000); Festus Aboagye, *ECOMOG: A Sub-Regional Experience in Conflict Resolution, Management, and Peacekeeping in Liberia* (Accra: Sedco, 1999); Fumni Olonisakin, "UN Cooperation with Regional Organization Peacekeeping: The Experience of ECOMOG and UNOMIL in Liberia," *International Peacekeeping* 3, no. 3 (1996): 33–51.

2. For more on the UN's cooperation with regional entities, see United Nations, *Cooperation Between the United Nations and Regional Organizations/Arrangements in a Peacekeeping Environment: Suggested Principles and Mechanisms* (New York: Department of Peacekeeping Operations, Lessons Learned Unit, March 1999).

3. Whereas in 1992 Boutros Boutros-Ghali downplayed the role of regional organizations in UN peacekeeping in his *Agenda for Peace,* thirteen years later the 2005 World Summit Outcome made specific reference to the value added to peace operations by regional organizations, focusing particularly on their ability to respond rapidly in the times of crisis. See United Nations, *2005 World Summit Outcome,* UN Doc. A/RES/60/1, 24 October 2005, p. 23.

4. Bruce Jones and Feryal Cherif, "Evolving Models of Peacekeeping: Policy Implications and Responses," 2004, http://pbpu.unlb.org/pbpu/library/bruce%20jones%20paper%20with%20logo.pdf.

5. The UN Operation in Burundi (ONUB) was itself deployed on the back of the African Union's first peace operation: the AU Mission in Burundi (AMIB).

6. Austria, Belgium, Brazil, Canada, Cyprus, Germany, Greece, Hungary, Ireland, Italy, the Netherlands, Portugal, South Africa, Spain, Sweden, and the United Kingdom contributed small numbers of troops to Artemis. For more on the mission, see United Nations, *Operation Artemis: The Lessons of the International Emergency Multinational Force* (New York: Department of Peacekeeping Operations, Best Practices Section, Military Division, October 2004).

7. A similar civilian-military divide characterizes the international presences in Iraq, though the mandated multinational force in Iraq is not a peacekeeping operation per se.

8. See European Union, EU Council Joint Action 2007/677/CFSP, 15 October 2007; United Nations, UN Doc. S/RES/1778, 25 September 2007.

9. The AU Mission in Somalia (AMISOM), the AU Mission in Support of Elections in Comoros (AMISEC), and the Force Multinational de la Communauté Économique et Monétaire de l'Afrique Centrale (FOMUC) also received external financial support, primarily from the EU's African Peace Facility.

10. For an in-depth analysis of the complexities of peacekeeping in Sudan, see Alhaji M. S. Bah and Ian Johnstone, "Peacekeeping in Sudan: The Dynamics of Protection, Partnerships, and Inclusive Politics," May 2007, http://www.cic.nyu.edu/internationalsecurity/docs/cic_paper2_sudan_final.pdf.

11. See UN Security Council Resolution 1769, UN Doc. S/2007/468, 30 July 2007. For additional details on the mandate, see also United Nations, *Report of the Secretary-General and the Chairperson of the African Union Commission on the Hybrid Operation in Darfur,* UN Doc. S/2007/307/Rev.1, 5 June 2007.

12. For more information, see United Nations, *Lessons Learned Study on the Start-Up Phase of the United Nations Mission in Liberia* (New York: Department of Peacekeeping Operations, Best Practices Section, April 2004). See also *ECOMIL After Action Review,* final report (Accra, August 2004).

13. *Operation Artemis,* p. 14.

14. For more on the facility, see "Mid-Term Evaluation of the African Peace Facility Framework Contract" (Report no. 9ACP RPR 22), December 2005, €250 million, http://www.dgroups.org/groups/cool/docs/apf-evaluation-final_report ecdpm_version_for_ecorys_190106.pdf.

3 Mission Reviews

Afghanistan

Efforts to stabilize Afghanistan faced serious challenges in 2007. Insecurity, corruption, and narcotics production and trafficking continued to worsen despite military operations.

During the year in review, international and national security forces continued operations designed to clear districts of Taliban fighters, and inflicted damage on the movement's command structure. However, Afghan administration and police have often been unable to hold territory after the withdrawal of the Afghan National Army and North Atlantic Treaty Organization–led International Security Assistance Force (ISAF). Nor was violence limited to the south; insurgents were active in several districts in and around Kabul itself, and increased their use of guerrilla and terrorist tactics.

Insurgency was not alone to blame for the deterioration in security. From the national to the district level, poor governance—including corruption and impunity of police and other government officials—was a growing problem. The patience of the Afghan people with government appeared to be wearing thin.[1] However, efforts to reform the police received new momentum with the deployment of a European Union police mission, and new resources to overhaul the Afghan National Police.

The cultivation of poppies—which provides the raw material for heroin production—surged to a new record high this past year. The lucrative drug economy not only financed violence and corruption, but also continued to motivate spoilers—within and outside government—for whom legitimate government authority is a threat to business.

Background: OEF, ISAF, and UNAMA

The ongoing operations in Afghanistan have their proximate origins in the 11 September 2001 terrorist attacks on the United States. The military response by the US-led coalition forces under Operation Enduring Freedom (OEF) unseated the Taliban government.[2] OEF remained focused on counterterrorism operations inside Afghanistan, leaving responsibility for rebuilding the Afghan state—and providing the requisite security—to other operations.

The signatories of the Bonn Agreement gave primary responsibility for security to the Afghan authorities, but they also recognized that developing effective institutions would take time. In the interim, they called for deployment of a UN-mandated international security force. ISAF was subsequently established pursuant to UN Security Council Resolution 1386 (2001). Its mandate was "to assist the Afghan Interim Authority in the maintenance of security in Kabul and its surrounding areas, so that the Afghan Interim Authority as well as the personnel of the United Nations can operate in a secure environment."[3] Forty-five hundred international troops were sent to Afghanistan for an initial six months under British command.

In March 2002, Security Council Resolution 1401 established the UN Assistance Mission in Afghanistan (UNAMA), which was mandated to support the political transition to a permanent Afghan government, to maintain peace and stability through the good offices of the Special Representative of the Secretary-General (SRSG), and to assist in aid coordination. UNAMA followed a "light footprint" approach, based on the principle that the Afghan government would lead the stabilization and reconstruction effort.

ISAF was initially deployed only in Kabul and the immediate vicinity, where it patrolled the city and provided security to key political events, including the 2002

Emergency Loya Jirga and 2003 Constitutional Loya Jirga. For its first year and beyond, the peace operation in Afghanistan was effectively without a security component in the provinces. A significant change occurred in August 2003, when the North Atlantic Treaty Organization (NATO) took command of ISAF. Under NATO, ISAF began deploying to the provinces in 2004, taking over existing provincial reconstruction teams (PRTs) in the north, and moving to the west in 2005.

With the transfer of ISAF command to NATO, however, also came the complication of dealing with the political concerns and constraints of the twenty-six members of NATO's decisionmaking body, the North Atlantic Council. These translated into caveats on the use of some members' forces, essentially limiting their deployment to more stable areas of the country.

With its absorption of US-led coalition forces, including 12,000 US troops in 2006, ISAF evolved from its predominant role as an umbrella for the nationally led PRTs. It constituted the main international military presence in Afghanistan in 2007, split into five regional commands: north, south, east, west, and central. As of October 2007, there were some 41,000 troops under ISAF command, including the force protection component of twenty-five PRTs and national contingent commands—making it the largest peace operation in the world.

Map No. 4255.5 Rev. 2   UNITED NATIONS
September 2007

Department of Field Support
Cartographic Section

International Security Assistance Force (ISAF)

- Authorization and Start Date   20 December 2001 (UNSC Res. 1386)
- Head of Mission   General Dan K. McNeill (United States)
- Budget $176.5 million (October 2006–September 2007)
- Strength as of 30 September 2007   Troops: 41,118

EU Police Mission in Afghanistan (EUPOL Afghanistan)

- Authorization Date   30 May 2007
- Start Date   June 2007
- Head of Mission   Jürgen Scholz (Germany)
- Budget $17.6 million (June 2007–May 2008)
- Strength as of 30 September 2007   Civilian Police: 70

Key Developments

Security and Political

Operation Enduring Freedom has downsized significantly, leaving fewer than 10,000 troops responsible for hunting terrorists and training Afghan security forces. Corresponding expansion of ISAF into volatile border regions has shifted its security assistance role toward greater offensive engagement with insurgents. Meanwhile, with the completion of the political transition prescribed by the Bonn Agreement,[4] the role of UNAMA has now changed to coordinating and monitoring the security, development, and governance goals agreed on by the international community and the government of Afghanistan under the 2006 Afghanistan Compact.

During the year in review, international and national security forces continued operations in

UN Assistance Mission in Afghanistan (UNAMA)

- Authorization and Start Date — 28 March 2002 (UNSC Res. 1401)
- SRSG and Head of Mission — Tom Koenigs (Germany)
- Senior Military Advisor — Brigadier Philip Jones (United Kingdom)
- Senior Police Advisor — Roberto Bernal (Philippines)
- Budget — $123.5 million (1 January 2006–31 December 2007)
- Strength as of 31 October 2007 — Military Observers: 15
  Police: 3
  International Civilian Staff: 223
  Local Civilian Staff: 1,040
  UN Volunteers: 31

For detailed mission information see p. 230.

the south, southeast, and east of the country, clearing districts of Taliban fighters and inflicting damage on the movement's command structure. Intelligence made possible the arrest and targeting of key leadership in both Afghanistan and Pakistan. But, in some instances, Afghan authorities have been unable to hold territory after the withdrawal of the military.

Military operations struggled to support the overarching political goals of statebuilding, by protecting nascent government institutions and creating space for development, while avoiding political pitfalls. From the military perspective, OEF and ISAF faced calculations between short-term tactics to aggressively pursue insurgents, and long-term strategy to win over Afghans to the cause of the government. Yet continued civilian casualties from military operations have further eroded Afghan support for foreign troops. Aggressive tactics—especially air strikes—also created tensions between ISAF and OEF forces over their respective sensitivities toward civilian populations. Some actors who were engaged in political and reconstruction activities argued that military tactics unintentionally exacerbated local political tensions.

ISAF now has the geographic reach that many initially envisioned, but its presence in regions previously devoid of an international military or a strong government has provoked an armed response from insurgents and other would-be spoilers. During the years when there was no international security presence, warlords, drug traffickers, and insurgents consolidated their hold. ISAF forces in the north, the west, and the central highlands region continue to play a stabilization role, but in the south and the southeast they are engaged in a violent counterinsurgency.

Because of caveats on the use of some NATO contingents' troops, ISAF forces in the south were largely unable to draw on troops or assets based elsewhere in the country for reinforcement. This was increasingly a source of tension within NATO, with some members arguing that the caveats meant placing force protection ahead of mission needs.[5] High casualty rates sustained by the Dutch and Canadian contingents in particular created difficulties for those governments in maintaining domestic support for their troops' continuing deployment.

Taliban fighters increasingly are relying on guerrilla tactics, improvised explosive devices, and suicide bombing as a way to avoid direct combat. Nationwide, suicide attacks and kidnappings have accelerated; nine months into the year, both the number of attacks and the number of casualties appeared set to overtake those of 2006.[6]

Recognizing the cross-border dimension of the insurgency, Afghan and Pakistani tribal leaders convened a Peace Jirga in August 2007. More striking, in September, President Hamid Karzai mooted peace talks with senior Taliban leadership. OEF counterterrorism operations will likely influence their decision; few insurgent leaders have been willing to participate in the national reconciliation program in place since 2006.

Governance and Corruption

As noted, the cultivation of poppies surged to a new record high this past year. Some

8,200 tons of opium were produced—34 percent more than in 2006, and a twofold increase over 2005.[7] The lucrative drug economy not only finances violence and corruption, but also continues to motivate spoilers—within and outside government—for whom legitimate government authority is a threat to business.

There is ongoing discussion between NATO and the UN regarding a greater role for ISAF in counternarcotics. Meanwhile, the Afghan government is under pressure from the United States to authorize controversial aerial spraying of poppy fields, which some fear could drive farmers to support the Taliban.

Efforts to reverse what some saw as Afghanistan's slide toward a narcostate focused on furthering the rule of law. Ending corruption within the government would be a vital step toward redressing the current backslide. Although police reform is receiving renewed attention, questions linger as to whether it is moving in the right direction. Vetting of police officers has largely stalled, while international trainers are in short supply. The Ministry of Interior as a whole remains plagued by problems, undermining its effectiveness and its legitimacy in the eyes of Afghans.

This is part of a wider problem. There are few effective governmental institutions through which to deliver security and essential services to the population, most importantly at the subnational level. Citizen engagement with the state is instead often marked by corrupt and predatory officials.

Reform of the police received renewed effort with the deployment of a European Union police mission in June 2007 (EUPOL Afghanistan). The mission is off to a slow start, however. Afghan recruits have been in short supply, Turkey has held up agreement between NATO and the EU over security guarantees for provincially deployed trainers, and the EU mission commander resigned three months into his appointment. Critics observe that an increased EU civilian role might substitute for a more robust military role by wary member states. The

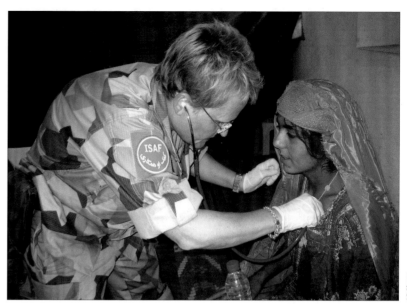

Swedish ISAF soldier examines an Afghan woman in the Faiz Abad district of Seberghan province north of Kabul, 16 June 2007.

United States is planning to spend a total of $2.5 billion during 2007–2008 to overhaul the police, including retraining all 72,000 officers. Progress here, too, has been modest, while the use of US military personnel for police training has raised concerns about militarization of the police—underscoring fundamental differences in vision over police reform and the urgent need for harmonization of approaches.

Reconstruction and Security: The Provincial Reconstruction Teams

Insecurity has narrowed the range of civilian actors operating in the south and southeast and limited the operational capacities of the remaining agencies. In this gap, reconstruction activities are channeled through provincial reconstruction teams (PRT).

The PRTs—small, provincially based deployments of civilians and military personnel first introduced in 2002—were an early attempt to jointly merge development and security roles in support of statebuilding. Since their inception, there has been disagreement over their function. Many within the assistance community have argued that the PRTs, by pro-

---

Box 3.1.1 Peacekeeping Principles and Guidelines: The UN's Capstone Doctrine

UN peacekeeping has been a major tool in the management of interstate and intrastate conflicts for nearly sixty years. But despite the critical role that peace operations have come to play, especially in the post–Cold War period, the only documented body of principles instructing UN peacekeepers in the field and at headquarters is a set of vague guidelines produced in 1995, *Peace Operations 2010.*[1] The year 2007, however, saw some progress in this area with the UN's release of a new set of principles and guidelines for its peacekeeping operations, known as the Capstone Doctrine. A product of the UN's Peacekeeping Best Practices Section, this document represents the first major doctrinal contribution produced by Department of Peacekeeping Operations (DPKO).

The development of a clear doctrine for UN peacekeepers is part of DPKO's larger reform agenda, as set out in *Peace Operations 2010.* The reform agenda aims to improve DPKO's ability to launch new peacekeeping missions with increased professionalism, and increasing the efficiency of its management of existing missions. In this context, the Capstone Doctrine, which is still pending approval by Under-Secretary-General Jean-Marie Guéhenno, aims to serve as an overarching guide for DPKO until it is reviewed again in 2010.

The fruit of an extensive consultative process, and drawing on the UN's history in the field as well as landmark reports such as *An Agenda for Peace* and the Brahimi Report, the Capstone Doctrine captures the dramatic evolution of UN peacekeeping over the past six decades. The comparative advantages and limitations exhibited by UN peacekeeping—lessons learned—inform Capstone's fundamental standards, which will instruct practitioners in the conduct of UN peacekeeping operations. The Capstone Doctrine provides instructions on a wide range of issues, including the evolving international environment, administration and planning, the complex dynamics of managing integrated missions, and supporting host populations. While the document attempts to provide the most comprehensive multidimensional doctrinal guidance, covering the complex nature of contemporary peace operations, it does not provide military doctrine, as that will remain the prerogative of member states.

Recognizing the continued evolution of peacekeeping doctrine and the need for further refinement, the Capstone Doctrine by no means represents the final word on the matter, but it is hoped that the doctrine will initiate deeper consideration and debate within UN headquarters, in the field, and among the UN's peacekeeping partners. In this vein, future iterations of the Capstone Doctrine will benefit from regular engagement with member states, particularly troop-contributing countries, the permanent members of the Security Council, as well as experts.

Source: United Nations, *Capstone Doctrine, Draft 3* (New York: Department of Peacekeeping Operations, June 2007), http://pbpu.unlb .org/pbps/pages/public/viewprimarydoc.aspx?docid=481.

Note: 1. United Nations, *Peace Operations 2010* (New York: Department of Peacekeeping Operations, 1995), http://www.un.org/depts/dpko/dpko/ articles/article191006.html.

---

viding humanitarian and development assistance, blur the line between the military and nongovernmental organizations (NGOs). Instead, it has been argued, they should focus on stabilization functions—security sector reform, presence patrols, and force multiplication—and limit their engagement on reconstruction to large-scale projects or government infrastructure.

Through engagement with the UN, the Afghan government, and the NGO community, the PRT concept evolved and expanded, although differences among individual commanders, lead-country approaches, and areas of operation mean variations in PRTs' respective approaches. Nonetheless, even proponents of the use of PRTs in insecure regions concede that PRT activities are not always the most appropriate, and that willingness to enter dangerous areas is not a substitute for prior experience in development. Some civilian officials, while recognizing that such projects are important, argue that there should be greater oversight over how this money is spent. In particular, there is a continual risk that embarking on development projects without an understanding of the local market or political context—and thus of the potential impact of the project—can undermine, rather than support, local stability. The Afghan government has leveled criticism that PRT projects often fail to address government-identified community priorities. During 2007, though, ISAF was making greater efforts to follow the interim Afghanistan National Development Strategy.

Reconstruction and Development

The interim Afghanistan National Development Strategy (ANDS) of 2006 laid out priorities for development and means of achieving the Afghan government's vision. The parallel Afghanistan Compact represents the political agreement between the Afghan government and international community to achieve the ANDS benchmarks. Together, they provide the overall framework for rebuilding the country.

Over the past year, the government held public, subnational consultations on the full ANDS—slated for completion in 2008—in all provinces. The Joint Coordination and Monitoring Board (JCMB), which oversees the Compact, largely focused on establishing structures and reporting mechanisms, so far limiting its impact on the ground. Meanwhile, insecurity and poor governance have driven a "quick fix" approach among donors, diverting attention from the Compact. Policy and funding decisions are often made outside the JCMB. As with security and governance, the development benchmarks outlined in the Compact will likely not be met on time unless the Afghan government and international community summon the necessary political will and resources for reform of government institutions and the JCMB, which has been criticized for, among other things, being too inclusive and therefore unwieldy.

Strategic Coordination

If there was one theme that focused efforts in 2007, however, it was the challenge of strategic coordination—specifically the effort to reconcile what should be complementary, but at times proved to be competing, goals of counterinsurgency and statebuilding.

Though the challenge of strategic coordination is not unique to Afghanistan, the operation in Afghanistan is complex and, in many respects, unique. It is a partnership among the Afghan government, UNAMA, ISAF, the US coalition forces under OEF, and myriad other multilateral and bilateral actors. Each has a different mandate, different capabilities, and different access to resources.

Coordination among international and national actors alone will not determine whether efforts to stabilize and rebuild Afghanistan succeed. However, absent a hierarchy among OEF, ISAF, and UNAMA, coordination was vital to ensuring that these distinct missions acted in concert, rather than at cross-purposes, in pursuing their political, peacemaking, and reconstruction goals. As managing insecurity became a greater priority, coordination among international military forces and civilian political and development organizations has become increasingly salient—both for improving the efficacy of counterinsurgency operations and for increasing space for political and development activities.

Yet, as Lieutenant-General David Richards, former commander of ISAF, warned during his tenure, "Lack of unity and co-ordination between the numerous different organizations and agencies often manifests itself in a situation close to anarchy, both military and civil."[8] In addition to separate organizational mandates, effective coordination between military and civilian organizations faced further challenges, including fundamental differences in cultures and approaches. The practice of using relatively short rotations, especially of military personnel, worked against a long-term contextual understanding of the situation on the ground, and also prevented the development of interpersonal relationships between counterparts. These factors affected ad hoc and institutionalized coordination from the international to the district level throughout the year.

From the national to the provincial level, numerous coordination mechanisms have been established to "deconflict" activities, prevent duplication of efforts, and improve strategic alignment between the statebuilding and counterinsurgency goals of the Afghan government and military and civilian actors. The Joint Coordination and Monitoring Board, established in April 2006, oversees and assesses implementation of the Afghanistan Compact. Other examples include the PRT Executive Steering Committee, which serves as a forum for discussion about coordination of the PRTs, and the PRT Working Group, a subsidiary of the committee that consults with the broader group of government, NGOs, and the UN. At the regional level, the first conference between ISAF Regional Command–East and UNAMA—held in April 2007—marked a significant step in coordinating ISAF's security role with the governance and development work of UNAMA.

NATO's senior civilian representative, appointed in 2003, represents the North Atlantic Council locally and liaises with ISAF, the Afghan government, UNAMA, other civilian agencies, and donor governments. The senior civilian representative does not have any authority over the commander of ISAF, however, arguably replicating a political-military split within ISAF itself.

Two relatively new mechanisms at the national level—the Policy Action Group and the Comprehensive Approach Team—warrant attention for their potential roles in reversing insecurity and its causes.

The Policy Action Group. In response to the deterioration of security in southern Afghanistan, the Policy Action Group (PAG) was established in July 2006. The PAG is convened by the National Security Council and brings together the president; key ministers, including those of Defense and Interior; UNAMA; ISAF; the US coalition forces; and important diplomatic representatives. It functions as a crisis management decisionmaking body that meets on a biweekly basis and attempts to make real-time decisions and take coordinated action. Proponents argue that the PAG provides one of the few forums that convenes key figures, providing a unique possibility to deliver results.[9]

The PAG is focused on enabling sustained development in four key provinces: Kandahar, Helmand, Zabul, and Uruzgan. The impetus was the intensity of the insurgency encountered by ISAF following its deployment to the south. However, the ANDS and the Afghanistan Compact were predicated on the country being at peace or becoming peaceful, conditions not present in these provinces. Proponents of the PAG argue that both processes are conflict-insensitive and therefore do not provide for timely response to crises.[10] The PAG, viewed as a way to coordinate government and international efforts in high-risk districts in order to rapidly provide an environment for development, has emphasized targeted reform of the government administration, establishment of auxiliary police units, and focusing support to "Afghan development zones"—areas secured by ISAF and Afghan security forces in which governance, reconstruction, and development are synchronized. Initial concern that the PAG replicated existing coordination structures of the ANDS and the JCMB appear to have been allayed, as the PAG has situated itself as an enabler of the ANDS.

Perhaps the PAG's biggest flaw is that, due to poor subnational governance, its priorities are not articulated from the provincial level to the center, and therefore problems discussed at the highest levels may not be reflective of local priorities. Likewise, the National Security Council no longer has regional offices and has limited potential to transfer enhanced capacity from the center to the provincial and district levels, where it is most needed.

Another concern is that the bilateral composition of the PAG is not regionally inclusive. Despite both recognition that Afghanistan's problems require regional solutions, and the acknowledgment in August 2007 by Pakistan's president, Pervez Musharraf, that the Taliban has used tribal areas as safe havens, no regional countries participate in the PAG. The strength of the PAG thus far has been its operation as an efficient, high-level crisis management body, but its capacity to produce tangible improvements on the ground have yet to be proven.

The Comprehensive Approach Team. The Comprehensive Approach Team (CAT) is convened on a regular basis by the planning cell within ISAF and includes ISAF forces, UNAMA other UN agencies, and NGOs. The usual point of engagement between ISAF and civilians is through the NGO Civil-Military Working Group, which provides a forum for NGOs to voice concerns about military, government, and donor reconstruction and development projects. The CAT, by contrast, is focused on military operations. Whereas civilians are usually excluded from the military planning process, CAT meetings provide a forum for the UN and NGOs to directly interact with ISAF's military planners, both to influence the direction of its military operations and to provide a perspective on its six-month planning process.

The transparency of the inner workings of the planning process marks a radical departure from previous processes in Afghanistan, and has resulted in increased confidence among ISAF, the UN, and NGOs. A new ISAF plan under development incorporates feedback from the civilian side of the peacekeeping and assistance operation. ISAF and UNAMA are now able to determine where participation has been meaningful, while the process also provides an opportunity to improve areas where engagement is still difficult.

Conclusion

There is increasing recognition by both the government of Afghanistan and the international community that the counterinsurgency cannot be won by military means alone. As a result of constructive engagement, trust and coordination between the international civilian and military actors in Afghanistan are improving. It remains to be seen whether these processes will yield tangible results that are able to change realities on the ground.

At the same time, the international community may need to scale back its expectations, while increasing its time horizons. Both counterinsurgency and the underlying state-building objective it serves are long-term endeavors. A sustained international presence may be required for some time to come. And the declining security situation and difficulties in establishing stable governmental structures in the country underscore that Afghanistan and its international partners still face a peace*making* challenge, along with continued peacekeeping and peacebuilding needs.

Notes

1. See Asia Foundation, "Statebuilding, Political Progress, and Human Security in Afghanistan: Reflections on a Survey of the Afghan People" (Kabul, 2007).

2. Unlike other international actors that operate at the formal invitation of the Afghan government, there is no status of forces agreement between the government and the coalition forces.

3. UN Security Council Resolution 1386. ISAF's mandate additionally "*requests* the leadership of the International Security Assistance Force to provide periodic reports on progress towards the implementation of its mandate through the Secretary-General" (italics in original).

4. The Bonn Agreement is formally known as the Agreement on Provisional Arrangements in Afghanistan Pending the Re-establishment of Permanent Government Institutions.

5. International Crisis Group, "Countering Afghanistan's Insurgency: No Quick Fixes," Asia Report no. 123 (Kabul, 2 November 2006), p. 15.

6. By 1 October 2007, 100 suicide bombings had killed 290 people, a rate expected to surpass the 123 bombs and 305 deaths of 2006. Kirk Semple, "Bomber Attacks Bus of Afghan Soldiers; 30 Dead," *New York Times,* 1 October 2007. In the first eight months of 2007, "reported security incidents"—which includes bombings, firefights, and intimidation—were up to 600 per month versus some 500 per month in the same period in 2006, a 20 percent increase. Likewise, 2,500–3,000 people—a quarter of them civilians—had been killed by insurgency-related violence by 1 October 2007, also a 20 percent increase over

the same period in 2006. Fatality rates for NATO and US soldiers were up nearly 20 percent, to 161 deaths. Finally, attacks and bombings killed 379 Afghan police in the first eight months of 2007, compared with 257 in 2006. David Rhode, "Afghan Police Suffer Setbacks as Taliban Adapt," *New York Times,* 2 September 2007.

7. UN Office on Drugs and Crime, "Afghanistan Opium Survey 2007," Executive Summary, p. iv, http://www.unodc.org/pdf/research/afg07_exsum_web.pdf.

8. Quoted in International Crisis Group, "Countering Afghanistan's Insurgency," p. 18.

9. Personal interview with a UNAMA official, Kabul, 16 September 2007.

10. Ibid.

Democratic Republic of Congo

The 2006 national elections in the Democratic Republic of Congo (DRC), which led to the election of Joseph Kabila as president, seemed to presage a new era for the country, one with the promise of political accommodation and a move toward democratic systems. Given substantial progress in 2005 and 2006 in consolidating the political process, the UN Organization Mission in the Democratic Republic of Congo (MONUC) and the international presence as a whole signaled an intent to focus efforts in 2007 on concluding the process of disarmament, demobilization, and reintegration (DDR) and on launching a security sector reform (SSR) program. Also, MONUC and other actors such as the European Union have undertaken serious efforts to rebuild the country's police force, leading to some improvements in the overall human rights situation, and in launching more coordinated economic recovery efforts.

Efforts on these fronts proceeded with mixed results, and were substantially complicated by renewed violence in the east, involving the government, the renegade general, Laurent Nkunda, and several militias. The violence dampened expectations, and cast renewed doubts over the outcomes from the hard-won peace. For much of the year, MONUC was compelled to reorient its efforts toward responding to mass displacement and humanitarian crisis in the Kivus. Indeed, the DDR process and the renewed violence were intertwined, as the government treated noncompliance with DDR agreements as an occasion for launching new military activity against insurgents. This generated some early successes for the government, though many within MONUC and other international ob-

servers were initially concerned that the government did not have the capacity to successfully implement its military strategy, and that its approach risked further fueling conflict, especially in the east. By December 2007, however, MONUC had determined that it would support renewed operations by the government in the east. The country entered a volatile new phase, and MONUC shifted its doctrinal and operational stance toward robust operational support to the elected government.[1]

Background

Despite the signing of a 1999 cease-fire agreement, the multiparty war in the DRC, dubbed "Africa's First World War," only came to an end in 2002 with the signing of

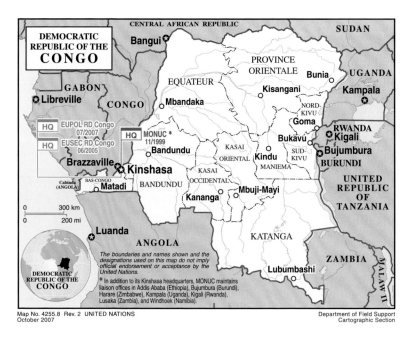

UN Organization Mission in the Democratic Republic of Congo (MONUC)

• Authorization and Start Date	30 November 1999 (UNSC Res. 1279)
• SRSG and Head of Mission	William Lacy Swing (United States)
• Force Commander	Lieutenant-General Babacar Gaye (Senegal)
• Police Commissioner	Daniel Cure (France)
• Budget	$1,115.7 million (1 July 2007–30 June 2008)
• Strength as of 31 October 2007	Troops: 16,655 Military Observers: 733 Police: 994 International Civilian Staff: 931 Local Civilian Staff: 2,062 UN Volunteers: 577

For detailed mission information see p. 220.

EU Advisory and Assistance Mission for Security Reform in the Democratic Republic of Congo (EUSEC RD Congo)

• Authorization Date	2 May 2005 (Council Joint Action 2005/355/CFSP)
• Start Date	June 2005
• Head of Mission	General Pierre-Michel Joana (Italy)
• Budget	$8.0 million (October 2006–September 2007)
• Strength as of 30 September 2007	Civilian Staff: 46

EU Police Mission in the Democratic Republic of Congo (EUPOL RD Congo)

• Authorization Date	12 June 2007 (Council Joint Action 2007/405/CFSP)
• Start Date	July 2007
• Head of Mission	Adilio Custodio (Portugal)
• Budget	$1.8 million (October 2006–September 2007)
• Strength as of 30 September 2007	Civilian Police: 23 Civilian Staff: 9

the Global All-Inclusive Accord. The agreement called for the establishment of a transitional government with a two-year timeline,

and for the convening of national elections. Joseph Kabila became the president of the interim government, which also comprised four vice presidents, representing the president's party, the People's Party for Reconstruction and Development (PPRD), the Rassemblement Congolais pour la Démocratie (RCD-Goma), the Movement for the Liberation of Congo (MLC), and the unarmed opposition and civil society.

MONUC was authorized by Security Council Resolution 1279 (1999), and given a mandate: to establish contact with the signatories of the Lusaka Cease-Fire Agreement, including the state signatories; liaise with the Joint Military Commission; provide information on the security situation in its area of operation; and facilitate the delivery of humanitarian assistance to displaced persons, refugees, children, and other war-affected persons. MONUC's mandate has evolved from its initial role as an observer to a more robust posture, especially since the adoption of Resolution 1493 (2003), which authorized the mission to use force in the protection of civilians.

The crisis in the east in 2003, which was partially precipitated by the withdrawal of Ugandan forces from the town of Bunia, threatened to degenerate into a humanitarian crisis as various militias battled each other to fill the void. This prompted the EU, at the request of the UN Secretary-General, to deploy the International Emergency Multinational Force, also known as Operation Artemis, in June 2003. Operation Artemis—the EU's first out-of-area operation—was mandated to provide security for a three-month period, pending reinforcement of the thin MONUC presence in the area. In May–June 2004, a group of local dissidents led by General Laurent Nkunda overran the town of Bukavu in South Kivu, despite MONUC's presence. MONUC's perceived failure to prevent the takeover affected its credibility with the local population, who took to the streets protesting against the mission. However, public confidence in MONUC's capabilities was partly restored when, in 2005, it mounted robust operations against "spoilers" in the area.

The mission has since maintained a strong presence in the volatile east.

Continued instability in the country's eastern provinces delayed the planned transition to an elected government from 2003 until 2006, when the country held its first multiparty elections in forty years. The elections were facilitated by MONUC as well as by a second EU short-term military support operation, the EU Force Democratic Republic of Congo (EUFOR RD Congo), deployed from July to November 2006.

With its 16,665 troops and 994 police, MONUC is at present the largest UN peacekeeping operation in the field.

Major Developments

Security and Political

The government of President Kabila, emboldened by the legitimacy from the widely acclaimed presidential and parliamentary elections of 2006, entered 2007 determined to conclude the process of disarming, demobilizing, and reintegrating all of the armed groups in the country. The government issued an ultimatum to former RCD-Goma leader Azarias Ruberwa, General Laurent Nkunda, and MLC leader Jean-Pierre Bemba that they allow their armed personal aides and militias to demobilize in March 2007. In their place, the government offered twelve police bodyguards to each leader. While Ruberwa complied, Jean-Pierre Bemba resisted the move, after which the government launched an attack on his headquarters in Kinshasa. According to diplomatic sources, over 600 people were killed, and Bemba was forced to seek refuge in the South African embassy before being granted permission to travel to Lisbon to seek medical treatment. Afterward, the remnants of Bemba's forces were subjected to summary demobilization and dispersed out of Kinshasa.

The casualty toll from these clashes, however, paled in comparison to the deaths and displacements caused by renewed fighting in the troubled Kivu provinces. The fighting in the

east during the second half of 2007 pitted rebels loyal to General Laurent Nkunda against several groups, including the national army (Forces Armées du République Démocratique du Congo [FARDC]) and the Forces Démocratiques de la Libération du Rwanda [FDLR]).[2] The fighting also involved scattered groups of traditional Mayi Mayi, some of whom allegedly joined the government in the regional towns of Bukavu, Maniema, and Goma.[3] The fighting and resultant displacements forced MONUC to concentrate 85 percent of its forces there to protect civilians and help stave off humanitarian disaster.

The continuing crisis prompted William Swing, the Special Representative of the Secretary-General (SRSG), to visit the area in September on a confidence-building tour designed to reassure local leaders and government officials in Kaleme, Moba, and Pweto of the determination of the international community to maintain peace in the region. Some success was noted after the visits of the SRSG to the Ituri area. MONUC subsequently called on the government to develop a coherent political, diplomatic, and military plan to address the situation in the two Kivus.[4]

Economic Reconstruction

Despite the instability in the east, MONUC's presence has paved the way for the commencement of immediate postconflict reconstruction and long-term peacebuilding activities in other parts of the country. The establishment of the Country Assistance Framework (CAF) in the postelection period was designed to harmonize the various programs and activities of the large number of agencies involved in reconstruction efforts. The CAF, which fused the UN Development Assistance Framework (UNDAF) with the World Bank's Country Assistance Strategy (CAS), is a coordinating framework aimed at reducing the transaction costs on the government of the DRC and among the various bilateral and multilateral agencies involved in reconstruction work in the country. It consists of over seventeen bilateral and multilateral members, including MONUC and other members of the UN system. The CAF, which covers the period from 2007 to 2010, is tailored to the priorities identified in the country's poverty reduction strategy paper, which covers the same period. Some bilateral donors have expressed concern that basing the CAF on the World Bank's poverty reduction strategy provides too narrow a lens for development in a still-insecure setting like the DRC.

DDR and SSR Effort:
The Brassage Process

The original roadmap for security sector reform in the DRC, laid out in February 2004, had six key elements: (1) development of a comprehensive national security sector policy, (2) coordination of SSR and DDR bodies under this common vision and strategy, (3) a plan for police reform, (4) creation of laws concerning national defense and the armed forces, (5) execution of a realistic military integration plan linked to comprehensive DDR, and (6) a coherent, timely, effective, and sustainable plan for deployment of integrated FARDC units, and the refurbishment of military training.

Accordingly, MONUC established a joint commission (jointly chaired by the SRSG and

MONUC peacekeepers carry weapons handed over by fighters loyal to former rebel leader Jean-Pierre Bemba in Kinshasa, 23 March 2007.

the DRC government) that coupled with a contact group (chaired by the EU and Belgium) to review policy, track progress, support needs, and advise and assist the government. This process led to the creation of two primary national plans for SSR in the DRC, one for DDR, and one for integrating the army.

In its national DDR efforts, MONUC and the government adopted a model known as "brassage," the core thrust of which was to reorganize former rebel units in two respects. First, the goal was to dismantle the rebel command and control lines, integrating former combatants to the new lines of FARDC authority. Second, the rapid disarmament and demobilization plan also involved the physical relocation of combatants to different regions of the country. The first phase of the brassage ran from September 2004 to September 2005, after which the second phase included limited military assistance by MONUC to the FARDC for enforced demobilization.

Under MONUC's mandate to facilitate DDR, 44,046 former combatants had been disarmed by December 2006, while 96,478 had been demobilized. Of the latter number, 50,541 had chosen to be reintegrated into the new army, resulting in fourteen of an intended eighteen integrated brigades.

MONUC also facilitated the provision of basic police training to 53,000 Congolese, with 32,000 receiving basic equipment from the UN Development Programme (UNDP). While police training was initially focused on providing security for the 2006 elections, the initiative has continued. The adoption of Resolution 1756 (2007) renewed attention to strategic planning on justice and correction issues, which had received little attention in the past.

Despite the challenges in the east, the government pledged to launch an SSR program as part of its "governance contract," placing particular emphasis on the rule of law.

In February 2007, a contact-group meeting in Pretoria transferred leadership of SSR programming to the Congolese government. In July 2007, the first government-led meet-

REUTERS/Ho New

ing produced a ministerial vision for defense reform that consisted of four pillars: (1) creation of a deterrent force (often referred to as a rapid reaction force), (2) development of a "vision of excellence" for the army by restoring discipline, training, and judicial oversight, (3) creation of an army that contributes to the reconstruction of the country, and (4) creation of an army that is self-supporting and can feed soldiers and dependants. Accordingly, the contact group agreed to host a roundtable on SSR in October 2007. During this period, however, schisms and splits within the army structure became evident, over events in the east but also over visions for the future of and ownership over SSR. Tensions between actors, and an overall lack of coordination and leadership, delayed SSR progress. These issues culminated in the postponement of the planned roundtable when both the chief of staff and the minister of defense presented competing plans for reform, at various levels of clarity, reflecting deep policy divisions between major bilateral donors.

While MONUC is preparing to conventionally train former rebel combatants in the integrated fourteen brigades by September 2009—as the new national army—the Congolese government is itself carrying out a similar process with at least six more brigades, and has mobilized assistance through bilateral arrangements with other countries such as Angola, South Africa, Belgium, and the United States. Training was scheduled to start in September 2007 and continue until September 2009, and will be linked with the major guiding policy statement on development and security for the five-year period (2007–2011) as released during the presidential inaugural speech on 6 December 2006.

Meanwhile, MONUC and UNDP were also involved in an innovative, cross-border program for the disarmament and return of foreign forces on Congolese soil in a model called disarmament, demobilization, reintegration, resettlement, and rehabilitation (DDRRR). The UN facilitated the departure of 15,000 armed foreign elements during the first phase of this program. Significantly, the MONUC-UNDP initiative has followed these ex-combatants, including former members of the Forces Armées Rwandaises (FAR) and the genocidal Interhamwe militia, as well as their families, to recipient countries such as Rwanda, Burundi, and Uganda, and has partly assisted in their resettlement and rehabilitation. A further 24,927 combatants, of whom 1,001 are women, have also been disarmed, while 20,000 militia in the Ituri region have been demobilized. This group of nearly 45,000 is now awaiting repatriation and resettlement to their countries of origin.

A significant complication in the DDR process arose with accusations of substantial corruption in the Commission Nationale de Désarmement, Démobilisation et Réinsertion (CONADER). The government agreed to restructure the widely discredited commission.

Despite the aforementioned progress, by December 2007 there were still 34,786 troops from the Kinshasa garrison and the Republican Guards who needed to be demobilized. Furthermore, efforts to implement a DDR process in the east, which commenced on 4 January 2007 following an agreement struck in Kigali, Rwanda, collapsed soon thereafter.

The Mixage Process and Renewed Violence in the East

A new framework for DDR in the east emerged in December 2006, following a meeting in Kigali between General Nkunda and President Kabila's special adviser, General John Nkumbi. This meeting resulted in an agreement to establish new brigades, under the aegis of the FARDC, through a process known as "mixage," based on two principles. First, Nkunda would remain in command of his troops and be absorbed with his forces almost intact. Second, the newly created force of the FARDC was to be given the task of hunting down and eliminating the so-called negative forces—including FDLR combatants, Nkunda's (and his alleged backer, Rwanda's) longtime opponents. Integration began in mid-January 2007, and by 27 March the mixed brigades were deemed operational.

However, by April the relationship between Nkunda and the government had deteriorated so much that the government suspended integration of the last brigade, and the Mayi Mayi withdrew, accusing Nkunda of planning attacks against non-Tutsi groups. Shortly after, the mixed brigades loyal to Nkunda launched a series of offensives against the FDLR, allegedly committing numerous human rights abuses. On 5 May, Nkunda announced that the mixage process was over, blaming the government on numerous grounds, including a lack of logistical support for counter-FDLR operations, and failing to withdraw the arrest warrant against him.

Three major factors were responsible for the breakdown of the mixage process. First, no formal documentation existed, and both sides were unwilling to publicly clarify the terms of the "agreement," particularly regarding timetables for disarmament. The complex relationships between the government and groups hostile to Nkunda, such as the Mayi Mayi, as well as with respect to broader communal tensions, made the agreement seem unworkable from the outset. Second, it was clear that Nkunda and his officers had exploited the Kigali agreement and used it to consolidate their positions, making it difficult for the FARDC to exert influence and control in the region. Third, the payout to combatants under this process was a paltry $50 per month over three months, compared to $300 for the same period that was paid to ex-combatants in Liberia, and even those monies were partially unavailable because of the restructuring of CONADER and difficulties with the World Bank. Thousands of troops were effectively stranded by this lack of funds and rendered susceptible to other readily available alternative sources for survival. Nkunda exploited the natural and mineral resources of the Kivus, as well as (allegedly) financial support from Tutsi businesspeople in eastern Congo, and was able to offer soldiers better stipends on a more regular basis than the government.

With the mixage process in tatters, Nkunda's forces allegedly began targeting government officials and institutions, as well as humanitarian workers. Officials from CONADER were forced to flee the area. Emboldened by his military success, Nkunda subsequently announced the formation of a political party, the Congrès National pour la Défense du Peuple (CNDP).[5]

The next months saw increased military buildup by both sides, escalating rhetoric, and mounting pressure from the international community for a political solution. Negotiations led nowhere and widespread violence broke out on 28 August 2007, when Nkunda loyalists attacked pro-Kinshasa elements. The fear of regional spillover led to a renewed round of diplomacy, and ultimately to the issuance of a joint Rwandan-Congolese communiqué on "a common approach to end the threat posed to peace and stability." The communiqué appeared to signal new common ground on the approach to the FDLR, and by early December 2007 this had freed the government to pursue Nkunda, while addressing Rwanda's longstanding concerns. On 21 November, in a joint press conference between MONUC's force commander, General Babacar Gaye, and the FARDC's chief of staff, General Dieudonne Kayembe, General Gaye stated simply that: "All peaceful ways have been explored without result . . . this is another phase where there is no solution but to force troops into brassage, without delay or conditions."[6]

This marked a significant shift from MONUC's earlier position of not supporting operations against Nkunda. At the time of writing, MONUC was poised to support new operations by the government in the east. The consequences of such a posture, and of the operations that may ensue, will shape events in 2008, and perhaps beyond.

Conclusion

The year in review started with MONUC engaged in DDR, SSR, and economic recovery activities, in a context of cautious optimism about the process of stabilizing a hard-won peace. DDR through the brassage model ap-

---

Box 3.2.1 Child Protection Advisers in UN Peacekeeping Operations

Efforts to protect children in conflict and postconflict societies, especially those hosting UN peace operations, have made remarkable progress since the mid-1990s. The Secretary-General's August 1996 note to the General Assembly, titled "The Impact of Armed Conflict on Children" (UN Doc. A/51/306), raised awareness about the issue and led to the appointment of a Special Representative for Children and Armed Conflict in 1997. Between 1999 and 2004, the number of reports by the Secretary-General to the Security Council that mentioned child protection rose significantly. The adoption of Resolution 1261 (1999) was significant, as it called for "training on the protection, rights, and welfare of children" to be included in UN activities. This resulted in the creation of a new category of peacekeeping personnel known as child protection advisers (CPAs).

The first CPAs were deployed in the UN Assistance Mission in Sierra Leone (UNAMSIL) during 2000. Operating under the overall guidance of mission heads, the principal tasks of CPAs included advising the senior mission leadership and other mission components on a comprehensive approach to child protection, advocating child rights and protection with other relevant partners on the ground, collaborating with child protection personnel both inside and outside the mission, and reporting on violations and other related issues. To date, CPAs have been deployed in seven missions, with a strength of sixty posts in six missions during 2007. Current large-scale CPA deployments include thirty-four posts in the UN Mission in Sudan (UNMIS) and seventeen in the UN Organization Mission in the Democratic Republic of Congo (MONUC).

In May 2007, the Peacekeeping Best Practices Section of the UN Department of Peacekeeping Operations (DPKO) commissioned a survey of the activities and impact of CPAs in field. The survey results were derived from responses by current and former CPAs, interviews held with stakeholders at UN headquarters, including the Office of the Special Representative of the Secretary-General for Children and Armed Conflict, and field visits to MONUC and UNMIS. Notably, the survey found the following:

- Monitoring and reporting activities of CPAs have brought attention to the needs of children affected by all stages of conflict, particularly in regard to the UN peace and security agenda.
- Collaboration with various partners has facilitated a general mainstreaming of child protection issues in other mission components.

- CPAs have been instrumental in implementing the UN's zero-tolerance policy toward sexual exploitation and abuse.

While the accomplishments of the CPAs have been significant, they have also been limited by several factors, including the inability of CPAs to advocate and identify resources for national child protection institutions and raise awareness among the whole spectrum of mission components. The survey found that, despite clearly defined terms of reference for CPAs, the inconsistency in child protection mandates provided to each mission and the varied deployment of CPAs per mission have led to confusion over their role in relation to other actors. Other obstacles include dissimilar profiles and selection processes of CPAs, a nonexistent DPKO operational support capacity, and an inability to fully and consistently collaborate with other child protection professionals on the ground. The survey indicated that all of these issues can be resolved through increased coordination and clarification from the DPKO, the Office of the Special Representative of the Secretary-General for Children and Armed Conflict, and the UN Children's Fund (UNICEF).

Source: Funmi Olonisakin, *Lessons Learned Study: Child Protection—The Impact of Child Protection Advisers in UN Peacekeeping Operations* (New York: United Nations, Department of Peacekeeping Operations, Peacekeeping Best Practices Section, May 2007).

---

peared to have worked relatively well in some parts of the country. The Kabila government's handover of Germain Katanga, leader of the Forces de Résistance Patriotique d'Ituri (FRPI) militia, to the International Criminal Court (ICC) was also welcomed as a significant step toward dealing with impunity for war crimes committed during the country's conflict. Katanga is the second Congolese militia leader to be handed over to the ICC; the first was Thomas Lubanga Dyilo, leader of the Union des Patriotes Congolais (UPC), who was handed over to the ICC in 2006.

On the other hand, while the government was applauded for the handover, local human rights groups in the DRC have accused it of bias, as some notorious warlords have been compensated with lucrative government positions. The transfer of Katanga to the ICC co-incided with reports of human rights violations by the FARDC and other militias involved in the war in the east. By late September 2007, international attention was also drawn to reports of increased incidents of gender-based violence by all sides to the conflict in the Kivus, including the FARDC.

As the year drew to a close, however, it was once again the crisis in the east that dominated political and security issues in the DRC. Whether the government-backed January 2008 peace conference in the provincial town of Goma succeeds in dealing with the crisis in the region, or whether the government reverts to a policy of forceful demobilization and disarmament will shape the prospects for peace consolidation. As became evident by late 2007, real security sector reform will be impossible given the instability in the east. For MONUC, the decision to support government operations in the east will likely substantially shape the challenges the mission may face in the year to come—and perhaps peacekeeping doctrine more broadly.

Notes

1. MONUC's stance in supporting the elected government was reminiscent of that taken by the UN Assistance Mission in Sierra Leone (UNAMSIL), backed up by a contingent of UK Royal Marines, in supporting the elected government of Sierra Leone when the government and the mission were attacked by rebels in 1999.

2. Barbara Among, "Surge in Kivu Conflict amid Calls for Protection of Civilians," *The East African,* 17–23 September 2007, p. 8.

3. Fred Oluoch, "Amnesty Hits at DRC Govt over Mass Killings in Kivu," *The East African,* 17–23 September 2007, p. 9.

4. Stephanie Wolters, "Trouble in the Eastern DRC: The Nkunda Factor," *Situation Report,* Institute for Security Studies, 3 September 2007, p. 8.

5. Presentation by Major-General Cammeart, former MONUC commander, at the ISS, September 2007.

6. See transcript of the press conference given on 21 November 2007, in Goma, by General Dieudonne Kayembe, FARDC chief of staff, and General Babacar Gaye, MONUC force commander.

3.3

Kosovo

In March 2007, Martti Ahtisaari, the UN Special Envoy for Kosovo, completed a comprehensive proposal outlining "supervised independence" for the province. In addition to detaching Kosovo from Serbian de jure sovereignty, the plan foresaw an operational shift from the existing peacekeeping framework, centering on NATO and the UN, to a reduced but significant international presence led by the EU and NATO. The technical details of this process had been under intensive discussion since mid-2006, when European planners arrived in Kosovo. Both the UN Interim Administration Mission in Kosovo (UNMIK) and NATO's Kosovo Force (KFOR) were committed to a smooth transition, and UN Secretary-General Ban Ki-Moon declared his full support for the Ahtisaari Plan.

A successful transition appeared important to the credibility of both UN and European peacekeeping. The deployment of NATO troops and UN police to Kosovo in 1999, following the ethnic cleansing of Albanians and NATO's air bombardment of the rump Yugoslavia, was the first major test for peacekeeping after the failures of the 1990s. UNMIK was the UN's most extensive executive mission to date, and was unique in including the EU and Organization for Security and Cooperation in Europe (OSCE) pillars[1]—dealing with economic and governance issues respectively—into an integrated mission structure under the UN Special Representative of the Secretary-General (SRSG). At its height in 1999, KFOR (institutionally separate from UNMIK) involved 50,000 personnel—nearly 10,000 more than are currently deployed under NATO command in Afghanistan.

Although the international commitment to Kosovo declined between 1999 and 2007, the province—which comprises only 4,293 square miles and a population of just over 2 million, 90 percent of it ethnically Albanian and about 5 percent ethnically Serb—has remained host to a significant peacekeeping presence. At the start of 2007, KFOR was still the third largest peace operation in the world, with over 16,000 troops. The UN had 2,000 police there (one-fifth of its global police deployments) and over 2,400 international and local civilian staff (its third biggest civilian complement after those in the Democratic Republic of Congo and Sudan).

For the EU, replacing this presence with a lighter-weight alternative looked to be an important test of the European Security and Defense Policy (ESDP), combined with its broader commitment to stabilize (and perhaps offer membership to) the entire Western Balkans. The Ahtisaari Plan foresaw two separate missions: an ESDP police operation and an international civilian office supporting a double-hatted international/EU Special Representative empowered to annul political decisions contravening the status agreement. KFOR would become the international military presence, while the OSCE would maintain an autonomous monitoring presence around Kosovo prioritizing community and minority affairs. All these international elements were expected to stay at least five years.

Transitioning from the UNMIK-KFOR system to this new model would have been difficult enough in a permissive international and domestic political environment. While a similar shift took place in Bosnia and Herzegovina,

Box 3.3.1 Comprehensive Proposal for the Kosovo Status Settlement: The Ahtisaari Plan

After more than a year of intensive yet inconclusive status deliberations, the Secretary-General's Special Envoy, Martti Ahtisaari, presented his proposal for Kosovo's final status. The proposal delineated that the future Kosovo should be an independent state, supervised by the international community, namely the EU and NATO. In a more detailed, comprehensive proposal for the Kosovo Status Settlement, also known as the Ahtisaari Plan, the former Finnish president enumerated the settlement provisions necessary, and technical aspects of implementation of the supervised independence arrangement, in twelve annexes, each delving into the areas necessary to establish Kosovo as a sustainable member of the international community.

In more specific terms, the Ahtisaari Plan provides for the following, under international supervision:

- Kosovo shall be a multiethnic, democratically self-governing society, with full respect for the rule of law. Kosovo shall adopt a constitution to enshrine these principles. While settlement is not contingent on completion of the constitution, the plan details that several elements must be part of the constitution.
- Kosovo shall have the right to negotiate and conclude international agreements, including the right to seek membership in international organizations.
- More than forty key religious and cultural sites shall be surrounded by protective zones to prevent any disruptive commercial and industrial development or construction, and to preserve the cultural dignity of such sites. The Kosovo Status Settlement also mandates additional physical security for selected sites.

- The cultural heritage of all members of Kosovo society shall be protected, and Kosovo's governing institutions shall be multiethnic.
- Kosovo's government shall be decentralized and promote good governance, transparency, and effectiveness in public service. The decentralization elements are to include new municipal competencies for Kosovo Serb majority municipalities; extensive municipal autonomy in financial matters, including the ability to accept transparent funding from Serbia for a broad range of municipal activities and purposes; provisions on intermunicipal partnerships and cross-boundary cooperation with Serbian institutions; and the establishment of six new or significantly expanded Kosovo Serb majority municipalities.
- Kosovo shall have an inclusive and multiethnic justice system that is integrated, independent, professional, and impartial, ensuring access to all persons in Kosovo.
- All refugees and internally displaced persons from Kosovo shall have the right to return and reclaim their property and personal possessions.
- Kosovo shall create a professional, multiethnic, and democratic security sector. The Kosovo Police Force shall have a unified chain of command throughout the country, with local officers reflecting the ethnic composition of the municipality in which they serve.
- The Kosovo Protection Corps shall be dissolved, to be replaced by a new professional and multiethnic force, the Kosovo Security Force, within one year. The Kosovo Security Force shall have a maximum of 2,500 active members and 800 reserve members.

- An international civilian representative, double-hatted as the EU Special Representative, shall be appointed by an international steering group. The international civilian representative shall have ultimate supervisory authority over the implementation of the Kosovo Status Settlement, and shall be conferred the necessary powers to oversee and ensure successful implementation of the settlement. The mandate of the international civilian representative shall continue until the international steering group determines that Kosovo has implemented the terms of the settlement.
- A European Security and Defence Policy mission shall monitor, mentor, and advise on all areas related to the rule of law. It shall assist Kosovo in the development of efficient, fair, and representative police, judicial, customs, and penal institutions, and have the authority to assume other responsibilities to ensure the maintenance and promotion of the rule of law, public order, and security.
- A NATO-led international military presence shall provide a safe and secure environment throughout Kosovo, in conjunction with the international steering group and in support of Kosovo's institutions until such time as those institutions are capable of assuming the full range of security responsibilities.
- The Organization for Security and Cooperation in Europe, with an extensive field presence in Kosovo, shall assist in the monitoring necessary for successful implementation of the Kosovo Status Settlement.

On UN Security Council approval, the Ahtissari Plan stipulates that there will be a 120-day transition period, wherein:

Box 3.3.1 Continued

• The mandate of the UN Interim Administration Mission in Kosovo (UNMIK) shall remain in effect.
• The international civilian representative shall possess the authority to monitor implementation of the Kosovo Status Settlement and make recommendations to UNMIK on actions to be taken to ensure compliance.

• The Kosovo National Assembly, in consultation with the international civilian representative, shall be responsible for approving a constitution and the legislation necessary for the implementation of the Kosovo Status Settlement. The new constitution and legislation shall become effective immediately on conclusion of the transition period.

At the end of the 120-day transition period, UNMIK's mandate will expire and all legislative and executive authority vested in UNMIK will be transferred to the authorities of Kosovo, in accordance with the status settlement. Within nine months of the entry into force of the status settlement, general and local elections are to be held.

Sources: United Nations, *Comprehensive Proposal for the Kosovo Status Settlement,* UN Doc. S/2007/168/Add.1, 26 March 2007, http://www.unosek.org/docref/comprehensive_proposal-english.pdf, http://www.unosek.org/unosek/en/statusproposal.html.

it took over two years to complete.[2] By contrast, UNMIK worked on the basis of a 120-day transition period. Within an already tight timetable, planning was thrown into confusion in mid-2007 when it became clear that Serbian opposition to Kosovo's independence, and a deep divide between Russia and the United States and European Union on the issue, meant that there would be no consensus on fulfilling the Ahtisaari Plan. Instead, Kosovo seemed ready to declare its independence unilaterally.

The international presence's capacity to respond to such an outcome was complicated by the fact that the majority of transition planning had been conducted on the assumption that there would be a Security Council resolution. As this possibility receded, it seemed likely that a unilateral declaration of independence by the Kosovo Albanians (even if combined with a commitment to observe the substance of the Ahtisaari Plan) would not only split the Security Council, but also create divisions within the EU. Rather than base a smooth handover on unquestioned legal foundations, UNMIK, KFOR, and the EU now had to confront the possibility of devising a new peacekeeping framework for Kosovo in the face of Serbian opposition, a fiercely divided international community, an uncertain legal framework, and potential violence.

Status Negotiations

Although Kosovo, under UN administration, had remained Serbian sovereign territory since 1999 under Security Council Resolution 1244,

Map No. 4255.7 Rev 1   UNITED NATIONS
October 2007

Department of Field Support
Cartographic Section

UN Interim Administration in Kosovo (UNMIK)

- Authorization and Start Date — 10 June 1999 (UNSC Res. 1244) (note: paragraph 19 of the resolution states that international and civil and security presences are established for an initial period of twelve months, to continue thereafter until the Security Council decides otherwise)
- SRSG and Head of Mission — Joachim Rücker (Germany)
- Chief Military Liaison Officer — Major-General Raul Cunha (Portugal)
- Police Commissioner — Richard Monk (United Kingdom)
- Budget — $210.7 million (1 July 2007–30 June 2008)
- Strength as of 31 October 2007 — Military Observers: 40
  Police: 1,966
  International Civilian Staff: 473
  Local Civilian Staff: 1,957
  UN Volunteers: 135

For detailed mission information see p. 288.

NATO Kosovo Force (KFOR)

- Authorization Date — 10 June 1999 (UNSC Res. 1244)
- Start Date — June 1999
- Head of Mission — Lieutenant-General Xavier de Marnhac (France)
- Budget — $35.5 million (October 2006–September 2007)
- Strength as of 30 September 2007 — Troops: 15,109
  Civilian Staff: 35

OSCE Mission in Kosovo (OMIK)

- Authorization and Start Date — 1 July 1999 (PC.DEC/305)
- Head of Mission — Ambassador Werner Wnendt (Germany)
- Budget — $43.1 million (October 2006–September 2007)
- Strength as of 30 September 2007 — Civilian Staff: 207

the Yugoslav and Serbian governments consistently restated their rights over the province. But the Kosovo Albanians' desire for independence was not in doubt: a survey in the second quarter of 2007 found 95 percent support among them for a break with Serbia.[3] In this context, UNMIK, mandated under Resolution 1244 to build up local governance institutions, was widely perceived as building the institutional basis for a new state. Although a gradual transfer of competencies to local politicians began in 2000, particularly significant advances were made in 2005, when the first elements of Ministries of Justice and Interior were put in place.

In October 2005, the Security Council approved talks on Kosovo's future, to be led by the UN Special Envoy. The decision stimulated an unusual degree of cohesion among the often fragmented Kosovo Albanian political leadership, who formed the Unity Team, comprising negotiators who represented all the main political parties. After the death of popular president Ibrahim Rugova in January 2006, the role of unifier passed to Agim Çeku, a former guerrilla with good ties to the UN who became prime minister in March 2006. However, Ramush Haradinaj, an ex–prime minister on trial for war crimes in The Hague since 2005, has maintained significant influence over Kosovo Albanian decisions.

From the start, discussions over the province's future were characterized by intransigence on both sides. Martti Ahtisaari and his team (the UN Office of the Special Envoy for Kosovo [UNOSEK], a Vienna-based political office distinct from UNMIK) began negotiations between Serbia and the Kosovo Albanian leadership in January 2006, with the goal of concluding them in a year. He postponed publishing his proposals until after Serbian national elections in January 2007, but after consultations on draft proposals, he declared on 10 March 2007 that there was no basis for a negotiated agreement and that the Security Council must decide Kosovo's future.

The United States and the EU's members aimed to win a Security Council resolution granting Kosovo supervised independence on the basis of the Ahtisaari Plan, and the Kosovo Albanian leadership declared its backing for this option. UNMIK saw a need for rapid progress toward a resolution, as it faced independence protests and sporadic violence in the winter of 2006–2007. In November 2006, UNMIK's headquarters were attacked by a mob, and in January 2007 UN police fired rubber bullets at protesters, killing two (leading to the resignation of UNMIK's police commissioner). Although senior Kosovo Albanian leaders were united in calling for calm, Çeku and others warned that they could not guarantee order if Kosovo's future remained in limbo much longer.

However, Serbia continued to oppose any formulas for Kosovo involving de jure independence (especially as symbolized by an army or seat at the UN). In this it had the support not only of the majority ethnic Serbs in Kosovo, many of them reliant on wages paid from Belgrade, but also of Russia. From March to July 2007, the United States and European Union pushed for an independence resolution at the UN, but Russia insisted that further negotiation was necessary. Fearing a Russian veto, the European Union and the United States eventually acquiesced to a further consultation period, with a UN deadline for negotiated settlement of 10 December. The resulting efforts at negotiation were marked by a lack of common ground, and concluded in late November with no progress made.

Local Political Environment

Even prior to the breakdown over Kosovo's future, UNMIK had concerns about how to manage the proposed transition. This was partly for operational reasons: as of early 2006, there were significant concerns that the mission would hemorrhage civilian staff as its closure approached, constraining its ability to carry out its final duties. Anticipating this, a retention package was designed for UNMIK staff—including generous exit payments and relocation options to other missions—that proved effective. By September 2007, UNMIK had a 20

Special Envoy Martti Ahtisaari (center) presents the *Comprehensive Proposal for the Kosovo Status Settlement* at UNMIK Headquarters in Pristina, 2 February 2007.

percent civilian staff vacancy rate, well below the percentages for missions likely to stay in place for far longer, such as the UN Mission in Sudan (UNMIS) and the UN Integrated Mission in Timor-Leste (UNMIT) (although specialized posts, like international prosecutors, proved increasingly difficult to fill).

In reality, UNMIK's major problem was one of political credibility, not operational viability. With Kosovo's status a matter of intergovernmental negotiation, UNMIK's leverage was significantly eroded—a problem that some observers believed to be exacerbated by the mission leadership's explicit desire to promptly transfer operational responsibility to the EU.

During the 2006 status negotiations, the willingness of Kosovo Serb politicians to cooperate with the international presence, always limited, dwindled to nothing (although some Serb business and community leaders appeared ready to work with the Albanians). After the Ahtisaari Plan was published, UN staff also noted a decline in Kosovo Albanian readiness to discuss issues such as minority rights, presumably because UNMIK was no longer seen as having a say over the province's fate. Similarly, international officials involved in economic issues were skeptical that commitments by their domestic counterparts would be kept once UNMIK had departed. But the top-level UNMIK leadership were relieved that their domestic political counterparts continued to urge moderation after July, as they had feared a worse deterioration in relations at this stage.

The maintenance of good relations had been partially secured by engaging the Kosovo Albanian politicians in a transition planning and implementation process involving multiple committees convening representatives of the current international presence (UNMIK and KFOR), the proposed post-status presence (European officials), and domestic politicians. These committees covered issues ranging from security to drafting a constitution—although the latter could not be approved before Kosovo's status was decided. Although the transition planning and implementation discussions began in 2005, well before Ahtisaari's proposals were developed, its work program was adjusted to match his plan in 2007.

After the July failure to reach a status resolution, UNMIK launched a "reconfiguration" process on the basis of the transition planning and implementation process, aimed at demonstrating that political progress was still possible. But this consisted of relatively minor gestures—such as reducing the residual presence of UN civil affairs officers at the municipal level and handing over civil registration responsibilities to local officials—and UN officials admitted that they had already made virtually all the major concessions they could prior to a final status deal.

UNMIK's loss of leverage was partially offset by the establishment of the Preparation Team for the International Civilian Office, as proposed by Ahtisaari. This was approved by the European Council in September 2006, and deployed in October that year—although the intended Special Representative (Peter Feith, who had previously led the EU mission to Aceh, Indonesia) was not authorized to deploy without a status deal. The Preparation Team worked closely with the Kosovo Albanian government on legislation to complement

the Ahtisaari Plan, enjoying influence UNMIK had lost. Additional political support for UNMIK came from the US office (its de facto embassy) in Pristina, which often proved to be the most efficient "fixer" with the Kosovo Albanians, especially at a local level—a role also played, to a lesser extent, by the British office.

A further political complication centered on elections to Kosovo's National Assembly—as well as municipal and mayoral contests—scheduled to take place later in 2007. UNMIK had originally expected these to take place during or after a transition process, and both international officials and many Kosovo Albanian politicians felt that it might be better to declare a postponement until after a status decision. But pressure from those politicians likely to gain in the elections resulted in the Unity Team requesting that voting should go ahead—a decision approved by UNMIK in late August. Although the OSCE pillar argued that it would take a minimum of four months to make the necessary arrangements, 17 November was chosen as polling day, as any later date would be too close to the 10 December talks deadline. Nonetheless, the November elections that installed former Kosovo Liberation Army commander Hashim Thaci and his Democratic Party of Kosovo as leaders of the province reflected the ambivalence of both the voting public, who turned out in record low numbers, and the Serbian minority, who boycotted the elections altogether.

In political terms, UNMIK had been left adrift by the intergovernmental failure to agree on Kosovo's future, demonstrating the limits of the peace operation. Ban Ki-Moon told the Security Council in September that the mission had "largely achieved what is achievable under 1244"—going on to warn that "a further prolongation of the future-status process puts at risk the achievements of the United Nations in Kosovo since June of 1999."[4]

Security Situation

If UNMIK could not shape Kosovo's politics, both it and KFOR still had responsibility for Kosovo's security. While the winter's violence was not repeated as negotiations dragged on (the fall of 2007 did not see a spike in interethnic attacks, as had been the case in 2005 and 2006), the fear of a breakdown continued to haunt both UNMIK and KFOR. Memories of March 2004, when three days of rioting targeted at ethnic Serbs and the UN erupted without warning, increased the level of concern. But a majority of Kosovo Albanians had positive perceptions of both KFOR and UNMIK police by the summer of 2007: among Serbs, KFOR's trust rating had risen from just over 10 percent in 2004 to over 50 percent by June 2007, while UNMIK police's rating had leapt from under 5 percent to over 40 percent in the same period.[5] If the international presence had lost much of its political leverage, its provision of security continued to confer a degree of legitimacy on its role.

In this context, UNMIK and KFOR had to plan for any immediate flareup of violence and continue to build up sustainable security mechanisms that would evolve beyond transition—while the EU needed to ensure the credibility of its future police role. The EU Planning Team, preparing for the ESDP mission, had originally foreseen a force of fewer than 1,000 officers, but this figure was revised upward through 2007—by September the target was 1,825, some of them to be taken directly from UNMIK. It was assumed that the ESDP mission could reach 90 percent of this strength in four months.

UNMIK itself aimed to maintain its police presence at roughly 2,000 officers until transition. However, it continued to emphasize the need for the domestic Kosovo Police Service (KPS) to take primary responsibility for public order—a strategy adopted soon after the 2004 riots. By early 2007, the KPS had some 7,500 officers (although international officials argued that its target size should be nearer 5,000), but was still very weak in terms of planning. UNMIK officials prioritized resolving this shortfall through the year, creating new planning units across the KPS through the summer of 2007, but predicted that the EU would need to continue to play a proactive role in capacity building in this specific area.

In the short term, the KPS was also likely to be of limited utility in the most likely site for any flareup: the ethnically divided city of Mitrovica in northern Kosovo, where UNMIK police have continued to provide direct security. The KPS also appeared unreliable in three Serb municipalities to the northwest of Mitrovica, where Serb security services have run "parallel structures" since 1999. KFOR and UNMIK officials had long feared that this region would declare its secession from an independent Kosovo, even with a UN resolution. In the case of a unilateral declaration, this seemed a certainty—complicated by the fact that the Kosovo Serbs could argue that international law was on their side.

The possibility of formal partition—previously a taboo for US and EU negotiators, who feared its ramifications for Bosnia and Macedonia—was increasingly widely discussed at the international level through 2007. But KFOR and UNMIK had to decide how they would respond to secession in the north on the day after a contested declaration of independence. French KFOR troops reopened a base in the area, and the United States and Germany sent additional troops there in the winter of 2007–2008. The situation was complicated by the possibility that militias from Serbia proper might try to cross into northern Kosovo in a crisis, daring KFOR to use significant force against them (despite belligerent comments in Belgrade, an incursion by the Serb army itself was ruled out by the defense minister).

While a flareup of Serb-led violence in the north might test NATO, it would stretch it less than more widespread Albanian-led violence throughout Kosovo—especially if, as in 2004, this involved attacks on the 40,000–50,000 Serbs living in enclaves across the province and at Orthodox religious sites. UNMIK and other international officials remained optimistic that the Kosovo Albanian leadership, realizing the effect of such violence on their international reputations, would be able to prevent this scenario. A survey in the second quarter of the year found that only 3 percent of Albanian respondents would "pick up weapons" if the Ahtisaari Plan were vetoed in the Security Council, and 2 percent would resort to street violence (although a third would protest peacefully).[6] But if the immediate risk seemed low, the impact of events in the north could not be predicted.

Moreover, both KFOR and the projected ESDP police mission were overshadowed by questions about their coherence in the case of a unilateral declaration of independence. It was widely believed that a number of European countries might refuse to deploy police, or even allow their units in KFOR to use force, without a new Security Council mandate.

It was even possible that the deployment of the ESDP police mission could be blocked by a single dissenting government in the European Council, which requires unanimity on foreign policy and security issues. By the last quarter of 2007, diplomats in Brussels had found a formula offering the dissenters the option of "constructive abstention" to circumvent this worst-case scenario, but planners in Kosovo found it very hard to develop sound operational plans when there was uncertainty over the personnel available to them. Again, there were strong memories of 2004, when some KFOR units were restrained by caveats on their use. Attempting to provide reassurance, NATO conducted a large-scale exercise on the Croatian coast in October 2007, to demonstrate its resources and determination.

The need to handle potential short-term challenges distracted KFOR from focusing on its proposed post-transition duties as the international military presence. However, these in-cluded one particularly sensitive task: the development of the Kosovo Security Force (KSF). This was intended to be an alternative to the Kosovo Protection Corps (KPC), a civil defense organization largely staffed by former Kosovo Albanian guerrillas. While the KPC had long been perceived as an "army in waiting" by much of the population, its personnel are of mixed quality, many have engaged in criminal activity, and a good number are now too old for military service. The future of the KPC, and even its funding, were a matter of political friction through the year.

Conclusion

Regardless of how or when Kosovo's final status is resolved, it is certain that the province will remain host to a complex set of multidimensional peace operations for some time to come. The transition from UN and NATO-led to EU and NATO-led peace operations will present its own challenges, and how those challenges are handled will shape the future of Kosovo. A proper response to the challenges of the planned transition partly rests on the international community's ability to overcome political differences over Kosovo's final status. As the year drew to a close, Kosovo's status remained contested as the United States and some EU members favored the province's independence, while Russia, Serbia, and other EU members remained opposed, in the face of indications that the province might declare independence in early 2008.

Notes

1. Initially, the first of UNMIK's four "pillars" was led by the UN High Commissioner for Refugees (UNHCR), responsible for the return of all refugees and displaced persons to their homes in Kosovo. Once the UNHCR's function was complete, this pillar was phased out. See http://www.unmikonline.org/intro.htm.

2. The Bosnian transition consisted of the double-hatting of Lord Paddy Ashdown as High Representative and EU Special Representative in May 2002; the transfer of policing duties from the UN to EU in January 2003; and finally the handover of military responsibilities from NATO to the EU in December 2004.

3. US Agency for International Development and UN Development Programme, *Kosovo,* Early Warning Report no. 17 (April–June 2007), p. 13.

4. United Nations, *Report of the Secretary-General on the United Nations Interim Administration Mission in Kosovo,* UN Doc. S/2007/582, 28 September 2007, p. 7.

5. USAID and UNDP, *Kosovo,* p. 45.

6. Ibid., p. 22.

3.4

Liberia

Liberia has made substantial political progress toward sustained recovery since the election of Ellen Johnson-Sirleaf—the first elected female president in Africa—in 2005. The Johnson-Sirleaf government has taken steps toward improving the fragile security situation and revamping the country's socioeconomic fabric, which was destroyed during the nearly fourteen-year brutal civil conflict. However, while the country remained stable throughout 2007, a high unemployment rate, especially among youths, and the slow process of developing professional security forces, persist as major security concerns. Throughout the year in review, the UN Mission in Liberia (UNMIL) remained deployed and continued its support of the government's peace consolidation efforts.

In August 2007, noting the "great strides in consolidating peace and promoting economic recovery" in Liberia, the UN Secretary-General recommended a gradual, three-phase drawdown of its military forces in the country.[1] The Security Council passed Resolution 1777 (2007) shortly after the Secretary-General's report, approving the first phase of the drawdown, and granting a one-year extension to UNMIL. The first phase of the drawdown, which began in October 2007 and will run through September 2008, will see the departure of 2,450 troops. An additional 498 police officers will depart during the period April 2008 to September 2010. Despite the drawdown, by the end of 2010, UNMIL will still have over 9,000 uniformed personnel in Liberia, ranking among the larger global peace operations.

Map No. 4255.6 Rev. 1   UNITED NATIONS
September 2007

Department of Field Support
Cartographic Section

UN Mission in Liberia (UNMIL)

• Authorization and Start Date	19 September 2003 (UNSC Res. 1509)
• SRSG and Head of Mission	Ellen Margrethe Løj (Denmark)
• Force Commander	Lieutenant-General Chikadibia Isaac Obiakor (Nigeria)
• Police Commissioner	Mohammed Ahmed Alhassan (Ghana)
• Budget	$688.4 million (1 July 2007–30 June 2008)
• Strength as of 31 October 2007	Troops: 13,322
	Military Observers: 206
	Police: 1,172
	International Civilian Staff: 502
	Local Civilian Staff: 945
	UN Volunteers: 242

For detailed mission information see p. 296.

Background

Liberia had been at war since 1989, when the National Patriotic Front of Liberia (NPFL), led by Charles Taylor, invaded the country from bases in Côte d'Ivoire. The conflict claimed an estimated 200,000 lives, resulted in injury to thousands more, and uprooted approximately 1.8 million civilians from their homes. Additionally, the conflict severely impacted Liberia's immediate neighbors—Sierra Leone, Guinea, and Coté d'Ivoire—as they struggled to cope with waves of refugees from Liberia while dealing with their own domestic challenges.

The deployment of the ECOWAS Mission in Liberia (ECOMIL) in August 2003 paved the way for UNMIL. The UN mission was deployed in October 2005 to oversee implementation of the Comprehensive Peace Agreement (CPA), signed on 18 August 2004 by the Liberian government, Liberians United for Reconciliation and Democracy (LURD), the Movement for Democracy in Liberia (MODEL), Liberian political parties, and civil society, under the auspices of the Economic Community of West African States (ECOWAS). Authorized under Chapter VII of the UN Charter, UNMIL was given a mandate to oversee the cease-fire agreement; develop and implement a disarmament, demobilization, reintegration, and repatriation (DDRR) program; provide security at key locations; protect UN staff and Liberian civilians under imminent threat; provide humanitarian and human rights assistance; support security sector reform; assist in extending state authority throughout the country; and support the implementation of the peace process, including assistance to national elections held in 2005.

Key Developments

Security

Liberia's peace is still quite fragile, with serious consequences for not only the Johnson-Sirleaf government, but also UNMIL, as its eventual withdrawal depends on Liberia's ability to manage its own affairs, including the provision of security. Despite relative stability, during 2007 there were reports of plans to overthrow the government, and on 17 July the government announced the arrest of George Koukou, former speaker of the National Transitional Legislative Assembly, and of Major General Charles Julu, former army chief of staff, on suspicion of plotting to overthrow the government. The two men were charged with treason and are still in detention. A third Liberian, Colonel Andrew Dorbor, had meanwhile been arrested in neighboring Côte d'Ivoire, allegedly trying to buy arms for the planned coup.

Potential regime insecurity is matched by personal insecurity. Violent crime, including armed robbery leading to serious assault and even death, appears to be on the increase. UNMIL reported nineteen incidents of armed assaults on individuals and twenty incidents of armed attacks on residences in August 2007 in Monrovia alone, and outside Monrovia some dramatic incidents of communal violence have been reported. But senior UNMIL and government officials caution that the high crime figures are the result of better reporting and do not really represent a spike in incidents of crime. Nevertheless, some serious incidents have occurred—notably on 20 June, when ex-combatants, protesting delays in the payment of their subsistence allowances, mounted simultaneous demonstrations in the towns of Buchanan, Ganta, and Gbarnga. This was followed by another incident in September, when former combatants of the national army (the Armed Forces of Liberia [AFL]), attempted a nighttime riot in the heart of Monrovia, blocking major roads and intersections. UNMIL police and Liberian personnel intervened in strength to clear them away.

The insecurity prompted President Johnson-Sirleaf to announce the launch of Operation Calm Down Fear, supplementing the earlier Operation Sweeping Wave, and to increase the number of patrols and spot-checks on vehicles in Monrovia. But these robust steps were undermined by the sheer lack of a dependable national security apparatus. An UNMIL technical assessment mission made on-the-spot visits to several police stations in the country in June and reported back on the lack of basic equipment such as communication facilities.

Security Sector Reform

Liberia is still a long way from creating a dependable security infrastructure. Attempts at creating a national army from scratch—with a proposed troop strength of 2,000—are being spearheaded by two US private security companies, DynCorp and Pacific Architect Engineers, with US government financial support. DynCorp is responsible for the recruitment and provision of basic training to the recruits at the Barclay and Camp Ware training centers, while Pacific Architect Engineers is responsible for providing advanced training of the recruits and the construction of the barracks, as well as the battalion and brigade headquarters, at Camp Kessely near Monrovia. The training of military personnel has been remarkably slow, as by October 2007 only 11 officers and 634 noncommissioned officers had completed the advanced individual training. The program also proved controversial, with some observers questioning the policy of having a private security force train a national professional army.

Meanwhile, the rebuilding of the Liberian National Police (LNP), led by UNMIL, has progressed faster: over 3,500 police officers graduated from the national academy in July 2007. Through UNMIL's quick-impact projects, police stations in several counties have been rehabilitated. Other stations in about half a dozen other counties are currently being rehabilitated. In addition to providing basic training for 3,500 police officers—including an all-female class of 110 police recruits—UNMIL, together with the UN civilian police, has initiated programs designed to strengthen the supervisory capacity of the LNP.

The presence of an all-female police contingent from India in UNMIL is believed to

Members of UNMIL's all-female formed police unit conduct a cordon and search operation in Monrovia, 4 April 2007.

Panos/ Aubrey Wade

have had a positive impact on UNMIL's drive to recruit more women to the LNP. However, the fact that many women lack the basic education to be accepted into the police force hampers such efforts. To tackle this problem, UNMIL launched an initiative aimed at providing women with intensive schooling within a short period of time to help them qualify for recruitment to the LNP. Meanwhile, forging an integrated command structure for the LNP has been slow, and it is difficult to assess, at this stage, the quality and impact of the training on the new police force.

Efforts to revamp Liberia's justice sector have registered slow progress, and the country's judiciary remains in a state of disrepair. An acute shortage of qualified personnel and woeful infrastructure are some of the major impediments to rebuilding a credible justice sector. Despite these challenges, UNMIL has since May 2006 provided training for 336 magistrates, 220 justices of peace, 226 prosecutors, 147 magistrate court clerks, and 53 circuit and Supreme Court clerks. UNMIL's quick-impact projects have also rehabilitated nine courthouses, and work is ongoing on several others.

Governance and Resource Management

In 2006, with the conclusion of the DDR process, the UN shifted its efforts toward the rebuilding of governance institutions more broadly, as well as toward the consolidation of state authority. There are several clusters of engagement with Liberia's rebuilding process. The UN Development Programme (UNDP) leads the early recovery cluster, which—together with the International Labour Organization—focuses on job creation and skills training. The Civil Affairs section in UNMIL spearheads the clusters on the rule of law and infrastructure rebuilding: under this program, there are plans to help the country rebuild vital state institutions and to revamp the justice sector. In all fifteen counties, the UN has established County Support Teams that bring together the various UN activities around one clear shared goal: to strengthen local government at the county level. UNMIL's Civil Affairs section, which has been operating at the county level since the deployment of the mission, plays a lead facilitation role in most counties. Importantly, the County Support Team initiative—in addition to being a mechanism for coordination—contains a project element that allows for direct support to capacity building, infrastructure development, information management, and day-to-day support.

The task of decentralization was complicated by a number of factors, including the centrist tradition that has characterized Liberian governance since the birth of the nation; the extreme low level of capacity currently found at county and district levels; and a tendency among donors and the government to focus primarily on national planning processes and other central-level governance issues. Despite these impediments, some progress has been achieved, not least due to the combined mobilization of UNMIL Civil Affairs officers and UN County Team staff and program resources.

In other areas, the government launched an interim poverty reduction strategy paper, a framework document to guide Liberia's development, at a partner forum in Washington, D.C., in February 2007. Shortly after, several countries, led by the United States, stated they would help Liberia to clear its nearly $4 billion in external debt. The framework document sets out the national socioeconomic context, choices and priorities regarding capacity building for poverty reduction and long-term development, as well as the implementation challenges the cash-strapped country will face. The interim poverty reduction strategy will guide Liberia's development management process through June 2008. The process to elaborate a full poverty reduction strategy has begun, and a substantive draft is intended for completion by March 2008.

2007 also saw efforts by various international partners, in particular the United Nations, the World Bank, the US Agency for International Development, and the European Commission, in collaboration with Liberia's Ministry of Public Works, to use road rehabilitation as a means of generating jobs. During last year's dry season—October 2006 to April 2007—this experiment helped create approximately 39,000 temporary jobs. The government's Liberia Emergency Employment Program–Liberia Employment Action Program (LEEP/LEAP), run by the Ministry of Labor, has also played an important role in this regard. Since it began operations in 2006, LEEP/LEAP is said to have generated thousands of temporary jobs as well.

Meanwhile, the government continued to pursue its official zero-tolerance policy for corruption. It submitted a draft bill to establish an anticorruption commission, which was returned to the government in October for modification; it will be reintroduced when the legislature reconvenes in January 2008. The government's anticorruption drive led to the prosecution of former transitional president Gyude Bryant on corruption charges and the dismissal of key government officials for the same reasons. In March, a deputy minister and an assistant minister were fired for allegedly granting bogus mining licenses.

UN sanctions against timber and diamond exports have now been lifted, since the

---

Box 3.4.1 Gender and Policing in UN Peace Operations

Addressing gender disparities in UN peace operations has been a major preoccupation for the Department of Peacekeeping Operations. But in the seven years since adoption of Security Council Resolution 1325 (2000), which mandated greater female representation in all categories of UN peacekeeping, progress has been limited. By July 2007, women still accounted for only about 2 percent of military and 6 percent of police of the over 83,000 uniformed personnel deployed under UN command, with even greater disparities at the senior mission-management level. During 2007, however, there were several promising developments in the UN's attempt to achieve balanced gender representation, especially with respect to civilian police in peace operations.

In February 2007, the police component of the UN Mission in Liberia (UNMIL), the third largest in the field, was supplemented with the first all-female formed police unit, from India. The 103 armed policewomen were trained in India's often tumultuous northern regions, and thus are well suited for the law enforcement challenges in Liberia. While the presence of the unit is viewed as a milestone in the UN's efforts for balanced gender representation among its uniformed and civilian personnel, it has had an even greater impact on public percep-

tions about the role of the police, especially among Liberia's female population. This is especially crucial because the Liberian National Police were seriously discredited during the country's civil war.

Thus, in postwar Liberia, the country's national police force was viewed with a great deal of skepticism. This was more pronounced among Liberian women, who were often the victims of police abuse during the civil war. The arrival of the all-female formed police unit appears to have reversed some of these negative perceptions, given that, one month after the arrival of the contingent, three times the usual number of females applied to join the Liberian National Police. Six months later, 115 female recruits had begun training in the country's police academy. Encouraged by these results and in order to deal with the high levels of illiteracy among Liberia's female population, UNMIL began a special program of public education to prepare aspiring female candidates to join the Liberian National Police.

Along similar lines, the UN Stabilization Mission in Haiti (MINUSTAH) also began an initiative toward a more gender-balanced police force. In support of the Haitian National Police, MINUSTAH began a large-scale registration program in August 2007, aimed at recruiting about 150

women for the twentieth graduating class of the police academy. But much work still needs to be done, as only about 5 percent of Haiti's approximately 8,000-strong police force are women.

The continuing efforts to build the UN's standing police capacity also include a strong focus on gender. Approved in 2006, a staff of over twenty-five police experts, once fully operational, will assist in the startup of new missions and provide rapid technical and operational support to existing UN operations. The UN Police Division has emphasized that this vital component of UN peace operations will be gender-sensitive: 24 percent of staff officers will be women, and gender considerations will be central in all of the division's plans and activities, both when conducting assessments and when starting up new missions.

Finally, October 2007 saw the Security Council renew its support for the role of women in peacekeeping operations. Citing the encouraging success of the all-female formed police unit in Liberia and the progress in Haiti, the Security Council called on the Secretary-General to prepare a report on the full implementation of Resolution 1325, including information on the impact of armed conflicts on women, their protection, and their role in peace processes.[1]

Source: United Nations, Department of Peacekeeping Operations, Peacekeeping Best Practices Section.
Note: 1. United Nations, "Statement by the President of the Security Council," UN Doc. S/PRST/2007/40, 24 October 2007.

---

government has instituted the required legislative and transparency measures. Liberia exported its first batch of Kimberley Process–certified diamonds in early September. The diamonds were worth $222,000, with the government earning a paltry $6,000 from them in the form of export tax, but this is projected to rise as exports increase.

The Governance and Economic Management Assistance Program (GEMAP)

The Liberian government bills GEMAP as an affirmation of its "commitment to a balanced budget and the establishment of a social macroeconomic framework." The program was signed between Liberia's national transitional government and the International Contact Group for Liberia on 9 September 2005. UN Security Council Resolution 1626 (2005) endorsed the agreement, and since then UNMIL has become the coordinating arm between the Liberian government and its international partners in implementing GEMAP.

The program was initiated as a response to pervasive corruption and mismanagement under the national transitional government. In early 2005, a European Commission audit of five key state-owned enterprises (Roberts International Airport, Liberia Petroleum Refinery, the Bureau of Maritime Affairs, the National Port Authority, and the Forestry Development Authority) revealed gross inefficiency, corruption, and a complete lack of transparency in the conduct of officials. Proceeds from these institutions could amount to 75 percent of the state's revenue. Among other things, the European Commission audit found a high level of uncertainty in the reporting related to the general accounts of these institutions, inconsistencies in staff salary levels, operating expenses and allowances, and an unjustified tax exception system in which tens of millions of dollars were lost by the state every year. A team of investigators of "financial and economic crimes" sent by ECOWAS buttressed the European Commission's findings, noting that the national transitional government was presiding over a financial administrative system that sacrificed financial probity to appease former warlords and ex-combatants.

These disclosures prompted some commentators to call for the imposition of external authority over the management of Liberia's natural resources and state finances. This, unsurprisingly, was deemed unacceptable by the government. But business as usual was also deemed unacceptable. GEMAP—which has expatriate officials operating what amounts to a "dual key" system with Liberian officials over the financial management of Liberia's key revenue-generating institutions—was the compromise arrangement. Even so, many Liberians, including senior state officials, still saw GEMAP as a highly intrusive program that would fail to

meaningfully develop Liberia's economic and governance institutions. The president herself shared this view publicly before her election, as did former president Amos Sawyer, who heads the Governance Reform Commission.

Once in office, however, President Johnson-Sirleaf embraced GEMAP. Five key state institutions operate under dual Liberian and international management, both of whose signatures are required for all transactions. The Economic Governance Steering Committee, responsible for overseeing the implementation of GEMAP, is chaired by the president, with the US ambassador as the vice president, and meets on a monthly basis at the Executive Mansion. A representative of UNMIL, who serves as facilitator, is always present at these meetings. The policy-setting GEMAP Technical Team meets bimonthly. The agenda of the Economic Governance Steering Committee is normally set by the US ambassador, although the government also participates. Even the national budget has to be thoroughly vetted by the Technical Committee, without meaningful participation by the legislature.

Real gains have been achieved from GEMAP. Revenue collection and preinspection of goods, once activities prone to corruption in Freeport, have greatly improved, and state revenues are up by 74 percent over last year. The Cash Management Committee now functions far better than before, and there is some transparency in the management of state expenditures. The Central Bank of Liberia, another key area of GEMAP intervention, now functions better, according to the monthly status reports of the chief administrator of Liberia's Central Bank, which is financed by the International Monetary Fund.

Critics of GEMAP, however, contend that these achievements are temporary, and that the intrusive nature of the program will be counterproductive. There does not seem to be a firm timeline for its conclusion, nor much evidence of local capacity building. Expatriate GEMAP officials are paid many times more than their Liberian counterparts, and there is a sustained lack of collegiality between the expatriates and their Liberian counterparts in key areas, often stymieing progress. Tentative efforts are currently under way to tackle some of these problems—national Liberian officials now report on GEMAP reforms, and the government, not the US ambassador, now reports on GEMAP work to the Economic Governance Steering Committee. Other problems persist, however, including some incoherence in the running of GEMAP. The international partners—the United States, the European Commission, and various multilateral institutions and governments—fund different sets of projects and personnel, and these consultants tend to report to those paying them, rather than to the Liberian government. The different layers of management do not seem to be fully accountable to the Liberian government.

Conclusion

Liberia is no longer the collapsed state it was when Taylor relinquished power in 2003. The continued presence of UNMIL has contributed to stabilizing the security situation, allowing the government to undertake crucial political steps aimed at stabilizing the country and restoring the economy. Confidence in UNMIL and the government is high, often manifested in a general sense of optimism by the civilian population. While there is thus cause for hope, developments in 2007 gave equal grounds for caution in assessing the medium-term prospects for the state and the economy. Significant concerns remain, including the slow process of rebuilding the country's security apparatus, notably the Armed Forces of Liberia; the slow pace of restoring government authority across the country; and the high unemployment rate.

More positively, as the year came to an end, renewed efforts to establish a truth and reconciliation commission, the increased stability in neighboring Sierra Leone, and the modest progress in Côte d'Ivoire's peace process, seemed to bode well for Liberia's peace consolidation efforts. The continued engagement of UNMIL and the international community looks likely to continue, and should provide the Johnson-Sirleaf government with the necessary support for still-needed governance reforms, including progress on decentralization, and the rebuilding of the country's infrastructure.

Note

1. See UN Security Council, *Fifteenth Progress Report of the Secretary-General on the United Nations Mission in Liberia,* UN Doc. S/2007/479, 8 August 2007.

Middle East

Following the Israel-Hezbollah war in July and August 2006, and despite the creation of a new political framework in the subregion with UN Security Council Resolution 1701, the Middle East as a whole continued to slide deeper into crisis in 2007. In Lebanon, a prolonged political crisis, repeated assassinations of prominent political figures, and several months of fighting between the Lebanese Armed Forces and an Al-Qaida-inspired Islamist faction (Fatah al-Islam) in a Palestinian refugee camp, combined with reports of illegal arms traffic across the Syrian-Lebanese border, contributed to creating a sense of instability and insecurity. Violence among Palestinian factions in the occupied Palestinian territory increased, which culminated in a week of clashes and the military takeover of the Gaza Strip by Hamas in June. Against this background, and also combined with heightening tension over Iran's nuclear program, as well as fears of a Syrian-Israeli confrontation in the summer of 2007, international peace operations remained caught up in the deepening regional turmoil. On the other hand, in the later part of 2007, levels of violence in Iraq began to decline, though this was not matched with a positive political process. At the same time, the renewal of contacts between Israel and the moderate Palestinian leadership in the West Bank and a victorious end to the fighting between the Lebanese Armed Forces and Fatah al-Islam in Lebanon gave some hope for stabilization and a renewal of the peace process in the Middle East.

UNIFIL: Background and Mandate

First established in 1978 by Security Council Resolutions 425 and 426, the UN Interim Force in Lebanon (UNIFIL) was initially tasked with confirming the withdrawal of Israeli forces, restoring international peace and security, and assisting the government of Lebanon in ensuring the return of its effective authority to the south of the country. In May 2000, UNIFIL assisted in confirming Israel's withdrawal of its forces in accordance with Resolution 425 behind a "Blue Line" identified by the UN.

Conditions remained unstable, however, as the Lebanese government was unable to deploy forces in the south. In 2004, Security Council Resolution 1559 reiterated the demand for an extension of the Lebanese government's authority throughout all of Lebanon, also calling for a withdrawal of Syrian troops (accomplished in the spring of 2005) and "the disbanding and disarmament of all Lebanese and non-Lebanese militias." In the context of the assassination of former Lebanese prime minister Rafiq Hariri, the UN was further mandated to conduct an investigation; in May 2007, amid the continuing Lebanese political crisis, the Security Council decided to establish an international tribunal to try those involved in the Hariri assassination.

War erupted in the south of Lebanon in July 2006 when Hezbollah launched an attack against an Israeli patrol and abducted two soldiers. A major military campaign ensued, ending after five weeks of intense bombing and rocket fire targeting civilians on both sides with the adoption of Security Council Resolution 1701. That resolution established a new and expanded mandate for UNIFIL, adding to its original responsibilities the tasks of monitoring the cessation of hostilities, ensuring that no foreign forces would be present in

Lebanon without government consent, assisting the Lebanese Armed Forces in preserving an area free of armed personnel (other than UNIFIL and Lebanese government troops) between the Blue Line and the Litani River, and fully implementing the Taif Accords, which require the disarmament of all armed groups in Lebanon. The resolution also added a number of political tasks that the UN was charged with, including facilitating negotiations over the contested Sheb'a Farms and the release of the two abducted Israeli soldiers and Lebanese prisoners in Israel.

UNIFIL: Key Developments and Challenges

In the year since the cessation of hostilities between Israel and Hezbollah, conditions in south Lebanon have been relatively stable, and the arrangements established with Security Council Resolution 1701 have largely held. Hezbollah has frequently reiterated its commitment to the resolution's implementation, and has focused on building political strength—though it has also replenished its military arsenal, albeit not within UNIFIL's area of operation in south Lebanon. At the same time, a permanent cease-fire is yet to be achieved, and many of the key elements called for in Resolution 1701 remain to be implemented. In addition, the prolonged political crisis in Lebanon, mounting tension and fears of renewed civil strife, and what may have been only a first manifestation of an Al-Qaida-inspired Islamist challenge, have significantly impacted UNIFIL. The mission was targeted by a roadside bomb attack in June 2007, which killed six soldiers from a Spanish battalion. A second major incident highlighting the continued precarious security of the mission occurred on 16 July, when a UNIFIL military police vehicle of the Tanzanian contingent was attacked, though no casualties resulted. Another attempt to attack UNIFIL peacekeepers was thwarted successfully by the Lebanese authorities in Tyre in October.

Map No. 4288 Rev. 1 UNITED NATIONS
September 2007

Department of Field Support
Cartographic Section

UN Interim Force in Lebanon (UNIFIL)

• Authorization and Start Date	19 March 1978 (UNSC Res. 425/426)
• Force Commander	Major-General Claudio Graziano (Italy)
• Budget	$713.6 million (1 July 2007– 30 June 2008)
• Strength as of 31 October 2007	Troops: 13,264 International Civilian Staff: 304 Local Civilian Staff: 583

For detailed mission information see p. 263.

UNIFIL's troop complement grew through a phased deployment. In February 2007, Italian general Claudio Graziano replaced Alain Pellegrini of France as force commander, and by mid-2007 UNIFIL had enlarged to roughly 13,500 military personnel from thirty countries, out of an authorized 15,000. This included 1,600 serving in its Maritime Task Force. Troop contributors (eight of which were represented on the Security Council in 2007, an unusually large number) generally remained committed to the mission's mandate and configuration, despite questions by some actors as to whether UNIFIL's mandate would evolve into an open-ended one, and as concerned the costs of, in particular, the Maritime Task Force.

UNIFIL's most notable characteristic remained the extensive European participation, a relative exception for UN operations. One manifestation, the Strategic Military Cell (a management mechanism at headquarters created to meet the insistence of European troop contributors on a separate command structure), made important contributions to supporting planning needs, according to two Secretariat reviews—though those reviews also emphasized its "mission-specific" and "temporary" character, as well as the need to establish interoperability between it and existing Department of Peacekeeping Operations (DPKO) structures, where coordination difficulties had surfaced.

In the months after the war, much emphasis was placed on consolidating the new status quo into a more permanent arrangement and on attaining greater stability in the area. By and large, the area remained quiet, and UNIFIL established effective cooperation with the newly deployed Lebanese Armed Forces. That cooperation enabled the establishment of an arms-free zone in south Lebanon, as provided for in Resolution 1701, and without any visible presence of Hezbollah in UNIFIL's area of operation. In February 2007, UNIFIL successfully contained the situation when Israeli troops crossed the technical fence along the Blue Line and a skirmish with the Lebanese Armed Forces almost ensued. UNIFIL's force commander also convened regular meetings between Lebanese and Israeli military officials designed to lead to an Israeli withdrawal from the northern part of Ghajar village (situated astride the Blue Line), where Israel maintained a military presence after the cessation of hostilities. In addition, UNIFIL officials undertook efforts to mark the Blue

Line on the ground in order to prevent unintended border violations by either side.

UNIFIL officials also worked hard to establish good relations with the civilian population in south Lebanon. In the first few months after its expansion, UNIFIL patrols faced occasional stone-throwing by local youths, and there were reports of Hezbollah activists denying peacekeepers freedom of movement. These incidents led to an increased engagement to foster dialogue with the local authorities—as well as, on occasion, the deliberate use of a firm posture vis-à-vis efforts to deny freedom of movement. As UNIFIL reached full troop strength and recruitment of civilian staff progressed, its political and civil affairs office, civil affairs teams, civilian-military cooperation unit, public information offices, and military community outreach unit all began working to improve relations with local communities and to implement confidence-building measures. Emphasizing its role as supporting the Lebanese Armed Forces enabled the mission to clarify its mandate and dispel tension. This was consistent with a consensus within the mission, albeit one not always shared by every member of the Security Council, that Hezbollah's eventual disarmament would take place only through a domestic political process. UNIFIL and national contingent quick-impact projects further helped to foster the support of local communities.

An equally important measure enhancing UNIFIL's security in its immediate environment has been the mission's contribution to the clearing of landmines and of the estimated 1 million unexploded cluster munitions used by Israel during the 2006 war. By June 2007, twenty-two UNIFIL teams were active alongside the Lebanese Armed Forces and seventy-five UN-contracted clearance teams operating under the UN Mine Action Coordination Centre, though their work was hampered by the fact that Israel continued to withhold targeting data, which would have facilitated the clearing effort.

Despite these efforts, implementation of important aspects of Resolution 1701 ran into difficulties. By October 2007, Israel had still not withdrawn from the northern half of Ghajar. Disagreements between Israeli and Lebanese officials had delayed UNIFIL's work to demarcate the Blue Line until the fall. Israel also continued its daily violations of Lebanese sovereignty in the form of frequent over-flights. And although a UN cartographer was expected by June to provide a geographical definition of the Sheb'a Farms, claimed by Lebanon but considered by the Security Council to be Israeli-occupied Syrian territory, it was only in October that the Secretary-General's report on the implementation of Resolution 1701 spelled out the territorial boundaries of the area. A political process to change the status of the area, however, did not appear to be imminent amid reports that Israel rejected any revisions to the UN's standing definition of the Sheb'a Farms as occupied Syrian territory.

UNIFIL was also affected by the security situation in Lebanon, which began deteriorating significantly toward the end of 2006, thus placing new demands on the Lebanese Armed Forces in arenas other than the south and creating new threat potential for UNIFIL. On 21 November 2006, Pierre Gemayel, the minister of industry and scion of one of Lebanon's most prominent Christian families, was assassinated by gunmen. Two weeks previously, all Shi'ite ministers (as well as one Christian) had resigned from the cabinet. As the government's constitutional legitimacy was increasingly drawn into question, the opposition began staging demonstrations at the prime minister's office in downtown Beirut from 1 December. In February 2007, two buses were bombed near a Christian village; three people died. In June and September 2007, two further prominent anti-Syrian members of parliament, Walid Eido and Antoine Ghanem, were killed in bomb blasts in downtown Beirut.

By early summer 2007, the Security Council had decided to establish an international tribunal to try the perpetrators and organizers of the Hariri assassination. Attention was increasingly focused on the next major issue driving the political crisis: the election of a new president when the term of pro-Syrian president Emile Lahoud would come to an

end. Efforts to hold the election, scheduled for late November, failed when opposition groups boycotted parliament. Despite both local and international mediation efforts, Lebanon remained tense, and amid a looming constitutional crisis there were reports of militias on all sides of the political spectrum rearming. Short of a last-minute compromise, renewed civil strife and the emergence of two competing governments seemed a realistic prospect.

The rise to prominence of extremist Islamist groups in Lebanon was identified at an early stage as a key security challenge to UNIFIL. A March 2007 report by the Secretary-General on the implementation of Resolution 1701 mentioned the "growing threat to the presence of the United Nations in Lebanon" from such groups for the first time. A bare two months later, the Lebanese Armed Forces found themselves embroiled in a confrontation with Fatah al-Islam, a small, Al-Qaida-inspired group led by a Palestinian-Jordanian and alleged by some to have ties to Syrian intelligence, in the Nahr al-Bared refugee camp near Tripoli. The conflict would be hailed as a critical test for Lebanese authorities; and after 163 Lebanese soldiers and 222 militants were killed and thousands of Palestinian refugees fled, the Lebanese authorities managed after just over a hundred days to secure the camp.

On 17 June 2007, the firing of Katyusha rockets from southern Lebanon into northern Israel by unknown elements represented the most serious breach of the cessation of hostilities since the end of the war. This incident, the bombing of the Spanish peacekeepers seven days later, and the attack on a Tanzanian UNIFIL vehicle in July, all highlighted continuous concerns over UNIFIL's security amid the tense political climate in Lebanon.

UNIFIL's contribution to maintaining the cessation of hostilities in south Lebanon led to a request from the Lebanese government for a one-year renewal of its mandate in June 2007. Security Council Resolution 1773 of 24 August 2007 extended the mandate until 31 August 2008.

However, there remained further questions related to the wider implementation of Resolution 1701. There has been little meaningful progress on the issues of the captured Israeli soldiers and the Lebanese prisoners, although Israel and Hezbollah conducted a limited exchange in October. Discussion also persisted in the first half of 2007 over reports of arms trafficking across the Syrian-Lebanese border, with weapons destined for Hezbollah or for Syrian-backed militant Palestinian groups. Although Syria (and most troop-contributing countries) had made it clear that an expansion of UNIFIL's area of operations to the Syrian-Lebanese border was entirely unacceptable, the reports of weapons traffic indicated that the underlying issues leading to the 2006 war remained unresolved, and that renewed confrontation between Israel and Hezbollah or other militant groups continued to be a possibility. In response, the UN Secretary-General dispatched an expert team to assess the situation along the Syrian-Lebanese border, which identified a clear need for enhanced international assistance to improve border monitoring.

Some parties, notably Israel, also advocated greater and more forceful proactivism on the part of UNIFIL to detect and confiscate

weapons. At the same time, under the impact of the enduring political stalemate in Lebanon and a tense yet generally stable situation along the Blue Line, a broad consensus evolved in favor of continuity in UNIFIL's current mandate and engagement. This consensus recognizes the critical role that the Lebanese Armed Forces have to play in consolidating the arrangements in the south of the country, and that greater proactivism on the part of UNIFIL would undermine, rather than strengthen, the government of Lebanon and the Lebanese Armed Forces. Consequently the Security Council adopted a presidential statement in early August 2007 that expressed its concern over the continued flow of weapons across the border, but separated this statement purposely from the adoption of the resolution extending UNIFIL's mandate three weeks later.

Other Missions

UNDOF

As tensions increased between Israel and Syria in the early summer, the UN Disengagement Observer Force (UNDOF), established under the 1974 disengagement of forces agreement between Israel and Syria to provide a buffer between their forces in the Golan Heights, attracted greater-than-usual attention. In August, faced with military exercises and a buildup of forces on both sides, UNDOF contributed to calming the situation by clarifying that the increase in Israeli military activities in the Golan area was for training purposes, increased patrolling of the cease-fire line by the Israeli Defense Forces, and renovation of existing positions by both sides, and did not constitute preparation for a military confrontation. In early September, tension mounted with reports that Syrian anti-aircraft batteries had fired on Israeli aircraft intruding into Syrian airspace and dropping ammunitions, even though Israel had just stated publicly, a few days earlier, that it no longer feared a military conflict. Subsequent reports appeared to confirm that Israeli aircraft had targeted a facility inside Syria, though both

epa/Corbis

A French member of UNIFIL on patrol in the village of Al Tiry, southern Lebannon, 29 August 2007.

sides maintained a stony silence on the episode, as did, revealingly, their neighbors.

As has been routine for the past thirty years, the mandate of UNDOF, comprising 1,048 troops, was extended twice over 2007, without any alteration.

UNTSO

The UN Truce Supervision Organization (UNTSO), established in 1948 to monitor observance of cease-fires negotiated between Israel and its neighbors, remains as the UN's longest-serving observer mission worldwide. Its current and main task is the provision of observers and of logistical and financial support to UNIFIL and UNDOF, as well as the provision of a small observer group in Egypt at the request of its government. While UNTSO observers operating under UNIFIL were affected during the war in Lebanon in 2006, UNTSO did not undergo any formal changes to its mandate or its authorized strength.

EUBAM Rafah and EUPOL COPPS

While Lebanon remained the clear focus of the UN's efforts in the region in 2007, events elsewhere in the Middle East also captured much of the international community's attention. Against the background of factional strife and the failure of a power-sharing deal between Fatah and Hamas, by mid-2007 the Palestinian territory was split between Gaza, which remained under the control of Hamas, and the West Bank, where Palestinian Authority president Mahmoud Abbas appointed a new government.

Humanitarian conditions, particularly in Gaza, worsened, as border crossings remained closed for sustained periods. In this context, the continuation of the EU Border Assistance Mission at Rafah (EUBAM Rafah), comprising forty-four civilian police and deployed at the Egypt-Gaza crossing in Rafah, was drawn into question. The mission was extended for one year in May 2007, but suspended its operations under the impact of the intensified internecine violence and the closure of the Rafah crossing from 9 June onward. On 7 July, in an indication that it did not expect a

---

UN Disengagement Observer Force (UNDOF)

- Authorization and Start Date — 31 May 1974 (UNSC Res. 350)
- Force Commander — Major-General Wolfgang Jilke (Austria)
- Budget — $39.5 million (1 July 2007–30 June 2008)
- Strength as of 31 October 2007 — Troops: 1,043
  International Civilian Staff: 40
  Local Civilian Staff: 105

For detailed mission information see p. 246.

UN Truce Supervision Organization (UNTSO)

- Authorization and Start Date — 29 May 1948 (UNSC Res. 50)
- Chief of Staff — Major-General Ian Campbell Gordon (Australia)
- Budget — $30 million (1 January–31 December 2007)
- Strength as of 31 October 2007 — Military Observers: 150
  International Civilian Staff: 105
  Local Civilian Staff: 120

For detailed mission information see p. 351.

EU Border Assistance Mission at Rafah (EUBAM Rafah)

- Authorization Date — 5 November 2005 (Agreement on Movement and Access), 12 December 2005 (Joint Action 2005/889/CFSP)
- Start Date — October 2005
- Head of Mission — Major-General Pietro Pistolese (Italy)
- Budget — $14 million (October 2006–September 2007)
- Strength as of 30 September 2007 — Civilian Police: 44
  International Civilian Staff: 10

EU Police Mission for the Palestinian Territories (EUPOL COPPS)

- Authorization Date — 14 November 2005 (Joint Action 2005/797/CFSP)
- Start Date — January 2006
- Head of Mission — Colin Smith (United Kingdom)
- Budget — $4.8 million (October 2006–September 2007)
- Strength as of 30 September 2007 — Civilian Police: 11

Who Is Dying for Peace? An Analysis of UN Peacekeeping Fatalities

Walter Dorn*

Since 1948, over 2,400 peacekeepers have made the "supreme sacrifice" while serving in UN operations. Thus the UN has suffered a historical average of forty fatalities of uniformed and civilian peacekeepers per year. A more precise analysis reveals significant variations and trends that may help identify the causes and, hopefully, help prevent future loses.

With the end of the Cold War and the advent of modern multidimensional peacekeeping, the number of deployed peacekeepers jumped from the traditional level of about 10,000 to a peak almost eight times that number. Unfortunately, the number of fatalities experienced an even greater jump. The year 1993 was the worst for peacekeeping fatalities in UN history. In the dangerous operations in Somalia, Bosnia, Cambodia, and other UN locations, 225 personnel lost their lives, about half from malicious acts. Fortunately, the situation in peacekeeping has improved tremendously since 1993. In 2006, there were 107 deaths, even though the number of peacekeepers in the field was 10 percent greater than in 1993.

Malicious acts accounted for only 16 percent, while illness had become the prime killer, at 57 percent, for both military and civilian personnel. Accidents accounted for most of the remaining 27 percent.

The annual fatality rate for uniformed personnel has declined steadily since 1993, from 3.30 deaths per 1,000 serving, to 0.97 in 2006; a further decrease in the fatality rate, to 0.47, was projected for 2007. This encouraging trend is particularly pronounced in the new century: though the number of uniformed peacekeepers increased fivefold from 2000 to 2007, the number of fatalities did not rise accordingly, and even declined in recent years (see figure below).

For civilians working in UN operations, unfortunately, the same trend has not been observed. The fatality rate for international civilians increased from 1.0 per 1,000 in 2000, to 2.2 in 2006. The fatality rate for UN personnel hired locally was even higher, at 2.6 in 2006. Thus it is more risky to be a civilian in the field than to be a soldier. In 2006 the

fatality rate for civilians was more than double that of uniformed personnel.

Throughout the history of the UN, fatalities have been significant for both the developed and the developing world. India and Canada have suffered the most military fatalities (122 and 114, respectively, to the end of 2006). The United States and Argentina have experienced the greatest number of UN police fatalities (12 each). For international civilians, US and Indian fatalities top the list (12 and 7, respectively). The 2006 overall fatality rate for the developing world, however, was 77 percent higher than that for the developed world. This is especially significant because almost 90 percent of troops in the field are from the developing world. In recent years, illness has become the main cause of death. The UN would do well to directly address this issue of rising illness. A more thorough analysis of fatality statistics might be an important first step.

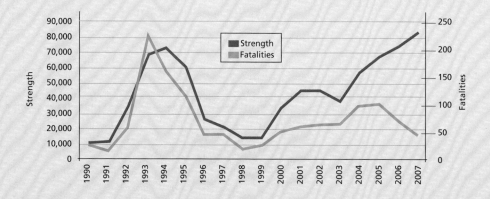

---

*Walter Dorn is professor of defense studies at the Royal Military College of Canada, and a consultant to the UN Department of Peacekeeping Operations.

Note: Figures for 2007 have been extrapolated from DPKO Situation Centre data available as of 30 September 2007.

return to previous conditions anytime soon, the EU decided to downscale EUBAM Rafah, whose members remained at their base in Ashkelon, Israel.

The EU Police Mission for the Palestinian Territories (EUPOL COPPS), the EU's second major civilian peace operation, was equally affected. EUPOL COPPS had been established in November 2005 and began operating in January 2006. The mission's efforts in the area of long-term reform and the provision of enhanced support to the Palestinian Authority in establishing sustainable and effective policing arrangements suffered following the Hamas electoral victory in January 2006. After the Hamas-Fatah split and the establishment of a new Palestinian government in the West Bank, however, EUPOL COPPS resumed its full operations within that area and thus contributed to the renewed momentum and hope for an Israeli-Palestinian breakthrough in the latter half of 2007.

TIPH

Much like the EU peace operations, the multinational Temporary International Presence in Hebron (TIPH) was affected considerably by the deteriorating conditions in the Palestinian territories. Established by Israeli-Palestinian agreement in 1994, and temporarily withdrawn and reestablished in 1997, TIPH is mandated with providing security for the residents of Hebron and promoting stability in the city through monitoring and reporting as well as various assistance activities. It is a small mission of only fifty-five personnel (reduced from seventy previously) from Norway, Sweden, Denmark, Italy, Switzerland, and Turkey, armed with light weapons.

In March 2007, a Swedish TIPH observer was hospitalized after being assaulted with a large stone by a Jewish settler. The same month, tensions erupted after TIPH criticized the contested takeover of a building in central Hebron by a settler group; the property was eventually vacated in April 2007.

At the same time, the renewal of the mission's presence in Hebron in 2007 became a symbol of hope for renewed dialogue. In August, shortly after the establishment of a new Palestinian government in the West Bank and the Israeli decision to reengage with the Palestinian Authority, TIPH's mandate extension became the first official agreement to be signed in a public ceremony by Israeli and Palestinian representatives.

MFO Sinai

The Multinational Force and Observers in Sinai (MFO Sinai) was established in 1981, pursuant to the withdrawal of the UN Emergency Force (UNEF) II in 1979 and the conclusion of the Israeli-Egyptian peace treaty. A proposal by the parties for a new UN force to oversee implementation of this agreement was rejected by the United Nations. MFO Sinai

Temporary International Presence in Hebron (TIPH)

- Authorization and Start Date: 15 January 1997 (Protocol Concerning the Redeployment in Hebron), 21 January 1997 (Agreement on the Temporary International Presence in Hebron)
- Head of Mission: Karl-Henrik Sjursen (Norway)
- Budget: $2.3 million (October 2006–September 2007)
- Strength as of 30 September 2007: Military Observers: 5, Civilian Police: 17, International Civilian Staff: 33

Multinational Force and Observers in Sinai (MFO Sinai)

- Authorization Date: 3 August 1981 (Protocol to the Treaty of Peace)
- Start Date: April 1982
- Head of Mission: Ambassador James A. Larocco (United States)
- Budget: $65 million (October 2006–September 2007)
- Strength as of 30 September 2007: Military Observers: 1,691, Civilian Staff: 15

began operations as a US-led multinational force in 1982, mandated to observe developments in three designated areas of the Sinai. In 2005, with the negotiation of the Access and Movement Agreement and Israel's "disengagement" from the Gaza Strip, its mission was amended to add a fourth function: observation and oversight of the Egyptian government's new commitments to patrol and prevent penetration of the Israel-Gaza boundary, in the context of Israel's withdrawal from Gaza. Notwithstanding Egypt's commitment and redeployment of forces to the area of the crossing, smuggling into the Gaza Strip continued unabated, and perhaps even accelerated, in 2007.

Although this last dimension of MFO Sinai's mandate is linked to conditions and developments in the Gaza Strip, the mission itself has to date not been affected by the turmoil in that area. The most significant incident for the force in 2007 occurred on 6 May, when a French-operated aircraft crashed on a training mission, killing eight French and one Canadian MFO personnel.

Conclusion

Persistently occupying a top spot on the international agenda, the Middle East remains an important area of engagement for UN and non-UN peace operations. The adoption of Security Council Resolution 1701 in 2006 and the deployment of an expanded "new" UNIFIL initially appeared to herald a new era in peacekeeping and was frequently cited in the early months of 2007 as a possible model and precedent for a similar force in the Gaza Strip. Both the deterioration of conditions there and Hamas's takeover in June, and the deep crisis in Lebanon, however, have underlined that while military deployments are important tools to help stabilize arenas in the Middle East, the key challenges confronting the region can only be addressed by political means. Thus, while the perception has strengthened—in Arab, Western, and even Israeli eyes—that peace operations can make an effective and important contribution to international peace and security in the region, this trend has simultaneously been accompanied by the realization that such operations can only fulfill their mandates successfully if embedded in broader political frameworks and processes. Consequently, in the second half of 2007, much of the regional and international focus was on initiatives to help overcome the Lebanese crisis, renewed Israeli-Palestinian talks, and the US-sponsored meeting in Annapolis on 27 November to help restore the tattered peace process.

3.6

Sudan

Sudan remains one of the most challenging peace operation theaters in the world, playing host to the UN in the south, an AU-led mission in Darfur, and the newly authorized hybrid UN-AU Mission in Darfur (UNAMID). Efforts to resolve the crisis in Sudan's western Darfur region, including providing adequate support to the AU Mission in Sudan (AMIS), remained a major preoccupation for the international community throughout the year. The compromise agreement that led to the authorization of a hybrid UN-AU peace operation—the first of its kind between the two institutions—was welcomed as a positive step in the tortuous search for solutions to the crisis, but implementation was painfully slow and marred by continuing Sudanese objections over the composition of the force. High-profile visits in September 2007 by Secretary-General Ban Ki-Moon and in October by a group of eminent elders led by former US president Jimmy Carter and Bishop Desmond Tutu, along with pressure from civil society groups, helped to highlight the gravity of the crisis and the need for international action. Secretary-General Ban identified Darfur as one of his priorities, and outlined a three-pronged strategy—the deployment of the hybrid UN-AU force, revitalizing the peace process, and providing humanitarian and reconstruction support to the victims of the crisis—to resolve the conflict. Meanwhile, on 11 October, the Sudan People's Liberation Movement (SPLM) suspended its participation in the government of national unity that was established after the signing of the Comprehensive Peace Agreement (CPA) in January 2005. The SPLM cited lack of implementation of key provisions of the CPA, such as boundary demarcation and wealth-sharing, as the reason for its actions. This move drew atten-tion to the faltering north-south peace process, which has been overshadowed by the Darfur crisis, prompting calls for a balanced approach to ensure that efforts to resolve the Darfur crisis would not deflect attention from the implementation of the CPA, which is crucial to peace in Sudan. Meanwhile, the SPLM returned to the Government of National Unity in December but a clash between the SPLA and an Arab militia around the same time, which left an estimated one hundred people dead, was a manifestation of the continued tensions between the parties.

AMIS: Mandate and Functions

AMIS was initially deployed in June 2004 with 60 observers and a protection force of

73

AU Mission in Sudan (AMIS)

• Authorization Date	28 May 2004 (Agreement with Sudanese Parties), 30 July 2004 (UNSC Res. 1556)
• Start Date	June 2004
• Head of Mission	Rodolphe Adada (Congo) (note: both Adada and General Agwai will remain active in their positions until the deployment of UNAMID, where they will retain their titles)
• Force Commander	General Martin Luther Agwai (Nigeria)
• Police Commissioner	Mohase Elias Tsibane (South Africa)
• Budget	$297.6 million (January–June 2007)
• Strength as of 30 September 2007	Troops: 5,222 Military Observers: 549 Civilian Police: 1,416

For detailed mission information see p. 357.

300 troops. After several attacks in October of that year, the AU Peace and Security Council expanded the force to 3,000 and gave AMIS a more robust mandate, including protection of civilians and proactive deployment against hostile groups, but it lacked the capacity to do so. In March 2005, AMIS was again expanded, to 6,171 military personnel and 1,586 civilian police.

The Darfur crisis continued unabated throughout 2007, overwhelming the approximately 7,000 uniformed personnel in the region. AMIS's deployment throughout the year was complicated by severe logistical and financial challenges and was disrupted by increased hostility from the various belligerent groups. This reality fed into the dominant debate of the year, over the nature and composition of a peacekeeping force to replace AMIS. Facing continued resistance from the government of Sudan to the deployment of a UN-led operation, a compromise was reached on the deployment of a hybrid UN-AU force in Darfur. Subsequently, the Security Council adopted Resolution 1769 (2007), authorizing deployment of UNAMID, comprising 26,000 troops.

AMIS: Key Developments in Darfur

Peacekeeping efforts in 2007 were complemented by efforts to revitalize the peace process, which had ground to a halt soon after the signing of the Darfur Peace Agreement (DPA) in May 2006. Consultations involving all parties, and led by Salim Ahmed Salim and Jan Eliasson of the Joint UN-AU Mediation Support Team, culminated in a meeting of the various nonsignatories of the DPA in Arusha, Tanzania, in July 2007. While the Arusha meeting concluded with an agreement between the majority of rebel groups and Khartoum to continue talks in Sirte, Libya, in October 2007, Abdul Wahid Mohammed Nur, founder of the Sudan Liberation Movement, boycotted the proceedings. The Tripoli peace talks received a serious blow when, barely a week before the start of the talks, the Justice and Equality Movement and several other groups announced that they would also boycott the meeting. The announcements came after an October meeting of several rebel groups in Juba, in south Sudan, failed to reach a consensus on the proposed peace talks. At the time of writing, efforts were under way to jumpstart the stalled peace talks in Libya, and some progress had been achieved in the deployment of UNAMID, with the establishment of joint headquarters and the arrival of new police and troop units. But with no commitment of attack helicopters and other force enablers, coupled with difficulties with the government, especially over the composition of the mission, the prospects for a rapid deployment of UNAMID remained slim.

Power- and Wealth-Sharing

Progress in implementing the DPA was limited, despite the appointment of Minni Minawi—the only rebel signatory to the agreement—as special assistant to the president and chairman of the Transitional Darfur Regional Authority. The process of establishing some of the key structures provided for in the DPA, such as the Darfur Assessment and Evaluation Commission, lagged significantly, and the few

---

Box 3.6.1 The African Standby Force: Progress 2007

It has been four years since the African Union adopted a policy framework and a roadmap for operationalization of the African Standby Force (ASF) as part of a broader continental security architecture. On completion, the ASF will be composed of five regional, multidisciplinary (military, police, and civilian) standby brigades. As defined in the policy framework, each brigade will be equipped to address six intervention scenarios, which among others include: providing military advice for a political mission, and intervening in situations involving war crimes, crimes against humanity, and genocide. Under the roadmap, AU policy for the ASF will be developed in two phases. The first phase, initially planned to be completed by 30 June 2005 (since extended), focuses on developing the strategic-level management capacity of the AU and the regional economic communities to undertake peace operations under Chapter VI of the UN Charter, and/or preventive deployment. The second phase focuses on developing the strategic management capacity of the AU and the regional economic communities to undertake complex peace operations, including robust military intervention.

While the somewhat ambitious target dates for operationalization of the ASF could not be met during 2007, policy formulation at the AU strategic level progressed remarkably during the year. This work, undertaken in close collaboration with the regional economic communities, has produced a uniquely African doctrine, established a set of standard operating procedures, and created logistical procedures, training and evaluation procedures, and command, control, communication, and information systems. Further policy development was pursued in formulating the ASF concept for rapid deployment, a continental ASF training plan to be completed in 2010. The year 2007 also saw the conclusion of a feasibility study on the development of ASF continental and regional logistical depots, which will support future ASF deployments. These policy instruments, which were developed with the technical and financial support of the AU's international partners, especially members of the extended Group of Eight, are pending approval by the African chiefs of defense and security.

Plans are under way to commence verification of the operational readiness of pledged troops from the various subregions. In 2006, eastern, western, central, and southern Africa made troop pledges of 3,500–4,000, 6,500, 4,000–6,000, and 3,655 respectively. It is crucial that verification begins in earnest in 2008 if the 2010 deadline for complete operationalization of the ASF is to be met. At the end of 2007, a draft document spelling out the verification method and process had been formulated, but was yet to be discussed with the regional economic communities.

Meanwhile, efforts to establish an initial planning capacity for the ASF at the AU headquarters in Addis Ababa registered modest progress, as several staff officers were recruited. However, the process of replacing the ASF's first chief of staff, General Ishaya Isah Hassan, who died in late 2006, has been very slow, leaving a gap in strategic military guidance for the ASF.

---

structures that were put in place hardly functioned. For instance, the Transitional Authority, established in October 2006, was only inaugurated in May 2007 amid a lack of clarity concerning its relationship with other local government entities in Darfur. Meanwhile, representatives of the Sudan Liberation Army–Minawi were appointed to several positions in the government of Khartoum. But the limited support for the DPA undercut the effectiveness of such appointments, as they were not representative of the various factions in Darfur.

Meanwhile, the Darfur-Darfur Dialogue and Consultation (DDDC)—proposed by the Darfur Peace Agreement—commenced with several preconsultation meetings involving local groups in Darfur. The DDDC's Preparatory Committee identified four stakeholder groups—native administration, internally displaced persons (IDPs), civil society, and intellectuals—and consultations were undertaken in order to identify representatives for each. Proper representation of all the stakeholders is viewed as key to the success of the DDDC, but the process has been complicated by the pervasive insecurity on the ground.

The deteriorating security situation forced AMIS to suspend efforts to assess the development and reconstruction needs as provided for by the DPA, significantly hampering wealth-sharing efforts. This led to the cancellation of a planned donor pledging conference that had been expected to follow the report of the Darfur Joint Assessment Mission. The conference

A peacekeeper injured in attacks on the AMIS base in Haskanita
is rushed to a waiting helicopter, Darfur, Sudan, 30 September 2007.

was viewed as a crucial step in raising funds to address the dire socioeconomic challenges that are partly believed to have precipitated the conflict.

Security Arrangements

Although AMIS maintained over 90 percent of its uniformed personnel on the ground, implementation of the security arrangements provided for by the DPA registered limited progress. Splintering and infighting among the rebel movements, as well as fighting against the government, undermined any efforts to implement the security provisions. Contrary to the DPA, the Janjaweed militia was not disarmed and remained active, persistently attacking innocent civilians throughout the year. Lack of access to areas controlled by nonsignatories to the DPA significantly limited verification of the locations of the parties and any monitoring of violations of the cease-fire agreement. In fact, by June 2007, verification of the parties' locations had only taken place in two out of the eight sectors.[1] The Cease-Fire Commission—a dual chamber for signatories and nonsignatories—was proposed as a compromise at the end of 2006, but was held hostage by government and rebel movements and proved largely ineffective during 2007. The government objected to the presence of representatives of the nonsignatories to the DPA on the commission, while the nonsignatories argued that the commission should be based on the N'Djamena Agreement of 2004.

These developments occurred at a time of increased hostility toward AMIS. Between March and September 2007, twenty AMIS peacekeepers were killed. The 29 September and 30 September attacks on an AU base in the town of Haskanita, which left ten peacekeepers dead, were the most deadly hostile actions recorded during this period. Although the motives of the attackers were unknown, the attacks reinforced the need for the hybrid UN-AU force to be sufficiently robust to deter such actions, as well as to adequately defend itself and the civilian population when faced with such hostility.

Interethnic and intraethnic fighting also surged in 2007, leading to the deaths of hundreds of civilians. The ethnic feuds were not limited to the rebel movements, but extended to Arab tribes believed by some to be the backbone of the Janjaweed. Additionally, there were reports of the government settling Arab nomads from neighboring countries in areas that were previously abandoned due to the conflict, raising significant concerns about the prospects of return for IDPs and refugees to those areas. A likely sticking point in the upcoming round of peace talks will therefore be the "right of return." Increasing militarization of IDP camps also emerged as a major security concern, as the presence of armed persons served as a pretext for attacks on the camps.

Humanitarian Situation

The unstable security situation triggered a fresh wave of refugees and IDPs, swelling the ranks of existing IDP and refugee populations. An estimated 250,000 civilians were displaced during the first three quarters of 2007, with some humanitarian agencies reporting substantially more displacements. Several thousand Chadian refugees crossed the border into Darfur due to cross-border fighting and massive displacement of civilian populations. Humanitarian access was hampered by the increased attacks on humanitarian workers and the poor road conditions during the rainy season. The deteriorating security situation led to the suspension of humanitarian activities in some areas, leaving thousands of civilians without any support systems. Despite these difficulties in providing aid, Darfur continued to play host to the world's largest humanitarian operation, aimed at assisting approximately 4.2 million conflict-affected people.

From AMIS to UNAMID

Faced with serious financial and logistical challenges, AMIS was nonetheless the only international force operating in Darfur during 2007. The mission continued to implement its mandate, but with great difficulty, as its personnel were deliberately targeted and often went for months without their allowances. Meanwhile, efforts to implement the light and heavy support packages—agreed to at the end of 2006 to bolster AMIS—continued throughout the year. By September 2007, the full complement of the light support package had been deployed, and it was anticipated that implementation of the heavy support package would have been completed before the deployment of the hybrid force in early 2008. However, deployment of the support packages was delayed by a combination of factors, including the poor security situation, and lack of accommodation and other facilities meeting UN standards.

After months of negotiations with the government of Sudan, the UN Security Council adopted Resolution 1769 (2007), authorizing the deployment of UNAMID.[2] Adopted under Chapter VII of the UN Charter, the mission is to consist of over 26,000 uniformed personnel: 19,555 military personnel (including 360 military observers and liaison officers), 3,772 police personnel, and 19 formed police units with 140 officers in each unit. The resolution emphasized the need to maintain the "African charac-

ter" of the mission, a condition that was put forward by the government of Sudan. The fact that the resolution was adopted under Chapter VII and included a mandate to protect civilians was viewed by many as an important first step, as protecting the vulnerable civilian population is widely recognized as the most pressing security challenge in Darfur. On the other hand, many expressed concern about the fact that Resolution 1769's section on the protection of civilians appeared to have been qualified, stipulating that the mission was authorized only to "take the necessary action" in protecting civilians and mission staff, rather than the usual authorization to "use all necessary means." In July 2007, the AU and the UN agreed on the appointment of Rodolphe Adada and General Martin Luther Agwai as the joint special representative and force commander of the hybrid UN-AU peacekeeping force, respectively.

The creation and deployment of UNAMID poses several important and unique challenges. Foremost is the ability of the mission to maintain the African character of the force without compromising its effectiveness. While AU member states have demonstrated a definite willingness to participate in peacekeeping missions in their own backyards, their overall capacity is less clear. In particular, most potential African troop contributors lack the force enablers, such as attack helicopters and armored personnel carriers, that are essential to UNAMID's effectiveness. In late 2007, offers from Sweden, Norway, and other countries to provide enabling contingents were being stymied by the government of Sudan. A second concern is that of command and control, especially regarding the strategic direction of the mission (an issue elaborated on in Chapter 2 in this Review). While the resolution emphasizes that the mission will adhere to the unity of command principle, there is no guarantee against rifts that may appear at the strategic level. As of November 2007, no mechanism had been established for resolution of potential disagreement between the AU and the UN. Third, the mandate does not specify how the mission will interact with the numerous humanitarian agencies on the ground without compromising the neutrality principle, an especially crucial concern given the hostile environment in Darfur. The fourth challenge is how the mission will secure enough water to support its personnel without depriving the local population of the much-needed resource in the arid environment of Darfur. The fifth challenge concerns cooperation of the government of Sudan with respect to issues such as land acquisition and authorizing night flights. The issue of night flights—which the government denied AMIS—is especially crucial in light of UNAMID's mandate to protect civilians, which will be significantly hampered if the mission's movement is limited at night. Finally, coordination among the UN, AU, and various other actors, including the newly authorized UN-EU peace operations in neighboring Chad and the Central African Republic, will be a critical challenge.

UNMIS: Background

The broad range of tasks and responsibilities that fall within the UNMIS mandate are typical of modern multidimensional UN peacekeeping operations. Authorized in 2005 by the UN Security Council, UNMIS has been charged with providing support to the implementation of the Comprehensive Peace Agreement. This support has been manifested primarily in the mission's role as honest broker, providing good offices to facilitate the dialogue between the strong central government of Sudan based in Khartoum, and the nascent government of southern Sudan in Juba. In addition to the mission's Chapter VII mandate to protect civilians under imminent threat of violence, UNMIS has been made responsible for monitoring compliance with cease-fire agreements, and for supervision of the redeployment of armed groups—as well as police restructuring, human rights monitoring, and support of government efforts to disarm, demobilize, and reintegrate former combatants. It is mandated to support preparations for the 2009 general election, and for the 2011 referendum on southern independence. Working closely with the UN High Commissioner for Refugees (UNHCR), the International Organization for Migration, and the World Food Programme, UNMIS officials have also coordinated the massive relief effort that has facilitated the return and reintegration of thousands of refugees and internally displaced persons this year.

UNMIS: Key Developments and Challenges

Military and police deployments were largely implemented in 2007, with deployment of military peacekeepers and civilian police reaching 97 percent and 96 percent of authorized strength, respectively, as of August. UNMIS undertook a decentralization of mission authority from Khartoum to the southern capital of Juba, with a view to strengthening the level of contact between UNMIS officials and the southern authorities. The mission continued to struggle with severe recruitment and retention challenges among its civilian staff, most notably the lack of a head of mission beginning in October 2006 when Special Representative of the Secretary-General (SRSG) Jan Pronk was declared persona non grata and expelled from the country. This personnel problem was exacerbated by the growing international attention to the crisis in Darfur, and the intense pres-

---

UN Mission in Sudan (UNMIS)

• Authorization and Start Date	24 March 2005 (UNSC Res. 1590)
• SRSG and Head of Mission	Ashraf Jehangir Qazi (Pakistan)
• Force Commander	Lieutenant-General Jasbir Singh Lidder (India)
• Police Commissioner	Kai Vittrup (Denmark)
• Budget	$846.3 million (1 July 2007–30 June 2008)
• Strength as of 31 October 2007	Troops: 8,827
	Military Observers: 583
	Police: 696
	International Civilian Staff: 865
	Local Civilian Staff: 2,580
	UN Volunteers: 253

For detailed mission information see p. 311.

sure for UNMIS to divert scarce human resources away from the Comprehensive Peace Agreement to the support of the Darfur Peace Agreement in the west. Only in September was Ashraf Qazi appointed to the position of UNMIS SRSG.

Power- and Wealth-Sharing

The year in review saw limited forward movement in the development of southern governance institutions. The parties came to an agreement on the procedural rules for the National Petroleum Commission, but the persistent mistrust between them meant that the enforcement of wealth-sharing agreements continued to be a challenge. Wealth-sharing agreements were further complicated by the slow disbursement of development funding from the World Bank–administered Multi-Donor Trust Fund and lower-than-expected oil revenues, both of which resulted in a budget deficit for the government of southern Sudan and strikes by teachers and veterans unhappy about the delays in their wages.

The demarcation of the north-south border continues to be highly controversial and has achieved minimal progress. During 2007, the Technical Border Committee conducted visits to the border region, and plans were under way for an UNMIS-supported workshop on international best practices for the border demarcation process. It is currently hoped that the final demarcation of the border will take place in the second quarter of 2008. The status of the contested area north of Abyei continues to be unresolved, and persistent restrictions on the movement of UNMIS patrols have challenged fulfillment of the mission's monitoring mandate in the area. Abyei, a region hotly contested by the north and south during the 2004 negotiations, and a potential flashpoint for interethnic violence, continues to threaten the success of the CPA.

While the lack of basic infrastructure and shortages of skilled professionals have hampered development of a functioning judiciary in the south, UNMIS, in conjunction with the UN Development Programme (UNDP) and local authorities, has sponsored a number of capacity-building initiatives to support the development of judicial, police, and prison reform. Positive developments were reflected in the anticorruption efforts of Slava Kiir, president of the government of southern Sudan, including a significant reshuffling of the southern cabinet, and the dismissal of the southern minister of finance. Additionally, the establishment of the National Human Rights and National Civil Service Commissions, the functioning of the Southern Sudan Peace and Reconciliation Commission, and the agreement between the government of national unity and the government of southern Sudan with regard to the respective jurisdictions of the two levels of government, marked significant strides in the transition to stability in the region. Election preparations took a step forward as well, when the pilot census was successfully completed in April. The official census, however, was pushed back from the planned date of November 2007 to January 2008, and UNMIS continues to monitor and support developments around the census and other electoral assistance activities. Internally, UNMIS has undertaken steps to enhance its capacity to support elections processes in preparation for the January census and the 2009 elections.

Security

The security situation in southern Sudan remains tenuous in the face of ongoing interethnic violence, banditry, and violent confrontations over cattle and grazing rights. At the same time, the Lord's Resistance Army—a Sudan-based Ugandan rebel group, four of whose leaders have been indicted by the International Criminal Court—was perceived by some as an ongoing security threat in 2007. UNMIS has attempted to address this generalized insecurity by working with local politicians and communities to promote community-based reconciliation, and by intensifying patrols in insecure areas. As refugee and IDP returns have continued to increase dramatically, there is further concern that competition over land and water resources, as well as over severely strained services such as education and healthcare, will become a new source of tension, particularly in and around the overcrowded towns of Juba and Malakal. Militia attacks have contributed to insecurity on the primary roads around Juba, and a peacekeeper was killed in an attack on a civilian demining team in the eastern equatorial region in January 2007, compounding concerns about the safety of UN and humanitarian staff. In November 2006 a violent clash between the Sudan Armed Forces and Sudan People's Liberation Army factions in Malakal resulted in over 150 deaths and the temporary relocation of nonessential UN staff, while a similar clash south of Abyei in January 2007 over the integration of troops from other armed groups displaced over 2,000 civilians. In both cases, UNMIS negotiated with the Sudan Armed Forces and the Sudan People's Liberation Army, as well as local leaders, to defuse the tensions and restore stability.

Security reforms were slow to materialize during the year in review, but by August the joint integrated units (JIUs)—which were created to provide the basis for national security under the terms of the CPA—had reached 77 percent of their expected strength. The capacity of the JIUs to deliver real security guarantees, however, has been uncertain. While a common code of conduct was agreed on by the parties in February, many JIUs lack discipline and logistical capabilities, and most continue to operate under parallel command and control structures. UNMIS has had a limited role in improving this situation, and in responding to specific shortcomings in the JIUs, as the joint defense board has not yet come to an agreement on a request for assistance. This weakness of the JIUs has been used to defend the slow pace of Sudan Armed Forces redeployment to the north, a crucial step that was meant to have been completed ahead of the 9 July 2007 deadline stipulated in the CPA. As of July 2007, only 66 percent of the troops stationed in south Sudan had been redeployed outside the region. Furthermore, there continues to be a significant Sudan Armed Forces

presence in the contested areas of southern Kordofan, the Blue Nile, and Abyei, as well as in the oil-rich Upper Nile.

The work of the National Council for Disarmament, Demobilization, and Reintegration (DDR) progressed slowly and, despite some promising steps during 2007, the national DDR strategy was not completed. The council did meet for the first time, in December 2006, and established a technical subcommittee for DDR, which UNMIS will support. Notable progress on the ground included the formal absorption of southern Sudan's defense forces into the ranks of the Sudan People's Liberation Army. In other positive security developments, the UNMIS civilian police continued to be co-located with local police officers, and worked to promote community policing strategies and international human rights standards. In June 2007, the first class of twenty-nine UN-trained police officers graduated from their program; they are expected to form the nucleus of the new Juba police force.

Conclusion

Efforts to deploy the hybrid UN-AU force in Darfur—which became operational on 31 December 2007—and revitalize the peace process while ensuring implementation of the CPA remained the focus of international engagement in Sudan throughout the year. While the authorization of UNAMID is a positive step in bringing stability to the region, its success depends on how rapidly the uniformed and civilian components of the mission are deployed. Sudan's continued intransigence, and the UN's approach to overcoming it, delayed deployments in the final months of 2007. UNAMID's ability to effectuate significant change in Darfur also depends on the ongoing political efforts to reach an inclusive and comprehensive peace agreement. Secretary-General Ban Ki-Moon's visit to the region in the summer of 2007 highlighted the intense international pressure being placed on the parties to achieve a meaningful political solution to the conflict. However, during Secretary-

General Ban's visit, Khartoum appointed Ahmed Haroun—a former government minister with a pending arrest warrant against him by the International Criminal Court—to chair a committee to oversee human rights violations in the country. One of the significant challenges in negotiating a comprehensive peace agreement in the year to come will be to address this lack of cooperation while maintaining an open dialogue with all parties.

Implementation of key provisions of the CPA in the north-south peace process, such as wealth-sharing, boundary demarcation, and disarmament of militias and other armed groups, achieved unsatisfactory progress. The postponement of the referendum planned for 2007 to January 2008 raised serious questions about the elections scheduled for 2009, as well as the 2011 referendum on the status of southern Sudan. Despite these delays and shortcomings, it is hoped that the deployment of the hybrid UN-AU mission in Darfur will generate enough progress to allow for a rebalancing of attention to include the faltering north-south peace process. The challenge for the international community is how to ensure that resolution of one of the conflicts is not achieved at the expense of the other.

Notes

1. *Report of the Chairperson of the African Union Commission and the Secretary-General of the United Nations on the Hybrid Operation in Darfur,* PSC/PR/2(LXXIX), 22 June 2007.

2. For details on UNAMID's mandate see, United Nations, Security Council Resolution 1769, UN Doc. S.2007/468, 30 July 2007.

Timor-Leste

The first full year of the UN Integrated Mission in Timor-Leste (UNMIT) was completed in 2007. Authorized in August 2006, UNMIT was deployed in the aftermath of two bloody months, April and May, that year, when large parts of state security institutions collapsed and the fledgling nation lurched dangerously toward civil conflict. Instead of completing its expected drawdown in 2006, the severe downturn in events required the UN to return in greater numbers with the likelihood of staying for several years.

UNMIT is a multidimensional mission with a wide mandate including political arbitration, security and judicial sector reform, and socioeconomic development. The mission's success will be assessed by its capacity to better help build effective and sustainable national institutions, compared to the efforts of predecessor missions. In particular, UNMIT's challenge will be to demonstrate its effectiveness in restoring public order, rebuilding trust in the police, and reforming the wider security sector.

Background

Soon after Timor-Leste declared independence from Portugal in 1975, Indonesia invaded and then annexed the territory. A brutal twenty-four-year occupation followed, during which over 100,000 Timorese suffered conflict-related deaths.[1] In August 1999, the people of Timor-Leste chose autonomy in a referendum supervised by the United Nations, resulting in Indonesia agreeing to the country's independence. Pro-Indonesian militias launched a campaign of violence soon after, leading to the deaths of approximately 2,000 Timorese and the dislocation of tens of thousands more.

Following military intervention by an Australian-led coalition under UN mandate, the UN Transitional Administration in East Timor (UNTAET) was established in October 1999 as the territory's administrative authority for an intermediary period, and to ensure a peaceful transition to independence. Although UNTAET was responsible for a relatively small territory compared to other UN peacekeeping missions, its mandate was colossal: in effect, to build a state from scratch. The would-be nation had few formal accouterments of sovereignty on which to build a state: no ministries, no institutions, no police, and just a handful of courts. For reasons of occupation and dislocation, indigenous resources to animate these institutions were limited, and a

Map No. 4255.11 Rev. 2   UNITED NATIONS
October 2007

Department of Field Support
Cartographic Section

mass exodus of Indonesian civil servants prior to and immediately following the territory-wide violence and destruction had left an enormous capacity vacuum. Two of the most credible indigenous institutions, the Conselho Nacional da Resistencia Timorense (CNRT) (the political umbrella), and the Forças Armadas da Libertação Nacional de Timor-Leste (FALINTIL), were on the one hand voluntarily disbanded, and on the other hand sidelined at the onset of the UNTAET mission.

During the three years of UN administration, Timorese politicians progressively assumed governing authority, establishing a national governing council and electing a parliament and president. On 20 May 2002, the country became independent, with resistance hero Jose Alexandre Kay Rala "Xanana" Gusmão sworn in as its first president and the government led by the Frente Revolucionária do Timor-Leste Independente (FRETILIN), one of the parties that had declared independence twenty-seven years previously. The challenges the new state would face were underscored by stark economic data released at the time: the UN's 2002 *Human Development Report* ranked Timor-Leste as the poorest country in Asia.

Following independence, UNTAET was succeeded by the UN Mission of Support in East Timor (UNMISET), with a mandate to provide interim law enforcement and public security, and to assist in the development of a new law enforcement agency, the East Timor Police Service (later called Policia Nacional de Timor-Leste [PNTL]). UNMISET was also mandated to contribute to the maintenance of the external and internal security of Timor-Leste, and provide assistance to core administrative structures critical to the viability and political stability of the country. A new Timorese defense force (the FALINTIL–Forças Armadas de Defesa de Timor-Leste [F-FDTL]) was created, but a large number of demobilized fighters were not incorporated into it. UNMISET was followed by the UN Office in Timor-Leste (UNOTIL) in 2005, a much smaller mission than its predecessors, and conceived as a bridging operation to transition from peacekeeping

to coordinated development assistance. UNOTIL was scheduled to end in May 2006, a decision influenced by member states' reluctance to fund it further.

The 2006 Crisis

The violence that erupted in Timor-Leste in 2006 demonstrated that the national and international efforts over six and a half years had not succeeded in developing and nurturing new state institutions. Judged with the benefit of hindsight, many of the institutions created by the UN and bequeathed to the new state were simply not fit for their purpose. The short time-frame was not the only factor: the manner in which the UN and donor countries

---

UN Integrated Mission in Timor-Leste (UNMIT)

- Authorization and Start Date: 25 August 2006 (UNSC Res. 1704)
- SRSG and Head of Mission: Atul Khare (India)
- Chief Military Liaison Officer: Colonel Graeme Roger Williams (New Zealand)
- Police Commissioner: Rodolfo Aser Tor (Phillipines)
- Budget: $153.2 million (1 July 2007–30 June 2008)
- Strength as of 31 October 2007: Military Observers: 32
Police: 1,464
International Civilian Staff: 333
Local Civilian Staff: 771
UN Volunteers: 118

For detailed mission information see p. 321.

International Security Forces (ISF)

- Authorization Date: 20 June 2006 (UNSC Res. 1690)
- Start Date: May 2006
- Force Commander: Brigadier John Hutcheson (Australia)
- Budget: $87.4 million (October 2006–September 2007)
- Strength as of 30 September 2007: Troops: 1,020

approached statebuilding in Timor-Leste can be faulted in other respects. During the UN transitional administration, Timorese participation in the process was frequently sidelined by the presence of a large number of international advisers and overreliance on "off the shelf" models, with limited consideration of their appropriateness in the Timorese context.

The newly created security sector institutions were especially frail, and tensions within and between the PNTL and the F-FDTL were important factors in the renewed violence. Compared to the police, the F-FDTL was relatively neglected by the international community (including in terms of the mandates given to UNTAET and UNMISET), and poorly funded by donors.[2] Alleged unfair treatment within the ranks ignited discontent. In February 2006, 400 officers (later 594) went on strike over discrimination in promotions and ill-treatment. The decision of the F-FDTL commander to dismiss these officers in March 2006 prompted demonstrations that descended into violence. The acrimony escalated in the following months, and acquired a regional character, as armed groups from Timor's eastern and western provinces clashed. The police forces split along similar geographic lines, reflecting a perception that Timorese from the west of the country had not carried their weight during the armed resistance. Youth gangs, often politically manipulated and sparked by tensions emanating from beliefs that the easterners had usurped residential property and market stalls in the capital, clashed throughout the city. In April–May 2006, thirty-seven people died, many houses were destroyed, and 150,000 Timorese—15 percent of the entire population—were displaced from their homes amid the violence.

Within the space of a few months, many of the institutions established with the assistance of the UN appeared to be rapidly unraveling. The tensions laid bare the long-standing animosities between and within the political elite, and the sharp rivalries between the police and the defense force. The government was largely paralyzed, with a split between Prime Minister Mari Alkatiri and President Gusmão over the appropriate governmental mechanisms for power-sharing. The PNTL and the F-FDTL were at best incapable of controlling, and at worst complicit in, crime and lawlessness. Under the circumstances, the small UNOTIL mission, without any military contingent, tried its best to assist the parties to resolve the crisis peacefully. In one of the most tragic events in this harrowing time for the UN, the police chief of the UNPOL mission was fired upon as he attempted to negotiate safe passage for PNTL officers hemmed in their headquarters by F-FDTL soldiers. Eight unarmed PNTL were shot dead in the attack.[3]

By late May, security had largely collapsed, prompting the president, the prime minister, and the president of the national parliament to request international assistance to help stabilize the situation. Defense forces from Australia and New Zealand arrived in Dili on 26 May, calming the situation in partnership with formed police units from Portugal and Malaysia. In these circumstances, a prior decision to downsize and withdraw the UN presence seemed untimely. A multidimensional assessment team led by a Special Envoy of the Secretary-General, Ian Martin (former Special Representative in the UN Mission in East Timor [UNAMET]), recommended a larger peacekeeping mission, one focused on security and judicial sector reform.

Security Council Resolution 1704 was passed on 25 August 2006, paving the way for the establishment of UNMIT. The mission's broad mandate include support of the 2007 elections, institutional reform of the police and armed forces, justice sector development, relocation of displaced persons, use of good offices to assist reconciliation of a fractured polity, and a coordinating role in executing the "compact" through which Timorese national development plans, the UN, and bilateral donors are to be dovetailed in the provision of humanitarian assistance and the promotion of sustainable development. Restoring public security is a mission priority, and the UN civilian police are the mission's most visible face. UN police will provide interim executive policing support,

Box 3.7.1 Challenges of Building National Police Structures: The UN's Portfolio of Law Enforcement Projects

The critical role of police personnel in UN peacekeeping operations was on display during the year in review, from Haitian National Police conducting a series of successful raids on gangs in the slums of Port-au-Prince alongside UN police, to the positive impacts of the deployment of an all-female Indian formed police contingent in the UN Mission in Liberia (UNMIL). The presence of the all-female police contingent is reported to have had a positive impact on public perceptions, as the number of female applicants who sought to join the Liberian National Police increased significantly following the deployment of the unit. In addition to their support in maintaining law and order, UN police personnel are playing a prominent role in developing the organic police capacity in postconflict societies. Since the 2000 report of the Panel on UN Peace Operations, commonly known as the Brahimi Report, which emphasized the crucial role of police personnel, this critical undertaking has not been matched by the provision of ade-

quate resources. It is against this backdrop that the Police Division of the UN Department of Peacekeeping Operations published *The Portfolio of Police and Law Enforcement Projects 2007,* to highlight both achievements and deficiencies of the current UN police programs.

The *Portfolio* details the administration, current funding, objectives, and challenges of seventy-three UN police projects across ten different peace operations. Most projects are given a timeline of one year for completion, including achievable benchmarks, but some projects may take up to three years to be completed. In 2007, UN police consisted of more than 9,000 officers, with an approximately $215 million funding requirement for in-mission projects. Slightly more than half of this amount was earmarked for equipment, and nearly a third for construction and rehabilitation projects, with the remaining for capacity building and service delivery projects. MINUSTAH had the highest estimated cost, at $44.5 million for nine

projects, with a large portion, over $18 million, going toward equipping the Haitian National Police. The highest individual estimated figure was $21.1 million in Burundi, for a project to develop the newly created Department of Civil Protection.

Based on ten UN-led peace operations, the *Portfolio* points to a chronic lack of human, material, and financial resources as impediments to police reform efforts in postconflict countries. Meanwhile, the challenges posed by increasing needs for larger numbers of UN police personnel, and proper training, have yet to be properly addressed. Currently, the responsibility to coordinate potential donor resources toward mission project goals falls to small in-mission committees tasked with coordinating all rebuilding projects. It is hoped that the *Portfolio* will serve as a reference tool for donors wanting to strengthen UN police efforts and support new and ongoing projects in several missions.

Source: United Nations, *The Portfolio of Police and Law Enforcement Projects 2007* (New York: Department of Peacekeeping Operations, Police Division, December 2006), http://www.un.org/depts/dpko/dpko/unpolprojects.html.

while simultaneously reconstituting the deeply politicized, institutionally weak PNTL.

The mission began in a somewhat changed political environment. José Ramos Horta acceded to the premiership after the resignation of Mari Alkatiri in June 2006, while two other ministers with direct responsibility for the police and the military resigned at the same time. Rogério Lobato, the former interior minister, was held culpable for his role in the events of April–May 2006 and sentenced to seven and a half years in jail.[4]

Key Developments

The presence of UNMIT has helped to restore relative calm to Timor-Leste, assisted in no

small measure by the presence of the 1,000 Australian and New Zealand troops operating in the International Security Forces, formerly Operation Astute. UNMIT police have played a primary role in the security efforts, with "blue beret" civilian police drawn from over forty countries. The police are currently engaged in vetting PNTL officers, removing officers implicated in the trouble of 2006, and retraining and mentoring the remainder, some of whom are already deployed.

In some respects, this police rebuilding process is something of a "do-over" opportunity for the UN police, a chance to prove that they are able to address the deficiencies that arose in the creation of the PNTL during the transitional administration period.[5] As the UN

A Portuguese UNMIT policeman guards election workers loading ballot boxes to be distributed to the sub-districts of Dili, 8 May 2007.

Independent Commission of Inquiry discovered in probing the events of 2006, the PNTL was deeply politicized and fragmented, with many of its officers having been drawn from among those who served under the Indonesian occupation.

The question currently facing Timor-Leste is whether the "blue berets" will be any better at creating an effective police institution than their predecessors were during the transitional administration. The UN police need to provide their officers—who are often in a country with which they are not linguistically or culturally familiar—with improved tools for police training and mechanisms to better transfer knowledge about the role of the police to the local population. The day-to-day transfer of knowledge, skills, and best practices remains a substantial ongoing challenge.

Their assignment is made doubly challenging because some members of the PNTL have shown themselves resistant to reform. According to a trusted human rights monitor, "many PNTL members do not report for their training courses or turn up for duty at the designated place."[6] Public trust in the PNTL remains low, and insecurity remains a prominent concern, especially in the major cities,

where a flammable mix of unemployment, youth bulge, and gang culture persists.

UNMIT's other major functions have included good office efforts to promote dialogue and reconciliation among the still-fractured leadership and population, and to provide support for presidential and parliamentary elections. Achievements in this regard were tempered by the underlying fragility of politics in the country. The elections effectively resulted in the individuals serving as president and prime minister swapping jobs. José Ramos-Horta was elected president in May 2007, defeating the candidate of Timor-Leste's governing party, FRETILIN, in a second-round run-off. FRETILIN's electoral setback continued in the June parliamentary poll, as it slipped from fifty-five seats (of eighty-eight) to twenty-one in the now sixty-five-member parliament. Although it remained the largest party in terms of seats, FRETILIN was unable to persuade enough other parties to join it in a coalition, leading to a deadlock in the formation of a government. In August 2007, an alliance of parties led by Gusmão was requested by the president to form the new government. The new administration has put forward a platform involving, among other things, tackling poverty, strengthening security, and returning the remaining 100,000 persons who were internally displaced during the 2006 violence to their homes. FRETILIN continues to question the new government's legitimacy.

Violence following the formation of the new government illustrates how brittle the ostensible calm in Timor remains. In protests in Dili and major cities, where FRETILIN supporters protested the results, an estimated 400 houses were torched, a UN convoy was ambushed, and hundreds of civilians were displaced in the ensuing violence.

Beyond insecurity, the new government faces profound challenges. Timor-Leste struggles with deep-seated social, economic, and governance problems: high unemployment, rapid population growth, inadequate infrastructure, a weak public sector with limited service capacity, and fragile state institutions.

Box 3.7.2 HIV/AIDS and UN Peacekeeping

In 2007, the UN's Peacekeeping Best Practices Unit, part of the Department of Peacekeeping Operations (DPKO), conducted its second HIV/AIDS "Knowledge, Attitude, and Practice" (KAP) survey of uniformed peacekeepers as part of its ongoing effort to measure the effectiveness of HIV/AIDS education programs for peacekeepers. Employing a model similar to that used in the first KAP, in the UN Mission in Liberia (UNMIL) in 2005, the Peacekeeping Best Practices Unit set out to survey the UN Stabilization Mission in Haiti (MINUSTAH) in May 2007, the results of which were published in August.

DPKO's KAP survey is in line with Security Council Resolution 1308 (2000), which requested member states to initiate HIV/AIDS prevention and awareness programs for peacekeepers and offer voluntary counseling and testing. Recognizing the inherent challenges this poses in terms of standardization of training modules, the DPKO, with the support of the UN Programme on HIV/AIDS (UNAIDS), developed a standard generic training module on HIV/AIDS to supplement training from member states. The MINUSTAH survey thus assessed the performance of these programs using the generic training module developed by DPKO and UNAIDS.

The MINUSTAH survey involved 1,166 uniformed male officers in the mission. Female officers were not included in the survey, as they represented a small percentage of staff and confidentiality could not be ensured. In carrying out the MINUSTAH survey, the Peacekeeping Best Practices Unit incorporated lessons learned from the UNMIL survey in 2005. For example, the 2005 survey of uniformed UNMIL personnel was administered only in English, while the MINUSTAH survey of 2007 was conducted in English, French, Spanish, and Portuguese, to allow for a wider subject pool and thereby remedy some of the shortfalls from the UNMIL survey.

The MINUSTAH survey revealed that between 47 and 74 percent of respondents demonstrated a comprehensive knowledge of HIV/AIDS. The predeployment section of the survey assessed that 89 percent of military personnel had received training on HIV issues in their home countries, while 65 percent had received training on the ground in Haiti. The figures for UN police were 73 percent and 83 percent, respectively. Although the UNAIDS program distributes awareness cards to mission personnel, less than half of those surveyed had received the cards, and only 17 percent of respondents were carrying their cards when they were interviewed. The variance between knowledge and training demonstrates the challenges for the latter in terms of streamlining prevention and awareness.

The survey also found that 11 percent of respondents considered themselves at high risk for contracting HIV, with 43 percent considering themselves at low risk and 42 percent considering themselves at no risk. However, nearly 90 percent of interviewees indicated an interest in a free, confidential HIV test in the mission area. The large number of respondents interested in the latter demonstrates the need for facilities to undertake voluntary counseling and testing, and placed an enormous responsibility on MINUSTAH to provide these services. The 2007 KAP survey had two notable limitations. First, the methodology was flawed, given the discrepancy between risk and testing highlighted in the survey's interview versus self-administered style, the latter of which elicits more honest responses but results in a lower response rate. Second, MINUSTAH civilian personnel and the local community were excluded from the survey. Nonetheless, as with the previous KAP surveys, the lessons of the MINUSTAH survey will be incorporated into future research.

The survey report made several recommendations for member states, DPKO, and MINUSTAH, including training and deployment of HIV/AIDS peer-educators by troop-contributing countries, providing guidance to troop and police contributors on testing and counseling standards, and emphasizing the importance that mission personnel carry their HIV/AIDS awareness cards at all times.

Source: Elisabeth Lothe and Megh Gurung, "HIV/AIDS Knowledge, Attitude, and Practice Survey: UN Uniformed Peacekeepers in Haiti" (New York: United Nations, Department of Peacekeeping Operations, Peacekeeping Best Practices Unit, August 2007).

Unemployment is approximately 50 percent, gross domestic product is $370 per capita per year, few industries exist apart from coffee, and the birth rate is 7.8 children per woman, among the highest birth rates in the world. Half of the population still has no access to safe drinking water, and the country remains Asia's most impoverished state. The UN's 2006 *Human Development Report* depicted a poor country getting even poorer, despite significant wealth generated by oil and natural gas exploitation in the Timor Sea.

To some extent, UNMIT's focus on public order and elections in its first year on the ground meant that other elements of its mandate received less attention. The "compact" between the government and the international community to ensure that the new mission's activities and resources complement the government's own budget resources and priorities was still under negotiations as the year in review drew to a close. A large part of Timor-Leste's future is linked with the use of revenues from oil and gas, expected to generate $35 billion over the next decade, but parliamentary guidelines erected around the use of these revenues, coupled with the government's lack of budgetary execution, have to date limited their effect. Only 35 percent of the 2005–2006 budget was executed, and a mere 5 percent of the capital development budget was fulfilled in 2006–2007. This chronic lack of capacity and continuing politicization within state structures results in poor service delivery to the populace, undercutting the legitimacy of public institutions.

Progress regarding security sector reform has been slow, due in part to the need to ensure the new government's buy-in. UNMIT's recruitment of staff for its Security Sector Support Unit was also delayed. While the planned Timorese-led comprehensive review of the security sector remains at an embryonic stage, some signs are nonetheless encouraging. Importantly, the need for reforming the security sector is accepted and embraced by the new government. Major challenges remain, not least the size, makeup, and role of the F-FDTL in any new security architecture.

Resolving the structure and function questions surrounding the F-FDTL will be a vital aspect of the ongoing reforms to the security sector.

Conclusion

One year into UNMIT's timeline, it is too early to judge outcomes and attribute marks of success and failure. The challenges to the new government of Timor-Leste and to the international agencies charged to support the consolidation of peace and development are great. Discernible progress has been achieved in containing of violence, but the underlying tensions and weakness of national institutions remain an ongoing threat. The violence that followed the inauguration of the new government, and FRETILIN's continuing contestation of the government's legitimacy, indicate that neither political nor social stability are secure.

The ultimate test will come after Australian and New Zealand troops withdraw. Considerably more time is needed, however, before the Timorese police and defense forces will able to replace them and economic progress lays the ground for the productive rather than disruptive engagement of Timorese youth. Given the scale of the challenge, a UN presence appears necessary for the foreseeable future. The way in which that presence is structured, and its relationship to the government and people of Timor-Leste is developed over the next several years, will determine how this essential peace operation is judged.

Notes

1. Commission for Reception, Truth, and Reconciliation in East Timor, *Chega!* final report (Dili, October 2005), p. 44.

2. Shepard Forman, "The Failings of Security Sector Reform in Timor-Leste," in *Annual Review of Global Peace Operations, 2007* (Boulder: Lynne Rienner, 2007).

3. Independent Special Commission of Enquiry for Timor-Leste, "Report of the United Nations Independent Special Commission of Enquiry on Timor Leste" (Geneva, 2 October 2006), paras. 77–85.

4. In August 2007, an ailing Lobato was allowed (by decision of an appellate court and the government) to leave his jail cell in Dili to seek medical treatment in Malaysia. It is unclear if he will return.

5. Ludovic Hood, "Missed Opportunities: The United Nations, Police Service and Defence Force Development in Timor-Leste, 1999–2004," in Gordon Peake, Eric Scheye, and Alice Hills, eds., *Managing Insecurity: Field Experiences of Security Sector Reform* (London: Taylor and Francis, 2007).

6. "Screening PNTL Back Into Service," *La'o Hamutuk Bulletin,* June 2007, p. 5.

4 Mission Notes

4.1

Abkhazia-Georgia

UN Observer Mission in Georgia (UNOMIG)

- Authorization and   24 August 1993
  Start Date   (UNSC Res. 858)
- SRSG and   Jean Arnault (France)
  Head of Mission
- Chief Military   Major-General Niaz Mohammad Khan
  Observer   Khattak (Pakistan)
- Senior Police Advisor   Oleksiy Telychkin (Ukraine)
- Budget $35 million (1 July 2007–30 June 2008)
- Strength as of   Military observers: 130
  31 October 2007   Police: 17
                           International Civilian Staff: 97
                           Local Civilian Staff: 181
                           UN Volunteers: 1

For detailed mission information see p. 343.

CIS Peacekeeping Force (CISPKF) in Abkhazia-Georgia

- Authorization Date   21 October 1994 (CIS Council of
                             Collective Security), 21 July 2004
                             (UNSC Res. 937)
- Start Date   June 1994
- Head of Mission   Major-General Sergey Chaban (Russia)
- Strength as of   Troops: 1,600
  30 September 2007

The year 2007 saw a partial thaw of the frozen conflict between Georgia and Abkhazia, but meaningful discourse between the two parties remained elusive. The lack of diplomatic progress on peace negotiations was compounded by disputes over the validity of local Abkhaz elections and the continued efforts to link Abkhazia's independence with the situation in Kosovo. Georgia-Russia tensions remained high throughout the year, driven largely by an incident involving rocket fire in the Kodori Valley (the 6 August missile incident in South Ossetia) and Russian withdrawal from the Conventional Forces in Europe Treaty.

After Abkhazia declared independence from Georgia in 1992, the UN Observer Mission in Georgia (UNOMIG) was established in August 1993 to verify compliance with the cease-fire agreement. In spring 1994, the two sides negotiated the "Agreement on a Cease-Fire and Separation of Forces," also known as the Moscow Agreement, which mandated the CIS Peacekeeping Force (CISPKF). Drawing on the over 1,000 Russian troops present in the conflict zone, the CISPKF was mandated to promote the safe return of refugees, provide a "security zone," and supervise implementation of the agreement. In July 1994, the UN Security Council adopted Resolution 937, expanding UNOMIG's mandate to include monitoring of the CISPKF, the cease-fire agreement, and Georgian troop withdrawal from the Kodori Valley.

Several incidents toward the end of 2006 led to heightened tensions in the conflict zone throughout 2007. On 25 October 2006, the Georgian government reported that three rockets were fired in the upper Kodori Valley in northern Abkhazia, an incident that the UN Secretary-General referred to as "very serious." Following the arrest in December 2006 of an Abkhaz official from Gali by the Georgian police, the Gali administration temporarily closed several crossing points into the district. UNOMIG responded by launching fifty-two special patrols to 273 destinations on both sides of the cease-fire line. Despite this increased UN presence in the region, sporadic violence continued into early 2007.

In February and March 2007, the Abkhaz administration conducted local and parliamentary elections, the validity of which was contested by much of the international community. The Group of Friends, composed of the United States, France, Germany, Russia, and the United Kingdom, continued their attempts to define the principles for a political settlement of the conflict. Though two meetings were convened, talks stalled over the issue of Georgian withdrawal of armed personnel from the upper Kodori Valley, and over the ongoing dispute over the disappearance of

David Sigua, an Abkhaz election official from Gali district.

The most serious incident in 2007 occurred on 20 September, when Georgian and Abkhaz forces engaged in direct clashes, leading to two dead and seven detained on the Abkhaz side. Another serious incident took place on 11 March, when the Georgian Ministry of Foreign Affairs informed UNOMIG that five helicopters had fired rockets from the upper Kodori Valley into the villages of Chkhalta and Adjara. A joint fact-finding report was released by UNOMIG at the end of

---

Box 4.1.1 Tajikistan

UN Tajikistan Office of Peacebuilding (UNTOP)

- Start Date — 1 June 2000
- End Date — 31 July 2007
- Executive Representative of the Secretary-General — Ambassador Vladimir Sotirov (Bulgaria)
- Strength as of 30 September 2007 — Civilian Staff: 31 (10 internationally recruited, 21 local)

OSCE Centre in Dushanbe

- Authorization Date — December 1993 (Rome Ministerial), October 2002
- Start Date — February 1994
- Head of Mission — Ambassador Vladimir Pryakhin (Russia)
- Budget — $5.2 million (October 2006–September 2007)
- Strength as of 30 September 2007 — Civilian Staff: 17

Two events in 2007 highlighted Tajikistan's dramatic transformation over the past fifteen years: the tenth anniversary of the end of the country's civil war (1992–1997), and the end of the mandate of the UN Tajikistan Office of Peacebuilding (UNTOP) on 31 July 2007. Since 2000, UNTOP had provided political advice to the Tajikistan government to follow up the UN Mission of Observers to Tajikistan (UNMOT). While both events are indicative of general progress in Tajikistan's postconflict recovery process, the post-UNTOP environment is rife with political tension characterized by a democratic deficit.

In May 2006, the UN Secretary-General requested a year-long mandate extension for UNTOP to ensure assistance for the November 2006 presidential elections. UNTOP developed and implemented a technical assistance project for the elections and coordinated activities with the Organization for Security and Cooperation in Europe (OSCE) Centre in Dushanbe. Limited access to the media during the campaign emerged as a major shortfall in the country's first postconflict elections, with five candidates vying for the presidency. Despite the challenges, the elections proceeded peacefully, resulting in a third consecutive seven-year term for President Imomali Rakhmon.

Throughout its seven-year history, UNTOP facilitated programs on a range of peacebuilding issues, including fostering national dialogue and reconciliation, strengthening democratic institutions, reintegrating former combatants, training police, and promoting human rights and rule of law. After a two-month mandate renewal in May 2007 to allow for a smooth handover of its activities to national authorities, UNTOP closed its doors, having successfully fulfilled its mandate.

Following the end of UNTOP's mandate, in December 2007 the UN opened a regional preventive diplomacy center in Ashgabat, Turkmenistan, to facilitate communication among regional organizations within Central Asia and to provide continued political advice and assistance. While this is a promising sign, Tajikistan remains the poorest country in Central Asia, and it is evident that continued engagement of international actors will be necessary to consolidate the gains registered with the support of the various UN missions in Tajikistan.

July, but did not identify the parties involved in the incident. Reports of the movement of unidentified armed personnel in the lower Kodori Valley during early 2007 were also a concern.

A further contentious issue in 2007 was the presence of two Georgian "patriotic youth camps" on the border with Abkhazia. Georgia and Russia also continued to dispute whether the Russian presence at a military base in Abkhazia constituted a violation of the Conventional Forces in Europe Treaty. Russia's withdrawal from the treaty on 14 July increased tensions, while diplomatic channels remained at a standstill.

4.2

Bosnia and Herzegovina

Elections in the last quarter of 2006 and the formation of a new national government in February 2007 gave hope that Bosnia and Herzegovina (BiH), after twelve years under international administration, would assume governing responsibilities and continue along the process of integration into the European Union. Relying on this progress and the generally stable environment in BiH, then–High Representative Christian Schwarz-Schilling intended to hand over most of the governing powers to local politicians by the end of June 2007, effectively closing his office and ending its authority over the majority of BiH institutions.

Despite these promising signs earlier in the year, 2007 was characterized by a general lack of progress in BiH, in both its internal and its external dimensions. As the year drew to a close, the international community remained heavily engaged in the day-to-day management of the country, ethnic matters still dominated and froze BiH political discourse, and a new High Representative was appointed with an eye toward potentially closing the office in 2008. And while the EU was able to cut its military peacekeeping presence in the country, from roughly 6,000 to about 2,500 troops, the lack of political progress signaled a continued international political presence, rather than a phasing down.

More than a decade after the end of the conflict, Bosnia remains host to a peacekeeping architecture that evolved out of the 1995 Dayton Accords. Originally intended to be a short-lived international presence, the late 1990s saw the entrenchment of the roles of NATO's Stabilization Force (SFOR), the UN's International Police Task Force (IPTF), an Organization of Security and Cooperation in Europe (OSCE) mission, and the ad hoc Office of the High Representative in maintaining post-

EU Force in Bosnia and Herzegovina (EUFOR Althea)	
• Authorization Date	12 July 2004 (EU Council Joint Action 2004/570/CFSP), 9 July 2004 (UNSC Res. 1551)
• Start Date	December 2004
• Head of Mission	Rear Admiral Hans-Jochen Witthauer (Germany)
• Budget	$44.7 million (October 2006–September 2007)
• Strength as of 30 September 2007	Troops: 2,504

conflict stability. The European Union has since taken on the bulk of security responsibilities, with the EU Police Mission in Bosnia and Herzegovina (EUPM) replacing the IPTF in January 2003, and a military mission (the EU Force in Bosnia and Herzegovina [EUFOR Althea]) taking over from SFOR in December 2004. These transitions took place during the tenure of Lord Paddy Ashdown as High Representative. Appointed in 2002, he was also "double-hatted" as the EU's Special Representative. He took a highly assertive approach to his mandate and intervened in domestic politics, dismissing a number of elected politicians.

On 31 January 2006, Christian Schwarz-Schilling succeeded Ashdown as High Representative. While Schwarz-Schilling promised to maintain an emphasis on EU accession, he pledged to do so with less intervention than his predecessor. The adoption of this less assertive approach failed to achieve the intended outcome of a transfer of responsibilities to local Bosnian authorities, and served to further underscore ethnic polarization. Consequently, the anticipated handover did not materialize.

EU Police Mission in Bosnia and Herzegovina (EUPM)

- Authorization Date   11 March 2002 (EU Council Joint Action 2002/210/CFSP)
- Start Date   January 2003
- Head of Mission   Brigadier-General Vincenzo Coppola (Italy)
- Budget $16.1 million (October 2006–September 2007)
- Strength as of 30 September 2007   Civilian Police: 167   Civilian Staff: 28

OSCE Mission to Bosnia and Herzegovina

- Authorization Date   8 December 1995 (Fifth Meeting of the Ministerial Council)
- Start Date   December 1995
- Head of Mission   Ambassador Douglas Alexander Davidsson (United States)
- Budget $22.2 million (October 2006–September 2007)
- Strength as of 30 September 2007   Civilian Staff: 76

NATO Headquarters Sarajevo

- Authorization Date   28 June 2004 (Communiqué of NATO Istanbul Summit), 22 November 2004 (UNSC Res. 1575)
- Start Date   December 2004
- Senior Military Representative   Major-General Richard O. Wightman, Jr. (United States)

Schwarz-Schilling was replaced by Miroslav Lajčák in July 2007.

Prospects for Bosnia's accession to the EU were temporarily dashed in October 2007 when, after a year of Serb and Croatian-Bosniak political disagreement on police reforms within the EU's standards and deadline, the Stabilization and Association Agreement—an EU preaccession treaty—was postponed. EU standards require that all legislative and budgetary matters for police be vested at the state rather than the local level, and that technical criteria rather than ethnic divisions determine areas of police operations. Upon the failure of BiH to meet the EU's police reform deadline, and in a dramatic policy shift, High Representative Lajčák announced that his office would move its focus away from accession to the EU, toward economic reforms, as the deadlock on police reform was indicative of EU accession not being a priority for the local authorities, leaving BiH as the only former Yugoslav state without a pre-EU membership agreement.

The announcement of Lajčák's reforms highlighted the growing political crisis in Bosnia but also brought about some political compromise. The measures, aimed at improving the functioning of BiH government and avoiding ethnically driven stalemates, were seen as overly intrusive and elicited widespread protests in the streets and the resignation of Prime Minister Nicola Spiric in November 2007. As the year came to a close, however, a breakthrough was made on police reforms, and Lajčák's reforms were accepted. Even with EU accession back on track, many still expressed concern over the political situation and its lack of progress.

By late 2005, the EUPM, originally mandated in 2003 to assist in the reformation of BiH police and support capacity building, had seen progress on its work with Serb and Bosnian-Croat politicians who agreed to the principle of a unified force. However, over the course of the next two years, hard-line stances emerged, and implementation of police reform stalled. As of October 2007, the EUPM maintained only 167 international personnel in BiH, and its mandate was due to expire at the end of the year.

In response to the relatively calm security situation in BiH, EUFOR Althea continued its draw down. At the start of 2007, the force numbered approximately 6,000 troops and EU governments had reportedly considered reducing it to 1,500. However, the force was reduced only to 2,500 troops in 2007, to ensure it would have the capacity to perform its twofold mandate: providing security in BiH as its priority, and serving as a rapid reaction

The boundaries and names shown and the designation used on this map do not imply official endorsement or acceptance by the United Nations.

WESTERN BALKANS

— International boundary
—·—·— Republic boundary
— — — Autonomous province boundary
··········· Inter-Entity boundary line
✪ National capital
◉ Republican capital
◎ Provincial capital

Dates below the abbreviated mission names represent dates of effect (for UN missions) and start dates (for non-UN missions).

0   50   100   150 km
0   50   100 mi

Map No. 4255.3 Rev.2 UNITED NATIONS
October 2007

Department of Field Support
Cartographic Section

reinforcement to NATO's KFOR in nearby Kosovo. This mandate was renewed by the UN Security Council for another year in November 2007. EU troops continued to cooperate with US forces, commanded by a residual NATO headquarters in Sarajevo, in their ongoing operations to capture war crimes suspects. A number of these suspects have been brought to justice, but notorious former Bosnian Serb leaders Radovan Karadžić and Ratko Mladić are still on the loose. Meanwhile, the International Criminal Tribunal for the former Yugoslavia continued its work, and in February 2007 acquitted Serbia of genocide in Bosnia but found that it had violated the Genocide Convention with respect to the Srebrenica massacre.

A "normal" functioning Bosnian state looks no closer at the end of 2007 than it did at the start of the year, and this holds serious implications for the international community's engagements there. While the demand for international security assistance has been halved, the stalemate on police reform, the inefficiencies of the BiH governing structures, and other related issues highlight the need to promote enhanced political engagements toward a unified Bosnia.

4.3

Burundi

Despite concerns over the hasty drawdown of the UN Operation in Burundi (ONUB) in 2006, the security situation remained relatively stable during the year in review, with the government of President Pierre Nkurunziza making some progress in improving good governance and human rights. Burundi participated in various regional initiatives, including joining the East African Community and signing the Pact on Security, Stability, and Development in the Great Lakes Region. The country was also chosen to host the headquarters of the International Conference on the Great Lakes—a sign of confidence in the peace process—and participated in efforts to revive the Economic Community of the Great Lakes Countries. Moreover, the government pledged to provide 1,700 troops to the AU Mission in Somalia (AMISOM), and the first batch of the contigent deployed in December 2007. However, progress in implementing the peace agreement between the government and the Peuple

Hutu–Forces Nationales de Libération (Palipehutu-FNL), which was signed in September 2006, was faltering. This raised the possibility of a return to open conflict and reversal of the modest gains made since the election of President Nkurunziza.

Background

Burundi descended into violence in 1993 following the assassination of the country's first democratically elected president. The conflict pitted the Tutsi-dominated military against a host of Hutu rebel movements, including the Conseil National pour la Défense de la Démocratie–Forces pour la Défense de la Démocratie (CNDD-FDD) and the Palipehutu-FNL. Hundreds of thousands were killed in the ensuing years of internal war. A new power-sharing transitional government was established after the signing of the Arusha Accords in August 2000. However, it was not until November 2003 that the CNDD-FDD declared a cease-fire and joined the transitional administration. Meanwhile, the FNL, which had remained a source of insecurity in Burundi's western provinces, signed a peace agreement with the government in September 2006.

The UN Operation in Burundi (ONUB) was initially deployed in June 2004, taking over from the AU Mission in Burundi (AMIB). The mandate of ONUB ended in December 2006, and the mission was replaced by the UN Integrated Office in Burundi (BINUB). Some ONUB contingents—with South Africa as the core contributor—were rehatted and became known as the African Union Special Task Force, which is mandated to provide support during the implementation of the cease-fire agreement between the government and the FNL. BINUB was mandated to support the government of Burundi in its peace consolidation efforts and to ensure a holistic approach by the UN in its support to the government. In this vein, BINUB has championed the development of an integrated UN peace consolidation strategy for the 2007–2008 period.

Developments in 2007

Related to this peace consolidation strategy, Burundi was chosen as one of the first two clients of the newly established UN Peacebuilding Commission. In October 2006, the Peacebuilding Commission endorsed four critical priorities for peace consolidation and reducing the country's risk of relapse into conflict: promoting good governance, strengthening the rule of law, reform of the security sector, and ensuring community recovery. The Peacebuilding Commission and the government of Burundi, with the support of international actors and civil society organizations, agreed on a strategic peacebuilding framework. Adopted in June 2007, the framework builds on existing political and development frameworks, and identifies critical peacebuilding priorities and specific commitments to be undertaken by the government of Burundi, the Peacebuilding Commission, and other stakeholders. In addition to creating an integrated peacebuilding strategy in Burundi, the Peacebuilding Commission drafted a priority plan, outlining necessary critical interventions in relation to the Peacebuilding Fund. The priority plan was finalized by the government of Burundi and BINUB, and was fully endorsed by the head of the Peacebuilding Support Office. As a result, the Peacebuilding Fund allocated $35 million to Burundi in January 2007. Twelve projects amounting to $27 million have been approved, primarily in the areas of human rights and security sector reform.

Other areas of progress were recorded. The Burundian government and the FNL reached agreement on the question of immunity—granting FNL leaders provisional immunity from prosecution—and the release of detained FNL members. A joint verification and monitoring mechanism was established, and its chairman, Brigadier-General M. E. Pheko from South Africa, arrived in Bujumbura. The first meeting of the mechanism was convened on 19 February 2007, but subsequent meetings were suspended following disagreements between the parties over preconditions put forward by the FNL for its continued participation in the mechanism. Meanwhile, preparations continued for the demobilization of the FNL, but efforts to reform the security sector registered minimal results.

The acquittal of the country's former transitional president, Domitien Ndayizeye, and his deputy Alphonse-Marie Kadege, who were arrested in August 2006 on allegations of an attempted coup, were seen as important steps in fostering reconciliation and upholding the rule of law. Additionally, the adoption of presidential decrees commuting all death sentences and releasing 2,588 prisoners was viewed as a demonstration of the government's commitment to improving the human rights situation. The establishment of a truth and reconciliation commission and a special tribunal—two bodies designed to deal with the widespread crimes committed during the twelve-year civil war— was agreed to by the government of Burundi, and negotiations on its modalities were ongoing throughout the year in review.

While fears of a relapse into violence after the withdrawal of ONUB proved unfounded, significant challenges remained in peace consolidation efforts. Lack of progress in the implementation of the cease-fire agreement and reports of the FNL's active recruitment drive raised concerns over the sustainability of the country's fragile peace. The dire humanitarian effects of devastating rains at the end of 2006 and beginning of 2007 increased the need for the government and its international partners to deliver the much-awaited peace dividends. The allocation of $35 million by the UN Peacebuilding Commission to support peacebuilding initiatives in the country was a step in the right direction. However, while progress in socioeconomic recovery is crucial, concluding a viable peace deal with the FNL and, most importantly, undertaking efforts toward reconciliation, will likely be central in determining whether Burundi's hard-won peace can be sustained.

Central African Republic

Hopes that the 2005 elections in the Central African Republic (CAR) would provide conditions for peacebuilding continued to dwindle in 2007 as renewed violence in the northern provinces of the country overwhelmed the republic's military and the Force Multinational de la Communauté Économique et Monétaire de l'Afrique Centrale (FOMUC). EU and UN preparations for a multidimensional mission in Chad and the Central African Republic made some progress in 2007 with the authorization of UN police and EU military missions. But tenuous peace agreements with rebel groups reached earlier in the year were disrupted by flows of refugees from Darfur and a dramatic increase in internally displaced persons.

Background

Decades of political instability in CAR reached a peak in 1996, when protests over unpaid salaries erupted into insurrections by the armed forces against the elected government of President Ange-Félix Patassé. Fighting was fueled by regional and ethnic tensions, as well as a struggle to control the timber and diamond industries.

Regional mediators brokered the Bangui Peace Agreement in January 1997, which was monitored first by the 800-strong Inter-African Mission to Monitor the Implementation of the Bangui Agreements (MISAB) and subsequently by the UN Mission in the Central African Republic (MINURCA). The peacekeepers provided security in and around Bangui, enabling the elections that saw Patassé returned as president in September 1999. The UN Peacebuilding Support Office in the Central African Republic (BONUCA)

Force Multinational de la Communauté Économique et Monétaire de l'Afrique Centrale (FOMUC)

- Authorization Date   2 October 2002 (Libreville Summit), 21 March 2003 (Libreville Summit, Amended)
- Start Date   December 2002
- Head of Mission and Force Commander   Brigadier-General Auguste Roger Bibaye Itandas (Gabon)
- Budget $12.5 million (October 2006–September 2007)
- Strength as of 30 September 2007   Troops: 378

UN Peacebuilding Support Office in the Central African Republic (BONUCA)

- Authorization Date   10 February 2000 (S/PRST/2000/5)
- Start Date   15 February 2000
- SRSG and Head of Mission   Lamine Cissé (Senegal)
- Strength as of 31 October 2007   International Civilian Staff: 26 Local Civilian Staff: 50 UN Volunteers: 3

---

was created in February 2000, following the withdrawal of MINURCA.

Established in 2002, FOMUC was originally conceived as a small observer mission mandated to monitor the security in Bangui and along the Chadian border. The force is composed of troops from Gabon, the Congo, and Chad. Despite being unable to prevent a 2003 coup in which General François Bozizé ousted Patassé, the mission has continued operating. During 2006, FOMUC refocused its efforts toward the unstable northern provinces of the country, where violence continued throughout the year in review.

Major Developments

Ongoing aggression in the northern parts of the country in 2007 was attributed to several rebel groups, all dedicated to the overthrow of the Bozizé government. Renewed attacks by the Armèe pour la Restauration de la Règublique et la Dèmocratie (APRD) in the northwestern town of Paoua in January 2007, alongside continuing violence in the northeast, meant that the more than 200,000 internally displaced persons in the region continued to be exposed to indiscriminate violence. Particularly troubling were several incidents in which UN and humanitarian workers were targeted, including a hostage incident on 19 May, an attack on a BONUCA convoy on 26 May, and the killing of a French member of Médecins sans Frontièrs by the APRD on 11 June.

At the outset of 2007, the UN Security Council reiterated its call for the establishment of a multidimensional presence in Chad and the Central African Republic. In February, the Secretary-General proposed a UN mission in Chad and the Central African Republic, an 11,000-strong force mandated to protect civilians, facilitate relationships among the countries in the region, and monitor human rights violations in eastern Chad and the northern area of the Central African Republic. But this proposal ran into trouble when the Chadian government failed to consent to the deployment of UN troops on its territory. Subsequently, a compromise was reached, paving the way for authorization for the deployment of UN police personnel and EU troops, which had still not happened at the end of the year in review. The Security Council adopted 1778 (2007) authorizing the deployment of the UN Mission in the Central African Republic and Chad (MINURCAT). For its part, the European Union authorized the deployment of the EU Force in the Republic of Chad and the Central African Republic (EUFOR TCHAD/RCA) on 15 October 2007. Among other things, MINURCAT was mandated to liaise with the security services such as the army, the gendarmerie, and judicial officials in order to contribute to building sustainable peace in the Central African Republic. MINURCAT's mandate also includes cooperating with BONUCA and FOMUC to deal with existing and potential developments that would have negative consequences on the humanitarian situation in the area. In addition to providing security to the thousands of refugees and internally displaced persons, the EU Force will also provide security to UN personnel and facilities.

Meanwhile, diplomatic channels between the government of the Central African Republic and some rebel groups were opened at the end of 2006 and early 2007, with the assistance of a Central African civil society organization, Group of the Wise. In February, the government signed cease-fire agreements with two rebel groups, the Front Démocratique pour le Peuple Centrafricain (FDPC) and the Union des Forces Démocratiques pour le Rassemblement (UFDR). However, the relative calm that followed these agreements was soon disrupted by the arrival of approximately 3,000 Sudanese nationals fleeing heavy fighting in Darfur in May 2007. Over 26,000 Central African Republic refugees also spilled over into neighboring Cameroon during the year, highlighting the wider threat to the region posed by the continuing conflict, and the urgency of the coordinated UN-EU deployments.

4.5

Chad

With internal and subregional conflict generating more than 281,000 refugees from Sudan and the Central African Republic in Chad, alongside approximately 150,000 internally displaced, an impending humanitarian disaster led to calls for a robust peacekeeping force in the region during 2007. Cross-border attacks by the Janjaweed militia from neighboring Darfur complicated an already complex situation, as the government of Chad battled several rebel groups, notably the United Front for Democratic Change; the Platform for Change, National Unity, and Democracy; and the Popular Rally for Justice. The conflicts in eastern Chad, in the northeastern region of the Central African Republic, and in Darfur, Sudan, continued to feed each other, forming a broader regional conflict vortex. Efforts to deploy a UN peace operation were hampered when the Chadian government consented to the deployment of UN civilian police, but objected to the presence of UN troops.

This led to a compromise agreement for the UN to deploy a civilian and police team and for the EU to deploy a limited troop presence. The Security Council adopted Resolution 1778, authorizing the establishment of the UN Mission in the Central African Republic and Chad (MINURCAT), on 25 September 2007. MINURCAT will consist of a total of 300 police and 50 military liaison officers with a mandate to assist in training the Chadian national police and to liaise with other security services such as the army, the gendarmerie, and judicial officials, with the aim of fostering an improved security atmosphere in both countries. The mission was also mandated to liaise with the AU Mission in Sudan (AMIS), the hybrid UN-AU Mission in Darfur (UNAMID), the UN Peacebuilding

---

UN Mission in the Central African Republic and Chad (MINURCAT)

- Authorization Date   25 September 2007 (UNSC Res. 1778)
- Proposed Start Date   Early 2008
- Proposed Budget $182.4 million (1 July 2007–30 June 2008)
- Proposed Strength   Police: 300
                         Military Liaison Officers: 50
                         International Civilian Staff: 10

**EU Force in the Republic of Chad
and the Central African Republic (EUFOR TCHAD/RCA)**

- Proposed Start Date   Early 2008
- Proposed Strength   Troops: 3,700

Support Office in the Central African Republic (BONUCA), and the Force Multinational de la Communauté Économique et Monétaire de l'Afrique Centrale (FOMUC) on existing and potential issues affecting the humanitarian situation in the area. This was followed by an EU Joint Council Action authorizing the deployment of the EU Force in the Republic of Chad and the Central African Republic (EUFOR TCHAD/RCA) on 15 October 2007. The EU mission, comprising 1,500–3,000 troops, was mandated to protect civilians, especially refugees and internally displaced persons, to facilitate the delivery of humanitarian supplies and to protect UN personnel and facilities. As the year drew to a close, efforts to deploy the UN and EU missions were slowly getting under way.

Chad fell into civil war soon after independence in 1960 and has been involved in internal and regional conflicts ever since. The government of President Idriss Déby, which came to power in 1989, has been the target of several rebellions, including an intense civil war with the Mouvement pour la Démocratie et la Justice au TCHAD (MDJT) between 1998 and 2002. After a failed peace agreement between Déby and the MDJT in 2002, a rapid proliferation of rebel groups occurred in Chad, spurred by waves of defecting soldiers from the Chadian army.

The recent conflict, however, has centered on the deteriorating relationship between Sudan and Chad and the massive cross-border population movements caused by the violence in Darfur. In 2005, following a number of major attacks on towns in eastern Chad by Chadian rebels based in Darfur, tensions between the governments rose rapidly amid mutual accusations of arming, supporting, and harboring the respective rebel groups. The Front Uni pour le Changement (FUC) engaged in increasingly bold raids against Chadian government positions, including a failed attempt to seize the capital city of N'Djamena in April 2006.

A cease-fire agreement with Sudan in January 2007 failed to prevent the ongoing cross-border violence, and on 31 March Janjaweed militiamen killed nearly 400 people in eastern Chad. While Presidents Omar al-Bashir and Idriss Déby did sign a peace agreement on 3 May, aimed at reducing tension between their countries, violence did not abate in 2007. An international force to monitor the border between the two countries, agreed to in Libya in early 2006, never materialized, with civilians on both sides bearing the brunt of the suffering.

Peace talks in Tripoli with Chadian rebels culminated in a peace agreement between the government and the four main rebel groups in the country on 25 October 2007. As the year drew to a close, it remained uncertain whether the Tripoli Peace Agreement and the deployment of the UN-EU missions in Chad and the Central African Republic would help stem the tide of violence in Chad and the subregion as a whole. Clashes in the east on the Darfur border, between government and rebel forces in the face of threats to EU peacekeepers if they were to side with the Déby government, coupled with difficulties encountered by the EU in generating crucial force multipliers such as attack helicopters, raised questions about the feasibility and effectiveness of the planned missions.

4.6

Comoros

African Union peacekeepers returned to Comoros in 2007, a little more than a year after the withdrawal of the AU Mission in Support of Elections in Comoros (AMISEC), which was authorized by the AU Peace and Security Council in March 2006. The elections of May 2006 were followed by a sense of calm and stability throughout the country. However, disagreements with the island of Anjouan over scheduled elections for presidents on each of the autonomous islands forced the AU to deploy its second peace operation to the island: the AU Electoral and Security Assistance Mission in Comoros (MAES) in May 2007. While MAES was initially mandated to provide security during the election period, the prospect of renewed hostilities meant that the mission's 300 peacekeepers remained deployed well into the close of the year.

When both Anjouan and Moheli islands declared independence from Comoros in 1997, federal security forces sent to restore order clashed with separatists, leaving forty dead and causing consternation among the archipelago's regional neighbors.

The Organization of African Unity (OAU) became involved in resolving the conflicts on the islands in the mid-1990s, with the deployment of the small Observer Mission to Comoros (OMIC) in 1998. The OAU-supported negotiations culminated in the Fomboni Accords in 2001, which provided for a referendum on a new constitution in advance of national elections. Under the Fomboni Accords, each island has substantial autonomy, with a four-year rotating presidency.

The complex electoral arrangement devised by the OAU in 2001—with the terms of

AU Electoral and Security Assistance Mission in Comoros (MAES)

- Authorization Date — 9 May 2007 (Communiqué of the AU Peace and Security Council)
- Start Date — May 2007
- Head of Mission — Francisco Madeira (Mozambique)
- Strength as of 30 September 2007 — Troops: 300

the presidents of each autonomous island coming to an end in 2007—was to be followed by elections for new presidents on each of the three islands on 10 June 2007. However, President Mohamed Bacar of Anjouan refused to relinquish power at the end of his term of office. Following the federal government's appointment of an interim president for Anjouan in early May, forces loyal to Bacar attacked federal offices and clashed with government forces stationed there, killing two. An AU envoy was immediately dispatched to assess the situation. With continuing tensions, the AU Peace and Security Council authorized the deployment of the 300-strong MAES peace operation, with a mandate to maintain security in support of free and fair elections.

The deployment of MAES, however, was contained to the main island of Grand Comore, and thus had little impact on the belligerent Anjouan. While authorities on Grand Comore and Moheli chose to delay the 10 June elections by one week, elections in Anjouan proceeded on schedule, with Bacar claiming 89 percent of the vote, in an election that that was deemed illegitimate by the international community.

Bacar continued to ignore calls by the AU for the elections to be held again, prompting the Peace and Security Council to impose travel and financial sanctions on the renegade Anjouanese authorities in October 2007. The AU broadened MAES's mandated tasks to include, among other things, enforcement of the sanctions. As the year drew to a close, MAES peacekeepers had begun patrolling the waters around Anjouan to enforce the AU-authorized travel ban.

Côte d'Ivoire

Efforts to resolve the crisis in Côte d'Ivoire registered partial progress in 2007. The precarious situation that existed at the end of 2006 was replaced by a surprising political accommodation between arch-rivals President Laurent Gbagbo and Guillame Soro, leader of the Forces Nouvelles. This was largely credited to the Ouagadougou Agreement, signed on 4 March 2007 under the auspices of President Blaise Compaoré of Burkina Faso and the chairman of the Economic Community of West African States (ECOWAS). Despite being a bilateral deal between the two main protagonists, Gbagbo and Soro, the agreement enjoys broad political support from the Ivorian opposition parties and civic groups. Support for the agreement was based in part on a popular sense of it being a homegrown initiative, as distinct from previous deals. Under the agreement, Soro was appointed prime minister on 26 March 2007, a move that instilled confidence in what has been seen as a faltering peace process. While progress has been slow in some areas, notably in disarming the militias and merging the Forces Nouvelles and the Ivorian armed forces, the agreement stood up to serious challenges, the most significant being the attack on Prime Minister Soro's plane in June that left four of his close aides dead.

Background

Côte d'Ivoire was plunged into conflict in September 2002 following a mutiny and a failed coup attempt by soldiers of the country's armed forces. The country has since played host to ECOWAS, UN, and French-led peace operations. Established in April 2004, the UN Operation in Côte d'Ivoire

---

UN Operation in Côte d'Ivoire (UNOCI)

- Authorization Date   27 February 2004 (UNSC Res. 1528)
- Start Date   4 April 2004
- SRSG and   Choi Young-Jin
  Head of Mission   (Republic of Korea)
- Force Commander   Major-General Fernand Marcel Amoussou
     (Benin)
- Police Commissioner   Major-General Gerardo Cristian Chaumont
     (Argentina)
- Budget $470.9 million
     (1 July 2007–30 June 2008)
- Strength as of   Troops: 7,833
  31 October 2007   Military Observers: 189
     Police: 1,137
     International Civilian Staff: 406
     Local Civilian Staff: 573
     UN Volunteers: 284

For detailed mission information see p. 333.

Operation Licorne

- Authorization Date   4 February 2003 (UNSC Res. 1464),
     24 January 2006 (UNSC Res. 1652)
- Start Date   February 2003
- Head of Mission   General Bruno Clément-Bollée (France)
- Budget $334.5 million
     (October 2006–September 2007)
- Strength as of   Troops: 2,400
  30 September 2007

(UNOCI) was mandated to support implementation of the Linas-Marcoussis Accords, signed in 2003. Since then, the mission has supported the implementation of several follow-on peace deals, including the Ouagadougou Agreement. French Operation Licorne forces deployed to operate alongside the ECOWAS Mission in Côte d'Ivoire (ECOMICI), an earlier mission, continued to complement the UN mission by providing additional rapid reaction capabilities.

Developments in 2007

The Ouagadougou Agreement addresses, among other things, identification and registration of voters, holding of elections, disarming of militias, the process of reestablishing state administration throughout the country, the removal of the zone of confidence, and perhaps most importantly, the merging of rebel and government forces through the establishment of an integrated command center. Unlike previous agreements, clear timelines were established for its implementation, and two new follow-up mechanisms were established. One is a standing consultative mechanism composed of Gbagbo, Soro, former president Konan Bedie, former prime minister Alassane Ouattara, and President Compaoré in his capacity as facilitator. The second follow-up mechanism—the Evaluation and Monitoring Committee—comprises the facilitator as the chair, and three representatives from the signatories to the agreement. The consultative mechanism was mandated to address all issues pertaining to the agreement, while the committee is charged with assessing and recommending ways of enhancing the peace process. In addition, Security Council Resolution 1765, of 16 July 2007, supported the establishment of an international consultative organ, composed of the Special Representative of the Secretary-General, the resident coordinator of the United Nations system, and representatives of the World Bank, the International Monetary Fund, the European Union, the African Union, the African Development Bank, ECOWAS, and France, in order to support the Ivorian parties and the facilitator in implementing the Ouagadougou Agreement. The resolution further noted that this organ shall participate in the

meetings of the Evaluation and Monitoring Committee, as an observer, and may be consulted at any time by the facilitator.

The dismantling of the zone of confidence that had separated the government-controlled south and the rebel-held north started with the removal of two UNOCI check points on 16 April 2007, marking the beginning of an important step in reuniting a country that had been divided since the outbreak of the crisis in September 2002. The zone of confidence has been replaced by a green line patrolled by new mixed police units, consisting of the national police and those from the Forces Nouvelles. By October 2007, UNOCI had established seventeen observation posts along the green line while maintaining its readiness to respond to security threats in the region.

While the removal of the zone of confidence demonstrates significant progress in the reunification of the country, the security situation remains precarious, especially in the western region. President Gbagbo's official launch of militia disarmament on 19 May—symbolized by a weapons-destruction ceremony—has been followed by painfully slow progress, and substantial delays in establishing the integrated Ivorian–Forces Nouvelles command structure. Nonetheless, disarmament of the Forces Nouvelles commenced on 30 July with a ceremony in the town of Bouake attended by President Gbagbo and six of his counterparts from the region. The deployment of the mixed police units and efforts to build a unified national defense force have been hampered by disagreements over the ranks and number of rebel forces to be integrated into the Ivorian armed forces. UNOCI continues to support disarmament efforts, despite its exclusion from the two new follow-up mechanisms provided for by the agreement. UNOCI's exclusion is not surprising in light of previous objections by several Ivorian parties—especially pro-Gbagbo groups—to what they viewed as the intrusive role of the UN.

While the 23 April 2007 commencement date for a process of citizenship identification—a contentious issue in the conflict—was missed, the process was officially launched on 25 October through the establishment of mobile courts in the west and north of the country. This was preceded by the appointment of judges and prefects, and consultations involving President Campaoré in his capacity as facilitator and chair of the Evaluation and Monitoring Committee. Domestic and international concerns have been raised over delays in the identification process for two reasons. First, the issue of national identity is at the core of the conflict, and its speedy resolution will enhance the peace process. Second, elections can only be held after the completion of the identification process.

In July 2007, the UN Security Council adopted Resolution 1765, terminating the mandate of the High Representative for elections, and mandated the Special Representative of the Secretary-General to oversee and certify the outcome of the pending elections. Preparations for elections moved slowly, as the process was closely linked with the delayed identification process. UNOCI's ongoing work with the electoral commission in the training of electoral personnel has been stymied by the absence of key elements such as a clear strategy for the overall management of the election process.

Nonetheless, efforts to restore state authority throughout the country made some progress in 2007, with over 12,000 of the approximately 24,000 civil servants displaced by the conflict redeployed to their stations, as well as the appointment of several senior regional administrative officers. However, a lack of infrastructure and continued insecurity slowed the process of reestablishing state authority across the country.

Collaboration between UNOCI and Operation Licorne continued, with the latter providing ongoing rapid reaction capabilities for the UN mission. The improved security situation led to the withdrawal of 1,000 Licorne troops from the country, but UNOCI's troop strength remained at the authorized level, pending reassessment as the security situation improves. UNOCI was in the spotlight in 2007 when troops deployed in the Bouake area were accused of widespread sexual abuse of women and girls, prompting the UN to launch

Thousands of Ivorians attend the "Flame of Peace" ceremony, where tons of surrendered weapons were burned, Bouake, Côte d'Ivoire, 30 July 2007.

an investigation into the allegations. A contingent of Moroccan troops involved in the scandal was suspended and confined to their base as investigations continued. The episode added to the spate of sexual scandals involving UN military and civilian peacekeeping personnel across the globe.

Thus, during the year in review, Côte d'Ivoire moved on from the "no war, no peace" situation that had characterized it over the past few years. The conversion of President Campaoré from an alleged "spoiler" into a peacemaker bodes well for the fragile peace process. But the key to a successful resolution of the crisis rests with the two protagonists: President Gbagbo and Prime Minister Soro. However, lack of progress in vital aspects of the peace process, such as unifying the armed forces, identification and registration of voters, disarmament of militias, and the continued insecurity in the western part of the country, raises serious concerns. While the parties have demonstrated commitments to implementing the peace agreement, further delays could erode the modest gains made thus far, especially as economic hardship persists.

4.8

Cyprus

UN Peacekeeping Force in Cyprus (UNFICYP)

- Authorization and Start Date   4 March 1964 (UNSC Res. 186)
- SRSG and Head of Mission   Michael Møller (Denmark)
- Force commander   Major-General Rafael José Barni
        (Argentina)
- Senior Police Advisor   Carla Van Maris (Netherlands)
- Budget $48.1 million
        (1 July 2007–30 June 2008)
- Strength as of   Troops: 860
  31 October 2007   Police: 62
        International Civilian Staff: 38
        Local Civilian Staff: 107

For detailed mission information see p. 254.

The UN Peacekeeping Force in Cyprus (UNFICYP) continued to oversee a largely stable cease-fire between Greek Cypriots (in the south) and Turkish Cypriots (in the north) during its forty-third year of operation. While the parties maintained diplomatic communication, which resumed in 2006, lack of significant progress on substantive issues placed renewed emphasis on UNFICYP's role and signaled no anticipated change in the mandate of the mission over the next year.

Established in March 1964, UNFICYP was initially mandated to prevent violence between the Greek and Turkish Cypriot communities. Following the resurgence of hostilities and intervention by Turkish military forces, a de facto cease-fire was established in 1974 and UNFICYP's duties were broadened to include cease-fire monitoring, buffer zone administration, and humanitarian activities. In

March 2003 the UN Secretary-General, at the request of the Security Council, submitted a comprehensive peace plan to the parties, initiating the resumption of talks in April 2004. The Turkish Cypriots accepted the plan in a referendum, but the Greek Cypriot electorate rejected it. In the absence of a political settlement of the underlying conflict, the Security Council continued to extend UNFICYP's mandate at six-month intervals, most recently on 15 June 2007.

UNFICYP fulfills its mandated tasks through investigating cease-fire violations and buffer zone infringements, ranging from minor military position enhancements and stone-throwing to the more serious discharging of weapons. Between November 2006 and May 2007, UNFICYP reported 473 such violations, up from 330 in the previous six months. However, UNFICYP has helped to preserve the status quo along the cease-fire lines and has worked to promote law and order and the resumption of normal civilian activity in the buffer zone. Presently, some 8,000 Cypriots live and work in the UN-administered zone, where there is a steady flow of both people and trade. UNFICYP's humanitarian work facilitates farming, ensures the supply of basic services, and encourages bicommunal contacts in the buffer zone. UNFICYP also assists Greek Cypriots, the small Maronite community in the north, and Turkish Cypriots in the south, in maintaining contact with their relatives.

During September 2007, Greek and Turkish Cypriot authorities resumed their UN-assisted negotiations on technical issues aimed at working toward the resumption of peace talks; however, for the second consecutive year, no decisions were made on substantive issues. At the conclusion of the talks, the parties reiterated their commitment to continue in the future, prompting both the Secretary-General and his Special Representative to pledge support to the process, while stressing that the onus for settlement lies in the hands of the Greek and Turkish Cypriots.

4.9

Ethiopia and Eritrea

Continued imposition of operational restrictions on the UN Mission in Ethiopia and Eritrea (UNMEE) drove the Security Council, for the second consecutive year, to reduce the mission's size and scope. In late 2006, the lack of progress toward demarcation of the disputed border between the parties compelled the Ethiopia-Eritrea Border Commission (EEBC), the neutral body created to rule on the disputed boundaries in 2000, to give the parties a November 2007 ultimatum for reaching an amenable solution to their dispute, or face having one imposed. The tense and potentially unstable situation along the temporary security zone that persisted throughout 2007 clearly tested the international community's ability to assist in resolving the conflict, leading observers to warn of the high potential for renewed conflict between the two countries.

Ethiopia and Eritrea went to war in 1998 over disputed border territory around the town of Badme. The Algiers Agreement of 2000 provided for the withdrawal and separation of forces by a temporary security zone along the Eritrean side of the border. UNMEE was mandated under Chapter VI of the UN Charter to monitor the withdrawal of forces from the zone, chair a joint military commission, and coordinate mine clearance. In 2003 the EEBC clarified that its 2002 ruling that would cede Badme to Eritrea—a decision that Eritrea sees as final, and one that Ethiopia regards as illegal and has refused to implement. As a result, tensions along the temporary security zone have steadily escalated, and the border demarcation process has stalled.

Since 2003, both Ethiopia and Eritrea have regularly acted in opposition to the Algiers Agreement, amassing military elements in and around the temporary security zone. A steady curtailment of UNMEE's freedom to observe has been imposed since 2005, resulting in what the Secretary-General has called a "serious gap in the Mission's information on the current situation." These restrictions, while most glaringly associated with Eritrea's 2005 ban on UNMEE helicopter observation, also include restrictions on land patrols in both Ethiopian territory and the temporary security zone. Where UNMEE staff members are allowed to work, they have reportedly been confronted with nonrecognition on the part of Eritrean military officers in the zone and by Ethiopian restrictions on demining operations.

In May 2006, citing what then–Secretary-General Annan called a "pattern of hostility" toward the mission, the Security Council authorized the reduction of UNMEE's military component to approximately 2,300 troops. By January 2007, and in the face of continued belligerence on the part of both parties, the Security Council further downgraded the mis-

---

UN Mission in Ethiopia and Eritrea (UNMEE)

- Authorization and Start Date
- Acting SRSG
- Force Commander

- Budget
- Strength as of 31 October 2007

31 July 2000
(UNSC Res. 1312)
Azouz Ennifar (Tunisia)
Major-General Mohammad Taisir Masadeh (Jordan)
$126.6 million (1 July 2007–30 June 2008)
Troops: 1,464
Military Observers: 212
International Civilian Staff: 147
Local Civilian Staff: 202
UN Volunteers: 63

For detailed mission information see p. 279.

sion's strength to 1,700 peacekeepers, including 230 military observers, a process that was completed by April 2007.

Despite its diminished size and range of activity, UNMEE continues to conduct land patrols, humanitarian activities, and demining over the accessible portion of the temporary security zone. UNMEE military contingents and observers conduct approximately eighty patrols per day, and in May 2007 served to defuse a potentially destabilizing situation in which Ethiopian soldiers threatened to open fire on Eritrean troops conducting reconnaissance.

A September 2007 meeting of the EEBC convened the parties in The Hague for a last-ditch effort to demarcate the border. There, Eritrea promised to fulfill all requirements demanded by the boundary commission, including lifting restrictions on UN peacekeepers and withdrawing its troops from the temporary security zone on the condition that Ethiopia accept the 2002 EEBC ruling, which the latter has long opposed. The meetings ended without progress, and without commitment to future meetings. However, there were concerns that an EEBC-imposed resolution to the boundary demarcation could spark renewed violence between the two protagonists, but the situation remained calm at the end of the year in review.

Haiti

Three years since its initial deployment, the UN Stabilization Mission in Haiti (MINUSTAH) was able to bring a measure of stability to the long-troubled island. With enhanced legitimacy found in support from the 2006-elected government, in 2007 MINUSTAH, alongside the fledgling Haitian National Police (HNP), set out on a large-scale and robust security campaign against the violent gangs who had obstructed efforts toward Haitian peace and development. The resultant gains led the Security Council to approve a significant reconfiguration of MINUSTAH's activities and composition in October 2007. Though the mission's mandate was simultaneously extended until October 2008, its work is far from complete, given the poor state of Haiti's governance structures and security sector.

Background

Haiti descended into violent disorder after President Jean-Bertrand Aristide was ousted in a military coup in 1991. In response, the Security Council sent the UN Mission in Haiti (UNMIH) to establish an effective police force in the country. However, due to noncooperation by the Haitian military regime, UNMIH could not be fully deployed. In July 1994, the Security Council authorized deployment of a 20,000-strong multinational force to ensure the return of legitimate Haitian authorities and promote a stable return to civilian rule. From 1994 to 2001, Haiti witnessed a succession of UN peacekeeping missions, including the UN Support Mission in Haiti (UNSMIH), the UN Transition Mission in Haiti (UNTMIH), and the UN Civilian Police Mission in Haiti (MIPONUH).

Presidential and parliamentary elections in 2000 saw President Aristide and his Fanmi Lavalas party victorious after a turnout of about 10 percent of voters. The opposition contested the results, and in late 2003 called for Aristide's resignation. In February 2004, armed conflict broke out, with insurgents quickly taking control of the northern part of the country, forcing Aristide to flee.

The Security Council authorized deployment of a US-led multinational interim force, tasked with supporting local police, facilitating humanitarian aid, and promoting the protection of human rights and rule of law. MINUSTAH replaced the interim force in 2004 and oversaw the establishment of a transitional government. MINUSTAH is mandated to maintain security; facilitate the creation of a stable government; disarm, demobilize, and reintegrate all armed groups; and reform the police and judiciary.

Since deployment, MINUSTAH has faced a precarious security situation, fueled by a combination of endemic poverty and violence by gangs and former members of Haiti's military (the ex-FAd'H). While the mission's mandate includes oversight and support for democratic elections, the high level of violence and the transitional administration's unwillingness to allow former president Aristide's Lavalas party a relevant role in governing militated against legitimate political processes in MINUSTAH's first years.

A dramatic rise in violence during 2005 prompted the Security Council to adopt Resolution 1608, which approved an increase in MINUSTAH's military and police components from 6,700 and 1,622 to 7,500 and 1,897, respectively, and requested that the Secretary-General begin planning a drawdown scheme for MINUSTAH's forces to follow planned elections, commensurate with the situation on the ground. With enhanced force numbers, MINUSTAH began launching operations against groups of gangs and bandits in the Cité Soleil slum of Port-au-Prince. These operations were successful in quickly quelling violent outbreaks, but not in eradicating the nucleus of the gangs. Meanwhile, MINUSTAH's traditional disarmament program proved inappropriate for the circumstances on the ground, yielding slow progress; thus the streets remained flooded with weapons.

MINUSTAH oversaw delayed elections in February 2006, bringing former Aristide ally René Préval to the presidency. The elections were followed by a brief lull in violence, but in the context of Haiti's widespread poverty, unemployment, and corruption-ridden government, the security situation quickly backslid. By July 2006, steady gang violence in Port-au-Prince and the surrounding areas reached its height with a massacre in the Martissant slum of Port-au-Prince, where wanton murders and widespread kidnappings by armed gangs prevailed.

Developments 2007

With persistent instability threatening consolidation of the modest gains after the elections, MINUSTAH, alongside the growing HNP, began operations at the end of 2006 aimed at rooting out the gangs of the Port-au-Prince slums. These operations, which continued into

---

UN Stabilization Mission in Haiti (MINUSTAH)

• Authorization Date	30 April 2004 (UNSC Res. 1542)
• Start Date	1 June 2004
• SRSG and Head of Mission	Hédi Annabi (Tunisia)
• Force Commander	Major-General Carlos Alberto dos Santos Cruz (Brazil)
• Police Commissioner	Mamadou Mountaga Diallo (Guinea)
• Budget	$535.4 million (1 July 2007–30 June 2008)
• Strength as of 31 October 2007	Troops: 7,060
	Police: 1,829
	International Civilian Staff: 494
	Local Civilian Staff: 1,122
	UN Volunteers: 194

For detailed mission information see p. 211.

---

the first half of 2007, were supported by the legitimacy of the elected government when Préval issued gang members an ultimatum: disarm peacefully or be forced to do so by MINUSTAH and the HNP. Between December 2006 and March 2007, MINUSTAH and the HNP launched nineteen operations in the notoriously violent Cité Soleil and Martissant slums, removing gang leaders from positions of power and installing the state's authority.

Unlike the previous attempts to address the gangs, the security operations of 2007 were driven by reliable local intelligence and were provided with the largest force strength in MINUSTAH's history. The operations were initially met with fierce armed resistance, though this dissipated as inroads were made into the gang havens. Capitalizing on this success, and with an eye toward sustaining the hard-won stability, MINUSTAH, together with the HNP, stepped up the presence and frequency of their joint police patrols in the cleared areas, established satellite police headquarters in Martissant, and symbolically transformed former gang-control centers into medical clinics. By July, 850 gang members had been arrested and their figureheads removed.

Against the backdrop of the improved security situation, in July 2007 MINUSTAH conducted a detailed threat assessment that, with the gang violence under control, identified three areas that could impede MINUSTAH's work, and more importantly, further progress in Haiti. Each of these areas—threats of civil unrest, renewed armed conflict, and the thriving smuggling and drug trades—reflected longer-term challenges and the necessity for change in MINUSTAH's operational focus to address the root causes of Haiti's persistent conflict.

Despite these relative successes, the Hatian government still suffers from weak institutions that are further limited by a lack of human, financial, and material resources. Still, during 2007, MINUSTAH continued to support the government by coordinating international assistance efforts, providing support for efforts to organize the parliament, and developing links between local and state political actors.

Politically, the Préval government enjoyed a high level of public support throughout 2007, reinforced by the successful antigang operations. Préval's approach continues to be inclusive and supportive of decentralization. In April, municipal elections were held with the support of MINUSTAH, installing mayors in Haiti's 140

municipalities. With stability on the rise, in May Préval announced a government-wide war on corruption and in June, with MINUSTAH's support, the HNP seized a large shipment of narcotics, arresting twelve people involved, half of whom were members of the HNP.

MINUSTAH's continued efforts to develop Haiti's vital rule-of-law institutions saw some progress during the year. At the end of August 2007, some 7,728 HNP officers were active on patrol, and an additional 633 officers in the police academy were anticipated to join the force by the end of the year. Efforts to build a maritime component of the HNP are also under way, with MINUSTAH's assistance. Vetting of HNP officers began in January 2007 with a review of 220 officers by HNP-MINUSTAH teams, and background checks on recruits resulting in the dismissal of 26 potential officers by September 2007. The ability of the HNP to work without MINUSTAH's assistance remains unclear, as the force suffers from an enormous skill deficit and does not have the capacity to patrol outside Port-au-Prince, and because only a little more than half of the 14,000 police required to patrol Haiti are active.

Provision of technical advice and support to the development and reform of Haiti's judicial system is another area that saw progress with MINUSTAH's support. And while still under consideration, two bills submitted by the minister of justice and public security, on the status of magistrates and the Superior Council, which were adopted by the Senate, demonstrate significant progress toward beginning concerted judicial reform and providing necessary elements to fight corruption and establish a professional judiciary.

During August 2007, President Préval urged MINUSTAH to continue its support to Haiti, but also requested that it reorient its focus away from security matters and toward building Hatian state institutions and providing support for border control. The Secretary-General endorsed this request in his August 2007 report on MINUSTAH and recommended that

minustah.org/Marco Dormino

MINUSTAH Police instructs a Haitian National Police Academy cadet, Port-au-Prince 5 September 2007.

Box 4.10.1 Colombia

The Organization of American States (OAS) continued to operate its Mission to Support the Peace Process in Colombia (known by its Spanish acronym, MAPP) throughout 2007. First deployed in 2004, MAPP is mandated to help verify the demobilization of the right-wing United Self-Defense Forces of Colombia (AUC). While the mission has achieved considerable success in its demobilization efforts—over 30,000 paramilitaries and some 18,000 weapons had been demobilized and surrendered by early 2007—in the second half of 2007 the OAS strongly warned that, if this process is not followed by a strong reintegration process, the demobilized ex-combatants may revert to violence, dragging Colombia back into widespread conflict.

Following a critical assessment of MAPP's performance by the OAS in late 2005, and growing criticism from Colombian nongovernmental organizations that the mission lacked the resources to go beyond basic demobilization verification, MAPP received enhanced funding, allowing it to grow from forty-four civilian staff in 2005 to eighty-three by the end of 2006. The enhanced mission strength yielded a heightened MAPP presence and activity in the field, bringing the demobilization process of the mission's mandate near completion in the first half of 2007.

In his ninth quarterly report to the Permanent Council on MAPP, OAS Secretary-General José Miguel Insulza commended the mission and Colombia for their benchmark progress in demobilizing the AUC, but also warned of the immense challenges that will result from this successful phase. Focusing largely on evidence collected by MAPP, Insulza stressed that the reintegration process had progressed at an alarmingly slow rate, resulting in the regrouping and rearming of demobilized combatants into new armed groups and gangs, and thus posing a serious threat to the peace process as a whole. Observations from MAPP's regional offices and mobile teams showed that the demobilized are not only relapsing into their violent past, but also operating in increasingly complex and clandestine frameworks.

The difficulties experienced in the reintegration process have exposed weaknesses in Colombia's institutions and in MAPP's ability to mount a successful reintegration program. The Colombian authorities and the international community therefore need to increase their efforts to address the question of reintegration if the modest gains registered through the demobilization efforts are to be sustained.

---

the Security Council maintain MINUSTAH's initial mandate, but approve the reorientation of the mission commensurate with realities on the ground and downsize and enhance the mission's troop and police components respectively. On 15 October, the Security Council adopted Resolution 1780, authorizing MINUSTAH's reorientation.

Despite these positive developments, in November 2007 MINUSTAH's activity was marred by a sexual exploitation scandal allegedly involving Sri Lankan peacekeepers. Following a subsequent UN investigation, 108 of Sri Lanka's 950 peacekeepers were repatriated. Among those repatriated was the battalion's second in command.

The peace that has been established in Haiti is a credit to MINUSTAH's work over the past three years, but it is the tenuous nature of this peace that will present new challenges to the mission and its ability to balance the maintenance of security while developing institutions to prevent Haiti from relapsing to its turbulent past. While the stabilization of Haiti during 2007 made remarkable progress, successful peacebuilding efforts will require sustained commitment by the international community.

4.11

India and Pakistan

The UN Military Observer Group in India and Pakistan (UNMOGIP) oversaw a persistently tense situation along the Jammu-Kashmir border throughout 2007, but continued talks between India and Pakistan on the status of the disputed area created a measured level of optimism for resolution of the prolonged territorial dispute.

UNMOGIP observes the cease-fire established by the Karachi Agreement of 27 July 1949, despite India's official position that UNMOGIP has had no operational role to play since the signing of the 1972 Simla Agreement, which established the line of control separating the two armies. The mission monitors that 1972 line, which has only been slightly revised since the 1949 Karachi Agreement. Over the years, India has restricted the activities and movement of UNMOGIP observers on its side of the line of control by requiring them to travel in Indian army convoys, and has rejected proposals for the UN to play a mediating role in the conflict. Despite this resistance, both governments have continued to provide UNMOGIP with accommodation, transportation, and security.

Following tensions in 2003 that raised the prospect of nuclear confrontation, political relations took a positive turn in January 2004, when an agreement was reached to commence a bilateral "composite dialogue" on an agreed range of issues, including those related to Jammu-Kashmir. Numerous confidence-building measures were initiated, and a minisummit was held in April 2005 to discuss the fate of Jammu-Kashmir. At the December 2006 talks, Pakistan's president, Pervez Musharraf, put forward a four-point plan to establish peace for Kashmir, involving demilitarization, by both sides, of the line of control, as well as self-government and joint control over the disputed areas in Kashmir. India responded cautiously to the terms of that plan, and talks continued through 2007.

Despite decreases in the overall incidence of violence in and around the line of control throughout 2007, it is unlikely that there will be any change in UNMOGIP's role in the year to come. India and Pakistan are in full control of the peace process, which is moving at a slow pace, and while the 2007 talks bode well for change, it is unlikely that this will have any immediate effect on UNMOGIP's status.

UN Military Observer Group in India and Pakistan (UNMOGIP)

- Authorization Date   21 April 1948 (UNSC Res. 47)
- Start Date   1 January 1949
- Acting Chief Military   Colonel Jarmo Helenius (Finland)
  Observer
- Budget $7.9 million
  (1 January 2007–31 December 2007)
- Strength as of   Military Observers: 44
  31 October 2007   International Civilian Staff: 22
  Local Civilian Staff: 49

For detailed mission information see p. 328.

Iraq

Iraq entered 2007 mired in sectarian, civil, and terrorist violence. Stalled political progress both was a function of and contributed to spiraling insecurity. By midyear, however, violence had begun to decline substantially, and by December 2007 indices such as the number of multiple-casualty bombings per month were registering their lowest levels since late 2004. While violence continues, such progress nevertheless prompted many analysts—crediting the decline in violence to a combination of local political dynamics in some regions, improved strategy under Force Commander David Petreaus, and the "surge" in US troop levels in and around Baghdad—to suggest that Iraq faced a moment of opportunity to make critically necessary political progress.

Beginning in May 2003, Iraq was governed by the Coalition Provisional Authority, led by the United States under its obligations as an occupying force following the ousting of Saddam Hussein's regime. Iraqi sovereignty was restored with the establishment of an interim government on 28 June 2004. The Multinational Force Iraq (MNF-I), which succeeded the coalition forces, was deployed at the request of the Iraqi government and authorized by Security Council Resolution 1546 (8 June 2004). Apart from the United States, which supplies the large majority of the MNF-I's troops, leading contributors as of late 2007 included the United Kingdom, South Korea, Poland, Australia, Georgia, Romania, and Denmark.

The MNF-I's mandate is subject to ongoing Iraqi consent, as was most recently expressed by Prime Minister Nouri al-Maliki in a letter to the Security Council on 7 December 2007. Its mission is to contribute to security in Iraq, including through combat operations against forces hostile to the transition and by training and equipping Iraqi security forces. Pursuant to the prime minister's letter, in December 2007 MNF-I's mandate was extended for one year with Security Council Resolution 1790 (18 December 2007).

The UN Assistance Mission for Iraq (UNAMI) was established in 2003. Following a 19 August 2003 bomb attack on the UN headquarters, which killed Special Representative Sergio Vieira de Mello and twenty-one staff members, the remaining staff relocated to Jordan and Kuwait. UNAMI staff began returning to the Baghdad headquarters in April 2004, to resume their mandated task of supporting the Iraqi people in forming new governing structures.

With Prime Minister al-Maliki installed through democratic elections in 2005, it was hoped that consensus around an agenda for national reconciliation would follow soon thereafter. However, the steady deterioration of both the political and the security situation in Iraq disappointed those hopes.

The well-documented spiral that ensued over the next two years drove US president George W. Bush in early 2007 to announce a change in the MNF-I's approach in Iraq. Otherwise known as "the surge," the plan called for the enlargement of the US commitment in and around Baghdad by approximately 30,000 troops, which brought the total number of US forces to over 170,000 when deployment was completed in June 2007. The heightened troop strength resulted in increased numbers of MNF-I counterinsurgency operations and an overall heightened, more sustained presence.

In parallel, the UN undertook an enhanced diplomatic approach at the onset of the year, initiating a series of meetings that culminated with the creation of the Interna-

Multinational Force in Iraq (MNF-I)

- Authorization Date   16 October 2003 (UNSC Res. 1511),
                        8 June 2004 (UNSC Res. 1546)
- Start Date   November 2003
- Force Commander   General David H. Petraeus (United States)
- Strength as of   Troops: 180,009
  30 September 2007

NATO Training Mission in Iraq (NTM-I)

- Authorization Date   8 June 2004 (UNSC Res. 1546),
                        30 July 2004 (Establishment of NATO
                        Training Implementation Mission in
                        Iraq), 16 December 2004 (modified
                        into full-fledged training mission)
- Start Date   August 2004
- Force Commander   Lieutenant-General James Dubik
                        (United States)
- Budget $21.6 million
                        (October 2006–September 2007)
- Strength as of   Troops: 160
  30 September 2007

UN Assistance Mission in Iraq (UNAMI)

- Authorization Date   14 August 2003 (UNSC Res. 1500),
                        expanded 8 June 2004 (UNSC Res.
                        1546), expanded 10 August 2007
- Start Date   14 August 2003
- SRSG   Staffan de Mistura (Sweden)
- Budget $245.8 million (1 January 2006–
                        31 December 2007)
- Strength as of   Troops: 223
  31 October 2007   Military Observers: 7
                        International Civilian Staff: 278
                        Local Civilian Staff: 354

For detailed mission information see p. 238.

tional Compact with Iraq in May 2007. The Compact is an agreement between the UN and the government of Iraq for continued efforts to consolidate what peace has been achieved and to pursue political, economic, and social development over the next five years.

On 10 August 2007, the Security Council adopted Resolution 1770, changing UNAMI's mandate and expanding its charge to involve greater political efforts in Iraq, including advising on and assisting in political facilitation and national reconciliation, and promoting regional cooperation between Iraq and the countries of the region, notably through the continued role of the United Nations in the International Compact with Iraq.

By the end of September 2007, civilian casualties in Iraq had declined to an estimated 1,100 per month. While still high, the figures of late 2007 are striking in contrast to those from January 2007 and November 2006, when 2,800 and 3,500 civilian casualties were recorded, respectively.[1]

Against this backdrop, and despite the acknowledgment of the prevailing restrictive security situation in which UNAMI operates, in his October 2007 report to the Security Council, Secretary-General Ban Ki-Moon cited an opportunity for UNAMI to exploit its comparative advantage and take a leading political role in Iraq. As the year came to a close, Iraq's leaders and the international community were faced with an opportunity but also a challenge: to foster and support the significant political steps that would be required to take advantage of the decline in insecurity and prevent a resurgence of violence.

Note

1. Brookings Institution, *The Iraq Index,* 31 October 2007, pp. 13–14, http://www.brookings.edu/saban/~/media/files/centers/saban/iraq%20index/index20071029.pdf.

4.13

Mindanao, Philippines

The stated commitments to restarting peace negotiations between the separatist Moro Islamic Liberation Front (MILF) and the government of the Republic of the Philippines boosted the prospect of peace in the first half of 2007. However, those hopes were dashed by intense fighting between the two parties throughout the year. Faced with these realities, the Malaysian-led International Monitoring Team (IMT) worked to achieve its mandated goals, but as the situation deteriorated further during the year, the mission was watching an all-out war and a diplomatic stalemate rather than the cease-fire and active peace process that it was mandated to facilitate.

The 1996 peace agreement signed by the secular-nationalist Moro National Liberation Front (MNLF) and the government established the Autonomous Region of Muslim Mindanao (ARMM). The agreement failed to address demands of the radical MILF branch of the MNLF, which desires an independent Muslim state. After several failed attempts at negotiations, the parties resumed peace talks, brokered by Malaysia on behalf of the Organization of the Islamic Conference, in 2004. In mid-2004 the MILF agreed to cooperate with the government's armed forces against the Al-Qaida-connected Jemaah Islamiah network and other terrorist elements, while the government dropped its criminal charges against MILF personnel over alleged bombings in 2003. By September 2004, the parties had agreed to the creation of the IMT. In November, fifty Malaysians and ten Bruneians were deployed to monitor the cease-fire and develop mechanisms for conflict prevention and resolution.

IMT contingents wear official military uniforms, bear no weapons, and are escorted by security personnel from the government or

---

International Monitoring Team (IMT)

- Authorization Date   22 June 2001 (Tripoli Peace Agreement)
- Start Date   October 2004
- Head of Mission   Major-General Datuk Mat Yasin bin Mat Daud (Malaysia)
- Strength as of   Military Observers: 60
  30 September 2007

---

the MILF. The monitors are paid by their respective governments, while the government of the Philippines covers their operational costs. Since its initial deployment, the IMT's mandate has been extended annually at the request of the MILF and the government of the Philippines.

After talks broke down on substantive issues of resource management and territory delineation during 2006, both the MILF and the government expressed their willingness to resume peace talks, with proposals for limited Mindanao autonomy as their centerpiece in early 2007. The scheduled talks were postponed several times throughout the year amid persistent violence, and were finally put off indefinitely following the MILF's massacre of fourteen government marines and the subsequent resumption of full-scale hostilities during August. In response to the MILF's attacks and suspicions of the presence of extremist terrorist group Abu Sayyaf on the island, Philippine president Gloria Macapagal-Arroyo announced a full-scale military offensive in Mindanao and redeployed Philippine military headquarters to the region. The ensuing clashes were reported to have led to many casualties and to have displaced over 20,000 residents.

While the IMT presence did little to limit the escalation in violence throughout the year, both the government and the MILF agreed to extend the mission's mandate until August 2008. However, with both sides to the conflict increasingly pursuing military options in the face of diplomatic stalemate, the IMT's impact will remain limited until the parties demonstrate the willingness to pursue a political settlement to the conflict.

Moldova-Transdniestria

Demands for Russia to withdraw troops stationed in Transdniestria increased during 2007, and a lack of meaningful negotiations sponsored by the Joint Control Commission (JCC) meant there was little hope for a solution to the fifteen-year conflict. Western countries increased pressure for a solution to the conflict, especially via greater participation in the EU for Moldova, while Russia's support of the 2006 referendum in favor of independence did not result in formal recognition of Transdniestria in 2007.

Geographically isolated within Moldova by the Dnestr River, and historically and linguistically tied to Ukraine and Russia, Transdniestria declared its independence from Moldova in September 1990. The collapse of the Soviet Union was followed by full-scale conflict between Dniestrian militias and the Moldovan government. Fighting raged throughout early 1992. By July, a Moscow-Chisinau peace agreement was reached, mandating a cease-fire, Russian recognition of Moldova's territorial integrity, and provisions for Dniestrian independence should Moldova join Romania. The agreement also established a 140-mile security zone along the Dnestr River, patrolled by a joint peacekeeping force composed of Russian, Transdniestrian, and Moldovan units.

Operations of the joint peacekeeping force have been overseen by the Joint Control Commission, composed of Russian, Moldovan, Transdniestrian, Ukrainian, and Organization for Security and Cooperation in Europe (OSCE) representatives. Since September 2005, the JCC has also included US and EU representatives as observers. In addition to monitoring the activities of the peacekeeping force, the

---

Joint Control Commission (JCC) Peacekeeping Force

- Authorization Date   21 July 1992
- Start Date   July 1992
- Head of Mission   Colonel Anatoly Zverev (Russia)
- Strength as of   Troops: 1,174
  30 September 2007   Military Observers: 10

JCC is responsible for overseeing the return of internally displaced persons and refugees, and for brokering confidence-building measures. An EU border assistance mission, in place since December 2005, is mandated to monitor the Transdniestrian section of the common border with Ukraine and Moldova.

The first meeting of the new "5 + 2" JCC arrangement was halted when Transdniestria suspended its participation in the negotiations in March 2006 after Ukraine imposed a joint border customs regime with Moldova. At the request of Transdniestria, Russia sent additional troops to the region, 1,200 of whom remained stationed there during 2007. With Russia's withdrawal of troops from Georgia already under way by the beginning of 2007, negotiations over the Conventional Forces in Europe Treaty focused mainly on the Russian presence in Transdniestria. In April, President Vladimir Putin suspended Russia's obligations under the treaty, a decision that effectively foreclosed the possibility of withdrawal of Russian troops from Transdniestria in 2007, bringing negotiations to a halt.

Moscow-Chisinau relations did witness a possible positive development as Russia announced that it would end the economically crippling wine and meat ban on Moldova at the outset of 2007. But delays in lifting the ban through the summer left the region's poorest country facing another year in dire economic straits.

Of note during 2007 was Europe's increased involvement in the region. In February, the EU increased pressure on Transdniestrian leaders by reissuing a visa ban against those members of the Transdniestrian leadership considered responsible for the lack of cooperation in finding a political settlement.

The EU's European Neighborhood and Partnership Instrument, published in February, also laid out a strong role for the European Union and European Commission in Moldova's efforts to end the conflict in Transdniestria, including assistance on customs and border issues and specific assistance on demilitarization. Without JCC-sponsored talks during the year in review, however, little progress was made toward resolving the dispute over Transdniestria.

4.15

Nepal

The UN Mission in Nepal (UNMIN) was authorized by Security Council Resolution 1740 in January 2007, and had an expected duration of only one year. It was mandated to monitor the management of arms and armed personnel and advise the government of Nepal on holding elections for the Constituent Assembly. The year was dominated by the twin pressures of mission startup and mission implementation, with the prospect, at year's end, of mandate renewal after the government postponed the Constituent Assembly election.

UNMIN was established to assist implementation of specific elements of the Comprehensive Peace Agreement (CPA), signed in November 2006, which ended the decade-long conflict between the Communist Party of Nepal (Maoist) and the government. The conflict, which began in 1996, pitted a Maoist insurgency against a government that was itself often split between Nepal's king and the parliament's fractious political parties. Over the course of the conflict, the Maoists extended their reach across significant swathes of Nepal, displacing local government in as much as 70 percent of the country. By the time the CPA was signed, roughly 13,000 had been killed, over 1,000 had disappeared, and tens of thousands had been displaced. The conflict's resolution was spurred by the king's seizure of authority in 2005, which generated new unity among the political parties (Seven-Party Alliance), created the foundation for a broad-based people's movement that in April 2006 ended the king's direct rule, led to restoration of parliament, and enabled the series of cease-fire and related agreements over the course of 2006 that culminated in the CPA.

UN Mission in Nepal (UNMIN)

- Authorization and Start Date — 23 January 2007 (UNSC Res. 1740)
- SRSG and Head of Mission — Ian Martin (United Kingdom)
- Chief Arms Monitor — Jan Erik Wilhelmsen (Norway)
- Budget — $88 million (26 March 2007–31 December 2007)
- Strength as of 31 October 2007 — Military Observers: 153; International Civilian Staff: 222; Local Civilian Staff: 179; UN Volunteers: 200

For detailed mission information see p. 306.

UNMIN was preceded, in August 2006, by the appointment of a Personal Representative of the Secretary-General and, in November 2006, by authorization for advance deployment of up to thirty-five arms monitors and twenty-five electoral personnel. In January 2007, the Security Council established UNMIN as a special political mission with a mandate to monitor the parties' management of arms and armed personnel, provide technical support for the election of the Constituent Assembly, and assist in monitoring nonmilitary aspects of cease-fire arrangements.

Despite the initial pressures of mission startup (compounded by the absence of an authorized budget until late March and limited precommitment spending authority), UNMIN moved quickly to begin implementing the core components of its mandate. Arms monitors established twenty-four-hour monitoring of weapons storage in the designated Maoist army and Nepalese army sites, comprehensive liaison with commanders on both sides, and routine monitoring at the seven Maoist army cantonment sites (and twenty-one satellite sites) and Nepalese army barracks. Maoist combatants at four of the seven cantonment sites have been registered and verified. UNMIN also established and chairs a joint monitoring coordinating committee designed as a primary forum for addressing violations of the agreement and resolving disputes between the armies.

UNMIN's electoral office, in turn, established a presence with Nepal's electoral commission at the national, regional, and local levels to advise it on preparations for the Constituent Assembly election, initially slated for June 2007. The in-country electoral advisers were supplemented by an expert electoral monitoring team that makes periodic assessment visits and reports independently to the UN Secretary-General. Despite progress on many of the preparatory steps required to hold the election, disagreement between the parties over core issues led to a first postponement of the election, from June until November. Over the summer, tensions between the parties intensified, as did tensions within them, especially for the Maoist leadership, who faced increasing pressure from hardliners within their ranks. Inability to overcome these differences led, in October, to a second postponement of the election, without a specified new date, and to the Maoists leaving the interim government.

Meanwhile, new risks surfaced in the form of rising communal and criminal violence, partly due to political mobilization among traditionally marginalized groups excluded from the initial peace agreement, and partly due to the continued vacuum of state presence beyond the capital, especially in relation to public security. These dynamics, together with the double electoral postponement, were generally seen as symptomatic of the underlying weaknesses and diminishing credibility of the peace process, which needed to be addressed as such.

The year drew to a close with a series of developments including the dissolution of the monarchy, which led the Maoists to rejoin the interim government thereby putting in motion plans to hold constituent assembly elections in the first half of 2008. Meanwhile, UNMIN's mandate remained unchanged, and the government requested a six-month extension, pending Security Council approval.

4.16

Sierra Leone

The July 2007 presidential and parliamentary elections in Sierra Leone, which led to the election of Ernest Bai Koroma as president, were a watershed in the country's effort to recover from years of brutal conflict. The elections—the first since the withdrawal of UN peacekeepers in December 2005—were a real test of the country's ability to manage its affairs without the presence of international troops. Sierra Leone's national electoral commission was applauded for conducting what most local and international observers described as free and fair elections, despite some isolated cases of fraud and violence. However, the new government inherits a society characterized by high unemployment, especially among youths; the absence of basic social services such as healthcare and electricity; high levels of corruption; and ethnic polarization, especially during the election periods. Despite these challenges, the security situation remained stable, except for isolated election-related violence. The arrest and subsequent transfer to The Hague of Liberia's former president Charles Taylor removed a lingering security concern for Sierra Leone and the West African subregion as a whole.

Major Developments

Sierra Leone descended into chaos following the outbreak of conflict in 1991. The war, unmatched in recent times in terms of brutality, lasted for eleven years, claimed the lives of an estimated 55,000 victims, and displaced over 60 percent of the country's population. During this period, the country played host to peace operations led by the Economic Community of West African States (ECOWAS) and the

---

UN Integrated Office in Sierra Leone (UNIOSIL)

- Authorization Date   31 August 2005 (UNSC Res. 1620)
- Start Date   1 January 2006
- ERSG   Victor da Silva Angelo (Portugal)
- Chief Military   Colonel Sven-Olof Broman (Sweden)
  Liaison Officer
- Senior Police Advisor   Rudolfo Landeros (United States)
- Budget $23.3 million (1 January–
     31 December 2007)
- Strength as of   Military Observers: 14
  31 October 2007   Police: 26
     International Civilian Staff: 75
     Local Civilian Staff: 199
     UN Volunteers: 24

For detailed mission information see p. 273.

United Nations. Launched in 1999, the UN Assistance Mission in Sierra Leone (UNAMSIL) played a major role in supporting elections in 2002, and in the restoration of security and state authority across the country, including through a disarmament and demobilization program for 76,000 former fighters. The last UNAMSIL troops departed Sierra Leone in December 2005, and the UN Integrated Office in Sierra Leone (UNIOSIL) was established in its place, with a mandate to support the government in consolidating the hard-won peace.

UNIOSIL provided crucial support to the national electoral commission as it prepared for the July 2007 elections. It worked with the political parties and collaborated with the UN Development Programme (UNDP) and Sierra Leone's national journalists association to develop a code of conduct for the country's media, a crucial step given that both print and radio played a central role in informing public opinion in the run-up to elections. In other areas, a national human rights commission was established as part of efforts to implement the recommendations of the Sierra Leone Truth and Reconciliation Commission.

Trials by the Special Court for Sierra Leone of those believed most responsible for serious human rights abuses during the conflict concluded in convictions against the accused from two of three sets of indictees. In June, the court sentenced three former members of the Armed Forces Ruling Council—the military junta that seized power in 1997—to jail terms ranging from forty-five to fifty years each. This was followed in October by sentences of six to eight years for two members of the Civil Defense Force militia, the Kamajors. The third accused from the Civil Defense Force—Sam Hinga Norman—died on 22 February while receiving medical treatment in Dakar, Senegal. The trial of the leaders of the Revolutionary United Front continued, while that of former Liberian president Charles Taylor resumed in January 2008.

A further development during the year in review was the UN Peacebuilding Commission's engagement with Sierra Leone, which continued to progress. The government of Sierra Leone identified four priority areas for its engagement with the Peacebuilding Commission: youth employment and empowerment, justice and security sector reform, democracy consolidation and good governance, and capacity building. Meanwhile, the government and the Peacebuilding Commission agreed on a timeline for creating an integrated peacebuilding strategy, and the Peacebuilding Fund allocated $35 million to Sierra Leone. By October 2007, seven projects had been approved under two priority areas—justice and security, and youth empowerment and employment—amounting to over $16 million.

Meanwhile, Sierra Leone made a modest but significant contribution to international peacekeeping. The country deployed three military observers—one to Timor-Leste and two to Nepal—and plans are under way for the deployment of several military observers to Darfur. While the number of personnel may appear negligible, the significance of the contribution should be considered against the backdrop of the country's recent troubled past.

The credibility with which the July elections and the subsequent run-off were conducted was a major step toward consolidating peace and democracy in Sierra Leone. Elected on a platform of change, the new government must confront the monumental challenges of revamping the country's economy, creating jobs, especially for the restive youth, and most importantly, restoring confidence in public institutions. While the new government has pledged to address these issues with the urgency that they require, continued cooperation with the international community remains crucial to the consolidation of peace in the country. In December, the Security Council extended the mandate of UNIOSIL for the final nine months, after which the mission will cease its operations in the country.

4.17

Solomon Islands

A relative calm prevailed in the Solomon Islands during 2007, but the stable security situation belied a difficult operational reality for the Regional Assistance Mission in the Solomon Islands (RAMSI). The mission, while a largely welcome presence among the corruption-weary civilian population of the Solomon Islands, faced increasing opposition from local political actors who called for RAMSI's withdrawal and the restoration of Solomon Island sovereignty.

Land disputes on the main island of Guadalcanal during 1998 led to violence between indigenous residents and settlers hailing from the island of Malaitia—leaving hundreds dead and 20,000 Malaitians displaced. In subsequent years, Guadalcanal Liberation Front (GLF) militants and the opposing Malaitia Eagle Force (MEF) continued to terrorize the capital of Honiara by enlisting in the government's special constable units and using the cover of government uniforms to continue militia activities.

The situation prompted then–prime minister Sir Alan Kemakeza to request support from Australia and then from the Pacific Islands Forum. After notifying the UN Security Council, the initial RAMSI force of 2,000 Australian-led troops and police was deployed on 24 July 2003. Invited by the Solomon Island parliament, RAMSI was to restore stability as its primary objective, and then assist in the continued development of governance, rule-of-law, and economic structures to the point where the Solomon Islands could again assume control.

RAMSI's impact on security was immediate: GLF and MEF commanders surrendered by August 2003, and 400 (one-third) of the

Regional Assistance Mission in the Solomon Islands (RAMSI)

- Authorization Date | 23 October 2000 (Pacific Islands Forum Communiqué)
- Start Date | July 2003
- Head of Mission | Tim George (Australia)
- Budget | $107 million (October 2006– September 2007)
- Strength as of 30 September 2007 | Troops: 214 Civilian Police: 306 Civilian Staff: 169

Royal Solomon Island Police (RSIP) were dismissed, with some facing prosecution. The Participating Police Force (PPF), the police arm of RAMSI, has worked with the remaining RSIP personnel to strengthen the capabilities of the police force and reestablish it as a vital national institution. Since 2003, the 315 PPF personnel, alongside the remaining RSIP personnel, have established seventeen police posts in all provinces, and have continued to train recruits at the RSIP police academy in Rove. The RSIP has incrementally taken on more policing responsibility, enabling the PPF in 2007 to refocus its efforts on further RSIP capacity building and sustainment rather than providing security as it had done in the past.

The quick restoration of stability similarly allowed RAMSI to reduce its military presence after its first year and concentrate efforts on justice sector development, economic growth, and governance reform. RAMSI has placed advisers among the Solomon Island government, some holding high-level positions in ministries and courts, with the aim of assisting the government to assume its full responsibilities.

The nonsecurity dimension of RAMSI and its largely Australian composition have proven to be divisive, as the desire to autonomously rule their nation has grown among Solomon Island politicians. The tensions between RAMSI and its host reached a highpoint in 2006, when, following a spate of riots in April that required the redeployment of Australian defense forces, newly elected prime minister Manasseh Sogavare lauded the mission for its response but also announced a review of RAMSI and a possible limitation of its involvement in the government. Later in the year, Sogavare expelled Australia's top diplomat for alleged interference in the investigation of the April riots. Subsequently the Sogavare government escalated its rhetoric concerning the withdrawal of RAMSI and dismissal of more RAMSI top staff.

However, RAMSI's critical role in the Solomon Islands was demonstrated when it provided the large majority of emergency disaster relief following the April 2007 tsunami, including a range of services far out of the national government's reach. With its presence proven crucial, RAMSI was approved for another twelve-month duration in July 2007. In December, the Solomon Islands' parliament adopted a vote of no confidence on Sogavare remaining as prime minister, a move that could pave the way for improved relations between the government and RAMSI, and one that might translate to tangible progress in the Islands stability.

4.18

Somalia

After more than a decade-long hiatus, peacekeepers returned to Somalia in 2007. This followed the ouster of the Union of Islamic Courts (UIC) by the Transitional Federal Institutions (TFI), with military support from Ethiopia. While the Ethiopian intervention quickly restored a measure of authority to the TFI, and made way for the partial deployment of the AU Mission in Sudan (AMISOM) in March 2007, the security vacuum that followed plunged Somalia back into chaos. Throughout the year, a dispersed and disaffected UIC functioned as a heavily armed and active insurgency, while a widespread humanitarian crisis loomed large and a multitude of divergent external interests converged in what looked like a proxy war. During the year in review there was little peace to keep in Somalia, and the restoration of stability seemed unlikely, absent a shift in both international engagement and the national reconciliation process. The situation was aggravated by power struggles between TFI president Abdullahi Yusuf Ahmed and Prime Minister Ali Mohamed Gedi that culminated in the resignation of Gedi on 29 October 2007.

Background

After his election in October 2004, Abdullahi Yusuf Ahmed appealed to the international community for a multinational peacekeeping force of up to 20,000 troops to restore security in the country and enable his institution's return from exile to Mogadishu, the capital. The request was eventually supported by the AU in early 2005 and then by the UN Security Council. The Inter-Governmental Authority on Development (IGAD) agreed to take the lead in

AU Mission in Somalia (AMISOM)

- Authorization Date   19 January 2007 (AU PSC/PRI Comm. LXIX); 6 December 2006 (UNSC Res. 1725)
- Start Date   March 2007
- Strength as of   Troops: 1,600
  30 September 2007

establishing a peace support mission, which was approved by the AU in February 2005.

However, local groups in Somalia, including the UIC, immediately expressed their opposition to the deployment of peacekeepers, especially those from neighboring countries. An initial AU assessment mission in February 2005 was met with violent protests. The Security Council cautioned that any peace support mission "would require the support of the Somali people," while IGAD promised not to include troops from the neighboring states of Ethiopia, Kenya, or Djibouti in the proposed mission.

IGAD authorized its Peace Support Mission in Somalia (IGASOM) in April 2005 with a mandate for robust "peace enforcement." The concept of operations was approved by the transitional parliament and authorized by the AU in May 2005. On 13 September 2006, the AU's Peace and Security Council approved the deployment plan of IGASOM: 8,000 troops to provide security for the TFI and create an environment conducive to inclusive dialogue and reconciliation. Deployment was not legally feasible until December 2006, when the UN Security Council amended its long-standing arms embargo on Somalia with Resolution 1725. The altered embargo authorized IGAD and AU states to establish a "protection and training mission" in Somalia, where neighboring states, including Ethiopia, would be prohibited from contributing troops to the mission.

Meanwhile, throughout 2006 the UIC embarked on a broad campaign against a loose association of secular warlords, asserting its jurisdiction over the majority of Somalia's south, including Mogadishu, and imposing Islamic *sharia* on the bulk of the Somali population by October 2006. While this campaign was conducted in a largely nonviolent manner—returning a level of stability to the country not seen since the late 1980s—the UIC's alleged connection to organized terror groups, especially Al-Qaida, drew the attention of neighbors and the international community, in particular Ethiopia and the United States.

In December 2006, Ethiopia, citing national security interests as its impetus, began strongly supporting the TFI with troops and equipment, and eventually engaged the UIC in open combat. Ethiopian forces swiftly defeated the UIC, causing its dissolution by 27 December. The victory, however, was superficial, as remaining UIC elements quickly assimilated into the general population, creating chaos over much of the country's territory and restricting TFI control to the borders of Mogadishu.

Major Developments

As quickly as the UIC had fallen, talk of Ethiopian withdrawal began in early 2007. In January, the AU's Peace and Security Council authorized deployment of AMISOM to support the TFI in restoring stability to the country. The UN Security Council endorsed AMISOM the following month and the force began deploying in March. But efforts to deploy the 8,000-strong AU force have been painfully slow. In fact, by October, only one contributor, Uganda, had deployed troops, approximately 1,600. Several countries—Nigeria, Ghana, Senegal, and Burundi—all pledged troops, but as the

year came to a close only Burundi had begun deploying. Ethiopian troops remained in country at the end of 2007, despite opposition to their presence by some local Somali groups, most notably the defunct UIC.

The AU peacekeepers have been targeted by insurgents, and have been largely confined to Mogadishu. As in the past, the country is awash in weapons reportedly supplied by various regional players, further complicating peacekeeping efforts. Scores of civilians have been displaced by the violence, with severe humanitarian consequences. Consequently, AU chairperson Alpha Omar Konare appealed to the UN to provide assistance to AMISOM along the lines of the Light and Heavy Support packages it provided to the AU Mission in Sudan (AMIS). Acting on the request, in August 2007 the Security Council called on the Secretary-General to begin exploring options for the possible deployment of UN troops to Somalia. Reporting to the Security Council in early November, UN Secretary-General Ban Ki-Moon, however, questioned the feasibility of deploying a UN peace operation in Somalia, and ultimately urged the international community to consider other options.

Progress toward an inclusive political framework followed a similarly difficult trajectory during the year. A six-week national reconciliation conference—delayed three times because of threats of violence, but finally convened on 15 July 2007—was deemed largely insignificant due to the glaring absence of the dominant Hawiye clan. At a rival conference held in the Eritrean capital, Asmara, in September, members of the dissolved UIC met and pledged to oust the TFI and its Ethiopian backers under the newly established Alliance for the Liberation of Somalia, a move that many observers saw as a call for increased insurgent activity.

As the year drew to a close, prospects for stability in Somalia remained bleak in the absence of either concerted efforts to reconcile the varied and competing national groups vying for control of the country, or the full deployment of a robust peacekeeping force.

4.19

South Ossetia–Georgia

While Georgia's establishment of a parallel administration in South Ossetia at the end of 2006 was designed to change the status quo and reduce support for the Tskhinvali administration, negotiations remained frozen during 2007 and a missile incident in August kept tensions high. Continued statements linking the outcome of the Kosovo status talks with South Ossetia's future contributed to unease in Tbilisi, while the lack of productive high-level talks by the Joint Control Commission (JCC) left negotiations at a stalemate.

Violent conflict erupted in Georgia's South Ossetia region in January 1991 after the Georgian government denied a request by Ossetian officials for autonomous status within Georgia. The war continued until June 1992, leaving some 1,000 dead, 100 missing, more than 65,000 internally displaced, and the South Ossetian administrative center, Tskhinvali, destroyed. The 1992 "Agreement on the Principles of Settlement of the Georgian-Ossetian Conflict Between Georgia and Russia" (also known as the Sochi Accords) established both a cease-fire and the Joint Control Commission. The JCC was created primarily to monitor the terms of the agreement, implement settlement measures, coordinate economic reconstruction, and facilitate the return of refugees and internally displaced persons. Composed of representatives from Georgia, Russia, and North and South Ossetia, the JCC was also tasked with coordinating the efforts of the Joint Peacekeeping Forces (JPKF), a peacekeeping battalion commanded by the Russians and composed of 1,500 troops, equally drawn from Russia, Georgia, and North and South Ossetia.

For twelve years there was no military confrontation between the sides, with South Ossetians establishing their own de facto state

---

CIS–South Ossetia Joint Peacekeeping Forces (JPKF)

- Authorization Date   24 June 1992
- Start Date   July 1992
- Head of Mission   Major-General Marat Kulakhmetov (Russia)
- Strength as of   Troops: 1,500
  30 September 2007

OSCE Mission to Georgia

- Authorization Date   6 November 1992
- Start Date   December 1992
- Head of Mission   Ambassador Terhi Hakala (Finland)
- Budget $14 million
  (October 2006–September 2007)
- Strength as of   Civilian Staff: 29
  30 September 2007

---

institutions, including a presidency, a parliament, and armed forces. In 2004, newly elected Georgian president Mikhail Saakashvili made restoration of Georgian territorial integrity his top priority. As part of a robust antismuggling campaign, Saakashvili closed the Ergneti market outside Tskhinvali and ordered a significant number of Georgian troops to the border of the region. Violence rapidly increased and threatened to drive the conflict into war. While an August 2004 cease-fire agreement ended the direct military confrontation in South Ossetia, the zone of conflict continues to be a volatile area, with frequent border skirmishes and criminal incidents.

Since November 2006, there have been two self-proclaimed, competing governments in South Ossetia. The Tskhinvali-based administration, led by Eduard Kokoity and backed by Russia, has sought independence from Georgia and is generally supported by South Ossetians. The Kurta-based administration, just a few miles north of Tskhinvali, is supported by Tbilisi and was created in a November 2006 parallel election in South Ossetia's Georgian community. Dmitri Sanakoyev, a former member of Kokoity's administration, was elected on a platform of allegiance to Tbilisi and support of the territorial integrity of Georgia. Tbilisi's support of Sanakoyev through 2007 was seen by Russia as an attempt to undermine Kokoity and therefore a direct threat to the peace process. Nonetheless, Tbilisi has continued to implement measures to solidify the parallel government, including an 8 May 2007 resolution to establish a temporary administrative unit in South Ossetia.

Beyond the informal JCC discussions held in June and July 2007, Saakashvali's 2005 plan to build confidence and demilitarize the conflict zone did not see meaningful progress during the year in review. Hopes of high-level talks between Tbilisi and Tskhinvali receded still further on 6 August, when Georgian authorities reported an unexploded bomb near the South Ossetian border. Tbilisi lodged a formal protest with Russia, and called for EU and UN investigations of the matter. Amid this heightened tension, the JCC-brokered meetings planned for mid-August fell through, underscoring the debate over whether the JCC is the appropriate mechanism for defrosting the conflict.

4.20

Sri Lanka

Intense fighting between the government of Sri Lanka and the Liberation Tigers of Tamil Elam (LTTE) raged for the second consecutive year during 2007, and in its fifth year of operation the Sri Lanka Monitoring Mission (SLMM), originally mandated to oversee a 2002 cease-fire between the two, observed and reported on the conflict. The intense fighting, aside from inflicting considerable military, rebel, and civilian casualties, also set off a large-scale humanitarian disaster on the island. The violence displaced some 200,000 civilians and severely constrained the regular flow of critical humanitarian aid. In light of the precarious security situation, the SLMM's role as a mere observer mission has increasingly come into question.

After decades of civil war between the government and the LTTE—a struggle over Sinhalese-Tamil ethnic identity and autonomy in the north—a cease-fire between the two sides was agreed in February 2002. The SLMM, comprised of monitors from Norway, Sweden, Finland, Denmark, and Iceland, was established to oversee the cessation of military operations, separation of forces, and the free movement of personnel and nonmilitary goods. The mission is headquartered in Colombo and maintains six district offices, a liaison office in Killinochchi, and points of contact in the north and east. District offices operate mobile units and patrol in their areas of responsibility. The SLMM has the authority to respond to complaints throughout Sri Lanka, but relies on the parties for access, information, and security.

Following the election of hard-line anti-Tamil president Mahinda Rajapakse in November 2005, and tensions that arose in the aftermath of the December 2004 tsunami, the LTTE dramatically increased attacks on government military elements, prompting reprisals by gov-

Sri Lanka Monitoring Mission (SLMM)	
• Authorization and Start Date	22 February 2002
• Head of Mission	Major-General Lars Johan Sølvberg (Norway)
• Budget	$7 million (October 2006–September 2007)
• Strength as of 30 September 2007	Military Observers: 35

ernment forces. Since then the conflict has become more violent and the environment within which the SLMM is to operate has been constrained. The Norwegian-mediated peace talks that resumed in 2006 after a three-year hiatus have dissolved and show no sign of resumption. After being placed on the EU's list of international terrorist organizations in June 2006, the LTTE demanded that all SLMM monitors from EU countries withdraw from the mission, which they did by the end of August, bringing the mission's strength down to thirty from its mandated sixty.

By the occasion of the SLMM's fifth operational anniversary in February 2007, its weekly reports read more like war tallies than the lists of cease-fire violations it recorded during its first three years. The ongoing civil war has shone a light not only on the SLMM's limited investigative capacity, but also on the parties' disregard for the cease-fire and its related oversight mechanism. While the SLMM maintained its commitment to assisting the government and the LTTE in finding a solution to the conflict, the mission was rendered ineffectual and left the country when the Sri Lankan government withdrew from the ceasefire in early 2008.

4.21

Western Sahara

After almost a decade of political deadlock, the situation in Western Sahara witnessed modest progress during 2007. In the second half of the year, the parties to the conflict entered Security Council–mandated negotiations toward a resolution of the dispute over self-determination. Meanwhile, the UN Mission for the Referendum in Western Sahara (MINURSO) continued to maintain general stability on the ground and to provide conditions favorable for negotiations. While this year's negotiations are only the beginning of what will most likely be a long process, the parties have overcome a considerable impasse, which speaks to both the enduring efforts of MINURSO and the necessity of continued international engagement.

MINURSO was established after two years of war in 1991 on the basis of an agreement between Morocco and the Frente Popular para la Liberación de Saguia el-Hamra y de Río de Oro (POLISARIO) calling for a referendum on Western Sahara's future. After years of stalled progress, in 2003 the Secretary-General's Personal Envoy, former US secretary of state James Baker, presented "The Peace Plan for Self-Determination of the People of Western Sahara," a scheme for governance-sharing that also allowed for the possibility of a referendum on independence. POLISARIO accepted the plan in July 2003; however, the government of Morocco stated it would not agree to any arrangement that could lead to an independent Western Sahara. The parties to the conflict remained at this impasse until 2007, without any mention by the Security Council of Baker's peace plan or any pressure placed on the government of Morocco to alter its approach.

Recognizing the political deadlock between POLISARIO and Morocco, in January 2006 the Secretary-General's Personal Envoy, Peter van Walsum, stated that the only recourse was through direct negotiations between the parties, facilitated by the UN. Then–Secretary-General Kofi Annan reiterated this recommendation in his October 2006 report to the Security Council, but no movement was made. Only following another recommendation for talks by new Secretary-General Ban Ki-Moon in his April 2007 report on Western Sahara did the Security Council act, issuing Resolution 1754 and calling on the parties to enter into negotiations. Since then, the parties have convened on two occasions— June and August 2007—in the presence of the Personal Envoy and Mauritania and Algeria.

Western Sahara was generally calm throughout 2007. MINURSO conducted 4,246 ground patrols and 289 air patrols between October 2006 and April 2007, far surpassing the amount

---

UN Mission for the Referendum in Western Sahara (MINURSO)

• Authorization and Start Date	29 April 1991 (UNSC Res. 690)
• SRSG and Head of Mission	Julian Harston (United Kingdom)
• Force Commander	Major-General Zhao Jingmin (China)
• Budget	$47.6 million (1 July 2007–30 June 2008)
• Strength as of 31 October 2007	Troops: 29 Military Observers: 185 Police: 6 International Civilian Staff: 95 Local Civilian Staff: 145 UN Volunteers: 24

For detailed mission information see p. 204.

of patrols conducted in the previous year during the same period. The increase in patrols is attributed to the development of a joint operation center and a joint mission analysis cell in late 2005. These innovations allowed the mission to improve operational efficiency, augmenting its ability to monitor the cease-fire without additional personnel. Despite these increases, both POLISARIO and Morocco maintained stringent restrictions on MINURSO, especially access to military positions and within units. As a consequence, the mission is only partially able to achieve its mandated tasks. Despite a lack of violence in the region during the year, there were regular reports of human rights abuses.

While the parties remain at odds on a variety of issues, in particular the definition of self-determination, both agree that maintaining the status quo is unacceptable. Negotiations are planned to begin in January 2008, thereby emphasizing the need for the continued engagement of MINURSO and the international community.

5 Global Statistics on UN Missions

The data in this chapter covers all UN missions in the period running from 1 July 2006 to the third quarter 2007. While a number of exceptions are noted, the coverage reflects the UN's 2006/2007 budgetary year (which concluded on 30 June 2007) in addition to information available on later months. In almost all cases, the data presented here is aggregated from the mission-by-mission material in Chapter 7. Where other sources have been used, they are indicated in the footnotes.

5.1 Total Troops in UN Missions: July 2006–October 2007

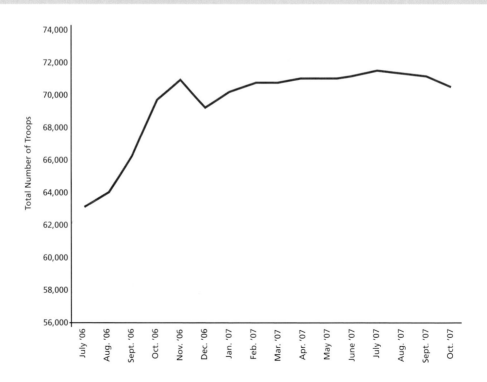

Source: DPKO FGS.
Note: Includes all UN DPKO peacekeeping missions, DPKO-led political missions (BINUB, UNAMA, UNIOSIL, UNMIN), and UNAMI.

5.2 Top Twenty Troop Contributors to UN Missions: 31 October 2007

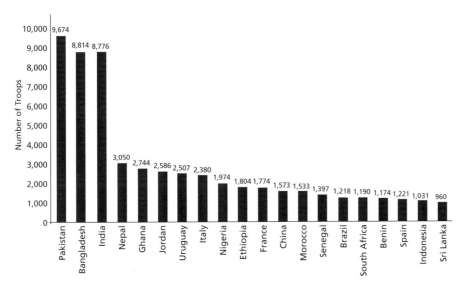

Source: DPKO FGS.

Note: Includes contributions to all UN DPKO peacekeeping missions, DPKO-led political missions (BINUB, UNAMA, UNIOSIL, UNMIN) and UNAMI.

5.3 Troops Deployed by UN Mission: 31 October 2007

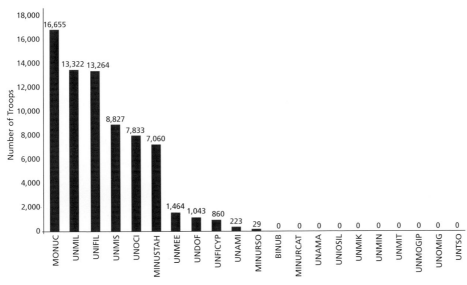

Source: DPKO FGS.

Top Twenty Troop Contributors to UN Missions

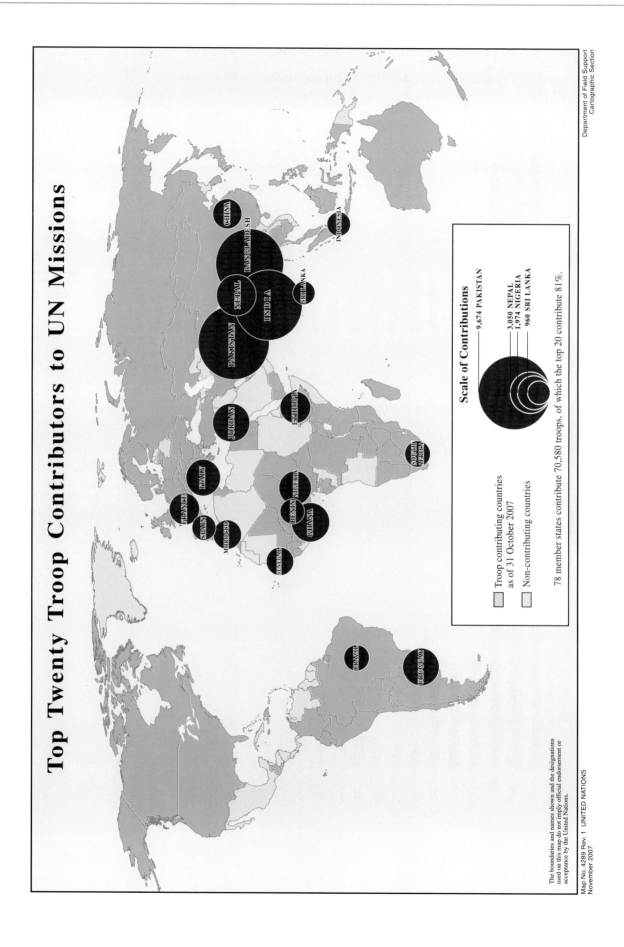

Scale of Contributions

9,674 PAKISTAN

3,050 NEPAL
1,974 NIGERIA
960 SRI LANKA

Troop contributing countries
as of 31 October 2007

Non-contributing countries

78 member states contribute 70,580 troops, of which the top 20 contribute 81%.

Map No. 4289 Rev. 1 UNITED NATIONS
November 2007

Department of Field Support
Cartographic Section

5.4 Total Military Observers in UN Missions: July 2006–October 2007

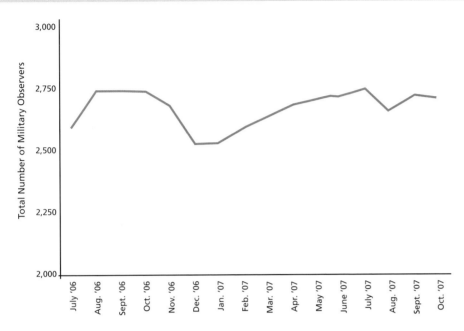

Source: DPKO FGS.

Note: Includes all UN DPKO peacekeeping missions, DPKO-led political missions (BINUB, UNAMA, UNIOSIL, UNMIN) and UNAMI.

5.5 Top Twenty Military Observer Contributors to UN Missions: 31 October 2007

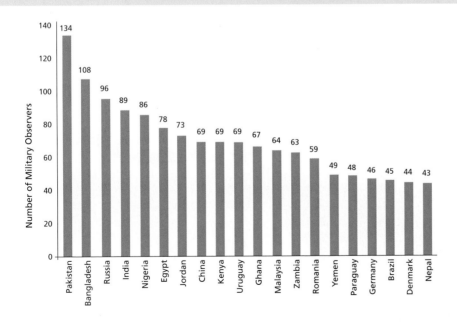

Source: DPKO FGS.

Note: Includes contributions to all UN DPKO peacekeeping missions, DPKO-led political missions (BINUB, UNAMA, UNIOSIL, UNMIN) and UNAMI.

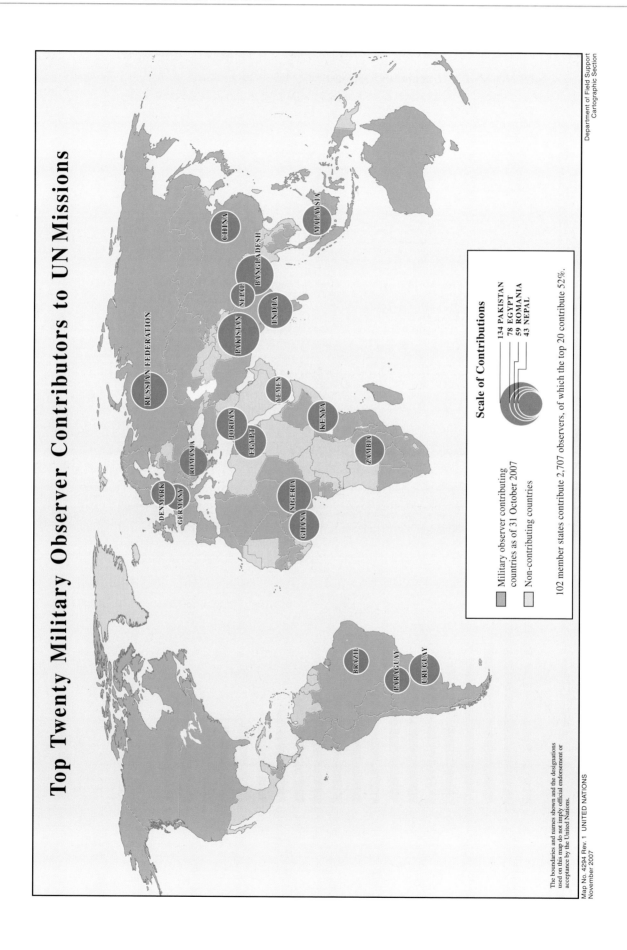

Top Twenty Military Observer Contributors to UN Missions

Scale of Contributions

134 PAKISTAN
78 EGYPT
59 ROMANIA
43 NEPAL

Military observer contributing
countries as of 31 October 2007

Non-contributing countries

102 member states contribute 2,707 observers, of which the top 20 contribute 52%.

Map No. 4294 Rev. 1   UNITED NATIONS
November 2007

Department of Field Support
Cartographic Section

5.6 Military Observers Deployed by UN Mission: 31 October 2007

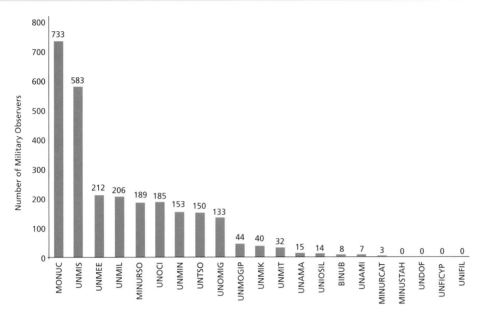

Source: DPKO FGS.

5.7 Total UN Police in UN Missions: July 2006–October 2007

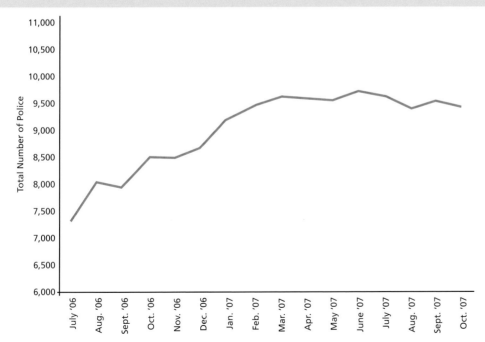

Source: DPKO PD.
Notes: Formed police units included. Includes all UN DPKO peacekeeping missions, DPKO-led political missions (BINUB, UNAMA, UNIOSIL, UNMIN), and UNAMI.

5.8 Top Twenty Police Contributors to UN Missions: 31 October 2007

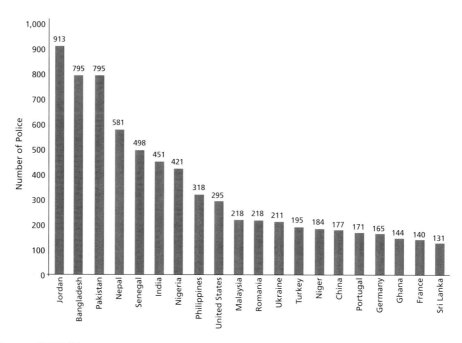

Source: DPKO PD.
Notes: Formed police units included. Includes contributions to all UN DPKO peacekeeping missions, DPKO-led political missions (BINUB, UNAMA, UNIOSIL, UNMIN) and UNAMI.

5.9 Police Deployed by UN Mission: 31 October 2007

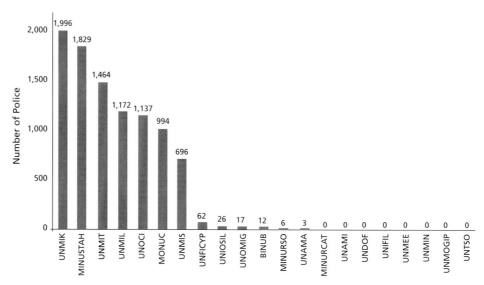

Source: DPKO PD.
Note: Formed police units included.

Top Twenty Police Contributors to UN Missions

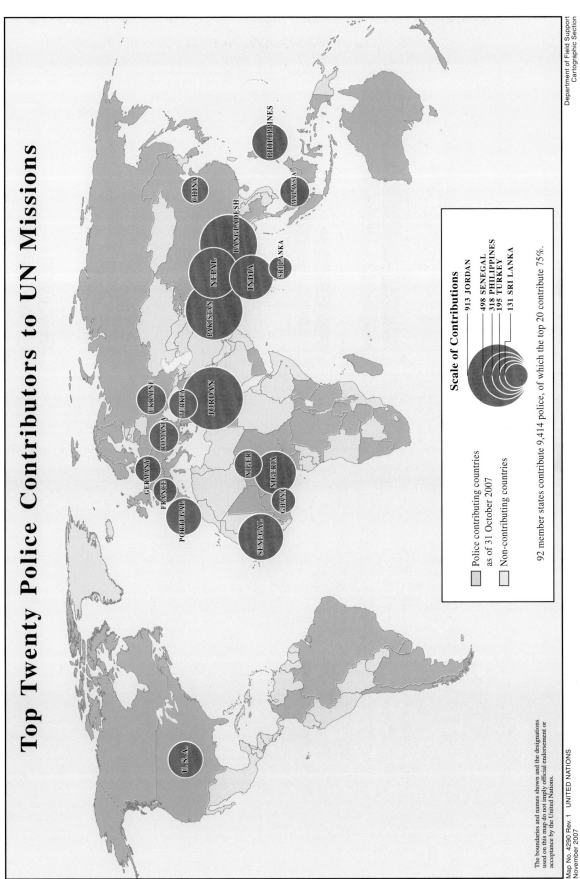

Scale of Contributions

913 JORDAN

498 SENEGAL
318 PHILIPPINES
195 TURKEY
131 SRI LANKA

Police contributing countries
as of 31 October 2007

Non-contributing countries

92 member states contribute 9,414 police, of which the top 20 contribute 75%.

Department of Field Support
Cartographic Section

The boundaries and names shown and the designations
used on this map do not imply official endorsement or
acceptance by the United Nations.

Map No. 4290 Rev. 1   UNITED NATIONS
November 2007

5.10 Formed Police by UN Mission: October 2006 and October 2007

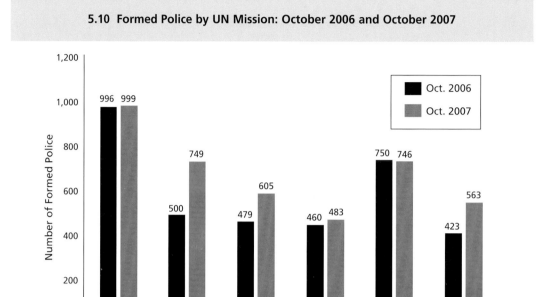

Source: DPKO PD.
Notes: MINUSTAH 2006 figures include a 40 person SWAT team. UNMIK 2006 figures include a 40 person canine unit.

5.11 Formed Police Contributions by UN Mission: 31 October 2007

	MINUSTAH	MONUC	UNMIK	UNMIL	UNMIT	UNOCI	Total
Jordan	290	—	—	120	—	375	785
Bangladesh	—	250	—	—	141	249	640
Pakistan	249	—	114	—	140	125	628
India	—	247	—	125	—	—	372
Nepal	125	—	—	240	—	—	365
Senegal	85	249	—	—	—	—	334
Nigeria	125	—	—	120	—	—	245
Portugal	—	—	—	—	142	—	142
Malaysia	—	—	—	—	140	—	140
Ukraine	—	—	139	—	—	—	139
China	125	—	—	—	—	—	125
Poland	—	—	115	—	—	—	115
Romania	—	—	115	—	—	—	115
Total	**999**	**746**	**483**	**605**	**563**	**749**	**4,145**

Source: DPKO PD.

5.12 Origin of UN Military Personnel by Region: 31 October 2007

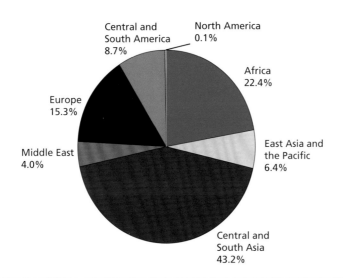

Region	Troops/Military Observers	Percentage of Total
Africa	16,381	22.4%
East Asia and the Pacific	4,662	6.4%
Central and South Asia	31,678	43.2%
Middle East	2,918	4.0%
Europe	11,191	15.3%
Central and South America	6,376	8.7%
North America	81	0.1%
Total	**73,287**	

Source: DPKO FGS.

Note: The regions used here and in the charts below are defined as follows: **Africa:** all members of the African Union and Morocco (but seen Middle East below.) **Central and South Asia:** all members of the South Asia Association for Regional Cooperation (including Afghanistan) and all members of the Commonwealth of Independent States to the east of the Caspian Sea, other than Russia. **East Asia and the Pacific:** all states in or bordering on the Pacific, the states of South-East Asia and Mongolia. **Central and South America:** all members of the Organization of American States other than Canada, the United States and Mexico. **Europe:** all states to the north of the Mediterranean, Armenia, Azerbaijan, Cyprus, Georgia, Malta, Russia and Turkey. **Middle East:** all members of the Gulf Cooperation Council, Lebanon, Iraq, Iran, Israel, Jordan, Syria, and Yemen. (While Egypt is included under Africa as a member of the AU, the contingent of UNTSO stations on the Suez Canal is counted under the Middle East deployment section to reflect its line of command.) **North America:** Canada, the United States, and Mexico.

5.13 Deployment of UN Military Personnel by Region: 31 October 2007

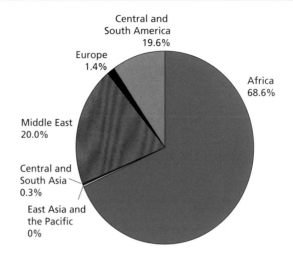

Region	Troops/Military Observers	Percentage of Total
Africa	50,263	68.6%
East Asia and the Pacific	32	0.0%
Central and South Asia	212	0.3%
Middle East	14,687	20.0%
Europe	1,033	1.4%
Central and South America	7,060	9.6%
North America	—	—
Total	**73,287**	

Source: DPKO FGS.

5.14 Origin of UN Police Personnel by Region: 31 October 2007

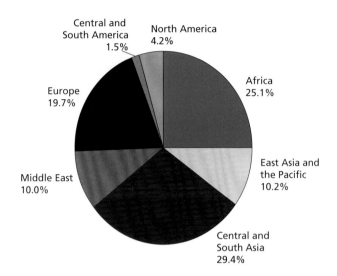

Region	Police	Percentage of Total
Africa	2,359	25.1%
East Asia and the Pacific	958	10.2%
Central and South Asia	2,768	29.4%
Middle East	937	10.0%
Europe	1,856	19.7%
Central and South America	140	1.5%
North America	396	4.2%
Total	**9,414**	

Source: DPKO PD.
Note: Formed police units included.

5.15 Deployment of UN Police Personnel by Region: 31 October 2007

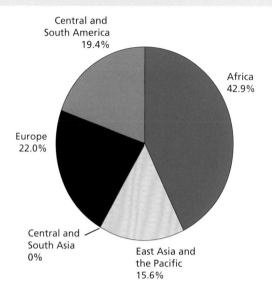

Region	Police	Percentage of Total
Africa	4,043	42.9%
East Asia and the Pacific	1,464	15.6%
Central and South Asia	3	0.0%
Middle East	—	—
Europe	2,075	22.0%
Central and South America	1,829	19.4%
North America	—	—
Total	**9,414**	

Source: DPKO PD.
Note: Formed police units included.

5.16 Origin of UN Military Personnel in Africa by Region: 31 October 2007

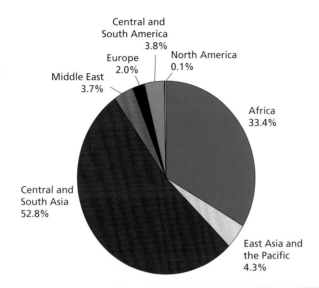

Region	Troops/Military Observers	Percentage of Total
Africa	17,511	33.4%
East Asia and the Pacific	2,227	4.3%
Central and South Asia	27,637	52.8%
Middle East	1,925	3.7%
Europe	1,064	2.0%
Central and South America	1,970	3.8%
North America	57	0.1%
Total	**52,391**	

Source: DPKO FGS.

5.17 Origin of UN Police Personnel in Africa by Region: 31 October 2007

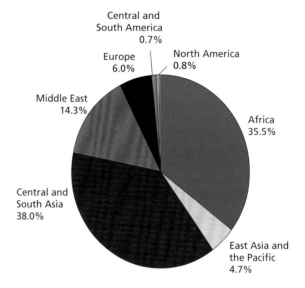

Region	Police	Percentage of Total
Africa	1,410	35.5%
East Asia and the Pacific	185	4.7%
Central and South Asia	1,510	38.0%
Middle East	569	14.3%
Europe	238	6.0%
Central and South America	29	0.7%
North America	30	0.8%
Total	**3,971**	

Source: DPKO PD.
Note: Formed police units included.

5.18 Origin of UN Military Personnel in the Middle East by Region: 31 October 2007

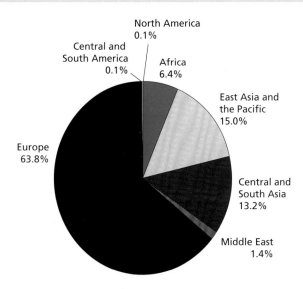

Region	Troops/Military Observers	Percentage of Total
Africa	945	6.4%
East Asia and the Pacific	2,203	15.0%
Central and South Asia	1,937	13.2%
Middle East	203	1.4%
Europe	9,375	63.8%
Central and South America	10	0.1%
North America	14	0.1%
Total	**14,687**	

Source: DPKO FGS.

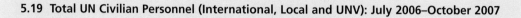

5.19 Total UN Civilian Personnel (International, Local and UNV): July 2006–October 2007

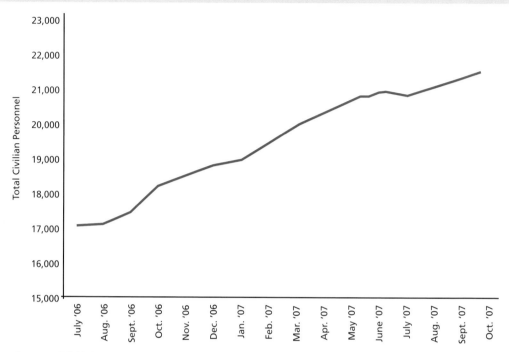

Sources: DPKO PMSS; UNV Programme.

Notes: Includes all UN DPKO peacekeeping missions, DPKO-led political missions (BINUB, UNAMA, UNIOSIL, UNMIN) and UNAMI. Staff at UN Logistics Base in Brindisi not included. Figures do not include staff from UN specialized agencies, funds and programmes.

5.20 UN International Civilian Staff and
DPKO Headquarters Personnel Occupational Groups: 31 October 2007

Occupation	International Civilian Staff	Percentage International Staff	DPKO HQ Staff	Percentage DPKO HQ Staff
Administration	884	14.9%	85	23.7%
Aviation	156	2.6%	—	—
Civil Affairs	237	4.0%	—	—
Economic Affairs	3	0.1%	—	—
Engineering	312	5.3%	—	—
Financial Management	233	3.9%	3	0.8%
Human Resources	217	3.7%	19	5.3%
Human Rights	185	3.1%	—	—
Humanitarian Affairs	66	1.1%	—	—
Information Management	22	0.4%	8	2.2%
Information Systems & Technology	480	8.1%	—	—
Legal Affairs	93	1.6%	—	—
Logistics	751	12.7%	—	—
Medical Services	58	1.0%	—	—
Military	—	—	52	14.5%
Police	—	—	40	11.1%
Political Affairs	429	7.2%	79	22.0%
Procurement	142	2.4%	—	—
Programme Management	121	2.0%	36	10.0%
Public Information	176	3.0%	3	0.8%
Rule of Law	181	3.1%	13	3.6%
Security	858	14.5%	—	—
Social Affairs	47	0.8%	4	1.1%
Training	—	—	17	4.7%
Transport	277	4.7%	—	—
Total	**5,928**		**359**	

Sources: DPKO PMSS; DPKO EO.
Notes: Mission Occupations includes all UN DPKO peacekeeping missions, DPKO-led political missions (BINUB, UNAMA, UNIOSIL, UNMIN) and UNAMI. Staff at UN Logistics Base in Brindisi not included. DPKO HQ occupations include both professional and general service staff.

5.21 UN Mission International Civilian Staff Occupations: 31 October 2007

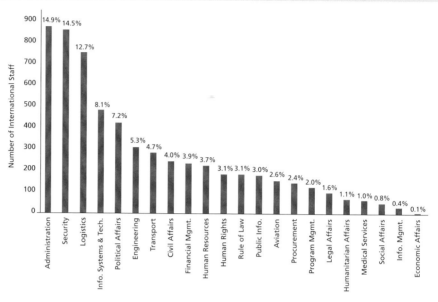

Sources: DPKO PMSS; DPKO EO.

Notes: Mission Occupations includes all UN DPKO peacekeeping missions, DPKO-led political missions (BINUB, UNAMA, UNIOSIL, UNMIN) and UNAMI. Staff at UN Logistics Base in Brindisi not included.

5.22 UN DPKO Headquarters Personnel Occupations: 31 October 2007

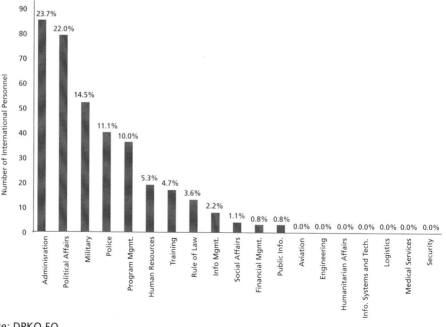

Source: DPKO EO.

Note: DPKO HQ occupations include both professional and general service staff.

5.23 Highest National Representation in UN Missions: 31 October 2007

UN Missions – International Professional and General Service Staff Total International Staff in Missions = 5,782				DPKO Missions – Local Professional and General Service Staff Total Local Staff in Missions = 12,775			
Rank	Country	Number of Intl'l Staff	Percentage of Total International Staff	Rank	Mission	Number of Local Staff	Percentage of Total Local Staff
1	United States	358	6.2%	1	UNMIN	2,580	20.2%
2	Kenya	243	4.2%	2	UNOCI	2,062	16.1%
3	Canada	217	3.8%	3	UNMEE	1,957	15.3%
4	Philippines	206	3.6%	4	MONUC	1,122	8.8%
5	United Kingdom	196	3.4%	5	UNAMA	1,040	8.1%
6	India	189	3.3%	6	UNMIK	945	7.4%
7	France	161	2.8%	7	UNMIS	771	6.0%
8	Ghana	144	2.5%	8	UNFICYP	583	4.6%
9	Sierra Leone	127	2.2%	9	UNAMI	354	2.8%
10	Ethiopia	123	2.1%	10	MINURSO	293	2.3%
11	Serbia	115	2.0%	11	BINUB	229	1.8%
12	Australia	110	1.9%	12	UNMIL	179	1.4%
13	Fiji	104	1.8%	13	UNIOSIL	172	1.3%
14	Nigeria	95	1.6%	14	MINUSTAH	145	1.1%
15	Pakistan	95	1.6%	15	UNTSO	120	0.9%
16	Croatia	84	1.5%	16	UNDOF	107	0.8%
17	Tanzania	81	1.4%	17	UNMIT	49	0.4%
18	Germany	80	1.4%	18	UNIFIL	46	0.4%
19	Italy	79	1.4%	19	UNOMIG	11	0.1%
20	Russia	79	1.4%	20	UNMOGIP	10	0.1%

Source: DPKO PMSS.
Notes: Includes all UN DPKO peacekeeping missions, DPKO-led political missions (BINUB, UNAMA, UNIOSIL, UNMIN) and UNAMI. Staff at UN Logistics Base in Brindisi not represented.

5.24 Highest National Representation in UN DPKO Headquarters: 31 October 2007

Total DPKO Headquarters Staff: 776
509 Professional Staff and 267 General Service Staff

Rank	Country	DFS	DPKO	DFS and DPKO	Percentage of Total DPKO HQ Staff
1	United States	89	62	151	19.5%
2	Philippines	26	22	48	6.2%
3	France	17	19	36	4.6%
4	United Kingdom	13	22	35	4.5%
5	India	18	9	27	3.5%
6	Canada	12	14	26	3.4%
7	Australia	11	9	20	2.6%
8	Germany	5	11	16	2.1%
9	Japan	4	10	14	1.8%
10	Pakistan	6	8	14	1.8%
11	Ghana	5	8	13	1.7%
12	Trinidad and Tobago	8	5	13	1.7%
13	Italy	3	9	12	1.5%
14	Kenya	7	5	12	1.5%
15	New Zealand	4	8	12	1.5%
16	Nigeria	5	7	12	1.5%
17	Denmark	5	6	11	1.4%
18	Ireland	8	3	11	1.4%
19	Romania	6	5	11	1.4%
20	Uruguay	6	5	11	1.4%

Source: DPKO EO.

5.25 Total Personnel in UN Missions: 31 October 2007

Mission	Troops	Military Observers	Police	International Staff	Local Staff	UNVs	Total
MONUC	16,655	733	994	931	2,062	577	21,952
UNMIL	13,322	206	1,172	502	945	242	16,389
UNIFIL	13,264	—	—	304	583	—	14,151
UNMIS	8,827	583	696	865	2,580	253	13,804
MINUSTAH	7,060	—	1,829	494	1,122	194	10,699
UNOCI	7,833	189	1,137	406	573	284	10,422
UNMIK	—	40	1,996	473	1,957	135	4,601
UNMIT	—	32	1,464	333	771	118	2,718
UNMEE	1,464	212	—	147	202	63	2,088
UNAMA	—	15	3	223	1,040	31	1,312
UNDOF	1,043	—	—	40	105	—	1,188
UNFICYP	860	—	62	38	107	—	1,067
UNAMI	223	7	—	278	354	—	862
UNMIN	—	153	—	222	179	200	754
MINURSO	29	185	6	95	145	24	484
UNOMIG	—	133	17	102	180	1	433
BINUB	—	8	12	117	229	46	412
UNTSO	—	150	—	105	120	—	375
UNIOSIL	—	14	26	75	199	24	338
UNMOGIP	—	44	—	22	49	—	115
UNAMID	—	—	—	—	—	58	58
MINURCAT	—	3	—	10	—	—	13
Total	**70,580**	**2,707**	**9,414**	**5,782**	**13,502**	**2,250**	**104,235**

Sources: DPKO FGS; DPKO PD; DPKO PMSS; UNV Programme.
Note: Police figures include formed police units.

5.26 UN Personnel Gender Statistics: 31 October 2007

Personnel Type	Male	Female	Percentage Male	Percentage Female
Troops	69,266	1,313	98.1%	1.9%
Military Observers	2,615	93	96.6%	3.4%
Police	8,827	587	93.8%	6.2%
International Civilian Staff	4,077	1,705	70.5%	29.5%
Local Civilian Staff	10,921	2,581	80.9%	19.1%
DPKO HQ Professional	295	194	60.3%	39.7%
DPKO HQ General Service	75	188	28.5%	71.5%
UN Logistics Base Brindisi	142	45	75.9%	24.1%
Total	**96,218**	**6,706**	**93.5%**	**6.5%**

Sources: DPKO FGS; DPKO PD; DPKO PMSS; DPKO EO.
Notes: International and local civilian staff includes all UN DPKO peacekeeping missions, DPKO-led political missions (BINUB, UNAMA, UNIOSIL, UNMIN) and UNAMI. Police figures include formed police units. The variation in troop and military observer totals between Tables 5.25 and 5.26 reflects a difference in staff categorization.

5.27 Total Monthly Fatalities in UN Missions: 1 July 2006–31 October 2007

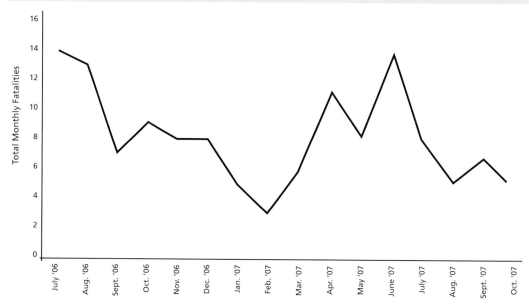

Source: DPKO Situation Center.

Notes: Includes all UN DPKO peacekeeping missions, DPKO-led political missions (BINUB, UNAMA, UNIOSIL, UNMIN) and UNAMI. UN Logistics Base in Brindisi not included.

5.28 Fatalities by UN Missions: 1 July 2006–31 October 2007

	Number of Fatalities	Percentage of Fatalities
MONUC	23	17.6%
UNMIS	20	15.3%
UNOCI	17	13.0%
UNMIL	15	11.5%
MINUSTAH	14	10.7%
UNIFIL	10	7.6%
UNAMA	6	4.6%
UNMEE	6	4.6%
UNTSO	5	3.8%
UNAMI	4	3.1%
UNIOSIL	3	2.3%
ONUB	2	1.5%
UNMIK	2	1.5%
UNMIT	2	1.5%
MINURSO	1	0.8%
UNOMIG	1	0.8%
BINUB	—	—
UNDOF	—	—
UNFICYP	—	—
UNMIN	—	—
UNMOGIP	—	—
Total	**131**	

Source: DPKO Situation Center.

5.29 Fatalities in UN Missions by Incident Type: 1 July 2006–30 September 2007

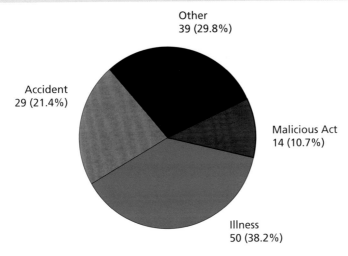

Other
39 (29.8%)

Accident
29 (21.4%)

Malicious Act
14 (10.7%)

Illness
50 (38.2%)

Source: DPKO Situation Center.
Notes: Includes all UN DPKO peacekeeping missions, DPKO-led political missions (BINUB, UNAMA, UNIOSIL, UNMIN) and UNAMI. UN Logistics Base in Brindisi not included. Malicious acts include both what were previously referred to as hostile acts and crime. Other includes what were previously qualified as self-inflicted.

5.30 Fatalities in UN Missions by Personnel Type: 1 July 2006–30 September 2007

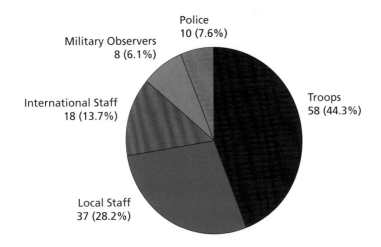

Police
10 (7.6%)

Military Observers
8 (6.1%)

International Staff
18 (13.7%)

Troops
58 (44.3%)

Local Staff
37 (28.2%)

Source: DPKO Situation Center.
Notes: Includes all UN DPKO peacekeeping missions, DPKO-led political missions (BINUB, UNAMA, UNIOSIL, UNMIN) and UNAMI. UN Logistics Base in Brindisi not included.

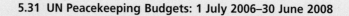

5.31 UN Peacekeeping Budgets: 1 July 2006–30 June 2008

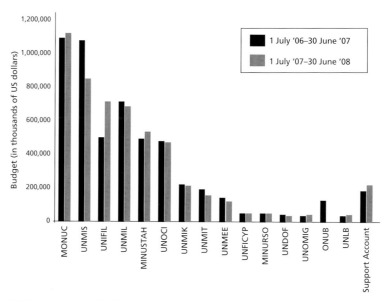

Sources: UN Documents A/C.5/61/22 and A/C.5/61/24; DPKO FMSS.

Notes: Figures above include only peacekeeping operations funded out of the peacekeeping budget; see table below for missions funded from the regular UN budget. The 1 July 2006–30 June 2007 UNMIT budget is commitment authority granted for the start-up of the mission. The 1 July 2006–30 June 2007 UNIFIL budget includes approved resources as well as an additional $50 million in commitment authority for the expansion of the mission.

5.32 Other Peace Operations Budgets: 1 January 2006–31 December 2007 (in thousands of US dollars)

	Appropriations
Peacekeeping Operations	18,604.1
BINUB	33,080.4
UNAMA	123,474.5
UNAMI	245,811.1
UNIOSIL	50,197.5
UNMIN	88,822.0
UNMOGIP	15,796.0
UNTSO	62,270.5
Total	**638,056.1**

Sources: UN Documents A/62/512/Add.3, A/62/512/Add.4, A/62/512/Add.5, and A/62/6(Sect.5); DPKO FMSS.

Notes: Peacekeeping Operations budget line item is for peacekeeping operations executive direction and management costs, programme of work and programme support.

5.33 2007 Top Twenty Providers of Assessed Contributions to UN Peacekeeping Budget

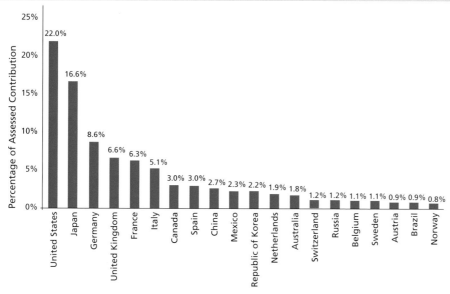

Source: DM OPPBA.

5.34 2007 Top Twenty Providers of Assessed Contributions to UN Regular Budget

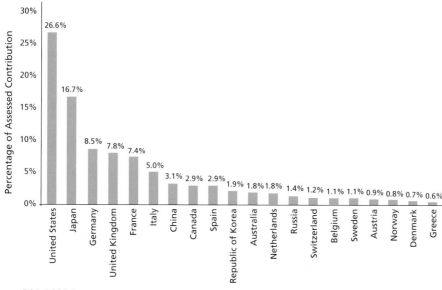

Source: DM OPPBA.

5.35 Top Twenty Assessed Financial Contributors to UN Peacekeeping Operations: 30 September 2007 (in thousands of US dollars)

Member State	2007 Effective Assessment Rate	Outstanding Contributions as at 31 December 2006	Assessments Issued in 2007	Collections Received in 2007	Credits Utilized in 2007	Oustanding Contributions as at 30 September 2007
United States	26.1%	677,419.5	1,473,654.8	837,916.3	(171,099.9)	1,142,058.2
Japan	16.6%	572,128.2	925,378.8	887,814.6	(111,003.1)	498,689.3
Germany	8.6%	—	472,007.2	370,228.7	(49,389.2)	52,389.3
United Kingdom	7.9%	3,445.2	431,176.1	341,550.9	(42,387.8)	50,682.7
France	7.5%	53,091.9	410,077.1	288,787.6	(41,716.7)	132,664.6
Italy	5.1%	2,252.9	278,545.8	164,992.9	(27,853.4)	87,952.3
China	3.2%	60,965.6	171,190.5	56,129.8	(15,549.0)	160,477.3
Canada	3.0%	—	163,068.9	147,029.6	(16,039.2)	—
Spain	3.0%	73,450.9	161,457.6	122,010.3	(13,586.0)	99,312.2
Republic of Korea	2.0%	85,270.7	106,642.4	160,268.0	(8,192.4)	23,452.7
Netherlands	1.9%	5,726.0	102,282.2	80,970.8	(9,636.1)	17,401.3
Australia	1.8%	734.2	97,505.6	78,247.3	(9,077.3)	10,915.2
Russia	1.4%	—	77,866.8	61,590.3	(7,610.0)	8,666.4
Switzerland	1.2%	—	66,796.5	52,543.7	(6,825.1)	7,427.8
Belgium	1.1%	15,777.7	60,472.3	37,155.3	(6,095.2)	32,999.5
Sweden	1.1%	—	58,610.3	46,378.1	(5,690.4)	6,541.8
Austria	0.9%	7,324.3	48,668.5	45,677.0	(4,897.9)	5,418.0
Norway	0.8%	0.2	42,599.5	33,660.6	(3,871.6)	5,067.5
Denmark	0.7%	0.1	40,557.1	31,948.4	(4,093.9)	4,514.9
Greece	0.6%	9,984.8	32,516.3	—	(3,375.5)	39,125.5

Source: DM OPPBA.

Note: Credits utilized are derived from unemcumbered balance of appropriations and other income for peacekeeping operations utilized at the time that assessments for the same operations were issued.

5.36 UN Mandate Renewals: 1 July 2005–31 December 2007

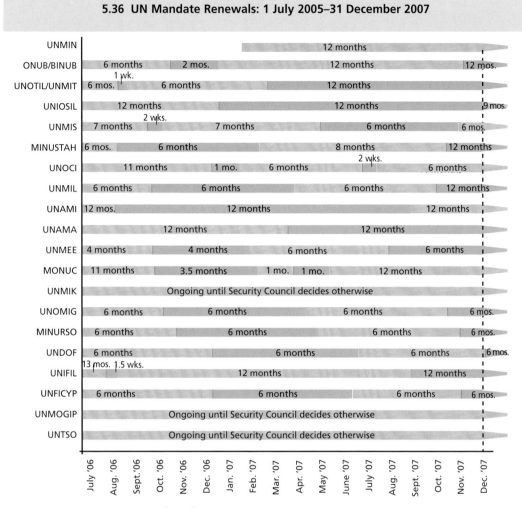

Sources: UN Security Council resolutions.

Notes: Mandate duration noted is mission authorization as per initial Security Council resolution. In some cases, mission authorization was renewed prior to the end of the previous mandate; in such cases the mandate duration may not match the timeline on the graph.

5.37 UN Operations Timeline: 1945–2007

Sources: UN Security Council resolutions.

6 Global Statistics on Non-UN Missions

This chapter presents data on peace operations conducted under the authority of regional organizations and non-standing coalitions of states; these data are compiled by the Stockholm International Peace Research Institute (SIPRI).

sipri

* * *

Listed here are 35 non-UN multilateral peace operations that started, were ongoing or terminated in 2007. The chapter lists only operations conducted by regional organizations or ad hoc coalitions of states with the stated intention to: (1) serve as an instrument to facilitate the implementation of peace agreements already in place, (2) support a peace process, or (3) assist conflict prevention and/or peace-building efforts.

SIPRI uses the UN Department of Peace-keeping Operations (DPKO) description of peacekeeping as a mechanism to assist conflict-ridden countries to create conditions for sustainable peace—this may include monitoring and observing ceasefire agreements; serving as confidence-building measures; protecting the delivery of humanitarian assistance; assisting with demobilization and reintegration processes; strengthening institutional capacities in the areas of judiciary and the rule of law (including penal institutions), policing and human rights; electoral support; and economic and social development. The chapter thus covers a broad range of peace missions to reflect the growing complexity of mandates of peace operations and the potential for operations to change over the course of their mandate. The chapter does not include good offices, fact-finding or electoral assistance missions.

The operations are divided into two loosely-defined categories: those with military and observer functions (Table 6.10) and those with primarily policing and other civilian functions (Table 6.11). Legal instruments underlying the establishment of an operation— UN Security Council resolutions or formal decisions by regional organizations—are cited in the third column. The start dates for the operations refer to dates of first deployments. The list of countries presented in this volume is incomplete and refer only to the main contributors to a mission. For a complete list of countries participating in each mission, consult the *SIPRI Yearbook*.

Mission fatalities are recorded as a total from the beginning of the mission until the last reported date for 2007 and as a total for 2007. Fatality figures are broken down by cause of death–hostilities, accidents and illness. Subtotals owing to hostilities accidents and illness may not add up to the total number of deaths in 2007 because some deaths have not yet been classified or were the result of other causes.

Data on multilateral peace operations are obtained from the following categories of open source: (1) official information provided by the secretariat of the authorizing organization; (2) information from the mission on the ground, either in official publications or in responses to annual SIPRI questionnaires; and (3) information from national governments contributing to the mission in question. These primary sources are supplemented with a wide selection of publicly available secondary sources consisting of specialist journals; research reports; news agencies; and international, regional and local newspapers.

Table 6.12 lists the estimated declared costs of the peace operations underway in

2007. Budget figures are for the period 1 October 2006–30 September 2007. Budget figures are given in millions of US dollars and conversions from budgets set in other currencies are based on the aggregated market exchange rates of the International Monetary Fund (IMF) for the reporting year and are expressed in current dollar terms. The issue of financing of peace operations is a complicated one and warrants a brief explanation on the different ways in which peacekeeping budgets are calculated and the manner in which they are financed.

Unlike UN budgets, figures for operations conducted by regional organizations such as the EU and NATO refer only to common costs. This includes mainly the running costs of EU and NATO headquarters (the costs of civilian personnel and operations and maintenance) and investments in the infrastructure necessary to support the operation. The costs of deploying personnel are borne by individual sending states and do not appear in the budget figures given here. Most EU missions are financed in one of two ways, depending on whether they are civilian or military missions. Civilian missions are funded through the Community Budget, while military missions or missions with military components are funded through the ATHENA mechanism to which only the participating member states contribute. In missions by other organizations, such as the ad hoc missions, budget figures for missions may include program implementation.

For these reasons, budget figures presented in this table are best viewed as estimates and the budgets for different missions should not be compared. There are certain limitations to the data. The main problems of reliability are due to varying definitions of what constitutes the total cost of an operation. The coverage of official data varies significantly between operations; sometimes a budget is an estimate while in other cases it is actual expenditure.

6.1 Top Twenty Troop Contributors to Non-UN missions: 30 September 2007

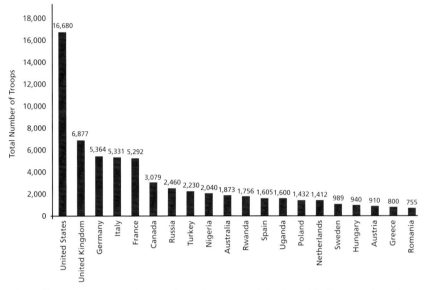

Notes: These figures represent the number of personnel deployed in large-scale units and may exclude some additional personnel deployed individually or in small scale units. For scaling reasons, MNF-Iraq figures are not included in this ranking.

6.2 Top Twenty Police Contributors to Non-UN Missions: 30 September 2007

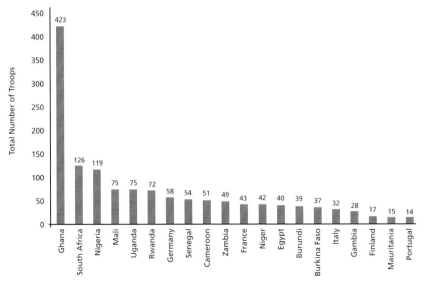

Note: As the figures for largest contributors represent personnel deployed in large scale units, there may be variations with actual field strength.

Top Twenty Troop Contributors to Non-UN Missions

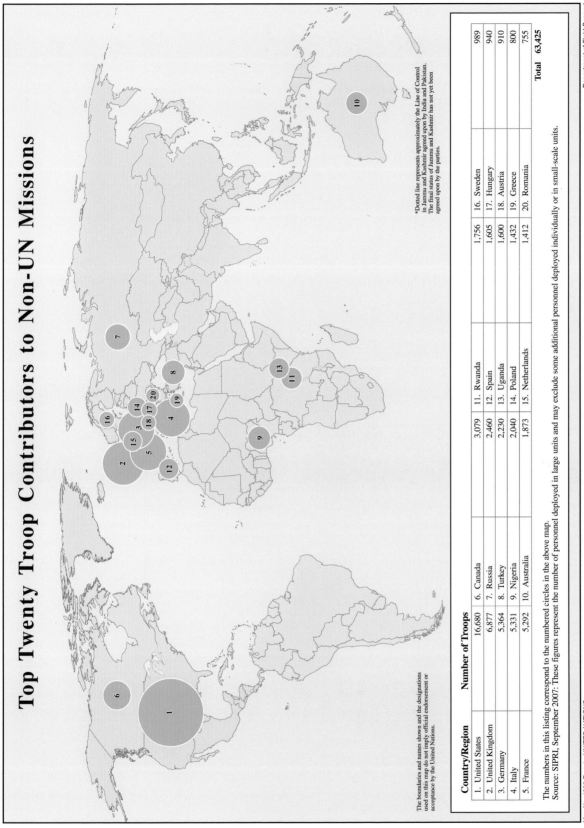

The boundaries and names shown and the designations used on this map do not imply official endorsement or acceptance by the United Nations.

*Dotted line represents approximately the Line of Control in Jammu and Kashmir agreed upon by India and Pakistan. The final status of Jammu and Kashmir has not yet been agreed upon by the parties.

Country/Region	Number of Troops		
1. United States	16,680	6. Canada	3,079	11. Rwanda	989	16. Sweden	1,756
2. United Kingdom	6,877	7. Russia	2,460	12. Spain	940	17. Hungary	1,605
3. Germany	5,364	8. Turkey	2,230	13. Uganda	910	18. Austria	1,600
4. Italy	5,331	9. Nigeria	2,040	14. Poland	800	19. Greece	1,432
5. France	5,292	10. Australia	1,873	15. Netherlands	755	20. Romania	1,412

Total 63,425

The numbers in this listing correspond to the numbered circles in the above map.
Source: SIPRI, September 2007: These figures represent the number of personnel deployed individually or in small-scale units.

Department of Field Support
Cartographic Section

Map No. 4288 Rev. 1   UNITED NATIONS
November 2007

Top Twenty Police Contributors to Non-UN Missions

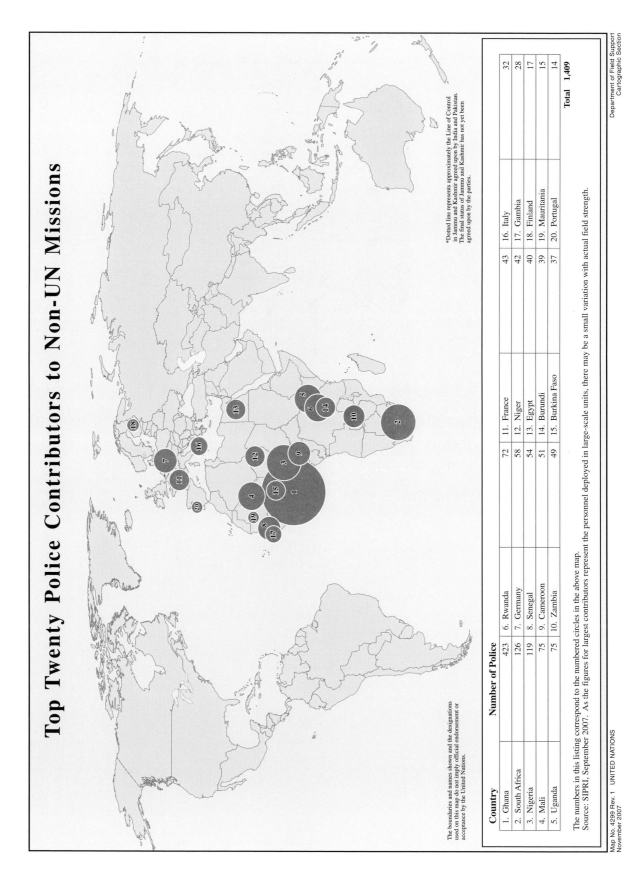

The boundaries and names shown and the designations used on this map do not imply official endorsement or acceptance by the United Nations.

*Dotted line represents approximately the Line of Control in Jammu and Kashmir agreed upon by India and Pakistan. The final status of Jammu and Kashmir has not yet been agreed upon by the parties.

Country	Number of Police			
1. Ghana	423	6. Rwanda	126	11. France	72	16. Italy	43
2. South Africa	119	7. Germany	75	12. Niger	58	17. Gambia	42
3. Nigeria		8. Senegal	75	13. Egypt	54	18. Finland	40
4. Mali		9. Cameroon		14. Burundi	51	19. Mauritania	39
5. Uganda		10. Zambia		15. Burkina Faso	49	20. Portugal	37
						Total	1,409

The numbers in this listing correspond to the numbered circles in the above map.
Source: SIPRI, September 2007. As the figures for largest contributors represent the personnel deployed in large-scale units, there may be a small variation with actual field strength.

Map No. 4299 Rev. 1 UNITED NATIONS
November 2007

Department of Field Support
Cartographic Section

6.3 Contributions of Military Personnel to Non-UN Missions: 30 September 2007

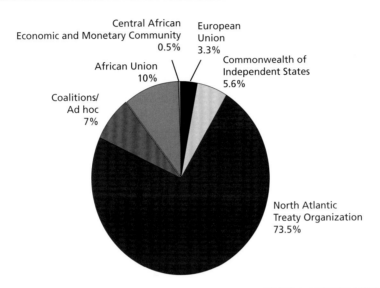

Organization	Troops/Military Observers	Percentage of Total
North Atlantic Treaty Organization	56,387	73.5%
African Union	7,714	10.0%
Coalitions/Ad hoc	5,425	7.0%
Commonwealth of Independent States	4,284	5.6%
European Union	2,554	3.3%
Central African Economic and Monetary Community	378	0.5%
Total	**76,742**	

Note: For scaling purposes, MNF-Iraq figures are not included in this ranking.

6.4 Deployment of Non-UN Military Personnel to Regions: 30 September 2007

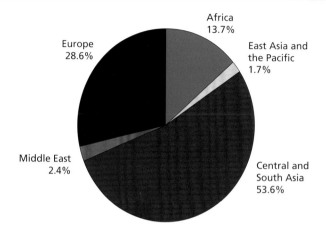

Organization	Troops/Military Observers	Percentage of Total
Africa	10,492	13.7%
East Asia and the Pacific	1,294	1.7%
Central and South Asia	41,153	53.6%
Middle East	1,856	2.4%
Europe	21,947	28.6%
Central and South America	—	—
North America	—	—
Total	**76,742**	

Note: For scaling reasons, MNF-Iraq figures are not included in this ranking.

6.5 Deployment of Non-UN Police by Organization: 30 September 2007

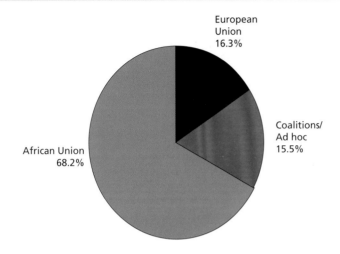

Organization	Police	Percentage of Total
African Union	1,425	68.2%
Coalitions/Ad hoc	323	15.5%
European Union	340	16.3%
Total	**2,088**	

6.6 Deployment of Non-UN Police to Regions: 30 September 2007

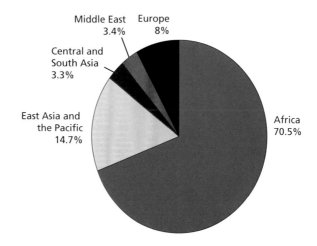

Region	Police	Percentage of Total
Africa	1,473	70.5%
East Asia and the Pacific	306	14.7%
Central and South Asia	70	3.3%
Middle East	72	3.4%
Europe	167	8.0%
Central and South America	—	—
North America	—	—
Total	**2,088**	

6.7 Deployment of Non-UN Troops in Africa by Organization: 30 September 2007

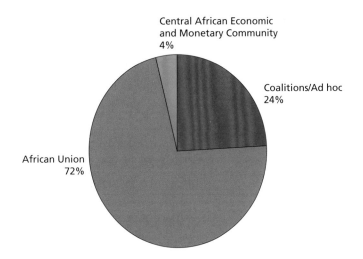

Organization	Troops	Percentage of Total
African Union	7,102	72%
Coalition/Ad hoc	2,400	24%
Central African Economic and Monetary Communinity	378	4%
Total	**9,880**	

6.8 Deployment of Non-UN Troops in Europe by Organization: 30 September 2007

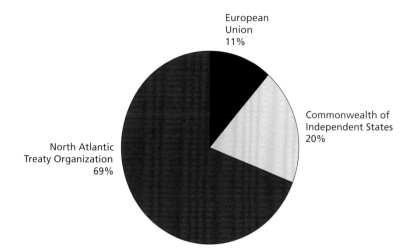

Organization	Troops	Percentage of Total
North Atlantic Treaty Organization	15,109	69%
Commonwealth of Independent States	4,274	20%
European Union	2,504	11%
Total	**21,887**	

6.9 Deployment of Non-UN Police in Africa by Organization: 30 September 2007

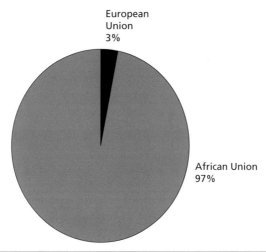

Organization	Police	Percentage of Total
African Union	1,425	97%
European Union	48	3%
Total	**1,473**	

6.10 2007 Non-UN Military and Observer Missions

Name	Location	Authorization Date	Start Date	Principal Troop Contributors	Principal Military Observer Contributors	Principal Civilian Police Contributors	Principal Civilian Staff Contributors	Troops, Military Observers, Civilian Police, Civilian Staff (Actual)	Total Deaths to Date/in 2007 (due to: hostilities, accidents, illness)
African Union Mission in Sudan (AMIS)	Darfur, Sudan	28 May 2004 (Agreement with Sudanese Parties)[1] 30 July 2004 (UNSC Res. 1556)	June 2004	Gambia (196), Kenya (46), Nigeria (2040), Rwanda (1756), Senegal (538), South Africa (592)	Nigeria (63), Rwanda (34), South Africa (39), Senegal (36), Ghana (23), Gambia (20), Kenya (45)	Cameroon (51), Ghana (423), Mali (75), Niger (42), Nigeria (119), Rwanda (72), Senegal (54), South Africa (126), Uganda (75), Zambia (49)[2]	—	Troops: 5,202 Military observers: 612 Civilian police: 1,425[3]	60/20 (20, –, –)
African Union Mission in Somalia (AMISOM)	Mogadishu, Somalia	19 January 2007 (AU PSC/PR/Comm (LXIX))[4] 21 February 2007 (UNSC Res. 1744)	March 2007	Uganda (1600)	—	—	—	Troops: 1,600	5/5 (4, 1, –)
AU Electoral and Security Assistance Mission to the Comoros (MAES)	The Union of the Comoros	9 May 2007 (PSC/MIN/Comm.1 (LXXVII))[5]	May 2007	Sudan, Tanzania	—	—	—	Troops: 300	../..
CEMAC Multinational Force in the Central African Republic (FOMUC)	Central African Republic	2 October 2002 (Libreville Summit) 21 March 2003 (Libreville Summit Amended)[6]	December 2002	Chad, Congo (Republic of), Gabon	—	—	—	378[7]	8/—
Joint Control Commission Peacekeeping Force July 1992	Moldova, Trans-Dniester	21 July 1992 (Moldova and Russia)[8]	July 1992	Moldova (403), Russia (360), Trans-Dniester (411)[9]	Ukraine (10)	—	—	Troops: 1,174 Military observers: 10	../..

Mission	Region	Date (Basis)	Contributors				Troops	
South Ossetia Joint Force	South Ossetia, Georgia	24 June 1992 (Georgia-Russia)[10]	Georgia (500) Russia (500), South Ossetia (500)[11]	—	—	—	Troops: 1,500	19/—
CIS Peacekeeping Forces in Georgia	Abkhazia, Georgia	21 October 1994 (CIS Council of Collective Security)[12] 21 July 1994 (UNSC Res. 937)[13]	Russia (1600)	—	—	—	Troops: 1,600	../..
EU Monitoring Mission (EUMM)	Western Balkans	7 July 1991 (Brioni Agreement)[14]	Austria (4), Finland (3), France (10), Germany (6), Greece (5), Ireland (5), Norway (3), Slovakia (2), Spain (4), Sweden (6), UK (2)	—	—	Military observers: 50[15]	11/—	

1. AMIS was initially established by the Agreement with the Sudanese Parties on the Modalities for the Establishment of the Ceasefire Commission and the Deployment of Observers in Darfur on 28 May 2004 as an observer mission and was endorsed by UNSC Res. 1556 with UN Charter Chapter VII powers. The mandate was expanded pursuant to a decision adopted at the 17th Meeting of the AU's Peace and Security Council (PSC). After the acceptance of the AU/UN hybrid force (UNAMID) by the Sudanese government in June 2007 the AU PSC authorized the extension of AMIS' mandate until 31 December 2007 (PSC, Communiqué on the Situation in Darfur, 22 June 2007).

2. The national breakdown of deployed civilian police is as of March 2007.

3. Additional civilian staff, international staff (3) and party representatives of the Government of Sudan, the Justice and Equality Movement, and the Sudan Liberation Movement/Army (232) are supporting the mission.

4. AMISOM was established by the AU PSC on 19 January 2007 and was endorsed by UNSC RES. 1744 (21 February 2007) with UN Charter Chapter VII powers. The mission is mandated to support the dialogue and reconciliation process in Somalia by supporting the Transitional Federal Institutions, facilitating the provision of humanitarian assistance, and contributing to the overall security situation. The AU and the UN approved the extension of AMISOM's mandate until March 2008.

5. MAES was established by the AU PSC on 9 May 2007 with a mandate to contribute to a secure environment for free, fair, and transparent presidential elections on the three islands in the Union of Comoros. On 13 August 2007, the PSC authorized an increase in the mission strength and extended the mission's mandate until 31 December 2007.

6. FOMUC was established by CEMAC at the Libreville Summit (2 October 2002) to secure the border between Chad and the Central African Republic (CAR) and to guarantee the safety of former President Patassé. Following the 15 March 2003 coup, its mandate was expanded by CEMAC at the Libreville Summit (21 March 2003) to include contributing to the overall security environment, assisting in the restructuring of CAR's armed forces and supporting the transition process.

7. FOMUC is supported by and co-located with a detachment of French soldiers. The mission is supported by locally recruited staff.

8. The Joint Control Commission Peacekeeping Force was established by the Agreement on the Principles Governing the Peaceful Settlement of the Armed Conflict in the Trans-Dniester region (21 July 1992). A Monitoring Commission with representatives from Moldova, Russia and the Trans-Dniester coordinates the activities of the joint peacekeeping contingent.

9. The participation of parties to a conflict in peace operations is typically not included in the table; however, the substantial involvement of the parties to the conflict in this operation is a distinctive feature of CIS operations and of the peace agreement, which is the basis for the establishment of the operation.

10. The South Ossetia Joint Force was established by the Agreement on the Principles Governing the Peaceful Settlement of the Conflict in South Ossetia (24 June 1992). A joint Monitoring Commission with representatives of Russia, Georgia, and the North and South Ossetia authorities was established to oversee implementation of the agreement.

11. See note 9 above.

12. The CIS Peacekeeping Forces in Georgia mission was established by the Georgian-Abkhazian Agreement on a Ceasefire and Separation of Forces (14 May 1994). The operation's mandate was approved by heads of state of the members of the CIS Council of Collective Security (21 October 1994) and endorsed by the UN through UNSC RES. 937 (21 July 1994). Its mandate was extended indefinitely from January 2004.

13. The Russian troops are deployed along the Georgian-Abkhazian border.

14. The EUMM was established by the Brioni Agreement (7 July 1991). Initially tasked to monitor the withdrawal of Yugoslav troops from Slovenia, the mission is now tasked to monitor political and security developments, borders, inter-ethnic issues and refugee returns; to contribute to the early warning mechanism of the European Council; and to contribute to confidence building and stabilization in the region of former Yugoslavia (CJA 2000/811/CFSP, 23 December 2000). After the closing of the field offices in Albania (December 2006) and Montenegro (June 2007), the field offices in Bosnia and Herzegovina, Macedonian, Serbia and Kosovo continued to operate during 2007. The mission closed on 31 December 2007 as detailed in Joint Action of November 2006 (CJA 2006/867/CFSP, 30 November 2006).

15. The figure includes seconded and contracted international staff. The mission is supported by locally recruited staff.

continues

6.10 Continued

Name	Location	Authorization Date	Start Date	Principal Troop Contributors	Principal Military Observer Contributors	Principal Civilian Police Contributors	Principal Civilian Staff Contributors	Troops, Military Observers, Civilian Police, Civilian Staff (Actual)	Total Deaths to Date/in 2007 (due to: hostilities, accidents, illness)
EU Military Operation in Bosnia and Herzegovina (EUFOR ALTHEA)	Bosnia and Herzegovina	12 July 2004 (Council Joint Action 2004/570/CFSP) 9 July 2005 (UNSC Res. 1551)[16]	December 2004	Albania, Austria (178), Bulgaria (115), France (73), Germany (235), Greece (75), Hungary (158), Italy (472), Poland (203), Spain (262), Turkey (253)[17]	—	—	—	Troops: 2,504[18]	5/—
EU Military Operation in Chad/CAR (EUFOR TCHAD/RCA)	Eastern Chad and north-eastern Central African Republic	15 October 2007 (CJA 2007/ 677/CFSP)[18] UNSC Res. 1778 (25 September 2007)	—	Austria (160), Belgium (100), France (1500), Ireland (350), Poland (400), Sweden (200)	—	—	—	Troops: 3,000[19]	./..
NATO Kosovo Force (KFOR)	Kosovo, Serbia[20]	10 June 1999 (UNSC Res. 1244)[21]	June 1999	Austria (569), Czech Republic (433), France (1841), Germany (2221), Greece (582), Hungary (468), Italy (2286), Spain (638), Turkey (762), USA (1526)	—	—	—	Troops: 15,109[22]	96/9 (–, 5, 2)
International Security Assistance Force (ISAF)	Afghanistan[23]	20 December 2001 (UNSC Res. 1386)[24]	December 2001	Australia (883), Canada (3079), France (978), Germany (2573), Italy (2908), Netherlands (1341), Poland (943), Turkey (1215), UK (6678), USA (15154)	—	—	—	Troops: 41,118[25]	293/123 (110, –, –)

Mission	Location	Date		Contributing countries			Lead nation	Strength	
NATO Training Mission in Iraq (NTM-I)	Iraq[26]	8 June 2004 (UNSC Res. 1546)[27]	August 2004	Bulgaria, Czech Republic, Denmark, Estonia, Hungary, Iceland, Italy, Lithuania, Netherlands, Norway, Poland, Portugal, Romania, Slovakia, Slovenia, Turkey, UK, Ukraine, USA	—	—	—	Troops: 160	—
Multinational Force and Observers (MFO)	Sinai, Egypt	3 August 1981 (Egypt and Israel)[28]	April 1982	—	Australia (25), Canada (28), Colombia (358), Fiji (338), France (18), Hungary (41), Italy (78), New Zealand (26), Norway (5), Uruguay (67), USA (687)	—	USA (15)	Military observers: 1,691 (–, 10, –) Civilian staff: 15	—

16. EUFOR ALTHEA is mandated to maintain a secure environment for the implementation of the 1995 Dayton Agreement, to assist in the strengthening of local capacity, and to support Bosnia and Herzegovina's progress towards EU integration. UNSC RES. 1722 (21 November 2006) extended the mandate until November 2007.

17. In accordance with the transition plan to downsize the mission, a Multinational Maneuver Battalion was redeployed to Sarajevo in March 2007. In addition, the Integrated Police Unit and liaison and observer teams (LOTs) retain their presence throughout BiH.

18. The operation was unable to deploy by year end and all information cited here is based on projected strength and deployment plans as of 31 October 2007. EUFOR TCHAD/RCA was established on 15 October 2007 by the EU Council and was endorsed by UNSC RES. 1778 (25 September 2007) with UN Charter Chapter VII powers. The mission is part of the multinational presence to eastern Chad and north-eastern CAR. It is mandated to support the UN Mission MINURCAT (UNSC RES. 1978) and contribute to the protection of civilians and UN personnel, and facilitate humanitarian aid efforts. The mission is initially mandated for 12 months.

19. The mission is supported by 452 locally recruited staff in the EUFOR Headquarters.

20. KFOR headquarters is located in Pristina and KFOR contingents are grouped into 6 task forces: MNTF Centre located in Lipljan is led by Sweden; MNTF North located in Novo Selo is led by France; MNTF South located in Prizren is led by Turkey; MNFT West located in Peje/Pec is led by Italy; MNTF East located in Urosevac is led by USA; and, finally MN Specialized Unit (MSU) located in Pristina is led by Italy.

21. KFOR's mandated tasks include deterring renewed hostilities, establishing a secure environment, supporting UNMIK and monitoring borders.

22. KFOR Headquarters is supported by 35 international and by 142 locally recruited staff.

23. The territory of Afghanistan is divided in five areas of responsibility: the Regional Command (RC) Capital in Kabul; RC North at Mazar-e Sharif, led by Germany; RC West at Herat, led by Italy; RC South at Kandahar, led by UK; and RC East at Bagram, led by the USA.

24. UNSC RES. 1776 (19 September 2007) extended the mandate until October 2008.

25. The following countries have contributed military and/or civilian personnel to the 25 PRTs: Australia, Belgium, Canada, Croatia, Czech Republic, Denmark, Estonia, Finland, France, Germany, Hungary, Iceland, Italy, Lithuania, Netherlands, New Zealand, Norway, Romania, Spain, Sweden, Switzerland, UK, USA.

26. The NATO Training Mission in Iraq is being carried out within Baghdad's secure "Green Zone" and in an undisclosed location outside of Iraq.

27. NTM-I is mandated to assist in the development of Iraq's security institutions. In 2007 NTM-I began mentoring and advising an Iraqi-led institutional training program.

28. The Multinational Force Observers was established according to the Protocol to the Treaty of Peace between Egypt and Israel, signed 26 March 1979.

continues

6.10 Continued

Name	Location	Authorization Date	Start Date	Principal Troop Contributors	Principal Military Observer Contributors	Principal Civilian Police Contributors	Principal Civilian Staff Contributors	Troops, Military Observers, Civilian Police, Civilian Staff (Actual)	Total Deaths to Date/in 2007 (due to: hostilities, accidents, illness)
Temporary International Presence in Hebron (TIPH 2)	Hebron	15 January 1997 (Hebron Protocol)[29]	January 1997	—	Turkey (5)	Denmark (3), Italy (10), Norway (4)	Denmark (6), Norway (13), Sweden (10), Switzerland (4)	Military observers: 5 Civilian police: 17 Civilian staff: 33	2/—
Sri Lanka Monitoring Mission (SLMM)	Sri Lanka	22 February 2002 (Government of Sri Lanka and the Liberation Tamil Tigers of Eelam)[30]	February 2002	—	Iceland (10), Norway (25)	—	—	Military observers: 35[31]	—
International Monitoring Team (IMT)	Philippines	November 2004 (Trilateral decision between Malaysia, Philippines and the MILF) 22 June 2001 (Tripoli Agreement on Peace)[32]	October 2004	—	Brunei Darussalam, Libya, Malaysia	—	Malaysia, Japan	Military observers: 60	./..
Operation Licorne	Côte d'Ivoire	24 January 2006 (UNSC Res. 1652) 4 February 2003 (UNSC Res. 1464)[33]	February 2003	France (2400)	—	—	—	Troops: 2,400[34]	24/1 (–, 1, –)

Mission	Date established (authority)	Date	Contributors			Strength	
Regional Assistance Mission in the Solomon Islands (RAMSI)	23 October 2000 (Pacific Islands Communiqué) (Biketawa Declaration)35	July 2003	Australia (140), New Zealand (44), Papua New Guinea, Tonga	Australia, Fiji (8), New Zealand (35), Papua New Guinea (10)	Australia, Fiji, New Zealand, Papua New Guinea, Tonga	—	Troops: 214 Civilian police: 306 Civilian staff: 169	2/—
Multinational Force in Iraq (MNF-I)	16 October 2003 (UNSC Res. 1511)37 8 June 2004 (UNSC Res. 1546 modified)	November 2003	Australia (1572), Azerbaijan, El Salvador, Georgia (2000), South Korea (1200), Mongolia, Poland (900), Romania (600), UK (5230)38, USA (168000)	—	—	Troops: 180,009	4130/1156 (1000 ,-,-)39
International Security Forces (ISF)	25 May 200640	May 2006	Australia (850), New Zealand (170)	—	—	Troops: 1,020	./..

29. The mission received its authority from the Protocol Concerning the Redeployment in Hebron (15 January 1997) and the Agreement on the Temporary International Presence in Hebron (21 January 1997). The mandate of the mission is to monitor and report breaches of international humanitarian law and contribute to a secure and stable environment. The mandate is renewed every six months pending approval from both the Palestinian and Israeli parties.

30. The Sri Lanka Monitoring Mission was instated to monitor the implementation of the Agreement on a ceasefire between the Government of the Democratic Socialist Republic of Sri Lanka and the Liberation Tigers of Tamil Eelam (CFA). The CFA was signed 22 February 2002. The mission constitutes an impartial entity that is to inquire into CFA violations. The governments of Norway and Sri Lanka, endorsed by the LTTE leadership, composed a Status of Mission Agreement (SOMA) where the position of the SLMM is delineated.

31. In addition 54 locally recruited staff members are contracted to the mission.

32. The mission was established after the Government of the Republic of the Philippines (GRP) and the Moro Islamic Liberation Front (MILF) signed the ceasefire agreement in July 2003. In November 2007 the Malaysian government reviewed IMT's mandate and decided that it will be prolonged.

33. Operation Licorne, was deployed under the authority of UNSC RES. 1464 (4 February 2003), under UN Charter Chapter VII and in accordance with UN Charter Chapter VIII, to initially support the ECOWAS mission in contributing to a secure environment and to facilitate implementation of the 2003 Linas–Marcoussis Agreement. UNSC RES. 1528 (27 February 2004) provides its current authorization and revised the mandate to work in support of UNOCI. UNSC RES. 1765 (16 July 2007) extended the mandate until 15 January 2008.

34. Following the signing of the Ouagadougou agreement in March 2007, about 1000 French troops were withdrawn; the remaining troops are now stationed in Abidjan and around Yamoussoukro.

35. RAMSI was established under the framework of the 2000 Biketawa Declaration in which members of the Pacific Islands Forum agreed to mount a collective response to crises, usually at the request of the host government.

36. For MNF-I purposes, the territory of Iraq is divided into 6 areas covered by the following units: MNF West, Multinational Division (MND) Baghdad, MND North and Central for which the USA is the lead nation; MND Central South, maintained by Poland; and MND Southeast, maintained by Australia and the UK.

37. The MNF-I was authorized by UNSC RES. 1511 (16 October 2003) to contribute to the maintenance of security and stability in Iraq, including for the purpose of ensuring necessary conditions for the implementation of UNAMIS's mandated tasks. The mandate of MNF-I was reaffirmed by UNSC RES. 1546 (8 June 2004) following the dissolution of the Coalition Provisional Authority and the subsequent transfer of sovereignty to the Interim Government of Iraq. UNSC RES. 1790 (18 December 2007) extended the mandate until 31 December 2008.

38. UK announced a reduction in troop strength by 1000 to 4500 to take effect at the end of 2007. A further drawdown to 2500 soldiers is expected in spring 2008.

39. The deaths of 156 coalition forces were caused by non-hostile actions.

40. The ISF, also known as Operation Astute, was deployed at the request of the Government of Timor-Leste to assist in stabilizing the security environment in the county and endorsed by UNSC RES. 1690 (20 June 2006). ISF cooperates closely with UNMIT.

6.11 2007 Non-UN Civilian Police and Civilian Missions

Name	Location	Authorization Date	Start Date	Principal Troop Contributors	Principal Military Observer Contributors	Principal Civilian Police Contributors	Principal Civilian Staff Contributors	Troops, Military Observers, Civilian Police, Civilian Staff (Actual)	Total Deaths to Date/in 2007 (due to: hostilities, accidents, illness)
EU Police Mission in Bosnia and Herzegovina (EUPM)	Bosnia and Herzegovina	11 March 2002 (Council Joint Action 2002/210/CFSP)[41]	January 2003	—	—	Finland (6), France (17), Germany (19), Italy (13), Netherlands (10), Poland (6), Romania (7), Slovakia (6), Turkey (9), UK (8)	Germany (9), Norway (1), UK (3)	Civilian police: 167 Civilian staff: 28[42]	3/—
EU Police Mission in Kinshasa (EUPOL Kinshasa)	Kinshasa, Democratic Republic of the Congo	9 December 2004 (Council Joint Action 2004/847/CFSP)[43]	April 2005	—	—	Belgium (2), France (12), Italy (4), Portugal (4), Romania (1), Spain (1), Turkey (1)	Belgium (1), France (1), Portugal (1), Sweden (1)	Civilian police: 25 Civilian staff: 4[44]	—
EU Advisory and Assistance Mission for DRC Security Reform (EUSEC RD CONGO)	Democratic Republic of the Congo	2 May 2005 (Council Joint Action 2005/355/CFSP)[45]	June 2005	—	—	—	Austria (2), Belgium (14), Cyprus (1), France (14), Germany (1), Italy (1), Luxembourg (1), Netherlands (1), Portugal (3), Sweden (2), UK (2)	Civilian staff: 46[46]	—

Mission	Location	Legal basis	Start				Contributing states		Strength
								Civilian staff:	
EU Border Assistance Mission for the Rafah Crossing Point (EU BAM Rafah)	Rafah Crossing Point	31 December 2005 (Council Joint Action 2005/889/CFSP)[47]	October 2003	—	—	—	Belgium (3), Denmark (2), Finland (3), France (5), Germany (3), Greece (2), Italy (10), Netherlands (2), Portugal (2), Romania (2), Spain (6), Sweden (3)	Estonia (1), Germany (1), Italy (4), Portugal, Spain (3), UK (1)	Civilian police: 44 Civilian staff: 10
EU Police Mission for the Palestinian Territories (EUPOL COPPS)	Palestinian Territory[48]	14 November 2005 (Council Joint Action 2005/797/CFSP)[49]	January 2006	—	—	—	Austria (1), Belgium (1), Finland (1), France (1), Germany (1), Italy (1), Sweden (2), UK (3)	—	Civilian police: 11[50]

41. At the request of the Bosnian authorities, the EU modified the mandate (including the size) of the mission, now focusing on combating major and organized crime, and extended it to the end of 2007 (CJA 2005/824/CFSP, 24 November 2005).

42. The figure includes seconded and contracted international staff. The mission is further supported by 219 locally recruited staff.

43. EUPOL Kinshasa was established as a follow on to the Integrated Police Unit (IPU) and was mandated to monitor, mentor and advise the Congolese police force. The mission closed on 30 June 2007.

44. The mission was supported by 9 locally recruited staff.

45. EUSEC DR Congo was established to complement EUPOL Kinshasa and contribute to security sector reforms in DRC. In 2007 the EU Council revised the mission's mandate to assist in the integration, restructuring and rebuilding of the Congolese army, provide technical assistance, and supervise EU projects and identify new ones. In carrying out its activities, EUSEC closely operates with the recently established EUPOL RD Congo and MONUC. The mission's mandate lasts until 30 June 2008 (CJA/406/CFSP, 12 June 2007).

46. The majority of the deployed personnel are military advisers. Of the 46, 28 are based in Kinshasa while 18 are located in the eastern parts of the DR Congo. In addition, the mission is supported by 36 locally recruited staff.

47. EU BAM Rafah was established on the basis of the Agreement on Movement and Access between Israel and the Palestinian Authority (15 November 2005). It is mandated to monitor, verify and evaluate the performance of the Palestinian Authority border control, security and customs officials at the Rafah Crossing Point with regard to the 2005 Agreed Principles for Rafah Crossing; and support the Palestinian Authority's capacity building in the field of border control. The mandate was extended until 24 May 2008 (CJA/2007/359/CFSP, 23 May 2007). On 9 June 2007 the Rafah Crossing Point closed following riots in the Gaza Strip. The mission maintains full operational capability.

48. The mission's headquarters are located in Ramallah with two field offices in the West Bank and in Gaza.

49. EUPOL COPPS is mandated to provide a framework for and advise Palestinian criminal justice and police officials and coordinate EU aid to the Palestinian Authority. The mission's 3-year mandate runs until 31 December 2008.

50. The figure includes an unspecified number of civilian experts. The mission is supported by 5 locally recruited staff. In October 2006 the mission will be reinforced, reaching its authorized strength.

continues

6.11 Continued

Name	Location	Authorization Date	Start Date	Principal Troop Contributors	Principal Military Observer Contributors	Principal Civilian Police Contributors	Principal Civilian Staff Contributors	Troops, Military Observers, Civilian Police, Civilian Staff (Actual)	Total Deaths to Date/in 2007 (due to: hostilities, accidents, illness)
Police Mission in Afghanistan (EUPOL Afghanistan)	Afghanistan[51]	30 May 2007 (Council Joint Action 2007/369/CFSP)[52]	June 2007	—	—	Belgium (1), Bulgaria (1), Croatia (2), Denmark (1), Finland (7), France (1), Germany (35), Ireland (2), Italy (4), Lithuania (3), Netherlands (1), Norway (1), Spain (1), Sweden (2), UK (5)	—	Civilian police: 70[53]	—
EU Police Mission in the Democratic Republic of the Congo (EUPOL RD Congo)	Democratic Republic of the Congo	12 June 2007 (Council Joint Action 2007/405/CFSP)[54]	July 2007	—	—	Belgium (3), France(7), Italy (3), Portugal (8), Romania (1), Spain (1)	Belgium (1), Finland (1), France (3), Germany (1), Portugal (1), Sweden (2)	Civilian police: 23 Civilian staff: 9[55]	—
OAS Special Mission for Strengthening Democracy in Haiti	Port-Au-Prince, Haiti	16 January 2002 (Permanent Council Decision CP/RES. 806)[56]	June 2004	—	—	N/A	N/A	Civilian police: 2 Civilian staff: 22	1/—
OSCE Spillover Monitor Mission to Skopje	Former Yugoslav Republic of Macedonia	18 September 1992 (16th Committee of Senior Officials)[57]	September 1992	—	—	—	Austria (2), France (2), Georgia (2), Germany (6), Hungary (2), Italy (8), Norway (2), Romania (2),	Civilian staff: 69[58]	1/1 (–, –, 1)

			Slovenia (2), Spain (6), Sweden (2), Turkey (4), UK (5), Ukraine (3), USA (7)	
OSCE Mission to Georgia	6 November 1992 (17th Committee of Senior Officials)[59]	December 1992	—	Austria (1), Bulgaria (4), Canada (1), Czech Republic (2), Estonia (1), France (4), Germany (2), Hungary (2), Poland (2), Romania (1), Russia (1), Slovakia (1), Spain (1), UK (3), Ukraine (1), USA (2)	—	Civilian staff: 2960[60]	—

51. The mission's personnel are deployed at central, regional and provincial levels.

52. EUPOL Afghanistan was established on the invitation of the Government of Afghanistan. The mission is tasked to strengthen the rule of law by improving civil policing and law enforcement under Afghan ownership. The mission has a 3-year mandate, which terminates 30 May 2010.

53. The mission is supported by 25 locally recruited staff.

54. EUPOL RD Congo was established as a follow-on mission to EUPOL Kinshasa. The mission, supporting overall security sector reforms in DR Congo, is tasked to assist the Congolese authorities in the reform process of the Police Nationale Congolaise (PNC) and in improving the functioning of the criminal justice system. EUPOL RD Congo closely cooperates with EUSEC RD Congo. The mission is mandated until 30 June 2008 (CJA 2007/405/CFSP, 12 June 2007).

55. The mission is supported by 9 locally recruited staff.

56. The OAS Special Mission for Strengthening Democracy in Haiti was established by OAS PC resolution CP/RES. 806 (1303/02) of 16 January 2002. It is mandated to contribute to resolution of the political crisis in Haiti, including by assisting the Government of Haiti to strengthen its democratic processes and institutions. OAS General Assembly Resolution A/RES 2058 (XXXIV-O/04) of 8 June 2004 amended the mandate to include assistance in the holding of elections, promoting and protecting human rights, and the professionalization of the Haitian National Police.

57. The OSCE Spillover Monitor Mission to Skopje was authorized by the FYROM Government through Articles of Understanding agreed by an exchange of letters, in November 1992. Its tasks include monitoring, police training, development and other activities related to the 1992 Ohrid Framework Agreement. PC.DEC/764 (14 December 2006) extended the mandate until 31 December 2007.

58. The mission is supported by five international contracted staff (Canada/Croatia/Bosnia and Herzegovina, Russia) and 188 locally recruited staff.

59. The OSCE Mission to Georgia was authorized by the Government of Georgia through an MOU of 23 January 1993 and by South Ossetia's leaders through an exchange of letters on 1 March 1993. Its initial objective was to promote negotiations between the conflicting parties. The mandate was expanded at the 14th PC Meeting (29 March 1994) to include monitoring the Joint Peacekeeping Forces in South Ossetia. PC.DEC/450 (13 December 1999) expanded the mandate to include monitoring Georgia's borders with the Russian Republic of Ingushetia. PC.DEC/522 (19 December 2002) expanded the mandate to include observing and reporting on cross-border movement between Georgia and the Russian Republic of Dagestan. PC.DEC/766 (14 December 2006) extended the mandate until 31 December 2007.

60. In addition, seven international contracted staff (Poland, Czech Republic, Ukraine, Bosnia and Herzegovina, Hungary, Germany) and 154 locally recruited staff are supporting the mission.

continues

6.11 Continued

Name	Location	Authorization Date	Start Date	Principal Troop Contributors	Principal Military Observer Contributors	Principal Civilian Police Contributors	Principal Civilian Staff Contributors	Troops, Military Observers, Civilian Police, Civilian Staff (Actual)	Total Deaths to Date/in 2007 (due to: hostilities, accidents, illness)
OSCE Mission to Moldova	Moldova	4 February 1993 (19th Committee of Senior Officials)[61]	April 1993	—	—	—	Belarus, Estonia (1), France (2), Germany (2), Norway (1), Poland (2), UK (1), USA (2)	Civilian staff: 12[62]	—
OSCE Centre in Dushanbe	Dushanbe, Tajikistan	1 December 1993 (Rome Ministerial Council Decision)[63]	February 1994	—	—	—	Bulgaria (1), Denmark (1), Germany (1), Italy (3), Lithuania (1), Norway (1), Russia (1), UK (2), Ukraine (1), USA (2)	Civilian staff: 14[64]	2/2 (-, 2, -)
OSCE Mission to Bosnia and Herzegovina	Bosnia and Herzegovina[65]	8 December 1995 (5th Meeting of the Ministerial Council)[66]	December 1995	—	—	—	Austria (3), Azerbaijan (2), Belgium (2), Bulgaria (2), Finland (2), France (7), Germany (4),	Civilian staff: 76[67]	—

Mission				Participating states	Civilian staff
				Ireland (2), Italy (11), Netherlands (3), Norway (1), Russia (5), Slovakia (2), Slovenia (1), Spain (2), Sweden (3), UK (2), USA (13)	
OSCE Mission in Kosovo (OMIK)	1 July 1999 (PC.DEC/305, 1 July 1999)[69]	July 1999	—	—	—
				Austria (12), Bosnia and Herzegovina (6), Canada (6), France (9),Germany (26), Greece (6), Italy (22), Netherlands (6), Poland (6), Romania (6), Spain (17), Sweden (7), USA (29)	Civilian staff: 207[70] 9/2 (-, 1, 1)
	Kosovo, Serbia[68]				

61. The OSCE Mission to Moldova was authorized by the Government of Moldova through an MOU (7 May 1993). Its tasks include assisting the conflicting parties in pursuing negotiations on a lasting political settlement and gathering and providing information on the situation. PC.DEC/763 (14 December 2006) extended the mandate until 31 December 2007.

62. Besides, one international contracted staff (Czech Republic), the mission is supported by 34 locally recruited staff.

63. The OSCE Centre in Dushanbe was established by a decision taken at the 4th meeting of the OSCE Ministerial Council, CSCE/4-C/December 1, Decision I.4 (1 December 1993). No bilateral MOU has been signed. The mission's mandate includes facilitating dialogue, promoting human rights and informing the OSCE about further developments. This was expanded in 2002 to include an economic and environmental dimension. PC.DEC/754 (23 November 2006) extended the mandate until 31 December 2007.

64. The mission is supported by two international contracted staff (Russia/Romania) and 71 locally recruited staff.

65. Mission's headquarters are in Sarajevo with four regional centers located in Banja Luka, Sarajevo, Mostar, Tuzla and 20 field offices.

66. The OSCE Mission to Bosnia and Herzegovina was established by a decision of the 5th meeting of the Ministerial Council (MC(5).DEC/1, 8 December. 1995), in accordance with Annex 6 of the 1995 Dayton Agreement. The mission is mandated to assist the parties in regional stabilization measures and democracy building. PC.DEC/747 (23 November 2006) extended the mandate until 31 December 2007.

67. The mission is supported by nine international contracted and 532 locally recruited staff.

68. The mission headquarters are located in Pristina with five Regional Centers situated throughout Kosovo, each covering a number of five to nine municipalities. In addition, 30 Municipal Teams, supervising the work of local authorities, were deployed to all municipalities as well as three pilot municipal units.

69. The OSCE Mission in Kosovo was established by the PC.DEC/305 (1 July 1999). Its mandate includes training police, judicial personnel and civil administrators and monitoring and promoting human rights. The mission is a component (pillar III) of UNMIK. PC.DEC/765 (14 December 2006) extended the mandate until 31 December 2007.

70. In addition 38 international contracted staff and 695 locally recruited staff are supporting the mission.

6.12 Cost of Non-UN Military, Observer, Civilian Police and Civilian Missions: October 2006–September 2007

Name	Location	Cost ($US Millions)
Non-UN Military and Observer Missions		
African Union Mission in Sudan (AMIS)	Darfur, Sudan	280.8
African Union Mission in Somalia (AMISOM)	Somalia	—
African Union Electoral and Security Assistance Mission to the Comoros (MAES)	Comoros	—
CEMAC Multinational force in the Central African Republic (FOMUC)	Central African Republic	12.5
Joint Control Commission Peacekeeping Force	Moldova-Trandniester	—
South Ossetia Joint Force	South Ossetia Georgia	—
CIS Peacekeeping Forces in Georgia	Abkhazia-Georgia	—
EU Military Operation in Bosnia and Herzegovina (EUFOR ALTHEA)	Bosnia and Herzegovina	44.7
EUFOR TCHAD/RCA	Chad and the Central African Republic	—
EU Monitoring Mission (EUMM)	Western Balkans	2.9
NATO Kosovo Force (KFOR)	Kosovo, Serbia	35.3
International Security Assistance Force (ISAF)	Afghanistan	176.5
NATO Training Mission in Iraq (NTM-I)	Iraq	21.6
Multinational Force and Observers (MFO)	Sinai, Egypt	65.0
Temporary International Presence in Hebron (TIPH 2)	Hebron	2.3
International Monitoring Team (IMT)	Philippines	—
Sri Lanka Monitoring Mission (SLMM)	Sri Lanka	7.4
Operation Licorne	Côte d'Ivoire	334.5
Regional Assistance Mission in the Solomon Islands (RAMSI)	Solomon Islands	107.0
Multi National Force in Iraq (MNF-I)	Iraq	107,000.0
International Security Forces (ISF)	Timor-Leste	87.4
Non-UN Civilian Police and Civilian Missions		
OAS Special Mission for Strengthening Democracy in Haiti	Haiti	—
OSCE Spillover Monitor Mission to Skopje	Former Yugoslav Republic of Macedonia	13.2
OSCE Mission to Bosnia and Herzegovina	Bosnia and Herzegovina	22.2
OSCE Mission in Kosovo (OMIK)	Kosovo, Serbia	43.1
OSCE Centre in Dushanbe	Tajikistan	5.2
OSCE Mission to Moldova	Moldova	2.41
OSCE Mission to Georgia	Georgia	14.0
EU Police Mission in Bosnia and Herzegovina (EUPM)	Bosnia and Herzegovina	16.1
EU Police Mission in Kinshasa (EUPOL Kinshasa)	Kinshasa, Democratic Republic of the Congo	4.3
EU Advisory and Assistance Mission for DRC Security Reform (EUSEC RD CONGO)	Democratic Republic of the Congo	8.0
EU Border Assistance Mission for the Rafah Crossing Point (EU BAM Rafah)	Rafah Crossing Point	14.0
EU Police Mission for the Palestinian Territories (EUPOL COPPS)	Palestinian Territories	4.8
EU Police Mission in Afghanistan (EUPOL Afghanistan)	Afghanistan	17.6
EU Police Mission in the Democratic Republic of the Congo (EUPOL RD Congo)	Democratic Republic of the Congo	1.8

6.13 Heads of Non-UN Military, Observer, Civilian Police and Civilian Missions: September 2007

Name	Location	Head of Mission
Non-UN Military and Observer Missions		
African Union Mission in Sudan (AMIS)	Darfur, Sudan	Rodolphe Adada (DR Congo)
African Union Mission in Somalia (AMISOM)	Somalia	Maj. Gen. Levy Karuhanga (Uganda)
African Union Electoral and Security Assistance Mission to the Comoros (MAES)	Comoros	Francisco Madeira (Mozambique)
CEMAC Multinational Force in the Central African Republic (FOMUC)	Central African Republic	Gen. Brig. Auguste Roger Bibaye Itandas (Gabon)
Joint Control Commission Peacekeeping Force	Moldova-Transdniester	Col. Anatoly Zverev (Russia)
South Ossetia Joint Force	South Ossetia Georgia	Maj. Gen. Marat Kulakhmetov (Russia)
CIS Peacekeeping Forces in Georgia	Abkhazia-Georgia	Maj. Gen. Sergey Chaban (Russia)
EU Military Operation in Bosnia and Herzegovina (EUFOR ALTHEA)	Bosnia and Herzegovina	Rear Admiral Hans-Jochen Witthauer (Germany)
EUFOR TCHAD/RCA	Chad and the Central African Republic	Lt. Gen. Patrick Nash (Ireland)
EU Monitoring Mission (EUMM)	Western Balkans	Maryse Daviet (France)
NATO Kosovo Force (KFOR)	Kosovo, Serbia	Lt. Gen. Xavier de Marnhac (France)
International Security Assistance Force (ISAF)	Afghanistan	Gen. Dan K. McNeill (USA)
NATO Training Mission in Iraq (NTM-I)	Iraq	Lt. Gen. James Dubik (USA)
Multinational Force and Observers (MFO)	Sinai, Egypt	Amb. James A. Larocco (USA)
Temporary International Presence in Hebron (TIPH 2)	Hebron	Karl-Henrik Sjursen (Norway)
International Monitoring Team (IMT)	Philippines	Maj. Gen. Datuk Mat Yasin bin Mat Daud (Malaysia)
Sri Lanka Monitoring Mission (SLMM)	Sri Lanka	Maj. Gen. Lars Johan Sølvberg (Norway)
Operation Licorne	Côte d'Ivoire	Gen. Bruno Clément-Bollée (France)
Regional Assistance Mission in the Solomon Islands (RAMSI)	Solomon Islands	Tim George (Australia)
Multinational Force in Iraq (MNF-I)	Iraq	Gen. David H. Petraeus (USA)
International Security Forces (ISF)	Timor-Leste	Brig. John Hutcheson (Australia)
Non-UN Civilian Police and Civilian Missions		
OAS Special Mission for Strengthening Democracy in Haiti	Haiti	Arthur Gray (Trinidad and Tobago)
OSCE Spillover Monitor Mission to Skopje	Former Yugoslav Republic of Macedonia	Amb. Giorgio Radicati (Italy)
OSCE Mission to Bosnia and Herzegovina	Bosnia and Herzegovina	Amb. Douglas Alexander Davidsson (USA)
OSCE Mission in Kosovo (OMIK)	Kosovo, Serbia and Montenegro	Amb. Werner Wnendt (Germany)
OSCE Centre in Dushanbe	Tajikistan	Amb. Vladimir Pryakhin (Russia)
OSCE Mission to Moldova	Moldova	Amb. Louis F. O'Neill (USA)
OSCE Mission to Georgia	Georgia	Amb. Terhi Hakala (Finland)
EU Police Mission in Bosnia and Herzegovina (EUPM)	Bosnia and Herzegovina	Brig. Gen. Vincenzo Coppola (Italy)
EU Police Mission in Kinshasa (EUPOL Kinshasa)	Kinshasa, Democratic Republic of the Congo	Adilio Custodio (Portugal)

continues

6.13 Continued

Name	Location	Head of Mission
EU Advisory and Assistance Mission for DRC Security Reform (EUSEC RD CONGO)	Democratic Republic of the Congo	Gen. Pierre-Michel Joana (Italy)
EU Border Assistance Mission for the Rafah Crossing Point (EU BAM Rafah)	Rafah Crossing Point	Maj. Gen. Pietro Pistolese (Italy)
EU Police Mission for the Palestinian Territories (EUPOL COPPS)	Palestinian Territories	Colin Smith (United Kingdom)
EU Police Mission in Afghanistan (EUPOL Afghanistan)	Afghanistan	Jürgen Scholz (Germany)
EU Police Mission in the Democratic Republic of the Congo (EUPOL RD Congo)	Democratic Republic of the Congo	Adilio Custodio (Portugal)

7 UN Mission-by-Mission Statistics

This chapter contains data on all current missions of the UN Department of Peacekeeping Operations (DPKO), as well as some Department of Political Affairs (DPA) missions supported by DPKO. It is based on public UN documents and sources, combined with data provided by DPKO and in some cases by the UN Department of Management (DM).

Variations in types of data sources and reporting dates between missions are often a result of differences in the structure, reporting and funding mechanisms for different types of UN peace operations:

- Peacekeeping missions funded by the General Assembly on the basis of a financial period running from 1 July to 30 June of the following year.
- Peacekeeping missions funded by the biennial UN budget, which runs from January in even years to December of odd years (UNMOGIP and UNTSO).
- Integrated missions, DPA political missions, and special political missions with a peacekeeping component supported by DPKO and funded through extrabudgetary resources, running on a single calendar-year basis (UNAMA, BINUB, UNAMI, UNIOSIL, UNMIN).

The features of our dataset are outlined below.

Key Facts
Notes on mandates and key personnel.

Personnel: July 2006–September 2007
These graphs cover personnel trends through the last UN peacekeeping financial year and through the first quarter of the 2006–2007 financial year on a month-by-month basis. Authorized military and police personnel strengths are based on authorized strengths in Security Council resolutions, relevant budgetary documentation, or were provided directly by the DPKO Force Generation Service (FGS) and the DPKO Police Division (PD). Actual military and personnel strengths were provided by the FGS and PD. Actual and authorized strengths for international staff and local staff were provided by the DPKO Personnel Management Support and Service (PMSS). United Nations Volunteer (UNV) actual and authorized strengths (based on exchange of letters and mission-specific agreements between UNV Programme and DPKO) were provided by the UNV Programme in Bonn.

Personnel: Since 2000
These graphs show average annual number of personnel and average annual number of authorized personnel since 2000 (up to June 2007 for missions funded by the peacekeeping budget and through September 2007 for other missions). For the July 2006–September 2007 period, actual military and police personnel figures were calculated based on information provided by the FGS or PD. Authorized military and police personnel figures were derived from Security Council Resolutions or obtained

from FGS and PD in cases where Security Council resolutions did not specify authorized strengths. International and local civilian staff actual and authorized strengths were calculated based on information provided by PMSS. UNV actual and authorized figures were provided by the UNV Programme.

Average actual and authorized figures for the January 2000–June 2007 period were obtained from official budgetary and financial performance reports covering that year, or from data collected directly from the relevant UN Departments for last year's edition of the *Review*. Exceptions include UNMOGIP and UNTSO, for which historical and actual personnel figures were derived from the UN's Proposed Programme Budget for the Biennium. Historical figures for UNAMA were obtained from the Reports of the Secretary-General on the Estimates in respect of special political missions, good offices and other political initiatives authorized by the General Assembly and/or Security Council. Historical military personnel figures for UNAMI are only available from DPKO on a regular monthly basis as of January 2006.

Military and Police Contributors: 30 September 2007

These data show all contributors to the mission on 30 September 2007, and were provided by the FGS and PD.

Military Units: 30 September 2007

These data show units in the field on the day in question by their type and country of origin, based on information provided by FGS. Military staff are not formed into traditional units in observer missions, political missions, and in the observer elements of larger missions; therefore these personnel are not recorded in this section.

International Civilian Personnel Occupations: 30 September 2007

These data, provided by PMSS, break down international civilian staff into occupational groups, as provided by PMSS.

Gender Statistics: 30 September 2007

These data show the total number of male and female troops, military observers, police, international staff, and local staff as of that date. Military data were provided by FGS, police data were provided by PD, and international and local staff data were provided by PMSS. Data for UNVs were not available.

Fatalities: Inception–September 2007

These data were provided by the DPKO Situation Center. Differences may exist between the historical data shown here and fatality data shown in last year's edition of the *Review* due to investigations and reviews of fatality reports undertaken by the Situation Center over the course of the year. Fatality incident types previously categorized as "hostile act" and "criminal act" have henceforth been combined into a single category—"malicious act." Fatality incident types previously categorized as "self-inflicted" have henceforth been combined into the "other" category.

Vehicles: 30 September 2007

These data cover both UN-owned vehicles and those vehicles owned by national contingents serving in the field under a Memorandum of Agreement and for which usage is reimbursed by the UN. Data on contingent-owned vehicles are obtained from a database managed by the DPKO Contingent Owned Equipment and Management Section. The following missions do not have Contingent Owned Equipment: BINUB, MINURSO, UNAMA, UNIOSIL, UNMIN, UNMOGIP and UNTSO. Data for UN-owned vehicles were provided by the DPKO Surface Transport Division.

Aircraft: 30 September 2007

These data have been provided by the DPKO Air Transport Section and identify aircraft by their type (transport fixed-wing, transport helicopter or attack helicopter) and supplier (commercial or government). The following missions do not have aircraft: UNAMI, UNDOF, UNMIK, UNMOGIP and UNTSO.

Budget and Expenditures: 2006–2008
All 2006–2008 data were provided by the DPKO Finance Management and Support Service (FMSS).

Peacekeeping missions funded by the peacekeeping budget show budget and expenditure data for the 2006–2007 financial year as well as the budget for the 2007–2008 financial year. The 2006–2007 budgets for UNMIT and UNIFIL include additional funds allotted through commitment authority as of mid-November 2006.

Peacekeeping missions funded from the regular biennial budget (UNTSO, UNMOGIP): these data show both the allotment and expenditures for the 1 January 2006–31 December 2007 period. Budgets for the 1 January 2008–31 December 2009 period were not available as of the date of publication.

Political/Special Political Missions (BINUB, UNAMA, UNAMI, UNIOSIL, UNMIN): these data show the appropriations and estimated expenditures for the 1 January 2006–31 December 2007 period, as well as allotted resources for the 2008 calendar year. Resources for the 2008 calendar year were not available for BINUB, UNMIN or UNIOSIL as of the date of publication. The 2006–2007 budget for BINUB includes additional funds allotted through commitment authority as of mid-March 2007. Detailed budget data was not available for UNMIN as of the date of publication.

Mission Expenditures: 2000–2006
Covering the financial years since 2000, this overview of expenditures has been derived from mission financing reports, financial performance reports, and reports on mission budgets. Information on UNAMA, UNMOGIP, and UNTSO has been provided by FMSS. Some discrepancies may appear between the 2005–2006 data provided here, which is derived from official performance reports on the budget, and those data provided in last year's edition of the *Review,* which

were provided by the FMSS prior to the publication of official performance reports. The mission expenditure tables for peacekeeping missions funded by the peacekeeping budget are broken down into the three following categories (although there was some variation in subcategories in 2000–2001[1]):

1. *Military and police personnel.* Includes missions' subsistence allowance, travel on emplacement, rotation and repatriation, death and disability compensation, rations and clothing allowances for military observers and police. This section also includes expenditures on major contingent-owned equipment and freight and deployment of contingent-owned equipment.

2. *Civilian personnel.* Covers salaries, staff assessment, common staff costs, hazardous duty stations allowances and overtime for international and local staff, as well as covers costs associated with United Nations Volunteers.

3. *Operational requirements.* Costs associated with general temporary assistance (salaries, common staff costs, staff assessment), government-provided personnel and civilian electoral observers (allowances and travel), consultants, official travel of civilian personnel, facilities and infrastructure, as well as self-sustainment costs of contingent-owned equipment. Also included are costs associated with ground, air, and naval transportation in mission, communications, IT, medical, special equipment, other supplies, services and equipment and quick impact projects.

Expenditures on Contingent Owned Equipment: July 2006–June 2007
These data, supplied by FMSS, cover contingents' expenditures on major equipment for which they can be reimbursed by the UN as well as self-sustainment (rations, etc.) for those missions financed by the peacekeeping budget. The following missions do not have Contingent Owned Equipment: BINUB, MINURSO, UNAMA, UNIOSIL, UNMIN, UNMOGIP and UNTSO. Data for UNAMI Contingent Owned Equipment are not available.

Voluntary Contributions:
July 2006–June 2007
These data cover those countries and organizations providing financial support to missions other than through assessed contributions. They are provided by the UN Department of Management's Office of Programme Planning, Budget and Accounts (OPPBA). The following missions do not have voluntary contributions: BINUB, MINUSTAH, UNAMA, UNAMI, UNDOF, UNIFIL, UNMEE, UNMIK, UNMIN, UNMIS, UNOCI, UNMOGIP, UNOMIG and UNTSO.

Note

1. Prior to the July 2001–June 2002 financial year, "Staff Assessment" was reported as an additional line item in "Gross Expenditures" for each mission. Since then, staff assessment has been included as part of the "Civilian Personnel" line item. For the sake of consistency, figures for the 2000–2001 financial years are shown using the current financial reporting method and include staff assessment expenditures as part of the civilian personnel expenditures. For those years, civilian personnel expenditures will thus appear to be higher than in the official UN financial reports.

7.1 BINUB (UN Integrated Office in Burundi)

BINUB Key Facts

Latest Key Resolution	19 December 2007 (date of issue); 1 January 2008 (date of effect) UNSC Res. 1791 (twelve month duration)
First Mandate	25 October 2006 (date of issue); 1 January 2007 (date of effect) UNSC Res. 1719 (twelve month duration)
ERSG	Youssef Mahmoud (Tunisia) SG letter of appointment 18 December 2006 Entry on duty 1 January 2007

BINUB Personnel: January 2007–September 2007

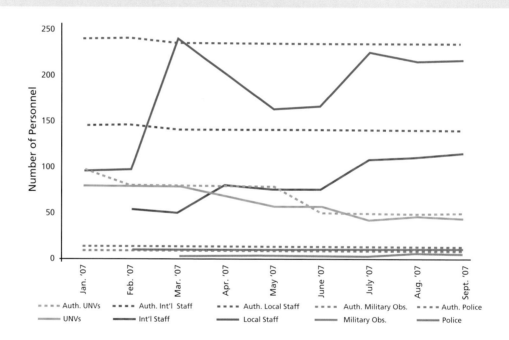

Sources: UN Document S/RES/1719; DPKO FGS; DPKO PD; DPKO PMSS; UNV Programme.

BINUB Military and Police Contributors: 30 September 2007

Contributing Country	Troops	Military Observers	Police	Total
Benin	—	—	2	2
Burkina Faso	—	—	2	2
Cameroon	—	—	2	2
Côte d'Ivoire	—	—	2	2
Madagascar	—	—	2	2
Turkey	—	—	2	2
Bangladesh	—	1	—	1
Netherlands	—	1	—	1
Nigeria	—	1	—	1
Pakistan	—	1	—	1
South Africa	—	1	—	1
Tunisia	—	1	—	1
Total	**—**	**6**	**12**	**18**

Sources: DPKO FGS; DPKO PD.

BINUB International Civilian Personnel Occupations: 30 September 2007

Occupation	International Staff	Percentage International Staff
Administration	21	18.1%
Aviation	—	—
Civil Affairs	—	—
Economic Affairs	—	—
Engineering	4	3.4%
Finance	6	5.2%
Human Resources	6	5.2%
Human Rights	9	7.8%
Humanitarian Affairs	—	—
Information Management	1	—
Information Systems and Technology	7	6.0%
Legal Affairs	—	—
Logistics	9	7.8%
Medical Services	3	2.6%
Political Affairs	8	6.9%
Procurement	4	3.4%
Programme Management	4	3.4%
Public Information	3	2.6%
Rule of Law	—	—
Security	25	21.6%
Social Affairs	2	1.7%
Transport	4	3.4%
Total	**116**	

Source: DPKO PMSS.

BINUB Personnel Gender Statistics: 30 September 2007

Personnel Type	Male	Female	Percentage Male	Percentage Female
Troops	—	—	—	—
Military Observers	6	—	100.0%	—
Police	11	1	91.7%	8.3%
International Civilian Staff	79	37	68.1%	31.9%
Local Civilian Staff	146	71	67.3%	32.7%
Total	**242**	**109**	**68.9%**	**31.1%**

Sources: DPKO FGS; DPKO PD; DPKO PMSS.

BINUB Fatalities: Inception–September 2007

	Personnel Type						
Time Period	Troop	MilOb	Police	Intl Staff	Local Staff	Other[a]	Total
2007 (Jan-Sep)	—	—	—	—	—	—	—
January-March	—	—	—	—	—	—	—
April-June	—	—	—	—	—	—	—
July-September	—	—	—	—	—	—	—
Total Fatalities	—	—	—	—	—	—	—

	Incident Type			
Time Period	Malicious Act	Illness	Accident	Other[b]	Total
2007 (Jan-Sep)	—	—	—	—	—
January-March	—	—	—	—	—
April-June	—	—	—	—	—
July-September	—	—	—	—	—
Total Fatalities	—	—	—	—	—

Source: DPKO Situation Centre.
Notes: a. Other refers to consultants, UNVs, etc.
  b. Incident type is unknown, uncertain, or under investigation. Other includes what were previously qualified as self-inflicted.

BINUB Vehicles: 30 September 2007

UN Owned Vehicles

Vehicle Type	Quantity
4x4 Vehicles	132
Ambulances	4
Automobiles	2
Buses	21
Material Handling Equipment	17
Trailers	4
Trucks	20
Vans	4
Total	**204**

Source: DPKO Surface Transport Section.

BINUB Aircraft: 30 September 2007

	Transport Fixed Wing	Transport Helicopter	Attack Helicopter
Commercial	—	1	—
Contingent Owned	—	—	—
Total	—	**1**	—

Source: DPKO Air Transport Section.

BINUB Budget and Expenditures (in thousands of US dollars)

Category	Appropriations Jan 06–Dec 07	Estimated Expenditure 2007
Military Observers	293.3	186.7
Military Contingents	—	—
Civilian Police	632.8	623.2
Formed Police Units	—	—
International Staff	15,698.0	12,762.3
Local Staff	2,864.4	3,290.3
United Nations Volunteers	1,823.7	1,650.2
General Temporary Assistance	—	—
Government-provided Personnel	—	—
Civilian Electoral Observers	—	—
Consultants	85.7	0.5
Official Travel	514.1	293.6
Facilities and Infrastructure	5,401.5	1,016.5
Ground Transportation	627.6	7.6
Air Transportation	2,403.6	1,742.3
Naval Transportation	—	—
Communications and Information Technology	2,204.3	(26.6)
Supplies, Services and Equipment	531.4	85.3
Quick-impact Projects	—	—
Gross Requirements	**35,227.5**	**21,631.9**
Staff Assessment Income	2,147.1	(2,528.9)
Net Requirements	**33,080.4**	**19,103.0**
Voluntary Contributions in Kind (budgeted)	—	—
Total Requirements	**33,080.4**	**21,631.9**

Source: DPKO FMSS.
Note: Financial figures are preliminary and subject to change.

7.2 MINURSO (UN Mission for the Referendum in Western Sahara)

MINURSO Key Facts

Latest Key Resolutions	31 October 2007 (date of issue and effect) UNSC Res. 1783 (six month duration) 30 April 2007 (date of issue and effect) UNSC Res. 1754 (six month duration)
First Mandate	29 April 1991 (date of issue and effect) UNSC Res. 690 (no determined duration)
SRSG	Julian Harston (United Kingdom) SG letter of appointment 31 January 2007 Entry on duty 31 January 2007
First SRSG	Johannes Manz (Switzerland)
Force Commander	Major-General Zhao Jingmin (China) SG letter of appointment 22 August 2007 Entry on duty 27 August 2007
First Force Commander	Major-General Armand Roy (Canada)

MINURSO Personnel: July 2006–September 2007

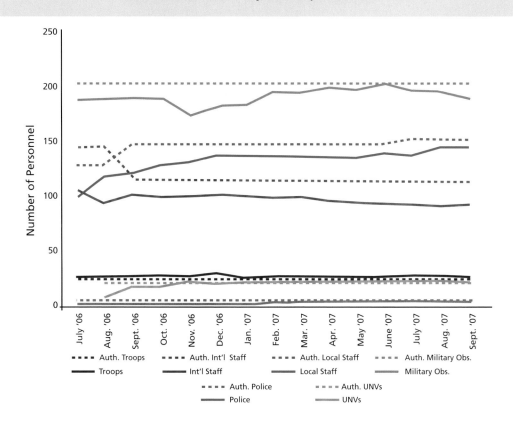

Sources: DPKO FGS; DPKO PD; DPKO PMSS; UNV Programme.
Note: Above figures do not include government provided personnel.

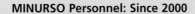

MINURSO Personnel: Since 2000

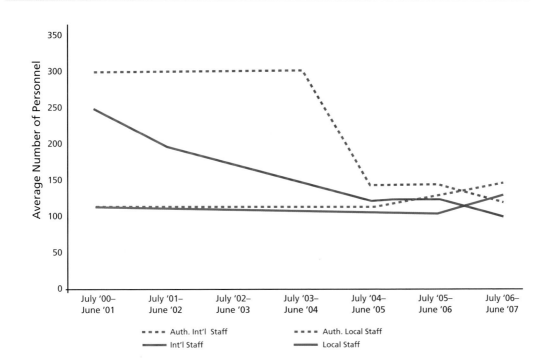

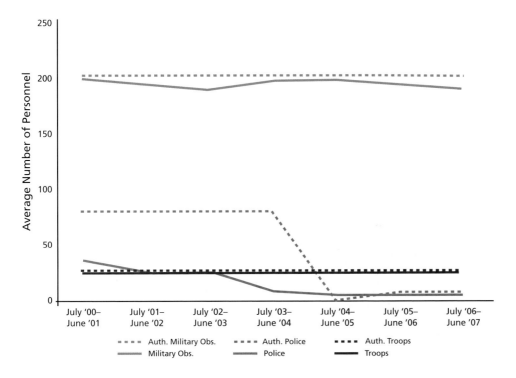

Sources: UN Documents A/56/818, A/57/674, A/58/642, A/59/619, A/60/634 and A/61/683; DPKO FGS; DPKO PD; DPKO PMSS; UNV Programme.
Note: Above figures do not include government-provided personnel.

MINURSO Military and Police Contributors: 30 September 2007

Contributing Country	Troops	Military Observers	Police	Total	Contributing Country	Troops	Military Observers	Police	Total
Malaysia	20	12	—	32	Italy	—	5	—	5
Russia	—	25	—	25	Kenya	—	5	—	5
Egypt	—	20	3	23	Nigeria	—	4	—	4
Ghana	7	9	—	16	Republic of Guinea	—	4	—	4
France	—	15	—	15	Ireland	—	3	—	3
China	1	13	—	14	Mongolia	—	3	—	3
Honduras	—	12	—	12	Austria	—	2	—	2
El Salvador	—	6	3	9	Djibouti	—	2	—	2
Bangladesh	—	8	—	8	Sri Lanka	—	2	—	2
Uruguay	—	8	—	8	Argentina	—	1	—	1
Croatia	—	7	—	7	Denmark	—	1	—	1
Pakistan	—	7	—	7	Greece	—	1	—	1
Hungary	—	7	—	7	Poland	—	1	—	1
Yemen	—	6	—	6	**Total**	**28**	**189**	**6**	**223**

Sources: DPKO FGS; DPKO PD.

MINURSO Military Units: 30 September 2007

Number	Unit Type	Country
1	Advanced Level I Medical Unit	Malaysia

Source: DPKO FGS.
Note: Military headquarters staff, staff officers and military observers not included.

MINURSO International Civilian Personnel Occupations: 30 September 2007

Occupation	International Staff	Percentage International Staff
Administration	8	8.5%
Aviation	3	3.2%
Civil Affairs	—	—
Economic Affairs	—	—
Engineering	6	6.4%
Finance	6	6.4%
Human Resources	3	3.2%
Human Rights	—	—
Humanitarian Affairs	—	—
Information Management	1	1.1%
Information Systems and Technology	13	13.8%
Legal Affairs	2	2.1%
Logistics	14	14.9%
Medical Services	—	—
Political Affairs	3	3.2%
Procurement	5	5.3%
Programme Management	—	—
Public Information	2	2.1%
Rule of Law	2	2.1%
Security	9	9.6%
Social Affairs	—	—
Transport	17	18.1%
Total	**94**	

Source: DPKO PMSS.

MINURSO Personnel Gender Statistics: 30 September 2007

Personnel Type	Male	Female	Percentage Male	Percentage Female
Troops	22	6	78.6%	21.4%
Military Observers	187	2	98.9%	1.1%
Police	3	3	50.0%	50.0%
International Civilian Staff	78	16	83.0%	17.0%
Local Civilian Staff	118	27	81.4%	18.6%
Total	**408**	**54**	**88.3%**	**11.7%**

Sources: DPKO FGS; DPKO PD; DPKO PMSS.

MINURSO Fatalities: Inception–September 2007

Personnel Type

Time Period	Troop	MilOb	Police	Intl Staff	Local Staff	Other[a]	Total
1992–1999	5	1	1	2	2	—	11
2000	—	—	—	—	—	—	—
2001	—	—	—	—	1	—	1
2002	—	—	—	—	—	—	—
2003	—	—	—	—	—	—	—
2004	—	—	—	—	1	—	1
2005	—	—	—	—	1	—	1
2006	—	—	—	—	—	—	—
January-March	—	—	—	—	—	—	—
April-June	—	—	—	—	—	—	—
July-September	—	—	—	—	—	—	—
October-December	—	—	—	—	—	—	—
2007 (Jan-Sep)	—	—	—	1	—	—	1
January-March	—	—	—	—	—	—	—
April-June	—	—	—	—	—	—	—
July-September	—	—	—	1	—	—	1
Total Fatalities	**5**	**1**	**1**	**3**	**5**	**—**	**15**

Incident Type

Time Period	Malicious Act	Illness	Accident	Other[b]	Total
1992–1999	—	3	8	—	11
2000	—	—	—	—	—
2001	—	—	—	1	1
2002	—	—	—	—	—
2003	—	—	—	—	—
2004	—	—	1	—	1
2005	—	—	1	—	1
2006	—	—	—	—	—
January-March	—	—	—	—	—
April-June	—	—	—	—	—
July-September	—	—	—	—	—
October-December	—	—	—	—	—
2007 (Jan-Sep)	—	1	—	—	1
January-March	—	—	—	—	—
April-June	—	—	—	—	—
July-September	—	1	—	—	1
Total Fatalities	**—**	**4**	**10**	**1**	**15**

Source: DPKO Situation Centre.
Notes: a. Other refers to consultants, UNVs, etc.
   b. Incident type is unknown, uncertain or under investigation Other includes what were previously qualified as self-inflicted.

MINURSO Vehicles: 30 September 2007

UN Owned Vehicles

Vehicle Type	Quantity
4x4 Vehicles	291
Airfield Support Equipment	6
Ambulances	4
Automobiles	10
Buses	14
Engineering Vehicle	1
Material Handling Equipment	26
Trailers	33
Trucks	27
Total	**412**

Source: DPKO Surface Transport Section.

MINURSO Aircraft: 30 September 2007

	Transport Fixed Wing	Transport Helicopter	Attack Helicopter
Commercial	3	3	—
Contingent Owned	—	—	—
Total	**3**	**3**	—

Source: DPKO Air Transport Section.

MINURSO Budget and Expenditures (in thousands of US dollars)

Category	Budgeted Jul 06–Jun 07	Expenditures Jul 06–Jun 07	Budgeted Jul 07–Jun 08
Military Observers	5,598.2	6,764.5	6,457.4
Military Contingents	715.4	1,010.8	993.6
Civilian Police	165.1	172.2	207.6
Formed Police Units	—	—	—
International Staff	13,404.4	11,845.7	13,164.2
Local Staff	2,960.9	2,258.6	2,732.2
United Nations Volunteers	782.1	747.0	761.0
General Temporary Assistance	169.8	67.4	226.3
Government-provided Personnel	45.8	34.4	42.4
Civilian Electoral Observers	—		—
Consultants	3.0	—	26.4
Official Travel	336.2	360.9	402.7
Facilities and Infrastructure	2,843.7	4,559.4	4,020.4
Ground Transportation	1,555.0	2,078.5	2,953.0
Air Transportation	11,313.8	10,611.4	11,143.0
Naval Transportation	—	—	—
Communications and Information Technology	1,839.6	1,788.0	2,361.5
Supplies, Services and Equipment	886.4	2,179.6	2,145.5
Quick-impact Projects	—	—	—
Gross Requirements	**42,619.4**	**46,318.4**	**49,787.3**
Staff Assessment Income	2,206.4	—	2,100.4
Net Requirements	**40,413.0**	**46,318.4**	**47,686.9**
Voluntary Contributions in Kind (budgeted)	3,315.6	2,776.0	3,315.6
Total Requirements	**45,935.0**	**49,094.4**	**53,102.9**

Sources: UN Documents A/61/744, A/61/852/Add.3 and A/C.5/61/24; DPKO FMSS.
Notes: Financial figures are preliminary and subject to change. Gross requirements for July 2006–June 2007 expenditures include pro-rated costs of $1,840.0 thousand. Gross requirements for July 2007–June 2008 budgeted include pro-rated costs of $2,150.1 thousand.

MINURSO Voluntary Contributions: July 2006–June 2007 (in thousands of US dollars)

Contributor	Contributions in Kind (budgeted)	Contributions in Kind (non-budgeted)	Contributions in Cash (budgeted)	Total
Morocco	2,302.0	—	—	2,302.0
Algeria	438.0	—	—	438.0
Frente Polisario	36.0	—	—	36.0
Total	**2,776.0**	**—**	**—**	**2,776.0**

Source: DM OPPBA.

MINURSO Mission Expenditures: July 2000–June 2006 (in thousands of US dollars)

Category	Jul 00–Jun 01	Jul 01–Jun 02	Jul 02–Jun 03	Jul 03–Jun 04	Jul 04–Jun 05	Jul 05–Jun 06
Military and Police Personnel	7,144.0	6,344.7	6,214.8	6,495.3	6,373.5	6,217.6
Civilian Personnel	22,523.2	19,720.8	18,191.5	17,472.9	16,162.6	15,807.2
Operational Requirements	10,239.6	13,025.0	14,002.7	14,882.6	18,861.9	20,323.6
Other	2,309.1	—	—	—	—	—
Gross Requirements	**42,215.9**	**39,090.5**	**38,409.0**	**38,850.8**	**41,398.0**	**42,348.4**
Staff Assessment Income	3,773.4	2,751.3	2,636.2	2,442.8	2,311.9	2,191.5
Net Requirements	**38,442.5**	**36,339.2**	**35,772.8**	**36,408.0**	**39,086.1**	**40,156.9**
Voluntary Contributions in Kind (budgeted)	3,670.7	1,806.1	2,567.4	3,084.0	3,885.2	3,761.3
Total Requirements	**45,886.6**	**40,896.6**	**40,976.4**	**41,934.8**	**45,283.2**	**46,109.7**

Sources: UN Documents A/56/818, A/57/674, A/58/642, A/59/619, A/60/634 and A/61/683; DPKO FMSS.

7.3 MINUSTAH (UN Stabilization Mission in Haiti)

MINUSTAH Key Facts	
Latest Key Resolutions	15 October 2007 (date of issue and effect) UNSC Res. 1780 (twelve month duration) (note: reconfiguration of the mission including a decrease in authorized troops and increase in authorized police as per the Secretary General's report S/2007/503 of 22 August 2007) 15 February 2007 (date of issue and effect) UNSC Res. 1743 (eight month duration)
First Mandate	30 April 2004 (date of issue); 1 June 2004 (date of effect) UNSC Res. 1542 (six month duration)
SRSG and Head of Mission	Hédi Annabi (Tunisia) SG letter of appointment 26 July 2007 Entry on duty 1 September 2007
First SRSG	Juan Gabriel Valdés (Chile)
Force Commander	Major-General Carlos Alberto dos Santos Cruz (Brazil) SG letter of appointment 8 January 2007
First Force Commander	Lieutenant-General Augusto Heleno Ribeiro Pereira (Brazil)
Police Commissioner	Mamadou Mountaga Diallo (Republic of Guinea)

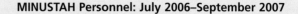

MINUSTAH Personnel: July 2006–September 2007

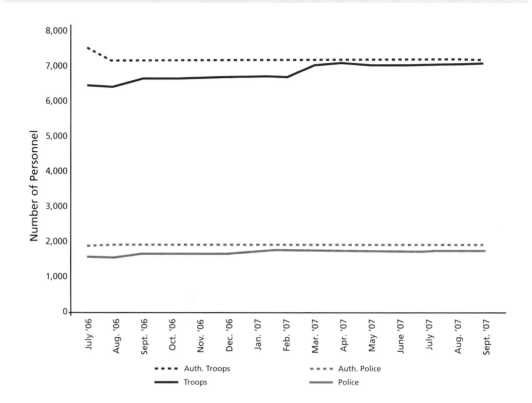

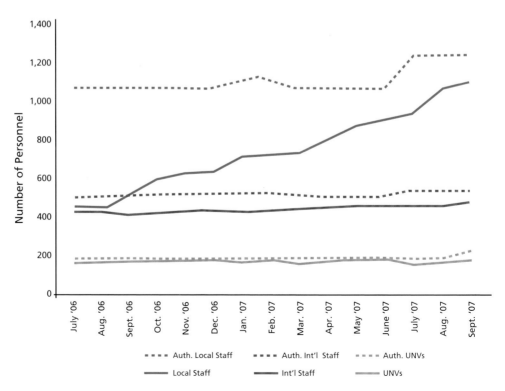

Sources: UN Document S/RES/1702; DPKO FGS; DPKO PD; DPKO PMSS; UNV Programme.

MINUSTAH Personnel: Since 2004

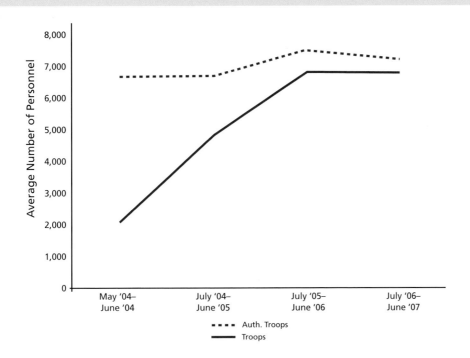

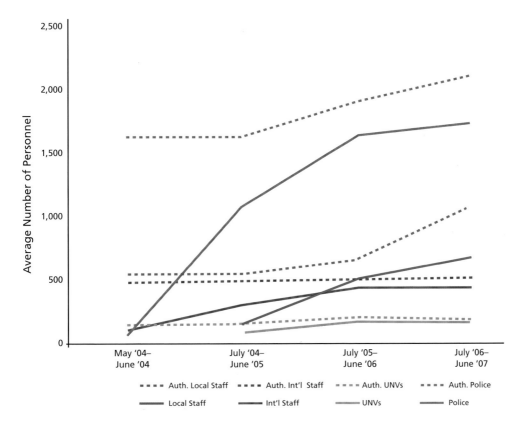

Sources: UN Documents S/RES/1542, S/RES/1608, S/RES/1702, A/60/646 and A/61/741; DPKO FGS; DPKO PD; DPKO PMSS; UNV Programme.

MINUSTAH Military and Police Contributors: 30 September 2007

Contributing Country	Troops	Military Observers	Police	Total	Contributing Country	Troops	Military Observers	Police	Total
Brazil	1,213	—	4	1,217	Benin	—	—	52	52
Nepal	1,109	—	146	1,255	Spain	—	—	39	39
Uruguay	1,148	—	4	1,152	Egypt	—	—	35	35
Jordan	755	—	292	1,047	Guinea	—	—	34	34
Sri Lanka	960	—	33	993	Paraguay	31	—	—	31
Argentina	562	—	4	566	Burkina Faso	—	—	28	28
Chile	501	—	13	514	Cameroon	—	—	27	27
Pakistan	1	—	249	250	Romania	—	—	25	25
Bolivia	217	—	—	217	Turkey	—	—	20	20
Peru	210	—	—	210	Rwanda	—	—	11	11
Philippines	157	—	13	170	Togo	—	—	11	11
Nigeria	—	—	131	131	Croatia	3	—	—	3
Senegal	—	—	131	131	Grenada	—	—	3	3
China	—	—	134	134	Russia	—	—	3	3
Guatemala	119	—	—	119	Columbia	—	—	2	2
France	2	—	74	76	Democratic Republic of Congo	—	—	2	2
Niger	—	—	76	76	El Salvador	—	—	2	2
Ecuador	67	—	—	67	Central African Republic	—	—	1	1
Canada	4	—	62	66	Chad	—	—	1	1
Mali	—	—	60	60	Madagascar	—	—	1	1
United States	3	—	50	53	Mauritius	—	—	1	1
					Total	**7,062**	**—**	**1,774**	**8,836**

Sources: DPKO FGS; DPKO PD.

Note: Police figures include formed police provided by China (125), Jordan (290), Nepal (125), Nigeria (125), Pakistan (249), and Senegal (85).

MINUSTAH Military Units: 30 September 2007

Number	Unit Type	Countries
2	Aviation Units	Argentina, Chile
2	Engineering Companies	Brazil, Chile-Ecuador Composite
1	Headquarters Company	Philippines
9	Infantry Battalions	Argentina, Brazil, Chile, Jordan, Nepal (2), Sri Lanka, Uruguay (2)
2	Infantry Companies	Bolivia, Peru
1	Level II Hospital	Argentina
1	Military Police Company	Guatemala
1	Platoon	Paraguay

Source: DPKO FGS.

Note: Military headquarters staff and staff officers not included.

MINUSTAH International Civilian Personnel Occupations: 30 September 2007

Occupation	International Staff	Percentage International Staff
Administration	78	16.2%
Aviation	14	2.9%
Civil Affairs	32	6.6%
Economic Affairs	—	—
Engineering	22	4.6%
Finance	22	4.6%
Human Resources	25	5.2%
Human Rights	17	3.5%
Humanitarian Affairs	6	1.2%
Information Management	1	0.2%
Information Systems and Technology	26	5.4%
Legal Affairs	6	1.2%
Logistics	79	16.4%
Medical Services	3	0.6%
Political Affairs	25	5.2%
Procurement	10	2.1%
Programme Management	6	1.2%
Public Information	18	3.7%
Rule of Law	18	3.7%
Security	53	11.0%
Social Affairs	4	0.8%
Transport	17	3.5%
Total	**482**	

Source: DPKO PMSS.

MINUSTAH Personnel Gender Statistics: 30 September 2007

Personnel Type	Male	Female	Percentage Male	Percentage Female
Troops	6,937	125	98.2%	1.8%
Military Observers	—	—	—	—
Police	1,730	44	97.7%	2.3%
International Civilian Staff	316	166	65.6%	34.4%
Local Civilian Staff	901	201	81.8%	18.2%
Total	**9,884**	**532**	**94.9%**	**5.1%**

Sources: DPKO FGS; DPKO PD; DPKO PMSS.

MINUSTAH Fatalities: Inception–September 2007

Personnel Type

Time Period	Troop	MilOb	Police	Intl Staff	Local Staff	Other[a]	Total
2004	—	—	—	—	—	—	—
2005	9	—	3	1	—	—	13
2006	6	—	—	3	3	—	12
January-March	3	—	—	1	1	—	5
April-June	—	—	—	—	—	—	—
July-September	—	—	—	1	2	—	3
October-December	3	—	—	1	—	—	4
2007 (Jan-Sep)	4	—	—	3	—	—	7
January-March	—	—	—	—	—	—	—
April-June	2	—	—	2	—	—	4
July-September	2	—	—	1	—	—	3
Total Fatalities	**19**	**—**	**3**	**7**	**3**	**—**	**32**

Incident Type

Time Period	Malicious Act	Illness	Accident	Other[b]	Total
2004	—	—	—	—	—
2005	6	3	3	1	13
2006	5	4	2	1	12
January-March	2	1	1	1	5
April-June	—	—	—	—	—
July-September	1	1	1	—	3
October-December	2	2	—	—	4
2007 (Jan-Sep)	—	1	2	4	7
January-March	—	—	—	—	—
April-June	—	1	1	2	4
July-September	—	—	1	2	3
Total Fatalities	**11**	**8**	**7**	**6**	**32**

Source: DPKO Situation Centre.
Notes: a. Other refers to consultants, UNVs, etc.
   b. Incident type is unknown, uncertain or under investigation. Other includes what were previously qualified as self-inflicted.

MINUSTAH Vehicles: 30 September 2007

Contingent Owned Vehicles		UN Owned Vehicles	
Vehicle Type	Quantity	Vehicle Type	Quantity
Aircraft/Airfield Support Equipment	12	4x4 Vehicles	719
Combat Vehicles	226	Aircraft/Airfield Support Equipment	5
Engineering Vehicles	97	Ambulances	4
Material Handling Equipment	27	Automobiles	25
Support Vehicles (Commerical Pattern)	506	Buses	52
Support Vehicles (Military Pattern)	539	Material Handling Equipment	27
Trailers	349	Trailers	2
Total	**1,756**	Trucks	66
		Vans	3
		Total	**903**

Sources: DPKO Contingent Owned Equipment and Property Management Section; DPKO Surface Transport Section.

MINUSTAH Aircraft: 30 September 2007

	Transport Fixed Wing	Transport Helicopter	Attack Helicopter
Commercial	1	5	—
Contingent Owned	—	6	—
		(2 Argentina, 4 Chile)	
Total	**1**	**11**	—

Source: DPKO Air Transport Section.

MINUSTAH Budget and Expenditures (in thousands of US dollars)

Category	Budgeted Jul 06–Jun 07	Expenditures Jul 06–Jun 07	Budgeted Jul 07–Jun 08
Military Observers	—	—	—
Military Contingents	191,211.9	176,231.8	180,823.8
Civilian Police	47,836.6	42,697.5	47,276.1
Formed Police Units	26,967.7	27,441.9	27,344.9
International Staff	77,031.1	70,187.1	80,746.4
Local Staff	15,500.2	15,843.5	24,147.5
United Nations Volunteers	7,457.3	8,511.8	11,500.3
General Temporary Assistance	2,493.6	4,062.1	2,424.5
Government-provided Personnel	—	—	802.0
Civilian Electoral Observers	—	—	—
Consultants	84.5	133.4	284.2
Official Travel	969.5	1,180.7	1,175.0
Facilities and Infrastructure	43,087.4	64,300.7	70,818.6
Ground Transportation	8,563.2	9,262.8	11,218.9
Air Transportation	25,378.4	18,231.7	24,260.7
Naval Transportation	192.0	239.3	198.0
Communications and Information Technology	25,108.9	29,521.7	35,212.4
Supplies, Services and Equipment	15,294.8	14,144.4	15,139.5
Quick-impact Projects	2,030.0	2,029.7	2,000.0
Gross Requirements	**489,207.1**	**505,200.9**	**561,344.9**
Staff Assessment Income	9,398.7	7,736.3	12,299.4
Net Requirements	**479,808.4**	**497,464.6**	**549,045.5**
Voluntary Contributions in Kind (budgeted)	—	—	—
Total Requirements	**489,207.1**	**505,200.9**	**561,344.9**

Sources: UN Documents A/61/852 Add.15 and A/61/869; DPKO FMSS.

Notes: Financial figures are preliminary and subject to change. Gross requirements for July 2006–June 2007 expenditures include pro-rated costs of $21,180.8 thousand. Gross requirements for July 2007–June 2008 budgeted include pro-rated costs of $25,972.1 thousand.

MINUSTAH Expenditures on Contingent Owned Equipment: July 2006–June 2007 (in thousands of US dollars)

Major Equipment	36,285.1
Self-sustainment	28,495.9

Source: DPKO FMSS.

MINUSTAH Mission Expenditures: May 2004–June 2006 (in thousands of US dollars)

Category	May 04–Jun 04	Jul 04–Jun 05	Jul 05–Jun 06
Military and Police Personnel	7,159.3	192,850.1	239,674.5
Civilian Personnel	1,246.5	56,050.5	88,831.9
Operational Requirements	26,150.3	128,334.7	151,130.2
Gross Requirements	**34,556.1**	**377,235.3**	**479,636.6**
Staff Assessment Income	60.7	5,347.3	8,664.8
Net Requirements	**34,495.4**	**371,888.0**	**470,971.8**
Voluntary Contributions in Kind (budgeted)	—	—	—
Total Requirements	**34,556.1**	**377,235.3**	**479,636.6**

Sources: UN Documents A/59/745, A/60/646 and A/61/741.

7.4 MONUC (UN Organization Mission in the Democratic Republic of the Congo)

	MONUC Key Facts
Latest Key Resolutions	21 December 2007 (date of issue and effect)
	UNSC Res. 1794 (ten day and twelve month duration)
	15 May 2007 (date of issue and effect)
	UNSC Res. 1756 (seven month and one-half month duration)
	13 April 2007 (date of issue and effect)
	UNSC Res. 1751 (one month duration)
	15 February 2007 (date of issue and effect)
	UNSC Res. 1742 (one month duration)
	22 December 2006 (date of issue and effect)
	UNSC Res. 1736 (one and one-half month strength increase)
First Mandate	30 November 1999 (date of issue and effect)
	UNSC Res. 1279 (three month duration)
SRSG	Willism Lacy Swing (United States)
	SG letter of appointment 16 May 2003
	Entry on duty 1 July 2003
First SRSG	Kamel Morjane (Tunisia)
Force Commander	Lieutenant-General Babacar Gaye (Senegal)
	SG letter of appointment 4 March 2005
	Entry on duty 23 March 2005
First Force Commander	Major-General Mountaga Diallo (Senegal)
Police Commissioner	Daniel Cure (France)
	Date of appointment 1 January 2005

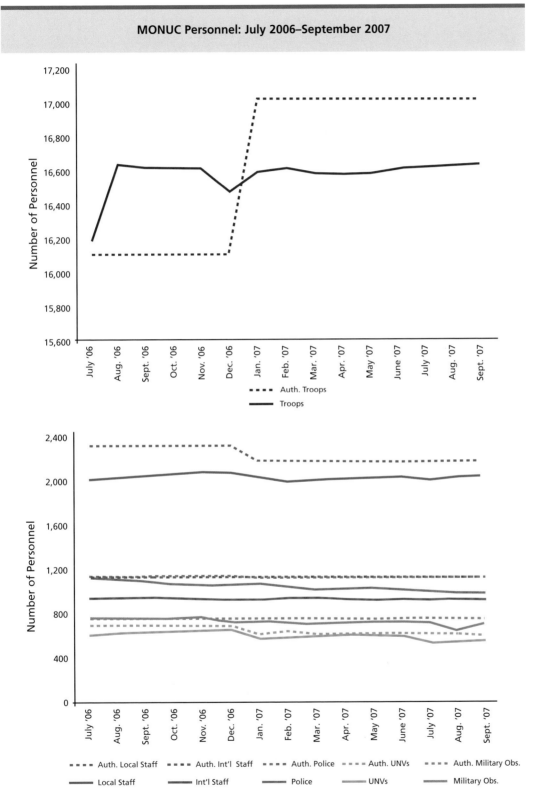

MONUC Personnel: July 2006–September 2007

Sources: UN Documents A/61/852 Add.11, S/RES/1742, S/RES/1751 and S/RES/1756; DPKO FGS; DPKO PD; DPKO PMSS; UNV Programme.

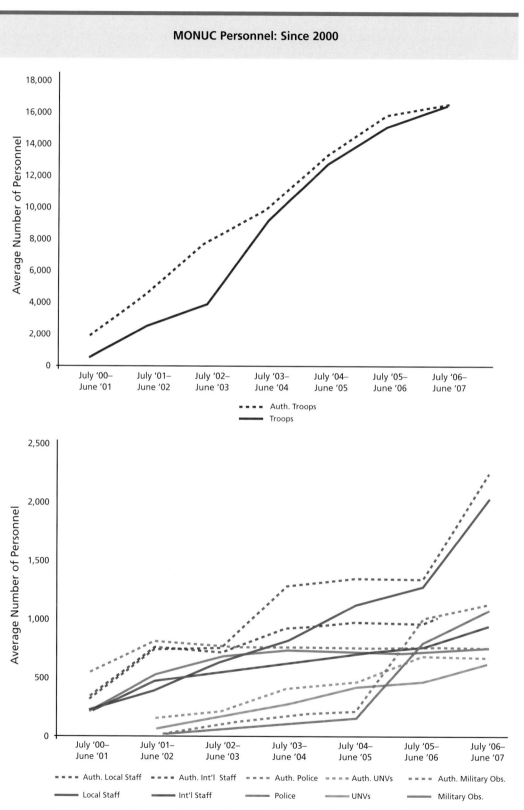

MONUC Personnel: Since 2000

Sources: UN Documents A/56/825, A/57/682, A/58/684, A/59/657, A/60/669, A/61/672, A/61/852 Add.11S/RES/1258, S/RES/1279, S/RES/1291, S/RES/1355, S/RES/1445, S/RES/1493, S/RES/1565, S/RES/1621, S/RES/1635, S/RES/1650, S/RES/1669, S/RES/1692, S/RES/1693, S/RES/1711, S/RES/1742, S/RES/1751 and S/RES/1756; DPKO FGS; DPKO PD; DPKO PMSS; UNV Programme.

MONUC Military and Police Contributors: 30 September 2007

Contributing Country	Troops	Military Observers	Police	Total	Contributing Country	Troops	Military Observers	Police	Total
India	4,381	54	247	4,682	Romania	—	23	1	24
Pakistan	3,579	56	—	3,635	Zambia	—	24	—	24
Bangladesh	1,326	24	250	1,600	Malaysia	—	17	—	17
Uruguay	1,324	45	—	1,369	France	—	6	9	15
South Africa	1,183	15	—	1,198	Paraguay	—	14	—	14
Nepal	1,030	20	—	1,050	Ukraine	—	6	5	11
Morocco	809	4	—	813	Canada	—	10	—	10
Benin	749	12	10	771	Guinea	—	—	10	10
Senegal	461	21	256	738	Sweden	—	5	5	10
Tunisia	462	25	—	487	Belgium	—	8	—	8
Ghana	461	24	—	485	Peru	—	7	—	7
China	218	16	—	234	Yemen	—	5	2	7
Bolivia	200	8	—	208	Serbia	6	—	—	6
Indonesia	175	15	—	190	United Kingdom	—	6	—	6
Malawi	111	23	—	134	Bosnia and Herzegovina	—	5	—	5
Guatemala	105	6	—	111	Madagascar	—	—	5	5
Jordan	66	25	4	95	Ireland	—	4	—	4
Niger	—	17	40	57	Sri Lanka	—	4	—	4
Cameroon	—	5	50	55	Argentina	—	—	3	3
Burkina Faso	—	8	36	44	Czech Republic	—	3	—	3
Mali	—	22	20	42	Denmark	—	2	—	2
Kenya	—	36	4	40	Mongolia	—	2	—	2
Egypt	—	22	5	27	Poland	—	2	—	2
Russia	—	28	3	31	Spain	—	2	—	2
Nigeria	—	27	—	27	Switzerland	—	2	—	2
Côte d'Ivoire	—	—	25	25	Turkey	—	—	1	1
					Total	**16,646**	**715**	**991**	**18,271**

Sources: DPKO FGS ; DPKO PD.
Note: Police figures include formed police provided by Bangladesh (250), India (247) and Senegal (249).

MONUC Military Units: 30 September 2007

Number	Unit Type	Countries
1	Air Cargo Handling Team	South Africa
5	Air Medical Evacuation Teams	Jordan, Morocco, Pakistan, Serbia, South Africa
1	Airfield Crash Rescue Team	South Africa
3	Airfield Service Units	Bangladesh, India, Uruguay
5	Engineering Companies	China, Indonesia, Nepal, South Africa, Uruguay
4	Headquarters Support & Signal Companies	Bangladesh, India, Pakistan, South Africa
7	Helicopter Units	Bangladesh, India (5), South Africa
17	Infantry Battalions	Bangladesh, Benin, Ghana, India (4), Morocco, Nepal, Pakistan (4), Senegal, South Africa, Tunisia, Uruguay
1	Infantry Guard Company	Malawi
1	Infantry Mechanized Unit	Bolivia
3	Level II Medical Units	China, Jordan, Morocco
1 partial	Level III Medical Unit	India
2	Military Police Companies	Bangladesh, South Africa
2	Riverine Units	Uruguay
1	Special Forces Company	Guatemala
1	Water Treatment Plant	Uruguay

Source: DPKO FGS.
Note: Military headquarters staff, staff officers, military observers, and Level I Medical Units not included.

MONUC International Civilian Personnel Occupations: 30 September 2007

Occupation	International Staff	Percentage International Staff
Administration	123	13.1%
Aviation	53	5.7%
Civil Affairs	20	2.1%
Economic Affairs	—	—
Engineering	48	5.1%
Finance	35	3.7%
Human Resources	38	4.1%
Human Rights	30	3.2%
Humanitarian Affairs	—	—
Information Management	—	—
Information Systems and Technology	81	8.6%
Legal Affairs	5	0.5%
Logistics	169	18.0%
Medical Services	14	1.5%
Political Affairs	92	9.8%
Procurement	21	2.2%
Programme Management	13	1.4%
Public Information	41	4.4%
Rule of Law	12	1.3%
Security	102	10.9%
Social Affairs	10	1.1%
Transport	30	3.2%
Total	**937**	

Source: DPKO PMSS.

MONUC Gender Statistics: 30 September 2007

Personnel Type	Male	Female	Percentage Male	Percentage Female
Troops	16,297	349	97.9%	2.1%
Military Observers	690	25	96.5%	3.5%
Police	966	46	95.5%	4.5%
International Civilian Staff	661	276	70.5%	29.5%
Local Civilian Staff	1,756	297	85.5%	14.5%
Total	**20,370**	**993**	**95.4%**	**4.6%**

Sources: DPKO FGS; DPKO PD; DPKO PMSS.

MONUC Fatalities: Inception–September 2007

Personnel Type

Time Period	Troop	MilOb	Police	Intl Staff	Local Staff	Other[a]	Total
1999	—	—	—	—	—	—	—
2000	—	—	—	—	—	—	—
2001	4	1	—	1	2	—	8
2002	3	2	—	2	1	—	8
2003	8	3	—	3	—	—	14
2004	18	2	—	—	2	—	22
2005	20	—	1	2	2	—	25
2006	18	1	1	1	7	—	28
January-March	8	—	—	—	—	—	8
April-June	7	—	—	—	1	—	8
July-September	2	1	1	1	1	—	6
October-December	1	—	—	—	5	—	6
2007 (Jan-Sep)	3	—	—	1	4	—	8
January-March	1	—	—	1	—	—	2
April-June	2	—	—	—	1	—	3
July-September	—	—	—	—	3	—	3
Total Fatalities	**74**	**9**	**2**	**10**	**18**	**—**	**113**

Incident Type

Time Period	Malicious Act	Illness	Accident	Other[b]	Total
1999	—	—	—	—	—
2000	—	—	—	—	—
2001	1	4	1	2	8
2002	—	5	3	—	8
2003	3	7	4	—	14
2004	3	8	11	—	22
2005	13	8	4	—	25
2006	9	15	2	2	28
January-March	8	—	—	—	8
April-June	1	5	2	—	8
July-September	—	6	—	—	6
October-December	—	4	—	2	6
2007 (Jan-Sep)	—	2	1	5	8
January-March	—	2	—	—	2
April-June	—	—	1	2	3
July-September	—	—	—	3	3
Total Fatalities	**29**	**49**	**26**	**9**	**113**

Source: DPKO Situation Centre.
Notes: a. Other refers to consultants, UNVs, etc.
  b. Incident type is unknown, uncertain or under investigation. Other includes what were previously qualified as self-inflicted.

MONUC Vehicles: 30 September 2007

Contingent Owned Vehicles		UN Owned Vehicles	
Vehicle Type	Quantity	Vehicle Type	Quantity
Aircraft/Airfield Support Equipment	85	4x4 Vehicles	1,443
Combat Vehicles	351	Aircraft/Airfield Support Equipment	44
Communications Vehicles	6	Ambulances	24
Engineering Vehicles	177	Automobiles	3
Material Handling Equipment	57	Boats	2
Naval Vessels	28	Buses	393
Support Vehicles (Commercial Pattern)	365	Engineering Vehicles	7
Support Vehicles (Military Pattern)	1,608	Material Handling Equipment	128
Trailers	535	Trailer	1
Total	**3,212**	Trucks	265
		Vans	23
		Total	**2,333**

Sources: DPKO Contingent Owned Equipment and Property Management Section; DPKO Surface Transport Section.

MONUC Aircraft: 30 September 2007

	Transport Fixed Wing	Transport Helicopter	Attack Helicopter
Commercial	22	17	—
Contingent Owned	—	22 (5 Bangladesh, 15 India, 2 South Africa)	8 (India)
Total	**22**	**39**	**8**

Source: DPKO Air Transport Section.

MONUC Budget and Expenditures (in thousands of US dollars)

Category	Budgeted Jul 06–Jun 07	Expenditures Jul 06–Jun 07	Budgeted Jul 07–Jun 08
Military Observers	43,874.0	44,369.5	44,618.2
Military Contingents	382,578.9	359,741.8	392,811.5
Civilian Police	21,173.8	18,214.7	20,841.8
Formed Police Units	18,199.0	17,197.2	18,388.2
International Staff	140,784.5	144,448.8	151,072.0
Local Staff	29,440.1	27,896.2	33,277.8
United Nations Volunteers	19,691.7	28,195.8	21,467.5
General Temporary Assistance	2,102.0	10,485.8	1,849.8
Government-provided Personnel	—	—	—
Civilian Electoral Observers	—	—	—
Consultants	317.2	899.3	317.2
Official Travel	4,056.9	7,271.6	4,154.0
Facilities and Infrastructure	93,058.8	94,898.0	93,056.1
Ground Transportation	17,165.1	18,552.9	22,109.8
Air Transportation	244,775.9	239,476.4	230,553.2
Naval Transportation	2,729.0	2,023.9	1,963.4
Communications and Information Technology	36,310.1	35,658.8	41,702.2
Supplies, Services and Equipment	33,985.8	34,797.6	36,471.6
Quick-impact Projects	1,000.0	999.1	1,000.0
Gross Requirements	**1,091,242.8**	**1,085,127.4**	**1,169,635.8**
Staff Assessment Income	18,760.0	19,985.6	20,989.1
Net Requirements	**1,072,482.8**	**1,065,141.8**	**1,148,646.7**
Voluntary Contributions in Kind (budgeted)	3,005.1	2,858.0	2,914.8
Total Requirements	**1,094,247.9**	**1,087,985.4**	**1,172,550.6**

Sources: UN Documents A/61/852 Add.11 and A/C.5/61/24; DPKO FMSS.
Notes: Financial figures are preliminary and subject to change. Gross requirements for July 2007–June 2008 budgeted include pro-rated costs of $53,981.5 thousand.

MONUC Expenditures on Contingent Owned Equipment: July 2006–June 2007 (in thousands of US dollars)

Major Equipment	61,210.7
Self-sustainment	71,245.8

Source: DPKO FMSS.

MONUC Voluntary Contributions: July 2006–June 2007 (in thousands of US dollars)

Contributor	Contributions in Kind (budgeted)	Contributions in Kind (non-budgeted)	Contributions in Cash (budgeted)	Total
Foundation Hirondelle	2,858.0	—	—	2,858.0
United States	—	36.0	—	36.0
South Africa	—	2.9	—	2.9
Total	**2,858.0**	**38.9**	**—**	**2,896.9**

Source: DM OPPBA.

MONUC Mission Expenditures: July 2000–June 2006 (in thousands of US dollars)

Category	Jul 00–Jun 01	Jul 01–Jun 02	Jul 02–Jun 03	Jul 03–Jun 04	Jul 04–Jun 05	Jul 05–Jun 06
Military and Police Personnel	29,656.1	97,177.0	156,973.6	262,734.7	379,763.4	448,543.1
Civilian Personnel	28,080.0	68,491.0	93,521.5	112,562.7	140,862.5	163,232.0
Operational Requirements	185,247.6	223,159.0	229,456.9	261,188.0	380,258.6	443,265.2
Other	474.6	—	—	—	—	—
Gross Requirements	**243,458.3**	**388,827.0**	**479,952.0**	**636,485.4**	**900,884.5**	**1,055,040.3**
Staff Assessment Income	3,013.7	6,777.6	10,037.6	12,114.2	14,882.7	17,035.5
Net Requirements	**240,444.6**	**382,049.4**	**469,914.4**	**624,371.2**	**886,001.8**	**1,038,004.8**
Voluntary Contributions in Kind (budgeted)	—	—	1,780.2	2,345.8	3,112.6	3,237.5
Total Requirements	**243,458.3**	**388,827.0**	**481,732.2**	**638,831.2**	**903,997.1**	**1,058,277.8**

Sources: UN Documents A/56/825, A/57/682, A/58/684, A/59/657, A/60/669 and A/61/672.

7.5 UNAMA (UN Assistance Mission in Afghanistan)

UNAMA Key Facts	
Latest Key Resolution	23 March 2007 (date of issue and effect) UNSC Res. 1746 (twelve month duration)
First Mandate	28 March 2002 (date of issue and effect) UNSC Res. 1401 (twelve month duration)
SRSG	Tom Koenigs (Germany) SG letter of appointment 16 December 2006, effective 16 February 2006
First SRSG	Lakhdar Brahimi (Algeria)
Senior Military Advisor	Brigadier Philip Jones (United Kingdom) Entry on duty 6 July 2006
Senior Police Advisor	Roberto Bernal (Philippines) Date of appointment 20 December 2005

UNAMA Personnel: July 2006–September 2007

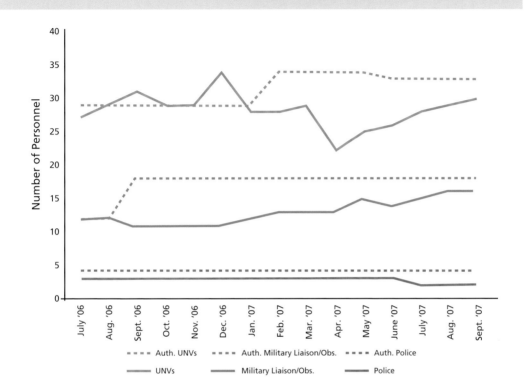

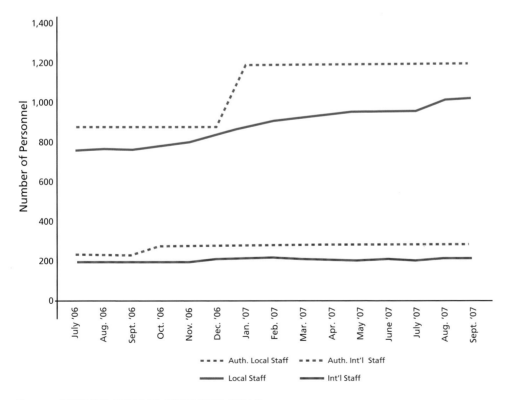

Sources: DPKO FGS; DPKO PD; DPKO PMSS; UNV Programme.

UNAMA Personnel: Since 2002

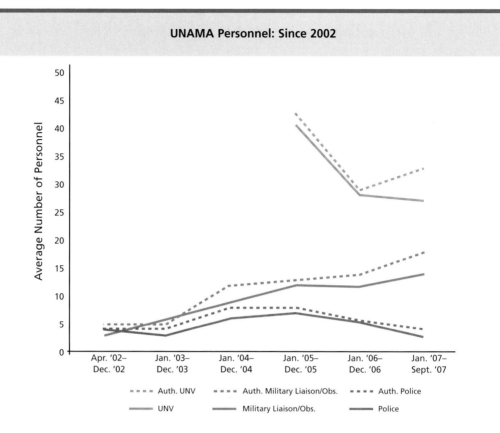

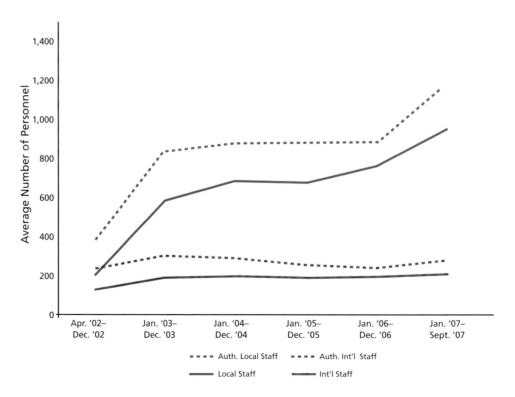

Sources: UN Documents A/C.5/56/25/Add.4, A/C.5/57/23, A/C.5/58/20 and A/59/534/Add.1; DPKO FGS; DPKO PD; DPKO PMSS; UNV Programme.

UNAMA Military and Police Contributors: 30 September 2007

Contributing Country	Troops	Military Observers	Police	Total
Bangladesh	—	2	—	2
Australia	—	1	—	1
Bolivia	—	1	—	1
Denmark	—	1	—	1
Germany	—	1	—	1
Lithuania	—	1	—	1
Nepal	—	—	1	1
New Zealand	—	1	—	1
Nigeria	—	—	1	1
Norway	—	1	—	1
Paraguay	—	1	—	1
Philippines	—	—	1	1
Poland	—	1	—	1
Republic of Korea	—	1	—	1
Romania	—	1	—	1
Sweden	—	1	—	1
United Kingdom	—	1	—	1
Uruguay	—	1	—	1
Total	—	**16**	**3**	**19**

Sources: DPKO FGS; DPKO PD.

UNAMA International Civilian Personnel Occupations: 30 September 2007

Occupation	International Staff	Percentage International Staff
Administration	26	12.0%
Aviation	2	0.9%
Civil Affairs	3	1.4%
Economic Affairs	—	—
Engineering	2	0.9%
Finance	11	5.1%
Human Resources	6	2.8%
Human Rights	19	8.8%
Humanitarian Affairs	1	0.5%
Information Management	—	—
Information Systems and Technology	10	4.6%
Legal Affairs	4	1.8%
Logistics	8	3.7%
Medical Services	1	0.5%
Political Affairs	40	18.4%
Procurement	5	2.3%
Programme Management	16	7.4%
Public Information	5	2.3%
Rule of Law	6	2.8%
Security	40	18.4%
Social Affairs	—	—
Transport	12	5.5%
Total	**217**	

Source: DPKO PMSS.

UNAMA Personnel Gender Statistics: 30 September 2007

Personnel Type	Male	Female	Percentage Male	Percentage Female
Troops	—	—	—	—
Military Advisors/Liaison Officers	16	—	100.0%	—
Police	3	—	100.0%	—
International Civilian Staff	150	67	69.1%	30.9%
Local Civilian Staff	966	61	94.1%	5.9%
Total	**1,135**	**128**	**89.9%**	**10.1%**

Sources: DPKO FGS; DPKO PD; DPKO PMSS.

UNAMA Fatalities: Inception–September 2007

Personnel Type

Time Period	Troop	MilOb	Police	Intl Staff	Local Staff	Other[a]	Total
2002	—	—	—	—	1	—	1
2003	—	—	—	—	1	—	1
2004	—	—	—	—	2	—	2
2005	—	—	—	—	—	—	—
2006	—	—	—	—	1	—	1
January–March	—	—	—	—	—	—	—
April–June	—	—	—	—	—	—	—
July–September	—	—	—	—	—	—	—
October–December	—	—	—	—	1	—	1
2007 (Jan–Sep)	—	—	—	1	4	—	5
January–March	—	—	—	—	—	—	—
April–June	—	—	—	1	3	—	4
July–September	—	—	—	—	1	—	1
Total Fatalities	—	—	—	1	9	—	10

Incident Type

Time Period	Malicious Act	Illness	Accident	Other[b]	Total
2002	—	—	1	—	1
2003	—	1	—	—	1
2004	—	2	—	—	2
2005	—	—	—	—	—
2006	—	—	—	1	1
January–March	—	—	—	—	—
April–June	—	—	—	—	—
July–September	—	—	—	—	—
October–December	—	—	—	1	1
2007 (Jan–Sep)	—	1	1	3	5
January–March	—	—	—	—	—
April–June	—	—	1	3	4
July–September	—	1	—	—	1
Total Fatalities	—	4	2	4	10

Source: DPKO Situation Centre.
Notes: a. Other refers to consultants, UNVs, etc.
b. Incident type is unknown, uncertain or under investigation. Other includes what were previously qualified as self-inflicted.

UNAMA Vehicles: 30 September 2007

UN Owned Vehicles

Vehicle Type	Quantity
4x4 Vehicles	271
Ambulances	3
Automobiles	8
Buses	56
Material Handling Equipment	8
Snowmobiles	4
Trucks	17
Vans	12
Total	**379**

Source: DPKO Surface Transport Section.

UNAMA Aircraft: 30 September 2007

	Transport Fixed Wing	Transport Helicopter	Attack Helicopter
Commercial	1	2	—
Contingent Owned	—	—	—
Total	**1**	**2**	**—**

Source: DPKO Air Transport Section.

UNAMA Budget and Expenditures (in thousands of US dollars)

Category	Appropriations Jan 06–Dec 07	Estimated Expenditures Jan 06–Dec 07	Requirements 2008
Military Observers	1,222.7	1,182.1	780.1
Police	291.0	319.6	368.0
International Staff	51,130.8	50,950.4	31,273.7
Local Staff	20,380.6	19,919.0	14,759.6
United Nations Volunteers	2,705.8	2,191.2	1,726.2
Consultants	411.5	447.2	227.3
Official Travel	2,070.9	2,465.3	1,127.7
Facilities and Infrastructure	11,390.1	13,127.3	8,476.6
Ground Transportation	5,448.9	5,029.7	5,514.5
Air Transportation	17,952.8	18,383.2	11,725.6
Communications	5,547.2	5,181.4	2,442.7
Information Technology	2,912.8	2,369.3	1,581.3
Medical	451.7	451.7	306.4
Other Supplies, Services, and Equipment	1,557.7	1,453.4	614.2
Total	**123,474.5**	**123,470.8**	**80,923.9**

Sources: UN Document A/62/512/Add. 4; DPKO FMSS.
Note: Financial figures are preliminary and subject to change.

UNAMA Mission Expenditures: April 2002–December 2005 (in thousands of US dollars)		
Category	2002–2003	2004–2005
Military Observers	298.8	742.6
Police	206.0	78.2
Posts	39,022.2	62,875.4
United Nations Volunteers	1,474.7	2,976.4
Consultants	893.0	372.5
Official Travel	1,561.6	1,136.8
Facilities and Infrastructure	9,606.4	9,607.0
Ground Transportation	4,143.0	8,112.9
Air Transportation	9,340.4	12,379.1
Communications	4,549.3	3,365.4
Information Technology	3,546.6	1,853.6
Medical	160.4	256.2
Other Supplies, Services and Equipment	5,047.6	2,468.2
Public Information Programme	210.4	198.5
Training	—	981.5
Total	**80,060.5**	**107,404.2**

Source: DPKO FMSS.

7.6 UNAMI (UN Assistance Mission for Iraq)

UNAMI Key Facts	
Latest Key Resolutions	10 August 2007 (date of issue and effect) UNSC Res. 1770 (twelve month duration and expansion of mandate) 28 November 2006 (date of issue and effect) UNSC Res. 1723 (twenty-one day and four month duration)
First Mandate	14 August 2003 (date of issue and effect) UNSC Res 1500 (twelve month duration)
SRSG	Staffan de Mistura (Sweden) SG letter of appointment 4 September 2007 Enty on duty 11 November 2007
First SRSG	Sergio Vieira de Mello
Senior Military Advisor	Colonel Peter Jeffrey (Australia) Date of appointment 7 July 2006

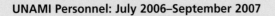

UNAMI Personnel: July 2006–September 2007

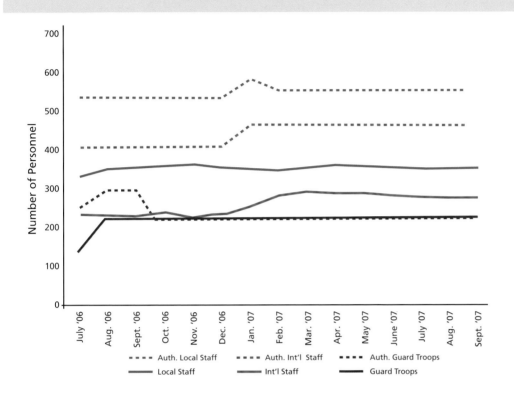

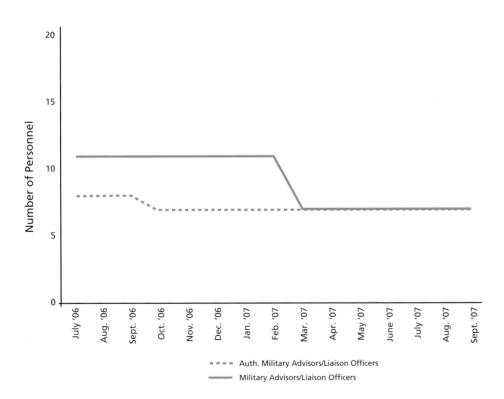

Sources: DPKO FGS; DPKO PMSS.

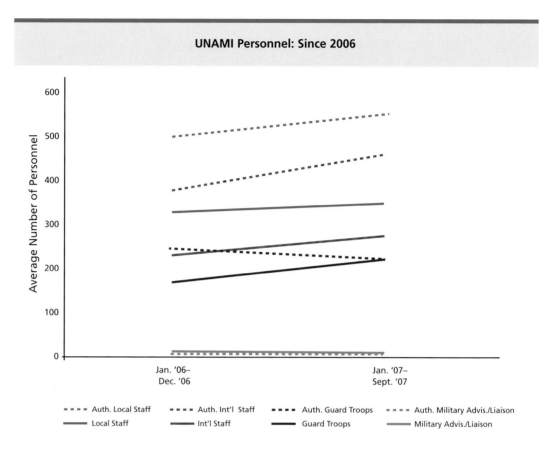

UNAMI Personnel: Since 2006

Sources: DPKO FGS; DPKO PMSS.

Note: Historical military personnel figures for UNAMI are only available from DPKO on a regular monthly basis as of January 2006.

UNAMI Military and Police Contributors: 30 September 2007

Contributing Country	Troops	Military Observers	Police	Total
Fiji	223	—	—	223
Denmark	—	3	—	3
Australia	—	1	—	1
Canada	—	1	—	1
New Zealand	—	1	—	1
United Kingdom	—	1	—	1
Total	**223**	**7**	**—**	**230**

Source: DPKO FGS.

UNAMI Military Units: 30 September 2007

Number	Unit Type	Country
3	Guard Units	Fiji

Source: DPKO FGS.
Note: Military headquarters staff and military observers not included.

UNAMI International Civilian Personnel Occupations: 30 September 2007

Occupation	International Staff	Percentage International Staff
Administration	25	9.1%
Aviation	5	1.8%
Civil Affairs	—	—
Economic Affairs	—	—
Engineering	10	3.6%
Finance	12	4.4%
Human Resources	14	5.1%
Human Rights	9	3.3%
Humanitarian Affairs	6	2.2%
Information Management	1	0.4%
Information Systems and Technology	18	6.5%
Legal Affairs	4	1.5%
Logistics	22	8.0%
Medical Services	2	0.7%
Political Affairs	26	9.5%
Procurement	8	2.9%
Programme Management	5	1.8%
Public Information	4	1.5%
Rule of Law	—	—
Security	96	34.9%
Social Affairs	1	0.4%
Transport	7	2.5%
Total	**275**	

Source: DPKO PMSS.

UNAMI Personnel Gender Statistics: 30 September 2007

Personnel Type	Male	Female	Percentage Male	Percentage Female
Troops	223	—	100.0%	—
Military Observers	7	—	100.0%	—
Police	—	—	—	—
International Civilian Staff	223	52	81.1%	18.9%
Local Civilian Staff	259	92	73.8%	26.2%
Total	**712**	**144**	**83.2%**	**16.8%**

Sources: DPKO FGS; DPKO PMSS.

UNAMI/UNOHCI Fatalities: January 2003–September 2007

Personnel Type

Time Period	Troop	MilOb	Police	Intl Staff	Local Staff	Other[a]	Total
2003	—	—	—	11	8	5	24
2004	—	—	—	—	—	—	—
2005	—	—	—	2	—	—	2
2006	1	—	—	—	1	—	2
January-March	1	—	—	—	—	—	1
April-June	—	—	—	—	—	—	—
July-September	—	—	—	—	1	—	1
October-December	—	—	—	—	—	—	—
2007 (Jan-Sep)	—	—	—	1	1	—	2
January-March	—	—	—	—	—	—	—
April-June	—	—	—	—	1	—	1
July-September	—	—	—	1	—	—	1
Total Fatalities	**1**	**—**	**—**	**14**	**10**	**5**	**30**

Incident Type

Time Period	Malicious Act	Illness	Accident	Other[b]	Total
2003	23	1	—	—	24
2004	—	—	—	—	—
2005	—	1	—	1	2
2006	—	2	—	—	2
January-March	—	1	—	—	1
April-June	—	—	—	—	—
July-September	—	1	—	—	1
October-December	—	—	—	—	—
2007 (Jan-Sep)	—	—	—	2	2
January-March	—	—	—	—	—
April-June	—	—	—	1	1
July-September	—	—	—	1	1
Total Fatalities	**23**	**4**	**—**	**3**	**30**

Source: DPKO Situation Centre.

Notes: UNAMI was incepted in August 2003. Prior to this, the United Nations Office of the Humanitarian Coordinator in Iraq (UNOHCI) was the lead presence in Iraq.

a. Other refers to consultants, UNVs, etc.

b. Incident type is unknown, uncertain or under investigation. Other includes what were previously qualified as self-inflicted.

UNAMI Vehicles: 30 September 2007

Contingent Owned Vehicles		UN Owned Vehicles	
Vehicle Type	Quantity	Vehicle Type	Quantity
Support Vehicle (Commercial Pattern)	1	4x4 Vehicles	174
		Airfield Support Equipment	1
Total	**1**	Ambulances	3
		Automobiles	2
		Buses	16
		Material Handling Equipment	8
		Trailers	11
		Trucks	10
		Vans	4
		Total	**229**

Sources: DPKO Contingent Owned Equipment and Property Management Section; DPKO Surface Transport Section.

UNAMI Budget and Expenditures (in thousands of US dollars)

Category	Appropriations Jan 06–Dec 07	Estimated Expenditures Jan 06–Dec 07	Requirements 2008
Military Liaison Officers	1,438.7	1,870.6	995.7
Military Contingents	28,794.5	21,027.3	13,925.0
International Staff	104,215.3	99,791.3	60,057.9
Local Staff	16,904.9	17,570.0	10,614.7
Consultants	864.9	695.0	896.6
Official Travel	3,432.9	5,705.2	2,195.8
Facilities and Infrastructure	31,014.3	36,465.1	13,534.0
Ground Transportation	12,223.3	14,978.3	16,842.5
Air Transportation	21,436.9	5,931.8	16,233.8
Communications	11,295.1	8,019.9	5,759.4
Information Technology	6,011.6	6,137.3	4,096.5
Medical	864.0	548.2	836.0
Other Supplied, Services, and Equipment	7,314.7	4,558.3	5,088.3
Total	**245,811.1**	**223,298.3**	**151,076.2**

Sources: UN Document A/62/512/Add. 5; DPKO FMSS.
Note: Financial figures are preliminary and subject to change.

UNAMI Mission Expenditures: August 2003–December 2005 (in thousands of US dollars)

Category	2003	2004	2005
Military Observers	—	75.3	320.3
Police	—	—	—
Posts	—	551.0	816.0
United Nations Volunteers	—	—	—
Consultants	—	170.8	804.3
Official Travel	146.6	931.2	1,332.7
Facilities and Infrastructure	1,416.4	6,670.2	44,582.3
Ground Transportation	1,190.7	2,343.4	7,983.1
Air Transportation	216.0	1,129.4	262.7
Communications	310.5	2,297.1	9,317.6
Information Technology	399.3	258.9	3,465.1
Medical	—	—	198.8
Other Supplies, Services and Equipment	1,539.2	1,557.7	2,435.7
Public Information Programme	—	5.0	240.6
Training	—	—	298.9
Total	**5,218.7**	**15,990.0**	**72,058.1**

Source: FMSS.

7.7 UNDOF (UN Disengagement Observer Force)

UNDOF Key Facts	
Latest Key Resolutions	14 December 2007 (date of issue); 1 January 2008 (date of effect) UNSC Res. 1788 (six month duration) 20 June 2007 (date of issue); 1 July 2007 (date of effect) UNSC Res. 1759 (six month duration) 15 December 2006 (date of issue); 1 December 2006 (date of effect) UNSC Res. 1729 (six month duration)
First Mandate	31 May 1974 (date of issue and effect) UNSC Res. 350 (six month duration)
Force Commander	Major-General Wolfgang Jilke (Austria) SG letter of appointment 16 January 2007 Entry on duty 17 January 2007
First Force Commander	Brigadier-General Gonzalo Briceno Zevallos (Peru)

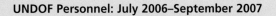

UNDOF Personnel: July 2006–September 2007

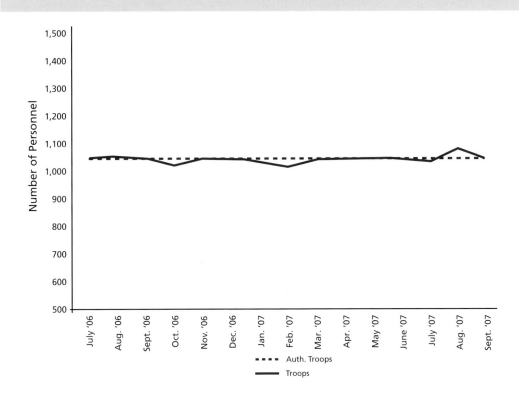

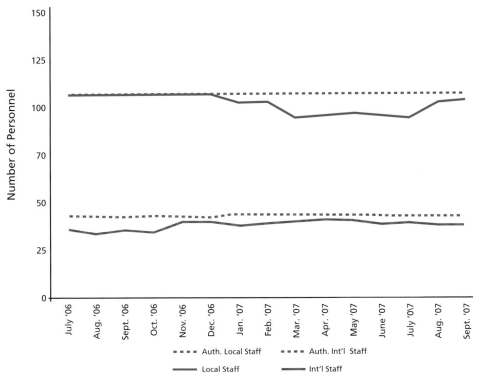

Sources: DPKO FGS; DPKO PMSS.

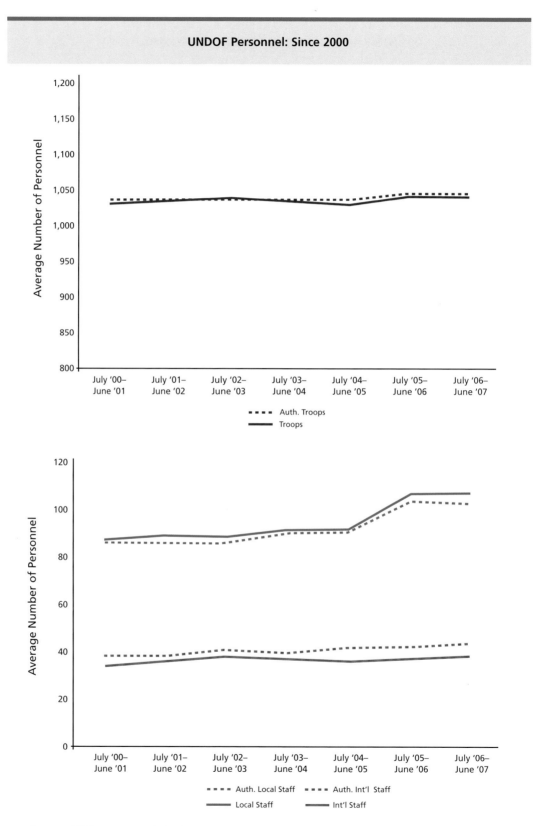

Sources: UN Documents A/56/813, A/57/668, A/58/641, A/59/625, A/60/628 and A/61/662; DPKO FGS; DPKO PMSS.

UNDOF Military and Police Contributors: 30 September 2007

Contributing Country	Troops	Military Observers	Police	Total
Austria	372	—	—	372
Poland	353	—	—	353
India	191	—	—	191
Slovakia	95	—	—	95
Japan	30	—	—	30
Canada	2	—	—	2
Total	**1,043**	—	—	**1,043**

Source: DPKO FGS.

UNDOF Military Units: 30 September 2007

Number	Unit Type	Country
2	Infantry Battalions	Australia, Poland-Slovakia Composite
1	Logistics Battalion	India-Japan Composite

Source: DPKO FGS.
Note: Military headquarters staff not included.

UNDOF International Civilian Personnel Occupations: 30 September 2007

Occupation	International Staff	Percentage International Staff
Administration	6	15.4%
Aviation	—	—
Civil Affairs	—	—
Economic Affairs	—	—
Engineering	4	10.3%
Finance	4	10.3%
Human Resources	2	5.1%
Human Rights	—	—
Humanitarian Affairs	—	—
Information Management	1	2.6%
Information Systems and Technology	9	23.1%
Legal Affairs	1	2.6%
Logistics	2	5.1%
Medical Services	—	—
Political Affairs	—	—
Procurement	3	7.7%
Programme Management	—	—
Public Information	—	—
Rule of Law	1	2.6%
Security	2	5.1%
Social Affairs	—	—
Transport	4	10.3%
Total	**39**	

Source: DPKO PMSS.

UNDOF Personnel Gender Statistics: 30 September 2007

Personnel Type	Male	Female	Percentage Male	Percentage Female
Troops	1,025	18	98.3%	1.7%
Military Observers	—	—	—	—
Police	—	—	—	—
International Civilian Staff	28	11	71.8%	28.2%
Local Civilian Staff	82	22	78.8%	21.2%
Total	**1,135**	**51**	**95.7%**	**4.3%**

Sources: DPKO FGS; DPKO PMSS.

UNDOF Fatalities: Inception–September 2007

Personnel Type

Time Period	Troop	MilOb	Police	Intl Staff	Local Staff	Other[a]	Total
1974–1999	38	—	—	1	—	—	39
2000	—	—	—	—	—	—	—
2001	—	—	—	—	—	—	—
2002	—	—	—	—	—	—	—
2003	—	—	—	—	—	—	—
2004	—	—	—	—	—	—	—
2005	2	—	—	—	—	—	2
2006	1	—	—	—	—	—	1
January-March	1	—	—	—	—	—	1
April-June	—	—	—	—	—	—	—
July-September	—	—	—	—	—	—	—
October-December	—	—	—	—	—	—	—
2007 (Jan-Sep)	—	—	—	—	—	—	—
January-March	—	—	—	—	—	—	—
April-June	—	—	—	—	—	—	—
July-September	—	—	—	—	—	—	—
Total Fatalities	**41**	**—**	**—**	**1**	**—**	**—**	**42**

Incident Type

Time Period	Malicious Act	Illness	Accident	Other[b]	Total
1974–1999	7	6	19	7	39
2000	—	—	—	—	—
2001	—	—	—	—	—
2002	—	—	—	—	—
2003	—	—	—	—	—
2004	—	—	—	—	—
2005	—	—	—	2	2
2006	—	—	—	1	1
January-March	—	—	—	1	1
April-June	—	—	—	—	—
July-September	—	—	—	—	—
October-December	—	—	—	—	—
2007 (Jan-Sep)	—	—	—	—	—
January-March	—	—	—	—	—
April-June	—	—	—	—	—
July-September	—	—	—	—	—
Total Fatalities	**7**	**6**	**19**	**10**	**42**

Source: DPKO Situation Centre.
Notes: a. Other refers to consultants, UNVs, etc.
b. Incident type is unknown, uncertain or under investigation. Other includes what were previously qualified as self-inflicted.

UNDOF Vehicles: 30 September 2007

Contingent Owned Vehicles		UN Owned Vehicles	
Vehicle Type	Quantity	Vehicle Type	Quantity
Engineering Vehicle	1	4x4 Vehicles	227
Excavator	1	Ambulances	10
Material Handling Equipment	1	Armoured Personnel Carriers	18
Support Vehicles (Commercial Pattern)	5	Automobiles	7
Support Vehicles (Military Pattern)	5	Buses	48
Trailers	1	Engineering Vehicle	1
Total	**14**	Material Handling Equipment	15
		Snow Tracks	3
		Trailers	31
		Trucks	64
		Vans	5
		Total	**429**

Sources: DPKO Contingent Owned Equipment and Property Management Section; DPKO Surface Transport Section.

UNDOF Budget and Expenditures (in thousands of US dollars)

Category	Budgeted Jul 06–Jun 07	Expenditures Jul 06–Jun 07	Budgeted Jul 07–Jun 08
Military Observers	—	—	—
Military Contingents	19,941.6	19,523.3	19,698.8
Civilian Police	—	—	—
Formed Police Units	—	—	—
International Staff	6,377.7	6,067.9	6,231.5
Local Staff	2,119.0	2,487.7	2,379.8
United Nations Volunteers	—	—	—
General Temporary Assistance	40.0	119.8	115.4
Government-provided Personnel	—	—	—
Civilian Electoral Observers	—	—	—
Consultants	14.0	0.3	14.0
Official Travel	227.0	243.6	338.6
Facilities and Infrastructure	4,094.7	4,171.1	4,165.0
Ground Transportation	3,954.2	3,413.0	3,235.5
Air Transportation	—	—	—
Naval Transportation	—	—	—
Communications and Information Technology	2,054.3	2,029.2	2,192.8
Supplies, Services and Equipment	1,042.7	1,493.1	1,291.1
Quick-impact Projects	—	—	—
Gross Requirements	**39,865.2**	**39,549.0**	**41,586.6**
Staff Assessment Income	1,066.6	1,139.2	1,110.6
Net Requirements	**38,798.6**	**38,409.8**	**40,476.0**
Voluntary Contributions in Kind (budgeted)	—	—	—
Total Requirements	**39,865.2**	**39,549.0**	**41,586.6**

Sources: UN Documents A/61/852/Add.1 and A/62/562; DPKO FMSS.

Notes: Financial figures are preliminary and subject to change. Gross requirements for July 2007–June 2008 budgeted include pro-rated costs of $1,924.1 thousand.

UNDOF Expenditures on Contingent Owned Equipment: July 2006–June 2007 (in thousands of US dollars)	
Major Equipment	300.2
Self-sustainment	509.1

Source: DPKO FMSS.

UNDOF Mission Expenditures: July 2000–June 2006 (in thousands of US dollars)					
Category	Jul 00–Jun 01	Jul 01–Jun 02	Jul 02–Jun 03	Jul 03–Jun 04	Jul 05–Jun 06
Military and Police Personnel	19,335.2	16,959.4	19,309.3	18,745.6	20,223.8
Civilian Personnel	5,088.0	6,348.7	6,892.7	7,597.2	7,867.5
Operational Requirements	9,046.8	11,114.8	12,773.7	13,401.0	12,025.6
Other	1,798.7	—	—	—	—
Gross Requirements	**35,268.7**	**34,422.9**	**38,975.7**	**39,743.8**	**40,116.9**
Staff Assessment Income	1,131.6	958.2	1,006.4	1,087.2	1,126.2
Net Requirements	**34,137.1**	**33,464.7**	**37,969.3**	**38,656.6**	**38,990.7**
Voluntary Contributions in Kind (budgeted)	—	—	—	—	—
Total Requirements	**35,268.7**	**34,422.9**	**38,975.7**	**39,743.8**	**40,116.9**

Sources: UN Documents A/56/813, A/57/668, A/58/641, A/59/625, A/60/628 and A/61/662.

7.8 UNFICYP (UN Peacekeeping Force in Cyprus)

UNFICYP Key Facts	

Latest Key Resolutions	14 December 2007 (date of issue);
	  15 December 2007 (date of effect)
	  UNSC Res. 1789 (six month duration)
	  15 June 2007 (date of issue and effect)
	  UNSC Res. 1758 (six month duration)
	  15 December 2006 (date of issue and effect)
	  UNSC Res. 1728 (six month duration)

First Mandate	4 March 1964 (date of issue and effect) UNSC Res. 186 (three month duration)

SRSG and Head of Mission	Michael Møller (Denmark)
	  SG letter of appointment 12 September 2005,
	  effective 1 December 2006

First SRSG	Carlos Alfredo Bernardes (Brazil)

Force Commander	Major-General Rafael José Barni (Argentina)
	  SG letter of appointment 6 February 2006
	  Entry on duty 5 March 2006

First Force Commander	Lieutenant-General P.S. Gyani (India)
Senior Police Advisor	Carla Van Maris (Netherlands) Date of appointment 18 September 2004

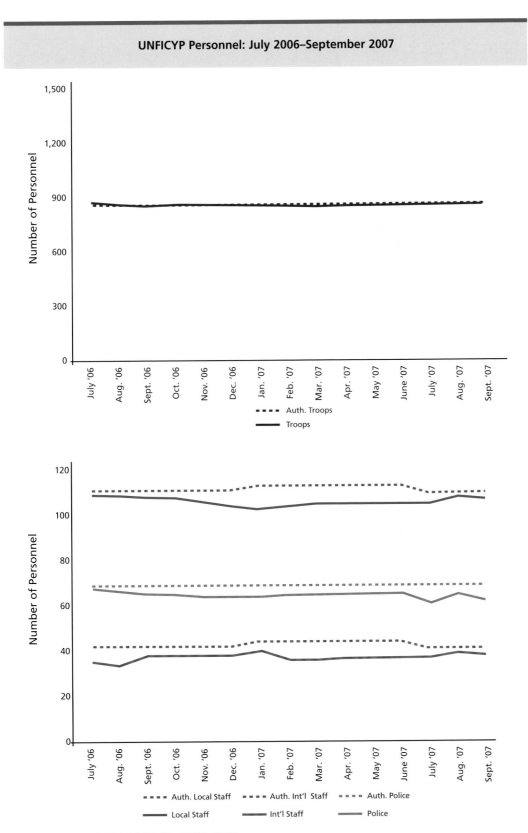

UNFICYP Personnel: July 2006–September 2007

······ Auth. Troops
——— Troops

····· Auth. Local Staff   ····· Auth. Int'l Staff   ····· Auth. Police
——— Local Staff   ——— Int'l Staff   ——— Police

Sources: DPKO FGS; DPKO PD; DPKO PMSS.

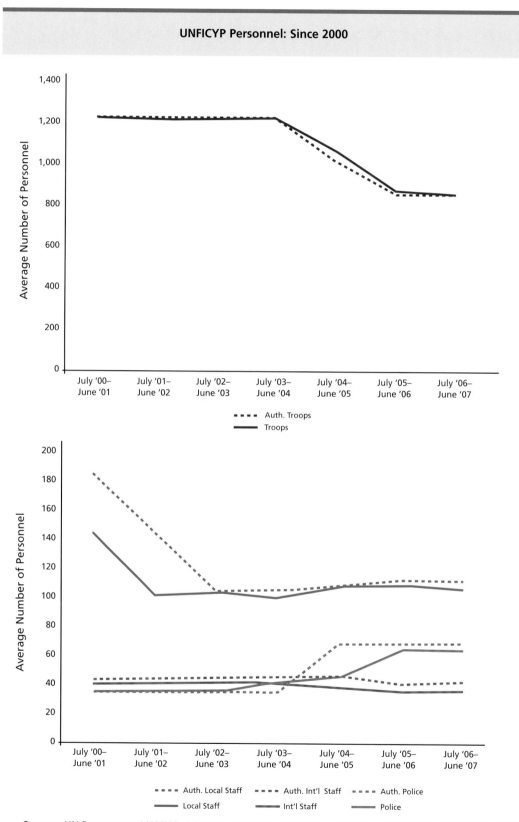

Sources: UN Documents A/56/782, A/57/667, A/58/631, A/59/620, A/60/584 and A/61/724; DPKO FGS; DPKO PD; DPKO PMSS.

UNFICYP Military and Police Contributors: 30 September 2007

Contributing Country	Troops	Military Observers	Police	Total
Argentina	287	—	4	291
United Kingdom	276	—	—	276
Slovakia	200	—	—	200
Hungary	84	—	—	84
Ireland	—	—	18	18
Australia	—	—	15	15
El Salvador	—	—	7	7
Netherlands	—	—	6	6
Austria	5	—	—	5
Croatia	—	—	4	4
Italy	—	—	4	4
Bosnia and Herzegovina	—	—	3	3
Canada	1	—	—	1
India	—	—	1	1
Total	**853**	**—**	**62**	**915**

Sources: DPKO FGS; DPKO PD.

UNFICYP Military Units: 30 September 2007

Number	Unit Type	Country
1	Aviation Unit	Argentina
1	Force Engineers Unit	Slovakia
1	Force Military Police Unit	Argentina-Hungary-Slovakia-United Kingdom Composite
3	Infantry Units	Argentina, Hungary-Slovakia Composite, United Kingdom
1	Mobile Force Reserve Unit	Argentina-Hungary-Slovakia-United Kingdom Composite

Source: DPKO FGS.
Note: Military headquarters staff and staff officers not included.

UNFICYP International Civilian Personnel Occupations: 30 September 2007

Occupation	International Staff	Percentage International Staff
Administration	9	23.7%
Aviation	—	—
Civil Affairs	3	7.9%
Economic Affairs	—	—
Engineering	2	5.3%
Finance	2	5.3%
Human Resources	2	5.3%
Human Rights	—	—
Humanitarian Affairs	—	—
Information Management	1	2.6%
Information Systems and Technology	5	13.2%
Legal Affairs	—	—
Logistics	1	2.6%
Medical Services	—	—
Political Affairs	4	10.5%
Procurement	2	5.3%
Programme Management	—	—
Public Information	2	5.3%
Rule of Law	3	7.9%
Security	2	5.3%
Social Affairs	—	—
Transport	—	—
Total	**38**	

Source: DPKO PMSS.

UNFICYP Personnel Gender Statistics: 30 September 2007

Personnel Type	Male	Female	Percentage Male	Percentage Female
Troops	813	40	95.3%	4.7%
Military Observers	—	—	—	—
Police	48	14	77.4%	22.6%
International Civilian Staff	25	13	65.8%	34.2%
Local Civilian Staff	62	45	57.9%	42.1%
Total	**948**	**112**	**89.4%**	**10.6%**

Sources: DPKO FGS; DPKO PD; DPKO PMSS.

UNFICYP Fatalities: Inception–September 2007

Personnel Type

Time Period	Troop	MilOb	Police	Intl Staff	Local Staff	Other[a]	Total
1963–1999	163	—	3	3	—	—	169
2000	1	—	—	—	—	—	1
2001	—	—	—	—	—	—	—
2002	—	—	—	—	—	—	—
2003	2	—	—	—	—	—	2
2004	1	—	—	—	1	—	2
2005	—	—	—	1	—	—	1
2006	—	—	—	—	1	—	1
January-March	—	—	—	—	1	—	1
April-June	—	—	—	—	—	—	—
July-September	—	—	—	—	—	—	—
October-December	—	—	—	—	—	—	—
2007 (Jan-Sep)	—	—	—	—	—	—	—
January-March	—	—	—	—	—	—	—
April-June	—	—	—	—	—	—	—
July-September	—	—	—	—	—	—	—
Total Fatalities	**167**	**—**	**3**	**4**	**2**	**—**	**176**

Incident Type

Time Period	Malicious Act	Illness	Accident	Other[b]	Total
1963–1999	15	41	91	22	169
2000	—	—	—	1	1
2001	—	—	—	—	—
2002	—	—	—	—	—
2003	—	—	2	—	2
2004	—	—	2	—	2
2005	—	1	—	—	1
2006	—	1	—	—	1
January-March	—	1	—	—	1
April-June	—	—	—	—	—
July-September	—	—	—	—	—
October-December	—	—	—	—	—
2007 (Jan-Sep)	—	—	—	—	—
January-March	—	—	—	—	—
April-June	—	—	—	—	—
July-September	—	—	—	—	—
Total Fatalities	**15**	**43**	**95**	**23**	**176**

Source: DPKO Situation Centre.
Notes: a. Other refers to consultants, UNVs, etc.
b. Incident type is unknown, uncertain or under investigation. Other includes what were previously qualified as self-inflicted.

UNFICYP Vehicles: 30 September 2007

Contingent Owned Vehicles		UN Owned Vehicles	
Vehicle Type	Quantity	Vehicle Type	Quantity
Combat Vehicles	9	4x4 Vehicles	9
Engineering Vehicles	4	Airfield Support Equipment	1
Material Handling Equipment	1	Ambulances	2
Support Vehicles (Commercial Pattern)	4	Bus	1
Support Vehicles (Military Pattern)	22	Engineering Vehicles	5
Trailers	6	Material Handling Equipment	20
Total	**46**	Trailers	16
		Trucks	30
		Total	**84**

Sources: DPKO Contingent Owned Equipment and Property Management Section; DPKO Surface Transport Section.

UNFICYP Aircraft: 30 September 2007

	Transport Fixed Wing	Transport Helicopter	Attack Helicopter
Commercial	—	—	—
Contingent Owned	—	3 (Argentina)	—
Total	**—**	**3**	**—**

Source: DPKO Air Transport Section.

UNFICYP Budget and Expenditures (in thousands of US dollars)

Category	Budgeted Jul 06–Jun 07	Expenditures Jul 06–Jun 07	Budgeted Jul 07–Jun 08
Military Observers	—	—	—
Military Contingents	17,198.6	18,417.7	18,900.0
Civilian Police	963.0	1,127.1	1,190.2
Formed Police Units	—	—	—
International Staff	5,856.2	6,069.8	6,019.6
Local Staff	5,844.3	6,850.8	6,601.7
United Nations Volunteers	—	—	—
General Temporary Assistance	332.9	155.2	79.0
Government-provided Personnel	—	—	—
Civilian Electoral Observers	—	—	—
Consultants	—	—	—
Official Travel	145.1	142.9	269.5
Facilities and Infrastructure	7,263.4	8,755.1	7,978.7
Ground Transportation	3,240.9	3,233.7	3,047.9
Air Transportation	1,567.2	1,576.5	1,589.1
Naval Transportation	—	—	—
Communications and Information Technology	1,496.2	1,345.2	1,564.5
Supplies, Services and Equipment	923.6	1,148.3	818.2
Quick-impact Projects	—	—	—
Gross Requirements	**44,831.4**	**50,760.3**	**50,318.5**
Staff Assessment Income	1,818.5	—	1,998.3
Net Requirements	**43,012.9**	**50,760.3**	**48,320.2**
Voluntary Contributions in Kind (budgeted)	1,439.0	1,475.0	1,471.0
Total Requirements	**46,270.4**	**52,235.3**	**51,789.5**

Sources: UN Documents A/61/774, A/61/852Add.4 and A/C.5/61/24; DPKO FMSS.
Notes: Financial figures are preliminary and subject to change. Gross requirements for July 2006–June 2007 expenditures include pro-rated costs of $1,938.0 thousand. Gross requirements for July 2007–June 2008 budgeted include pro-rated costs of $2,260.1 thousand.

UNFICYP Expenditures on Contingent Owned Equipment: July 2006–June 2007 (in thousands of US dollars)

Major Equipment	1,230.3
Self-sustainment	163.8

Source: DPKO FMSS.

UNFICYP Voluntary Contributions: July 2006–June 2007 (in thousands of US dollars)

Contributor	Contributions in Kind (budgeted)	Contributions in Kind (non-budgeted)	Contributions in Cash (budgeted)	Total
Cyprus	1,475.0	—	14,915.0	16,390.0
Greece	—	—	6,500.0	6,500.0
Total	1,475.0	—	21,415.0	22,890.0

Source: DM OPPBA.

UNFICYP Mission Expenditures: July 2000–June 2006 (in thousands of US dollars)

Category	Jul 00–Jun 01	Jul 01–Jun 02	Jul 02–Jun 03	Jul 03–Jun 04	Jul 04–Jun 05	Jul 05–Jun 06
Military and Police Personnel	22,150.2	20,169.2	22,583.1	22,980.3	21,685.5	18,131.3
Civilian Personnel	8,318.4	8,678.4	10,016.0	11,410.4	12,162.6	12,228.3
Operational Requirements	7,887.2	11,440.8	11,045.0	11,073.5	14,777.0	13,466.7
Other	2,090.0	—	—	—	—	—
Gross Requirements	40,445.8	40,288.4	43,644.1	45,464.2	48,625.1	43,826.3
Staff Assessment Income	1,914.7	1,489.0	1,721.7	1,865.3	1,984.7	2,001.0
Net Requirements	38,531.1	38,799.4	41,922.4	43,598.9	46,640.4	41,825.3
Voluntary Contributions in Kind (budgeted)	—	1,356.1	1,271.2	1,707.1	1,355.8	1,278.4
Total Requirements	40,445.8	41,644.5	44,915.3	47,171.3	49,980.9	45,104.7

Sources: UN Documents A/56/782, A/57/667, A/58/631, A/59/620, A/60/584 and A/61/724.

7.9 UNIFIL (UN Interim Force in Lebanon)

UNIFIL Key Facts	
Latest Key Resolution	24 August 2007 (date of issue); 1 September 2007 (date of effect) UNSC Res. 1773 (twelve month duration)
First Mandate	19 March 1978 (date of issue and effect) UNSC Res. 425/426 (six month duration)
Force Commander	Major-General Claudio Graziano (Italy) SG letter of appointment 16 January 2007 Entry on duty 17 February 2007
First Force Commander	Lieutenant-General Emmanuel A. Erskine (Ghana)

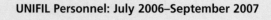

UNIFIL Personnel: July 2006–September 2007

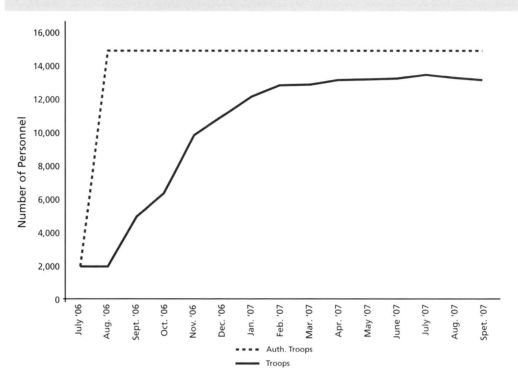

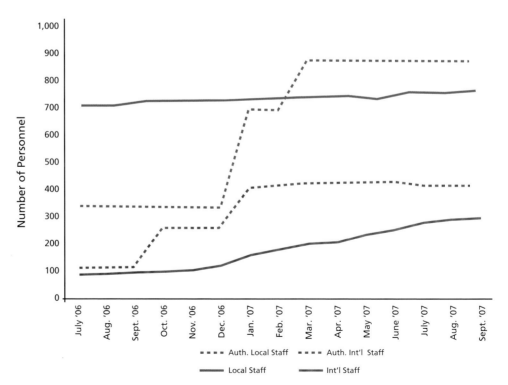

Sources: DPKO FGS; DPKO PMSS.

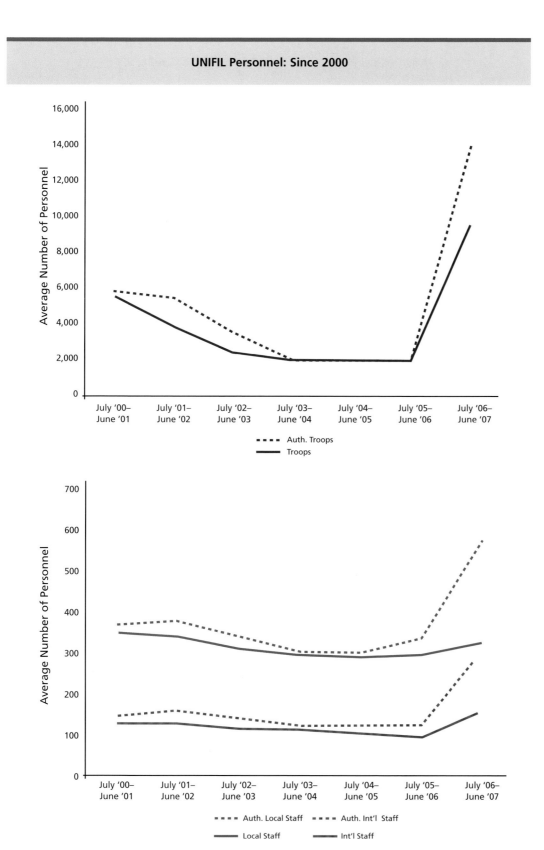

UNIFIL Personnel: Since 2000

Sources: UN Documents A/56/822, A/57/662, A/58/637, A/59/626, A/60/629 and A/61/829; DPKO FGS; DPKO PMSS.

UNIFIL Military and Police Contributors: 30 September 2007

Contributing Country	Troops	Military Observers	Police	Total
Italy	2,379	—	—	2,379
France	1,587	—	—	1,587
Spain	1,121	—	—	1,121
Germany	905	—	—	905
India	884	—	—	884
Ghana	868	—	—	868
Nepal	859	—	—	859
Indonesia	856	—	—	856
Turkey	746	—	—	746
Poland	482	—	—	482
Republic of Korea	363	—	—	363
Malaysia	362	—	—	362
China	343	—	—	343
Belgium	323	—	—	323
Greece	228	—	—	228
Finland	205	—	—	205
Qatar	203	—	—	203
Ireland	166	—	—	166
Netherlands	149	—	—	149
Portugal	146	—	—	146
Tanzania	77	—	—	77
Hungary	4	—	—	4
Cyprus	2	—	—	2
Guatemala	2	—	—	2
Luxembourg	2	—	—	2
Croatia	1	—	—	1
FYR of Macedonia	1	—	—	1
Total	**13,264**	—	—	**13,264**

Source: DPKO FGS.

UNIFIL Military Units: 30 September 2007

Number	Unit Type	Country
2	Aviation Units	Italy, Spain
1	Combat Support Service Company	Spain
1	Cartographic Staff	Hungary
1	Communications Unit	Spain
6	Engineering Companies	Belgium-Luxembourg Composite, China, France, Italy, Portugal, Turkey
1	Guard and Administrative Company	Malaysia
3	Headquarters Companies	Italy, Qatar, Spain
2	Infantry Battalions	Ghana, India
1	Infantry Company	Republic of Korea
1	Level I (plus) Hospital	India
2	Level II Hospitals	Belgium-Slovakia-Ukraine Composite, China
2	Logistics Companies	Italy, Poland
7	Mechanized Battalions	France (2), Indonesia, Italy (2), Nepal, Spain
2	Mechanized Companies	Ireland, Poland
2	Signals Companies	Italy, Spain
2	Corvette Components	Turkey
5	Fast Patrol Boat Components	Germany (4), Greece
4	Frigate Components	Germany, Greece, Netherlands, Turkey
4	Supply Ship Components	Germany (2), Norway, Turkey

Source: DPKO FGS.
Note: Military headquarters staff and staff officers not included.

UNIFIL International Civilian Personnel Occupations: 30 September 2007

Occupation	International Staff	Percentage International Staff
Administration	39	13.1%
Aviation	2	0.7%
Civil Affairs	6	2.0%
Economic Affairs	—	—
Engineering	26	8.7%
Finance	11	3.7%
Human Resources	12	4.0%
Human Rights	—	—
Humanitarian Affairs	—	—
Information Management	—	—
Information Systems and Technology	45	15.1%
Legal Affairs	2	0.7%
Logistics	60	20.1%
Medical Services	4	1.3%
Political Affairs	4	1.3%
Procurement	12	4.0%
Programme Management	1	0.3%
Public Information	6	2.0%
Rule of Law	4	1.3%
Security	34	11.4%
Social Affairs	1	0.3%
Transport	29	9.7%
Total	**298**	

Source: DPKO PMSS.

UNIFIL Personnel Gender Statistics: 30 September 2007

Personnel Type	Male	Female	Percentage Male	Percentage Female
Troops	12,878	386	97.1%	2.9%
Military Observers	—	—	—	—
Police	—	—	—	—
International Civilian Staff	225	73	75.5%	24.5%
Local Civilian Staff	442	129	77.4%	22.6%
Total	**13,545**	**588**	**95.8%**	**4.2%**

Sources: DPKO FGS; DPKO PMSS.

UNIFIL Fatalities: Inception–September 2007

Personnel Type

Time Period	Troop	MilOb	Police	Intl Staff	Local Staff	Other[a]	Total
1978–1999	233	1	—	2	1	—	237
2000	6	—	—	—	—	—	6
2001	3	1	—	—	—	—	4
2002	3	—	—	—	3	—	6
2003	1	—	—	—	—	—	1
2004	3	—	—	—	—	—	3
2005	—	—	—	—	—	—	—
2006	—	—	—	1	—	—	1
January-March	—	—	—	—	—	—	—
April-June	—	—	—	—	—	—	—
July-September	—	—	—	1	—	—	1
October-December	—	—	—	—	—	—	—
2007 (Jan-Sep)	8	—	—	1	—	—	9
January-March	1	—	—	1	—	—	2
April-June	7	—	—	—	—	—	7
July-September	—	—	—	—	—	—	—
Total Fatalities	**257**	**2**	**—**	**4**	**4**	**—**	**267**

Incident Type

Time Period	Malicious Act	Illness	Accident	Other[b]	Total
1978–1999	84	46	95	12	237
2000	1	—	5	—	6
2001	—	2	2	—	4
2002	—	3	3	—	6
2003	—	1	—	—	1
2004	—	—	3	—	3
2005	—	—	—	—	—
2006	—	—	—	1	1
January-March	—	—	—	—	—
April-June	—	—	—	—	—
July-September	—	—	—	1	1
October-December	—	—	—	—	—
2007 (Jan-Sep)	6	—	2	1	9
January-March	—	—	1	1	2
April-June	6	—	1	—	7
July-September	—	—	—	—	—
Total Fatalities	**91**	**52**	**110**	**14**	**267**

Source: DPKO Situation Centre.
Notes: a. Other refers to consultants, UNVs, etc.
b. Incident type is unknown, uncertain or under investigation. Other includes what were previously qualified as self-inflicted.

UNIFIL Vehicles: 30 September 2007

Contingent Owned Vehicles		UN Owned Vehicles	
Vehicle Type	Quantity	Vehicle Type	Quantity
Airfield/Airfield Support Equipment	11	4x4 Vehicles	406
Combat Vehicles	556	Airfield Support Equipment	1
Communications Vehicles	45	Ambulances	19
Engineering Vehicles	244	Armoured Personnel Carriers	45
Material Handling Equipment	50	Automobiles	109
Support Vehicles (Commercial Pattern)	247	Buses	56
Support Vehicles (Military Pattern)	1,419	Engineering Vehicle	1
Trailers	511	Material Handling Equipment	57
Total	**3,083**	Snow Tracks	2
		Trailers	38
		Trucks	141
		Vans	17
		Total	**892**

Sources: DPKO Contingent Owned Equipment and Property Management Section; DPKO Surface Transport Section.

Note: UNIFIL is supported by a maritime task force of 19 ships.

UNIFIL Aircraft: 30 September 2007

	Transport Fixed Wing	Transport Helicopter	Attack Helicopter
Commercial	—	1	—
Contingent Owned	—	15 (4 Germany, Greece, 6 Italy, Netherlands, 2 Spain, Turkey)	—
Total	**—**	**16**	**—**

Source: DPKO Air Transport Section.

UNIFIL Budget and Expenditures (in thousands of US dollars)

Category	Budgeted Jan 06–Dec 07	Expenditures Jul 06–Jun 07	Budgeted Jul 07–Jun 08
Military Observers	—	—	—
Military Contingents	258,965.5	235,814.9	375,536.2
Civilian Police	—	—	—
Formed Police Units	—	—	—
International Staff	21,417.8	30,078.9	67,288.3
Local Staff	14,877.7	20,238.2	40,701.9
United Nations Volunteers	—	—	—
General Temporary Assistance	2,883.8	3,496.7	1,429.6
Government-provided Personnel	—	—	—
Civilian Electoral Observers	—	—	—
Consultants	227.1	115.5	461.4
Official Travel	702.8	504.4	758.8
Facilities and Infrastructure	76,388.0	81,676.3	79,866.8
Ground Transportation	16,750.3	17,655.4	11,687.0
Air Transportation	5,140.0	5,527.0	7,182.7
Naval Transportation	53,133.7	55,468.1	86,627.0
Communications and Information Technology	28,390.1	28,892.2	20,849.5
Supplies, Services and Equipment	17,527.3	15,790.2	20,697.6
Quick-impact Projects	211.4	477.8	500.0
Gross Requirements	**496,615.5**	**499,787.7**	**748,204.6**
Staff Assessment Income	4,582.6	4,698.0	11,871.5
Net Requirements	**492,032.9**	**495,089.7**	**736,333.1**
Voluntary Contributions in Kind (budgeted)	—	—	—
Total Requirements	**496,615.5**	**499,787.7**	**748,204.6**

Sources: UN Documents A/61/852/Add.16 and A/61/870; DPKO FMSS.
Notes: The July 2006–June 2007 budget includes the approved budget and the $50 million in Commitment Authority for that period as of 31 October 2006. Financial figures are preliminary and subject to change. Gross requirements for July 2006–June 2007 expenditures include pro-rated costs of $4,052.1 thousand. Gross requirements for July 2007–June 2008 budgeted include pro-rated costs of $34,617.8 thousand.

UNIFIL Expenditures on Contingent Owned Equipment: July 2006–June 2007 (in thousands of US dollars)

Major Equipment	57,607.0
Self-sustainment	33,708.5

Source: DPKO FMSS.

UNIFIL Mission Expenditures: July 2000–June 2006 (in thousands of US dollars)

Category	Jul 00–Jun 01	Jul 01–Jun 02	Jul 02–Jun 03	Jul 03–Jun 04	Jul 04–Jun 05	Jul 05–Jun 06
Military and Police Personnel	112,944.0	69,170.0	51,098.7	40,465.1	40,509.1	40,777.8
Civilian Personnel	25,321.1	29,674.0	34,835.0	30,673.5	30,441.7	30,340.8
Operational Requirements	33,855.3	32,067.0	21,663.0	18,757.4	18,293.3	20,145.6
Other	6,938.5	—	—	—	—	—
Gross Requirements	**179,058.9**	**130,911.0**	**107,596.7**	**89,896.0**	**89,244.1**	**91,264.2**
Staff Assessment Income	4,752.1	4,231.8	4,520.2	4,340.3	4,164.1	4,078.5
Net Requirements	**174,306.8**	**126,679.2**	**103,076.5**	**85,555.7**	**85,080.0**	**87,185.7**
Voluntary Contributions in Kind (budgeted)	180.0	201.2	—	—	—	—
Total Requirements	**179,238.9**	**131,112.2**	**107,596.7**	**89,896.0**	**89,244.1**	**91,264.2**

Sources: UN Documents A/56/822, A/57/662, A/58/637, A/59/626, A/60/629 and A/61/829.

7.10 UNIOSIL (UN Integrated Office for Sierra Leone)

UNIOSIL Key Facts	

Latest Key Resolutions	31 December 2007 (date of issue and effect)
	  UNSC Res. 1793 (nine month duration and reduction of
	  staff resulting in mission termination at the end of mandate)
	22 December 2006 (date of issue); 1 January 2007
	  (date of effect)
	UNSC Res. 1734 (twelve month duration and temporary
	  ten month increase in strength)

First Mandate	31 August 2005 (date of issue); 1 January 2006 (date of effect) UNSC Res. 1620 (twelve month duration)

ERSG	Victor da Silva Angelo (first ERSG, Portugal)
	  SG letter of appointment 12 December 2005,
	  effective 1 January 2006

Chief Military Liaison Officer	Colonel Sven-Olof Broman (Sweden) Entry on duty 12 December 2005
Senior Police Advisor	Rudolfo Landeros (United States) Date of appointment 30 March 2006

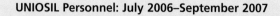

UNIOSIL Personnel: July 2006–September 2007

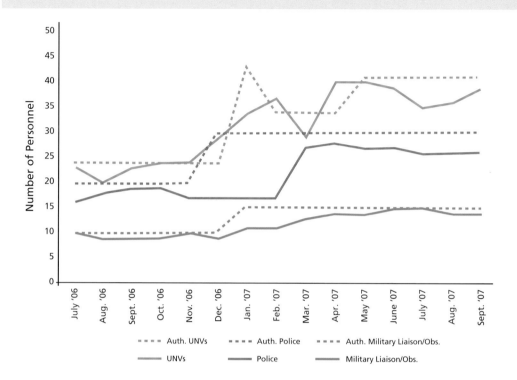

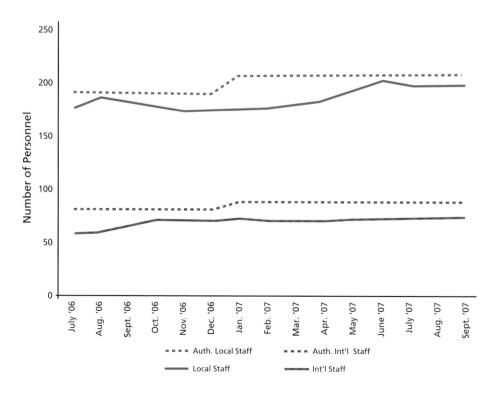

Sources: UN Documents S/RES/1620, S/RES/1734 and S/2005/273/Add.2; DPKO FGS; DPKO PD; DPKO PMSS; UNV Programme.

UNIOSIL Personnel: Since 2006

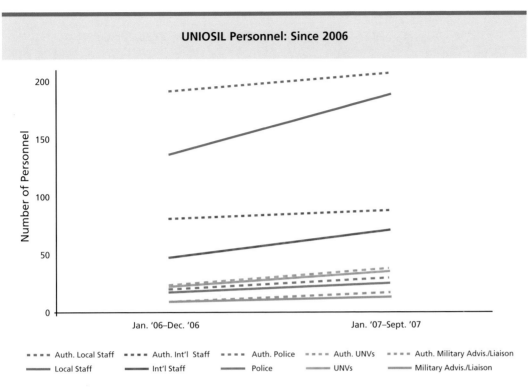

Legend:
- ····· Auth. Local Staff
- ---- Auth. Int'l Staff
- ---- Auth. Police
- ····· Auth. UNVs
- ---- Auth. Military Advis./Liaison
- —— Local Staff
- —— Int'l Staff
- —— Police
- —— UNVs
- —— Military Advis./Liaison

Sources: DPKO FGS; DPKO PD; DPKO PMSS; UNV Programme.

UNIOSIL Military and Police Contributors: 30 September 2007

Contributing Country	Troops	Military Observers	Police	Total
Nigeria	—	2	5	7
Sweden	—	1	3	4
Ghana	—	2	1	3
India	—	—	3	3
Nepal	—	1	2	3
Spain	—	—	3	3
United Kingdom	—	1	2	3
Gambia	—	—	2	2
Kenya	—	1	1	2
Portugal	—	—	2	2
Bangladesh	—	1	—	1
China	—	1	—	1
Croatia	—	1	—	1
Egypt	—	1	—	1
Malaysia	—	—	1	1
Pakistan	—	1	—	1
Turkey	—	—	1	1
Zambia	—	1	—	1
Total	**—**	**14**	**26**	**40**

Sources: DPKO FGS; DPKO PD.

UNIOSIL International Civilian Personnel Occupations: 30 September 2007

Occupation	International Staff	Percentage International Staff
Administration	12	16.0%
Aviation	2	2.7%
Civil Affairs	—	—
Economic Affairs	1	1.3%
Engineering	3	4.0%
Finance	7	9.3%
Human Resources	3	4.0%
Human Rights	5	6.7%
Humanitarian Affairs	—	—
Information Management	—	—
Information Systems and Technology	4	5.3%
Legal Affairs	1	1.3%
Logistics	8	10.7%
Medical Services	1	1.3%
Political Affairs	11	14.7%
Procurement	1	1.3%
Programme Management	—	—
Public Information	2	2.7%
Rule of Law	4	5.3%
Security	7	9.3%
Social Affairs	1	1.3%
Transport	2	2.7%
Total	**75**	

Source: DPKO PMSS.

UNIOSIL Personnel Gender Statistics: 30 September 2007

Personnel Type	Male	Female	Percentage Male	Percentage Female
Troops	—	—	—	—
Military Observers	14	—	100.0%	—
Police	22	4	84.6%	15.4%
International Civilian Staff	49	26	65.3%	34.7%
Local Civilian Staff	145	54	72.9%	27.1%
Total	**230**	**84**	**73.2%**	**26.8%**

Sources: DPKO FGS; DPKO PD; DPKO PMSS.

UNIOSIL Fatalities: Inception–September 2007

Personnel Type

Time Period	Troop	MilOb	Police	Intl Staff	Local Staff	Other[a]	Total
2006	—	1	—	—	2	—	3
January-March	—	—	—	—	1	—	1
April-June	—	—	—	—	—	—	—
July-September	—	1	—	—	—	—	1
October-December	—	—	—	—	1	—	1
2007 (Jan-Sep)	—	—	—	—	1	—	1
January-March	—	—	—	—	—	—	—
April-June	—	—	—	—	—	—	—
July-September	—	—	—	—	1	—	1
Total Fatalities	**—**	**1**	**—**	**—**	**3**	**—**	**4**

Incident Type

Time Period	Malicious Act	Illness	Accident	Other[b]	Total
2006	—	3	—	—	3
January-March	—	1	—	—	1
April-June	—	—	—	—	—
July-September	—	1	—	—	1
October-December	—	1	—	—	1
2007 (Jan-Sep)	—	—	—	1	1
January-March	—	—	—	—	—
April-June	—	—	—	—	—
July-September	—	—	—	1	1
Total Fatalities	**—**	**3**	**—**	**1**	**4**

Source: DPKO Situation Centre.
Notes: a. Other refers to consultants, UNVs, etc.
b. Incident type is unknown, uncertain or under investigation. Other includes what were previously qualified as self-inflicted.

UNIOSIL Vehicles: 30 September 2007

UN Owned Vehicles

Vehicle Type	Quantity
4x4 Vehicles	96
Airfield Support Equipment	2
Ambulances	2
Automobiles	2
Buses	13
Material Handling Equipment	8
Motorcycles	6
Trailers	6
Trucks	27
Vans	5
Total	**167**

Source: DPKO Surface Transport Section.

UNIOSIL Aircraft: 30 September 2007

	Transport Fixed Wing	Transport Helicopter	Attack Helicopter
Commercial	—	2	—
Contingent Owned	—	—	—
Total	—	**2**	—

Source: DPKO Air Transport Section.

UNIOSIL Budget and Expenditures (in thousands of US dollars)

Category	Budgeted Jan 06–Dec 07	Estimated Expenditures Jan 06–Dec 07
Military Observers	1,184.9	1,047.5
Military Contingents	—	33.8
Civilian Police	2,151.5	1,889.5
Formed Police Units	—	—
International Staff	21,743.3	19,389.7
Local Staff	2,524.0	2,616.4
United Nations Volunteers	2,638.0	2,310.3
General Temporary Assistance	—	—
Government-provided Personnel	—	—
Civilian Electoral Observers	—	—
Consultants	110.5	85.5
Official Travel	794.7	833.6
Facilities and Infrastructure	7,784.5	8,042.0
Ground Transportation	1,573.0	1,645.3
Air Transportation	7,839.1	8,842.8
Naval Transportation	—	—
Communications and Information Technology	4,009.1	3,501.7
Supplies, Services and Equipment	826.1	738.6
Quick-impact Projects	—	—
Gross Requirements	**53,178.7**	**50,976.7**
Staff Assessment Income	2,981.3	2,311.4
Net Requirements	**50,197.4**	**48,665.3**
Voluntary Contributions in Kind (budgeted)	—	—
Total Requirements	**53,178.7**	**50,976.7**

Source: DPKO FMSS.
Note: Financial figures are preliminary and subject to change.

7.11 UNMEE (UN Mission in Ethiopia and Eritrea)

UNMEE Key Facts	
Latest Key Resolutions	30 July 2007 (date of issue); 1 August 2007 (date of effect) UNSC Res. 1767 (six month duration) 30 January 2007 (date of issue and effect) UNSC Res. 1741 (six month duration and troop decrease)
First Mandate	31 July 2000 (date of issue and effect) UNSC Res. 1312 (six week duration)
Acting SRSG	Azouz Ennifar (Tunisia) Date of Appointment 1 May 2006
First SRSG	Legwaila Joseph Legwaila (Botswana)
Force Commander	Major-General Mohammad Taisir Masadeh (Jordan) SG letter of appointment 7 April 2006, effective 9 April 2006
First Force Commander	Major-General Patrick Cammaert (Netherlands)

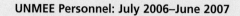

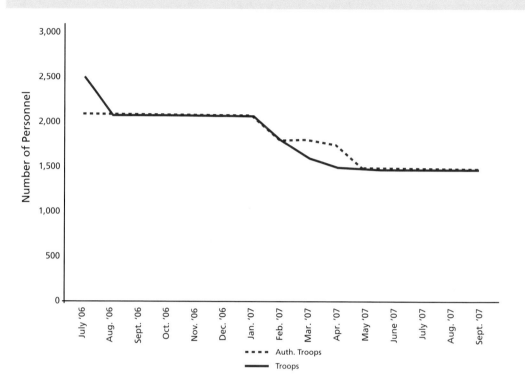

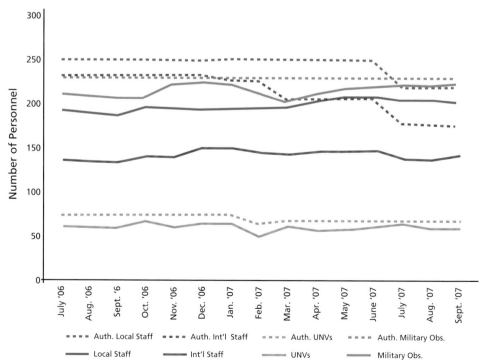

Sources: DPKO FGS; DPKO PMSS; UNV Programme.

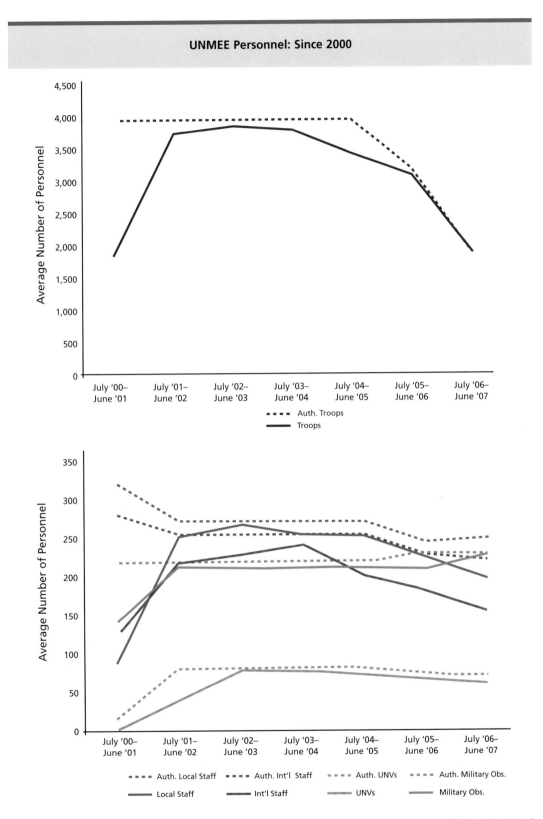

UNMEE Personnel: Since 2000

Sources: UN Documents S/RES/1320, S/RES/1622, S/RES/1681, A/56/840, A/57/672, A/58/633, A/59/616, A/60/615 and A/61/720; DPKO FGS; DPKO PMSS; UNV Programme.

UNMEE Military and Police Contributors: 30 September 2007

Contributing Country	Troops	Military Observers	Police	Total	Contributing Country	Troops	Military Observers	Police	Total
India	715	8	—	723	United States	—	5	—	5
Jordan	570	8	—	578	Bulgaria	—	4	—	4
Kenya	118	10	—	128	Croatia	—	4	—	4
Uruguay	37	5	—	42	Kyrgyzstan	—	4	—	4
Ghana	3	12	—	15	Mongolia	—	4	—	4
Bangladesh	5	8	—	13	Paraguay	—	4	—	4
Zambia	3	9	—	12	Peru	—	4	—	4
Malaysia	3	7	—	10	Sri Lanka	—	4	—	4
Tanzania	2	8	—	10	Denmark	—	3	—	3
Algeria	—	8	—	8	Greece	—	3	—	3
Nigeria	1	7	—	8	Iran	—	3	—	3
Tunisia	3	5	—	8	Norway	—	3	—	3
Brazil	—	7	—	7	Poland	—	3	—	3
Namibia	3	4	—	7	Russia	—	3	—	3
Nepal	—	7	—	7	Spain	—	3	—	3
China	—	6	—	6	Ukraine	—	3	—	3
Bolivia	—	5	—	5	Austria	—	2	—	2
Bosnia and Herzegovina	—	5	—	5	Czech Republic	—	2	—	2
Finland	—	5	—	5	Germany	—	2	—	2
Gambia	1	4	—	5	South Africa	—	2	—	2
Guatemala	—	5	—	5	Sweden	—	2	—	2
Pakistan	—	5	—	5	France	—	1	—	1
Romania	—	5	—	5	Switzerland	—	1	—	1
					Total	**1,464**	**222**	**—**	**1,686**

Source: DPKO FGS.

UNMEE Military Units: 30 September 2007

Number	Unit Type	Countries
1	Guard and Administrative Company	Kenya
1	Aviation Unit	Uruguay
1	Construction Engineering Company	India
1	De-mining Company	Kenya
2	Infantry Battalions	India, Jordan
1	Level II Hospital	Jordan
1	Military Police Unit	Jordan

Source: DPKO FGS.
Note: Military headquarters staff and military observers not included.

UNMEE International Civilian Personnel Occupations: 30 September 2007

Occupation	International Staff	Percentage International Staff
Administration	30	21.1%
Aviation	3	2.1%
Civil Affairs	—	—
Economic Affairs	—	—
Engineering	9	6.3%
Finance	9	6.3%
Human Resources	5	3.5%
Human Rights	5	3.5%
Humanitarian Affairs	—	—
Information Management	—	—
Information Systems and Technology	15	10.6%
Legal Affairs	2	1.4%
Logistics	18	12.7%
Medical Services	1	0.7%
Political Affairs	8	5.6%
Procurement	4	2.8%
Programme Management	—	—
Public Information	7	4.9%
Rule of Law	2	1.4%
Security	16	11.3%
Social Affairs	1	0.7%
Transport	7	4.9%
Total	**142**	

Source: DPKO PMSS.

UNMEE Personnel Gender Statistics: 30 September 2007

Personnel Type	Male	Female	Percentage Male	Percentage Female
Troops	1,455	9	99.4%	0.6%
Military Observers	214	8	96.4%	3.6%
Police	—	—	—	—
International Civilian Staff	104	38	73.2%	26.8%
Local Civilian Staff	133	70	65.5%	34.5%
Total	**1,906**	**125**	**93.8%**	**6.2%**

Sources: DPKO FGS; DPKO PMSS.

UNMEE Fatalities: Inception–September 2007

Personnel Type

Time Period	Troop	MilOb	Police	Intl Staff	Local Staff	Other[a]	Total
2001	2	—	—	—	1	—	3
2002	1	—	—	—	1	—	2
2003	2	—	—	1	1	—	4
2004	2	—	—	—	—	—	2
2005	1	—	—	1	—	—	2
2006	4	—	—	—	—	—	4
January-March	1	—	—	—	—	—	1
April-June	—	—	—	—	—	—	—
July-September	2	—	—	—	—	—	2
October-December	1	—	—	—	—	—	1
2007 (Jan-Sep)	1	—	—	1	1	—	3
January-March	—	—	—	—	—	—	—
April-June	1	—	—	—	1	—	2
July-September	—	—	—	1	—	—	1
Total Fatalities	**13**	—	—	**3**	**4**	—	**20**

Incident Type

Time Period	Malicious Act	Illness	Accident	Other[b]	Total
2001	—	2	1	—	3
2002	—	1	1	—	2
2003	—	4	—	—	4
2004	—	2	—	—	2
2005	—	1	1	—	2
2006	—	3	1	—	4
January-March	—	1	—	—	1
April-June	—	—	—	—	—
July-September	—	1	1	—	2
October-December	—	1	—	—	1
2007 (Jan-Sep)	—	1	—	2	3
January-March	—	—	—	—	—
April-June	—	1	—	1	2
July-September	—	—	—	1	1
Total Fatalities	—	**14**	**4**	**2**	**20**

Source: DPKO Situation Centre.
Notes: a. Other refers to consultants, UNVs, etc.
  b. Incident type is unknown, uncertain or under investigation. Other includes what were previously qualified as self-inflicted.

UNMEE Vehicles: 30 September 2007

Contingent Owned Vehicles		UN Owned Vehicles	
Vehicle Type	Quantity	Vehicle Type	Quantity
Aircraft/Airfield Support Equipment	3	4x4 Vehicles	434
Combat Vehicles	62	Ambulances	2
Communications Vehicle	1	Automobiles	33
Engineering Vehicles	30	Buses	56
Material Handling Equipment	2	Material Handling Equipment	17
Support Vehicles (Commercial Pattern)	92	Trailers	9
Support Vehicles (Military Pattern)	224	Trucks	77
Trailers	26	Vans	14
Total	**440**	**Total**	**642**

Sources: DPKO Contingent Owned Equipment and Property Management Section; DPKO Surface Transport Section.

UNMEE Aircraft: 30 September 2007

	Transport Fixed Wing	Transport Helicopter	Attack Helicopter
Commercial	2	1	—
Contingent Owned	—	2 (Uruguay)	—
Total	**2**	**3**	—

Source: DPKO Air Transport Section.

UNMEE Budget and Expenditures (in thousands of US dollars)

Category	Budgeted Jul 06–Jun 07	Expenditures Jul 06–Jun 07	Budgeted Jul 07–Jun 08
Military Observers	7,755.1	7,649.9	8,038.0
Military Contingents	55,347.2	54,740.4	37,418.7
Civilian Police	—	—	—
Formed Police Units	—	—	—
International Staff	22,113.6	20,135.6	20,964.9
Local Staff	1,245.8	1,187.5	1,304.0
United Nations Volunteers	2,365.6	2,237.8	2,127.1
General Temporary Assistance	622.3	30.6	133.4
Government-provided Personnel	—	—	—
Civilian Electoral Observers	—	—	—
Consultants	—	5.0	—
Official Travel	666.8	568.2	677.6
Facilities and Infrastructure	14,044.9	11,842.4	12,757.6
Ground Transportation	5,388.2	4,804.8	4,751.6
Air Transportation	8,897.3	7,707.2	8,233.2
Naval Transportation	—	—	—
Communications and Information Technology	5,907.0	4,986.7	5,480.0
Supplies, Services, and Equipment	13,031.3	10,722.4	11,597.3
Quick-impact Projects	—	—	—
Gross Requirements	**137,385.1**	**126,618.5**	**118,988.7**
Staff Assessment Income	2,751.0	2,718.1	—
Net Requirements	**134,634.1**	**123,900.4**	**118,988.7**
Voluntary Contributions in Kind (budgeted)	—	—	—
Total Requirements	**137,385.1**	**126,618.5**	**118,988.7**

Sources: UN Documents A/61/852/Add.9 and A/62/560; DPKO FMSS.
Notes: Financial figures are preliminary and subject to change. Gross requirements for July 2007–June 2008 budgeted include pro-rated costs of $5,505.3 thousand.

UNMEE Expenditures on Contingent Owned Equipment: July 2006–June 2007 (in thousands of US dollars)

Major Equipment	11,084.6
Self-sustainment	7,346.5

Source: DPKO FMSS.

UNMEE Mission Expenditures: July 2000–June 2006 (in thousands of US dollars)

Category	Jul 00–Jun 01	Jul 01–Jun 02	Jul 02–Jun 03	Jul 03–Jun 04	Jul 04–Jun 05	Jul 05–Jun 06
Military and Police Personnel	58,852.8	83,695.9	102,877.7	94,115.2	85,550.3	78,057.5
Civilian Personnel	12,429.1	27,756.2	31,042.2	34,311.3	31,112.2	27,778.4
Operational Requirements	80,993.8	73,555.6	75,699.2	55,173.7	63,667.8	50,160.2
Other	9,928.3	—	—	—	—	—
Gross Requirements	**162,204.0**	**185,007.7**	**209,619.1**	**183,600.2**	**180,330.3**	**155,996.1**
Staff Assessment Income	1,902.0	3,507.9	4,010.3	4,577.3	4,000.9	3,511.1
Net Requirements	**160,302.0**	**181,499.8**	**205,608.8**	**179,022.9**	**176,329.4**	**152,485.0**
Voluntary Contributions in Kind (budgeted)	—	—	—	—	—	—
Total Requirements	**162,204.0**	**185,007.7**	**209,619.1**	**183,600.2**	**180,330.3**	**155,996.1**

Sources: UN Documents A/56/840, A/57/672, A/58/633, A/59/616, A/60/615 and A/61/720.

7.12 UNMIK (UN Interim Administration in Kosovo)

UNMIK Key Facts	
First Mandate	10 June 1999 (date of issue and effect) UNSC Res. 1244 (paragraph 19 of the Resolution states that international civil and security presences are established for an initial period of twelve months, to continue thereafter until the Security Council decides otherwise.)
SRSG and Head of Mission	Joachim Rücker (Germany) SG letter of appointment 14 August 2006, effective 1 September 2006
First SRSG	Bernard Kouchner (France)
Chief Military Liaison Officer	Major-General Raul Cunha (Portugal) Entry on duty 24 November 2005
Police Commissioner	Richard Monk (United Kingdom) Entry on duty 5 March 2007

UNMIK Personnel: July 2006–September 2007

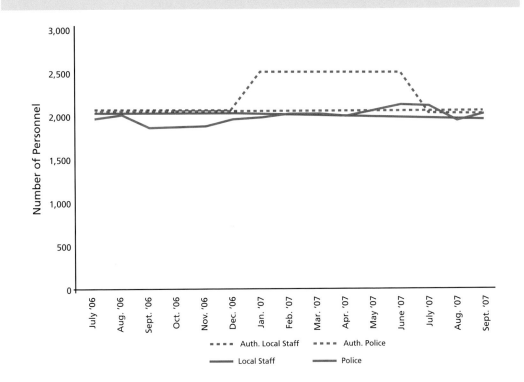

Auth. Local Staff ••••• Auth. Police
——— Local Staff ——— Police

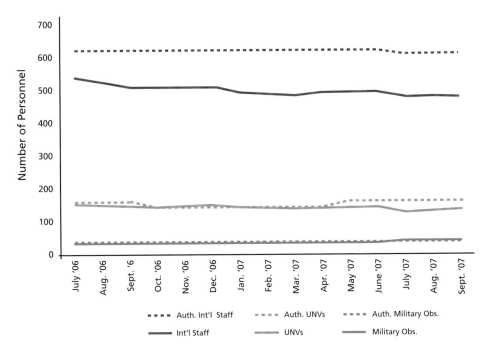

••••• Auth. Int'l Staff ••••• Auth. UNVs ••••• Auth. Military Obs.
——— Int'l Staff ——— UNVs ——— Military Obs.

Sources: DPKO FGS; DPKO PD; DPKO PMSS; UNV Programme.

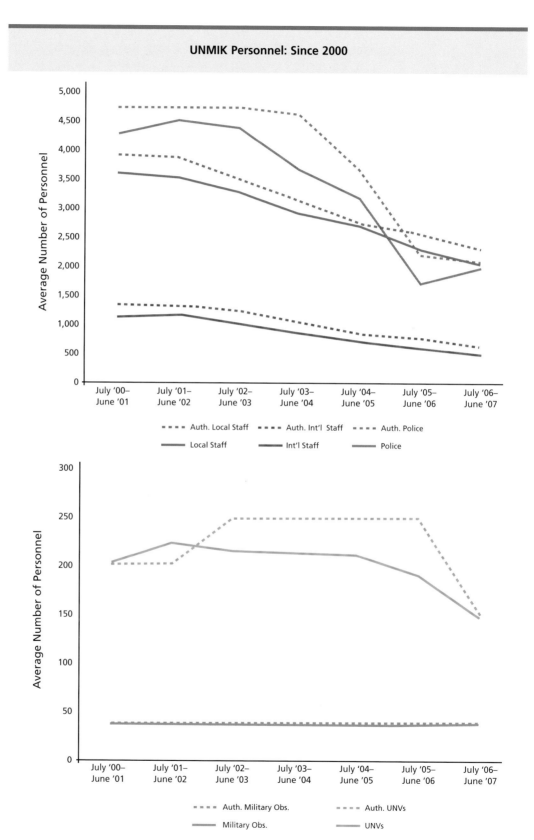

UNMIK Personnel: Since 2000

Sources: UN Documents A/55/724, A/56/763, A/57/678, A/58/634, A/59/623, A/60/637 and A/61/675; DPKO FGS; DPKO PD; DPKO PMSS; UNV Programme.

UNMIK Military and Police Contributors: 30 September 2007

Contributing Country	Troops	Military Observers	Police	Total	Contributing Country	Troops	Military Observers	Police	Total
United States	—	—	208	208	Kenya	—	2	15	17
Ukraine	—	2	188	190	Spain	—	2	15	17
Pakistan	—	2	181	183	Egypt	—	—	16	16
Romania	—	3	172	175	Hungary	—	1	15	16
Germany	—	—	157	157	Norway	—	1	14	15
Poland	—	1	122	123	Slovenia	—	—	15	15
Turkey	—	—	114	114	Finland	—	2	10	12
India	—	—	87	87	Argentina	—	1	10	11
Jordan	—	2	68	70	Zambia	—	1	10	11
Philippines	—	—	63	63	Croatia	—	—	9	9
United Kingdom	—	1	61	62	Greece	—	—	9	9
Bulgaria	—	1	50	51	Kyrgyzstan	—	—	9	9
France	—	—	50	50	Switzerland	—	—	8	8
Ghana	—	—	49	49	Lithuania	—	—	6	6
Bangladesh	—	1	41	42	Portugal	—	2	4	6
Russia	—	2	36	38	Malawi	—	1	4	5
Sweden	—	—	38	38	Ireland	—	4	—	4
Italy	—	—	30	30	Uganda	—	—	4	4
Denmark	—	1	24	25	Brazil	—	—	2	2
Austria	—	—	22	22	Timor-Leste	—	—	2	2
Nigeria	—	—	20	20	Bolivia	—	1	—	1
Czech Republic	—	1	18	19	Chile	—	1	—	1
Nepal	—	2	17	19	Malaysia	—	1	—	1
China	—	—	18	18	New Zealand	—	1	—	1
Zimbabwe	—	—	18	18	**Total**	—	**40**	**2,029**	**2,069**

Sources: DPKO FGS; DPKO PD.
Note: Police figures include formed police units provided by Pakistan (114), Poland (115), Romania (115), and Ukraine (154).

UNMIK International Civilian Personnel Occupations: 30 September 2007

Occupation	International Staff	Percentage International Staff
Administration	107	22.4%
Aviation	3	0.6%
Civil Affairs	53	11.1%
Economic Affairs	1	0.2%
Engineering	13	2.7%
Finance	18	3.8%
Human Resources	9	1.9%
Human Rights	1	0.2%
Humanitarian Affairs	—	—
Information Management	1	0.2%
Information Systems and Technology	33	6.9%
Legal Affairs	45	9.4%
Logistics	20	4.2%
Medical Services	7	1.5%
Political Affairs	30	6.3%
Procurement	9	1.9%
Programme Management	4	0.8%
Public Information	12	2.5%
Rule of Law	48	10.0%
Security	49	10.3%
Social Affairs	—	—
Transport	15	3.1%
Total	**478**	

Source: DPKO PMSS.

UNMIK Personnel Gender Statistics: 30 September 2007

Personnel Type	Male	Female	Percentage Male	Percentage Female
Troops	—	—	—	—
Military Observers	39	1	97.5%	2.5%
Police	1,897	132	93.5%	6.5%
International Civilian Staff	324	154	67.8%	32.2%
Local Civilian Staff	1,421	539	72.5%	27.5%
Total	**3,681**	**826**	**81.7%**	**18.3%**

Sources: DPKO FGS; DPKO PD; DPKO PMSS.

UNMIK Fatalities: Inception–September 2007

Personnel Type

Time Period	Troop	MilOb	Police	Intl Staff	Local Staff	Other[a]	Total
1999	—	—	5	2	—	1	8
2000	—	—	2	1	3	1	7
2001	—	—	1	1	—	—	2
2002	—	—	3	—	4	—	7
2003	—	—	4	1	2	—	7
2004	—	—	5	1	2	—	8
2005	—	—	4	—	2	—	6
2006	—	—	—	—	1	—	1
January-March	—	—	—	—	—	—	—
April-June	—	—	—	—	1	—	1
July-September	—	—	—	—	—	—	—
October-December	—	—	—	—	—	—	—
2007 (Jan-Sep)	—	—	1	—	1	—	2
January-March	—	—	—	—	1	—	1
April-June	—	—	—	—	—	—	—
July-September	—	—	1	—	—	—	1
Total Fatalities	—	—	**25**	**6**	**15**	**2**	**48**

Incident Type

Time Period	Malicious Act	Illness	Accident	Other[b]	Total
1999	1	—	7	—	8
2000	1	4	1	1	7
2001	—	2	—	—	2
2002	1	3	—	3	7
2003	3	3	—	1	7
2004	4	2	1	1	8
2005	1	3	1	1	6
2006	—	1	—	—	1
January-March	—	—	—	—	—
April-June	—	1	—	—	1
July-September	—	—	—	—	—
October-December	—	—	—	—	—
2007 (Jan-Sep)	—	1	—	1	2
January-March	—	—	—	1	1
April-June	—	—	—	—	—
July-September	—	1	—	—	1
Total Fatalities	**11**	**19**	**10**	**8**	**48**

Source: DPKO Situation Centre.
Notes: a. Other refers to consultants, UNVs, etc.
b. Incident type is unknown, uncertain or under investigation. Other includes what were previously qualified as self-inflicted.

UNMIK Vehicles: 30 September 2007

Contingent Owned Vehicles		UN Owned Vehicles	
Vehicle Type	Quantity	Vehicle Type	Quantity
Combat Vehicles	10	4x4 Vehicles	1,380
Support Vehicles (Commercial Pattern)	31	Airfield Support Equipment	2
Support Vehicles (Military Pattern)	62	Ambulances	9
Total	**103**	Automobiles	55
		Buses	117
		Engineering Vehicles	2
		Material Handling Equipment	44
		Trailers	27
		Trucks	70
		Vans	72
		Total	**1,778**

Sources: DPKO Contingent Owned Equipment and Property Management Section; DPKO Surface Transport Section.

UNMIK Budgets and Expenditures (in thousands of US dollars)

Category	Budgeted Jul 06–Jun 07	Expenditures Jul 06–Jun 07	Budgeted Jul 07–Jun 08
Military Observers	1,364.7	1,343.6	1,369.9
Military Contingents	—	—	—
Civilian Police	55,823.0	53,449.5	50,769.6
Formed Police Units	7,609.5	9,378.9	9,943.8
International Staff	74,712.0	70,210.8	73,512.1
Local Staff	45,269.6	44,405.1	45,354.7
United Nations Volunteers	6,344.8	6,186.9	6,094.4
General Temporary Assistance	718.9	416.1	427.3
Government-provided Personnel	—	—	—
Civilian Electoral Observers	—	—	—
Consultants	—	49.4	25.3
Official Travel	877.7	1,167.0	771.2
Facilities and Infrastructure	11,293.6	10,101.5	9,216.0
Ground Transportation	3,091.1	3,905.3	2,702.2
Air Transportation	821.0	850.8	1,638.2
Naval Transportation	—	—	—
Communications and Information Technology	8,075.7	6,485.5	6,983.8
Supplies, Services and Equipment	1,960.4	2,241.5	1,868.3
Quick-impact Projects	—	—	—
Gross Requirements	**217,962.0**	**219,627.1**	**220,897.2**
Staff Assessment Income	16,536.6	15,739.3	17,227.2
Net Requirements	**201,425.4**	**203,887.8**	**203,670.0**
Voluntary Contributions in Kind (budgeted)	—	—	—
Total Requirements	**217,962.0**	**219,627.1**	**220,897.2**

Sources: UN Documents A/61/852/Add.8 and A/C.5/61/24; DPKO FMSS.
Notes: Financial figures are preliminary and subject to change. Gross requirements for July 2006–June 2007 expenditures include pro-rated costs of $9,435.4 thousand. Gross requirements for July 2007–June 2008 budgeted include pro-rated costs of $10,220.4 thousand.

UNMIK Expenditures on Contingent Owned Equipment: July 2006–June 2007 (in thousands of US dollars)

Major Equipment	1,751.6
Self-sustainment	447.7

Source: DPKO FMSS.

UNMIK Mission Expenditures: July 2000–June 2006 (in thousands of US dollars)

Category	Jul 00–Jun 01	Jul 01–Jun 02	Jul 02–Jun 03	Jul 03–Jun 04	Jul 04–Jun 05	Jul 05–Jun 06
Military and Police Personnel	5,918.4	125,532.0	115,208.7	106,598.1	106,253.3	70,230.2
Civilian Personnel	280,113.5	184,775.0	170,595.0	163,458.9	156,162.2	135,815.5
Operational Requirements	73,816.0	49,941.0	44,164.1	45,452.2	32,081.5	27,707.9
Other	839.1	—	—	—	—	—
Gross Requirements	**360,687.0**	**360,248.0**	**329,967.8**	**315,509.2**	**294,497.0**	**233,753.6**
Staff Assessment Income	22,775.0	25,989.0	25,082.5	23,467.6	22,720.5	19,321.3
Net Requirements	**337,912.0**	**334,259.0**	**304,885.3**	**292,041.6**	**271,776.5**	**214,432.3**
Voluntary Contributions in Kind (budgeted)	—	—	—	—	—	—
Total Requirements	**360,687.0**	**360,248.0**	**329,967.8**	**315,509.2**	**294,497.0**	**233,753.6**

Sources: UN Documents A/56/763, A/57/678, A/58/634, A/59/623, A/60/637 and A/61/675.

7.13 UNMIL (UN Mission in Liberia)

UNMIL Key Facts	
Latest Key Resolutions	20 September 2007 (date of issue); 1 October 2007 (date of effect) UNSC Res. 1777 (twelve month duration and reduction of military personnel from October 2007 to September 2007 and reduction of police personnel from April 2008 to December 2010) 30 March 2007 (date of issue); 1 April 2007 (date of effect) UNSC Res. 1750 (six month duration and authorization for temporary redeployement of personnel among UNMIL and UNOCI)
First Mandate	19 September 2003 (date of issue and effect) UNSC Res. 1509 (twelve month duration)
SRSG	Ellen Margrethe Løj (Denmark) SG letter of appointment 22 October 2007
First SRSG	Jacques Klein (United States)
Force Commander	Lieutenant-General Chikadibia Isaac Obiakor (Nigeria) SG letter of appointment 21 November 2005 Entry on duty 1 January 2006
First Force Commander	Lieutenant-General Daniel Ishmael Opande (Kenya)
Police Commissioner	Mohammed Ahmed Alhassan (Ghana) Entry on duty 15 March 2005

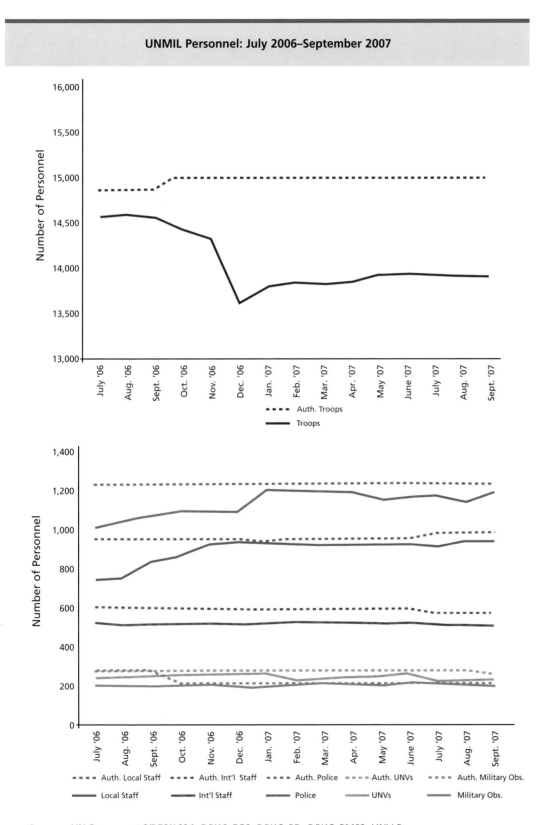

UNMIL Personnel: July 2006–September 2007

Sources: UN Document S/RES/1694; DPKO FGS; DPKO PD; DPKO PMSS; UNV Programme.

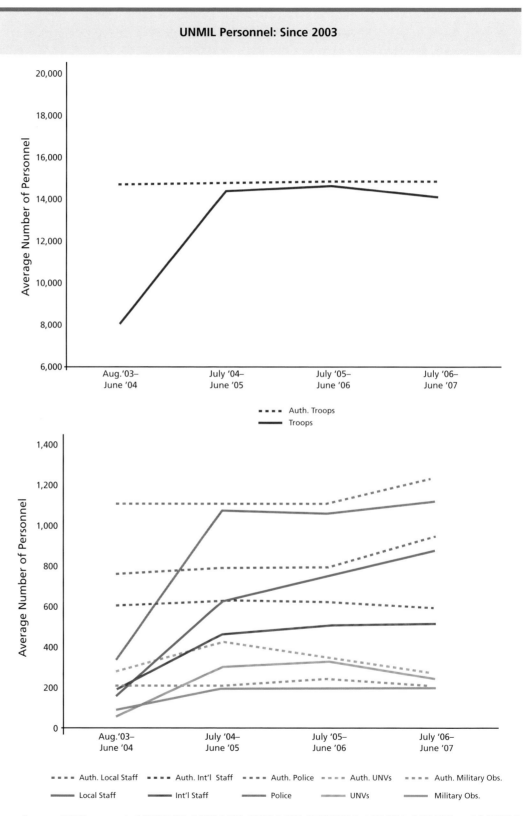

UNMIL Personnel: Since 2003

Sources: UN Documents S/RES/1509, S/RES/1626, S/RES/1667, S/RES/1694, A/59/624, A/60/645 and A/61/715; DPKO FGS; DPKO PD; DPKO PMSS; UNV Programme.

UNMIL Military and Police Contributors: 30 September 2007

Contributing Country	Troops	Military Observers	Police	Total	Contributing Country	Troops	Military Observers	Police	Total
Pakistan	3,402	15	31	3,448	Norway	—	—	10	10
Bangladesh	3,201	17	33	3,251	Czech Republic	—	3	5	8
Nigeria	1,957	17	163	2,137	Jamaica	—	—	7	7
Ethiopia	1,804	19	—	1,823	Argentina	—	—	6	6
Ghana	859	12	40	911	Kyrgyzstan	—	4	2	6
Namibia	613	2	6	621	Yemen	—	—	6	6
Senegal	602	3	—	605	Croatia	5	—	—	5
China	565	5	—	570	El Salvador	—	3	2	5
Ukraine	301	1	12	314	Germany	—	—	5	5
Nepal	43	3	261	307	Mali	1	4	—	5
Jordan	123	7	140	270	Peru	2	3	—	5
Mongolia	250	—	—	250	Poland	—	2	3	5
Philippines	170	3	34	207	Benin	1	3	—	4
India	—	—	125	125	Bolivia	1	3	—	4
Zambia	—	3	32	35	Ecuador	1	3	—	4
Zimbabwe	—	2	32	34	Paraguay	1	3	—	4
Kenya	4	3	26	33	Brazil	3	—	—	3
Gambia	—	2	30	32	Indonesia	—	3	—	3
Fiji	—	—	30	30	Moldova	—	3	—	3
United States	6	7	10	23	Niger	—	3	—	3
Turkey	—	—	21	21	Romania	—	3	—	3
Uganda	—	—	21	21	Togo	1	2	—	3
Malawi	—	—	14	14	United Kingdom	3	—	—	3
Sweden	—	—	14	14	Uruguay	—	—	3	3
Egypt	—	8	5	13	Bulgaria	—	2	—	2
Samoa	—	—	13	13	Denmark	—	2	—	2
Serbia	—	6	7	13	Ireland	2	—	—	2
Bosnia and Herzegovina	—	—	12	12	Montenegro	—	2	—	2
Russia	—	4	8	12	Republic of Korea	1	1	—	2
Rwanda	—	—	12	12	Finland	1	—	—	1
Sri Lanka	—	—	11	11	France	1	—	—	1
Malaysia	—	10	—	10	FYR of Macedonia	—	—	1	1
					Total	**13,924**	**201**	**1,193**	**15,318**

Sources: DPKO FGS; DPKO PD.
Note: Police figures include formed police units provided by India (125), Jordan (120), Nepal (240), and Nigeria (120).

UNMIL Military Units: 30 September 2007

Number	Unit Type	Countries
1	Aviation Unit	Ukraine
1	Communications Squadron	Nigeria
6	Engineering Companies	Bangladesh (3), China, Pakistan (2)
1	Quick Reaction Force	Pakistan
1	Guard Company	Mongolia
1	Heaquarters Company	Philippines
12	Infantry Battalions	Bangladesh (3), Ethiopia (2), Ghana, Namibia, Nigeria (2), Pakistan (2), Senegal
4	Level II Medical Hospitals	Bangladesh, China, Pakistan, Senegal
1	Level III Medical Hospital	Jordan
1	Military Police Company	Nepal
1	Road and Airfield Engineers Company	Pakistan
1	Transport Company	China

Source: DPKO FGS.
Note: Military headquarters staff and military observers not included.

UNMIL International Civilian Personnel Occupations: 30 September 2007

Occupation	International Staff	Percentage International Staff
Administration	77	15.1%
Aviation	15	2.9%
Civil Affairs	40	7.8%
Economic Affairs	—	—
Engineering	30	5.9%
Finance	14	2.7%
Human Resources	12	2.4%
Human Rights	16	3.1%
Humanitarian Affairs	6	1.2%
Information Management	1	0.2%
Information Systems and Technology	29	5.7%
Legal Affairs	6	1.2%
Logistics	84	16.5%
Medical Services	3	0.6%
Political Affairs	24	4.7%
Procurement	15	2.9%
Programme Management	12	2.4%
Public Information	12	2.4%
Rule of Law	11	2.2%
Security	78	15.3%
Social Affairs	4	0.8%
Transport	21	4.1%
Total	**510**	

Source: DPKO PMSS.

UNMIL Personnel Gender Statistics: 30 September 2007

Personnel Type	Male	Female	Percentage Male	Percentage Female
Troops	13,645	279	98.0%	2.0%
Military Observers	194	7	96.5%	3.5%
Police	1,098	95	92.0%	8.0%
International Civlian Staff	349	161	68.4%	31.6%
Local Civilian Staff	757	190	79.9%	20.1%
Total	**16,043**	**732**	**95.6%**	**4.4%**

Sources: DPKO FGS; DPKO PD; DPKO PMSS.

UNMIL Fatalities: Inception–September 2007

Time Period	Personnel Type						
	Troop	MilOb	Police	Intl Staff	Local Staff	Other[a]	Total
2003	5	—	—	—	—	—	5
2004	23	1	3	1	1	—	29
2005	26	—	3	3	4	—	36
2006	13	—	2	1	2	—	18
January-March	5	—	—	—	—	—	5
April-June	4	—	1	1	2	—	8
July-September	1	—	—	—	—	—	1
October-December	3	—	1	—	—	—	4
2007 (Jan-Sep)	5	—	2	—	3	—	10
January-March	2	—	—	—	2	—	4
April-June	2	—	—	—	1	—	3
July-September	1	—	2	—	—	—	3
Total Fatalities	**72**	**1**	**10**	**5**	**10**	**—**	**98**

Time Period	Incident Type				
	Malicious Act	Illness	Accident	Other[b]	Total
2003	—	1	4	—	5
2004	—	22	6	1	29
2005	—	28	7	1	36
2006	—	16	1	1	18
January-March	—	5	—	—	5
April-June	—	8	—	—	8
July-September	—	1	—	—	1
October-December	—	2	1	1	4
2007 (Jan-Sep)	—	6	—	4	10
January-March	—	2	—	2	4
April-June	—	1	—	2	3
July-September	—	3	—	—	3
Total Fatalities	**—**	**73**	**18**	**7**	**98**

Sources: DPKO Situation Centre.
Notes: a. Other refers to consultants, UNVs, etc.
b. Incident type is unknown, uncertain or under investigation. Other includes what were previously qualified as self-inflicted.

UNMIL Vehicles: 30 September 2007

Contingent Owned Vehicles		UN Owned Vehicles	
Vehicle Type	Quantity	Vehicle Type	Quantity
Aircraft/Airfield Support Equipment	4	4x4 Vehicles	1,173
Combat Vehicles	323	Aircraft/Airfield Support Equipment	3
Communications Vehicles	2	Ambulances	13
Engineering Vehicles	131	Automobiles	7
Material Handling Equipment	28	Buses	113
Support Vehicles (Commercial Pattern)	452	Engineering Vehicles	2
Support Vehicles (Military Pattern)	1,160	Material Handling Equipment	55
Trailers	454	Trailers	31
Total	**2,554**	Trucks	179
		Vans	3
		Total	**1,579**

Sources: DPKO Contingent Owned Equipment and Property Management Section; DPKO Surface Transport Section.

UNMIL Aircraft: 30 September 2007

	Transport Fixed Wing	Transport Helicopter	Attack Helicopter
Commercial	2	8	—
Contingent Owned	—	8 (Ukraine)	6 (Ukraine)
Total	**2**	**16**	**6**

Source: DPKO Air Transport Section.

UNMIL Budget and Expenditures (in thousands of US dollars)

Category	Budgeted Jul 06–Jun 07	Expenditures Jul 06–Jun 07	Budgeted Jul 07–Jun 08
Military Observers	10,899.4	10,805.2	11,061.8
Military Contingents	321,370.4	312,058.3	301,613.8
Civilian Police	39,743.1	30,251.4	30,700.6
Formed Police Units	6,899.0	13,041.3	14,467.1
International Staff	80,511.0	87,754.6	89,625.9
Local Staff	15,978.6	14,425.0	16,080.0
United Nations Volunteers	10,755.9	10,638.3	10,868.7
General Temporary Assistance	792.8	1,197.1	515.9
Government-provided Personnel	—	—	—
Civilian Electoral Observers	—	—	—
Consultants	675.6	507.4	855.6
Official Travel	1,614.1	2,536.4	2,203.5
Facilities and Infrastructure	80,871.7	68,737.5	69,749.7
Ground Transportation	20,512.4	15,220.1	19,343.9
Air Transportation	66,140.0	59,265.3	69,139.2
Naval Transportation	2,590.5	2,662.0	3,002.7
Communications and Information Technology	28,880.3	23,709.5	24,480.9
Supplies, Services and Equipment	25,378.6	22,449.6	23,674.1
Quick-impact Projects	1,000.0	995.8	1,000.0
Gross Requirements	**714,613.3**	**707,203.9**	**721,775.8**
Staff Assessment Income	10,291.9	—	11,719.6
Net Requirements	**704,321.4**	**707,203.9**	**710,056.2**
Voluntary Contributions in Kind (budgeted)	264.0	53.0	52.8
Total Requirements	**714,877.3**	**707,256.9**	**721,828.6**

Sources: UN Documents A/61/852/Add.7 and A/C.5/61/24; DPKO FMSS.
Notes: Financial figures are preliminary and subject to change. Gross requirements for July 2006–June 2007 expenditures include pro-rated costs of $30,949.1 thousand. Gross requirements for July 2007–June 2008 budgeted include pro-rated costs of $33,392.4 thousand.

UNMIL Expenditures on Contingent Owned Equipment: July 2006–June 2007 (in thousands of US dollars)

Major Equipment	55,376.3
Self-sustainment	57,209.3

Source: DM OPPBA.

UNMIL Voluntary Contributions: July 2006–June 2007 (in thousands of US dollars)

Contributor	Contributions in Kind (budgeted)	Contributions in Kind (non-budgeted)	Contributions in Cash (budgeted)	Total
Germany	53.0	—	—	53.0
Total	**53.0**	**—**	**—**	**53.0**

Source: DM OPPBA.

UNMIL Mission Expenditures: August 2003–June 2006 (in thousands of US dollars)

Category	Aug 03–Jun 04	Jul 04–Jun 05	Jul 05–Jun 06
Military and Police Personnel	269,436.1	393,267.7	377,419.5
Civilian Personnel	33,596.3	98,618.9	109,620.6
Operational Requirements	245,146.3	249,078.2	220,064.8
Other	—	—	—
Gross Requirements	**548,178.7**	**740,964.8**	**707,104.9**
Staff Assessment Income	3,113.1	9,768.1	10,877.6
Net Requirements	**545,065.6**	**731,196.7**	**696,227.3**
Voluntary Contributions in Kind (budgeted)	100.0	120.0	264.0
Total Requirements	**548,278.7**	**741,084.8**	**707,368.9**

Sources: UN Documents A/59/624, A/60/645 and A/61/715.

7.14 UNMIN (UN Mission in Nepal)

UNMIN Key Facts

First Mandate	23 January 2007 (date of issue and effect)
	UNSC Res. 1740 (twelve month duration)
SRSG and Head of Mission	Ian Martin (First SRSG, United Kingdom)
	SG letter of appointment 2 February 2007
Chief Arms Monitor	General Jan Erik Wilhelmsen (Norway)

UNMIN Personnel: January 2007–September 2007

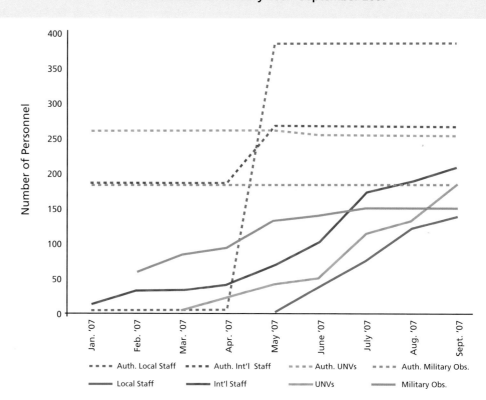

Sources: UN Document S/RES/1719; DPKO FGS; DPKO PD; DPKO PMSS; UNV Programme.
Note: As of September 2007 four police were on mission.

UNMIN Military and Police Contributors: 30 September 2007

Contributing Country	Troops	Military Observers	Police	Total	Contributing Country	Troops	Military Observers	Police	Total
Yemen	—	15	—	15	Gambia	—	4	—	4
Jordan	—	10	—	10	United Kingdom	—	4	—	4
Malaysia	—	7	1	8	Norway	—	3	—	3
Nigeria	—	8	—	8	Singapore	—	2	1	3
Russia	—	8	—	8	Sweden	—	3	—	3
Zambia	—	8	—	8	Uruguay	—	3	—	3
Brazil	—	7	—	7	Austria	—	2	—	2
Egypt	—	7	—	7	Croatia	—	2	—	2
Thailand	—	7	—	7	Denmark	—	2	—	2
Indonesia	—	6	—	6	Guatemala	—	2	—	2
Japan	—	6	—	6	Sierra Leone	—	2	—	2
Switzerland	—	5	1	6	Zimbabwe	—	2	—	2
Ghana	—	5	—	5	Ecuador	—	1	—	1
Paraguay	—	5	—	5	Finland	—	1	—	1
Republic of Korea	—	5	—	5	Kazakhstan	—	1	—	1
Romania	—	5	—	5	Philippines	—	—	1	1
South Africa	—	5	—	5	**Total**	—	149	4	153

Sources: DPKO FGS; DPKO PD.

UNMIN International Civilian Personnel Occupations: 30 September 2007

Occupation	International Staff	Percentage International Staff
Administration	17	8.0%
Aviation	6	2.8%
Civil Affairs	45	21.2%
Economic Affairs	—	—
Engineering	11	5.2%
Finance	6	2.8%
Human Resources	5	2.4%
Human Rights	—	—
Humanitarian Affairs	—	—
Information Management	1	0.5%
Information Systems and Technology	16	7.5%
Legal Affairs	1	0.5%
Logistics	22	10.4%
Medical Services	1	0.5%
Political Affairs	36	17.0%
Procurement	4	1.9%
Programme Management	3	1.4%
Public Information	8	3.8%
Rule of Law	3	1.4%
Security	15	7.1%
Social Affairs	3	1.4%
Transport	9	4.2%
Total	**212**	

Source: DPKO PMSS.

UNMIN Personnel Gender Statistics: 30 September 2007

Personnel Type	Male	Female	Percentage Male	Percentage Female
Troops	—	—	—	—
Military Observers	140	13	91.5%	8.5%
Police	4	—	100.0%	—
International Civilian Staff	145	67	68.4%	31.6%
Local Civilian Staff	103	38	73.0%	27.0%
Total	**392**	**118**	**76.9%**	**23.1%**

Sources: DPKO FGS; DPKO PD; DPKO PMSS.

UNMIN Fatalities: Inception–September 2007

Personnel Type

Time Period	Troop	MilOb	Police	Intl Staff	Local Staff	Other[a]	Total
2007 (Jan-Sep)	—	—	—	—	—	—	—
January-March	—	—	—	—	—	—	—
April-June	—	—	—	—	—	—	—
July-September	—	—	—	—	—	—	—
Total Fatalities	—	—	—	—	—	—	—

Incident Type

Time Period	Malicious Act	Illness	Accident	Other[b]	Total
2007 (Jan-Sep)	—	—	—	—	—
January-March	—	—	—	—	—
April-June	—	—	—	—	—
July-September	—	—	—	—	—
Total Fatalities	—	—	—	—	—

Source: DPKO Situation Centre.
Notes: a. Other refers to consultants, UNVs, etc.
b. Incident type is unknown, uncertain, or under investigation. Other includes what were previously qualified as self-inflicted.

UNMIN Vehicles: 30 September 2007

UN Owned Vehicles

Vehicle Type	Quantity
4x4 Vehicles	170
Ambulance	1
Buses	4
Material Handling Equipment	4
Total	**179**

Source: DPKO Surface Transport Section.

UNMIN Aircraft: 30 September 2007

	Transport Fixed Wing	Transport Helicopter	Attack Helicopter
Commercial	1	4	—
Contingent Owned	—	—	—
Total	**1**	**4**	—

Source: DPKO Air Transport Section.

UNMIN Budget and Expenditures (in thousands of US dollars)

Category	Appropriations Jan 06–Dec 07	Estimated Expenditures Jan 06–Dec 07	Requirements 2008
Miltary and Police Personnel Costs	5,304.7	3390.6	892.8
Civilian Personnel Costs	23,801.3	21756.3	8,177.3
Operational Costs	59,716.0	49592.4	7,718.5
Total Requirements	**88,822.0**	**74,739.3**	**16,788.6**

Source: DPKO FMSS.

7.15 UNMIS (UN Mission in the Sudan)

UNMIS Key Facts	

Latest Key Resolutions	31 October 2007 (date of issue and effect)
	  UNSC Res. 1784 (six month duration)
	31 July 2007 (date of issue to take effect no later than
	  31 December 2007)
	  UNSC Res. 1769 (note: mission will revert to initial strength
	  as authroized in UNSC Res. 1590 following the transfer of
	  authority from AMIS to UNAMID)
	30 April 2007 (date of issue and effect)
	  UNSC Res. 1755 (six month duration)
	6 October 2006 (date of issue and effect)
	  UNSC Res. 1714 (seven month duration)

First Mandate	24 March 2005 (date of issue and effect) UNSC Res. 1590 (six month duration)
SRSG	Ashraf Jehangir Qazi (Pakistan) SG letter of appointment 3 September 2007
First SRSG	Jan Pronk (Netherlands)

Force Commander	Lieutenant-General Jasbir Singh Lidder (India)
	  SG letter of appointment 4 January 2006
	  Entry on duty 9 January 2006

First Force Commander	Major-General Fazle Elahi Akbar (Bangladesh)
Police Commissioner	Kai Vittrup (Denmark) Date of appointment 10 September 2006

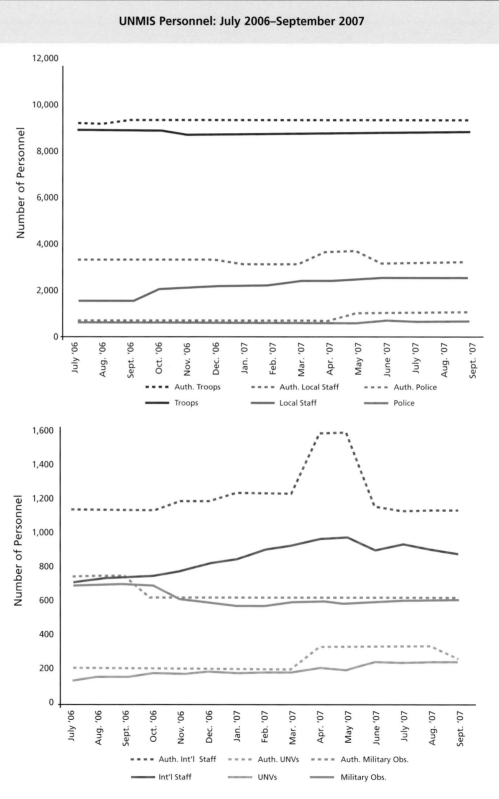

UNMIS Personnel: July 2006–September 2007

Sources: DPKO FGS; DPKO PD; DPKO PMSS; UNV Programme.
Note: UNV figures include national UNVs.

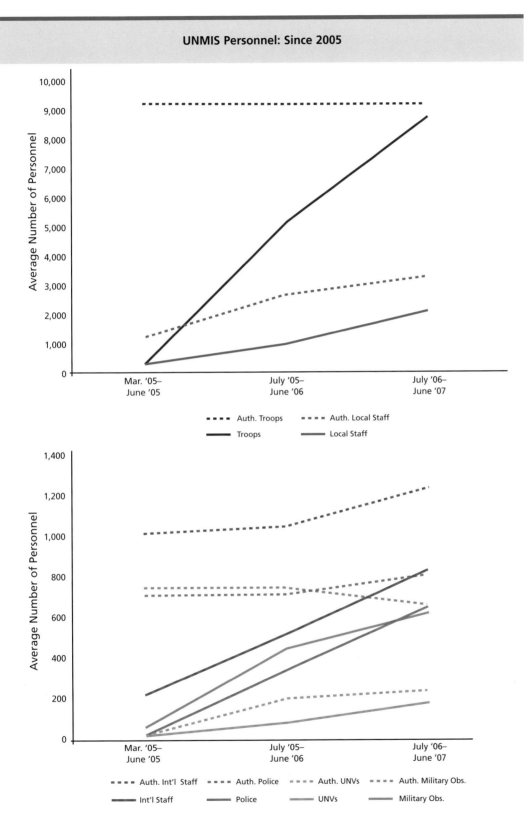

UNMIS Personnel: Since 2005

Sources: UN Documents A/61/689, S/RES/1590 and S/RES/1706; DPKO FGS; DPKO PD ; DPKO PMSS; UNV Programme.

UNMIS Military and Police Contributors: 30 September 2007

Contributing Country	Troops	Military Observers	Police	Total	Contributing Country	Troops	Military Observers	Police	Total
India	2,607	20	15	2,642	Thailand	2	12	—	14
Pakistan	1,569	20	39	1,628	Samoa	—	—	13	13
Bangladesh	1,535	20	32	1,587	United States	—	—	13	13
Kenya	831	7	20	858	Romania	—	12	—	12
Egypt	816	18	7	841	Argentina	—	—	11	11
China	446	14	8	468	El Salvador	—	5	5	10
Zambia	354	15	18	387	Kyrgyzstan	—	8	2	10
Rwanda	262	15	25	302	Mali	—	10	—	10
Cambodia	136	10	—	146	Namibia	—	9	1	10
Russia	122	14	10	146	Paraguay	—	10	—	10
Nepal	7	8	58	73	Guatemala	1	8	—	9
Nigeria	10	12	51	73	Republic of Guinea	—	9	—	9
Philippines	—	13	53	66	Gabon	—	8	—	8
Zimbabwe	3	14	28	45	Malawi	2	6	—	8
Ghana	3	—	40	43	Republic of Korea	1	7	—	8
Germany	6	31	5	42	Benin	—	7	—	7
Jordan	10	12	18	40	Burkina Faso	—	6	—	6
Netherlands	5	14	15	34	Greece	2	4	—	6
Canada	9	21	3	33	Jamaica	—	—	6	6
Norway	9	15	6	30	Belgium	—	5	—	5
Sri Lanka	—	3	24	27	Botswana	—	5	—	5
Brazil	—	24	2	26	Croatia	5	—	—	5
Australia	9	6	10	25	Senegal	5	—	—	5
Uganda	—	11	14	25	South Africa	4	—	—	4
Malaysia	4	8	11	23	United Kingdom	3	—	1	4
Yemen	4	16	3	23	Finland	1	—	2	3
Ukraine	—	6	16	22	Mozambique	—	3	—	3
Gambia	1	—	20	21	New Zealand	1	2	—	3
Tanzania	6	15	—	21	Bosnia and Herzegovina	—	—	2	2
Turkey	4	—	17	21	Moldova	—	2	—	2
Ecuador	—	20	—	20	Mongolia	—	2	—	2
Bolivia	1	16	—	17	Poland	—	2	—	2
Peru	—	17	—	17	Uruguay	—	—	2	2
Sweden	3	3	11	17	Italy	1	—	—	1
Denmark	5	10	1	16	France	1	—	—	1
Indonesia	—	10	6	16	Niger	1	—	—	1
Fiji	—	7	8	15	**Total**	**8,807**	**607**	**652**	**10,066**

Sources: DPKO FGS; DPKO PD.

UNMIS Military Units: 30 September 2007

Number	Unit Type	Countries
5	De-mining Companies	Bangladesh, Cambodia, Egypt, Kenya, Pakistan
1	Engineer Platoon	Zambia
5	Engineering Construction Companies	Bangladesh, China, Egypt, India, Pakistan
1	Headquarters Company	Rwanda
5	Infantry Battalions	Bangladesh, India (2), Kenya, Pakistan
2	Infantry Companies	Egypt, Zambia
4	Level II Medical Units	Bangladesh, China, India, Pakistan
1	Level III Medical Unit	Egypt
4	Military Aviation Units	India, Pakistan (2), Russia
1	Military Police Unit	Bangladesh
1	Riverine Unit	Bangladesh
1	Petroleum Platoon	Bangladesh
2	Signals Companies	India, Pakistan
5	Transport Companies	Bangladesh, China, Egypt, India, Pakistan
1	Transport Platoon	Zambia

Source: DPKO FGS.

Notes: Military headquarters staff and military observers not included. Level I Medical Units are not shown as they are integrated in the units above.

UNMIS International Civilian Personnel: 30 September 2007

Occupation	International Staff	Percentage International Staff
Administration	99	11.2%
Aviation	29	3.3%
Civil Affairs	24	2.7%
Economic Affairs	1	0.1%
Engineering	73	8.3%
Finance	28	3.2%
Human Resources	38	4.3%
Human Rights	47	5.3%
Humanitarian Affairs	43	4.9%
Information Management	6	0.7%
Information Systems and Technology	60	6.8%
Legal Affairs	3	0.3%
Logistics	106	12.0%
Medical Services	7	0.8%
Political Affairs	26	2.9%
Procurement	13	1.5%
Programme Management	36	4.1%
Public Information	19	2.2%
Rule of Law	18	2.0%
Security	140	15.9%
Social Affairs	13	1.5%
Transport	53	6.0%
Total	**882**	

Source: DPKO PMSS.

UNMIS Personnel Gender Statistics: 30 September 2007

Personnel Type	Male	Female	Percentage Male	Percentage Female
Troops	8,699	108	98.8%	1.2%
Military Observers	595	12	98.0%	2.0%
Police	607	45	93.1%	6.9%
International Civilian Staff	623	259	70.6%	29.4%
Local Civilian Staff	2,192	374	85.4%	14.6%
Total	**12,716**	**798**	**94.1%**	**5.9%**

Sources: DPKO FGS; DPKO PD; DPKO PMSS.

UNMIS Fatalities: Inception–September 2007

Personnel Type

Time Period	Troop	MilOb	Police	Intl Staff	Local Staff	Other[a]	Total
2005	1	—	—	—	1	—	2
2006	5	1	1	4	4	—	15
January-March	—	—	—	—	2	—	2
April-June	1	—	—	1	1	—	3
July-September	2	1	—	3	—	—	6
October-December	2	—	1	—	1	—	4
2007 (Jan-Sep)	3	—	1	—	5	—	9
January-March	1	—	—	—	—	—	1
April-June	2	—	1	—	2	—	5
July-September	—	—	—	—	3	—	3
Total Fatalities	**9**	**1**	**2**	**4**	**10**	**—**	**26**

Incident Type

Time Period	Malicious Act	Illness	Accident	Other[b]	Total
2005	—	1	1	—	2
2006	1	12	1	1	15
January-March	—	2	—	—	2
April-June	1	2	—	—	3
July-September	—	5	1	—	6
October-December	—	3	—	1	4
2007 (Jan-Sep)	2	3	1	3	9
January-March	1	—	—	—	1
April-June	1	2	—	2	5
July-September	—	1	1	1	3
Total Fatalities	**3**	**16**	**3**	**4**	**26**

Source: DPKO Situation Centre.

Notes: a. Other refers to consultants, UNVs, etc.

b. Incident type is unknown, uncertain or under investigation. Other includes what were previously qualified as self-inflicted.

UNMIS Vehicles: 30 September 2007

Contingent Owned Vehicles		UN Owned Vehicles	
Vehicle Type	Quantity	Vehicle Type	Quantity
Aircraft/Airfield Support Equipment	32	4x4 Vehicles	1,645
Combat Vehicles	88	Aircraft/Airfield Support Equipment	19
Communications Vehicles	2	Ambulances	18
Engineering Vehicles	213	Automobiles	4
Material Handling Equipment	36	Buses	160
Naval Vessels	22	Engineering Vehicles	13
Support Vehicles (Commercial Pattern)	215	Material Handling Equipment	245
Support Vehicles (Military Pattern)	936	Trailers	46
Trailers	439	Trucks	262
Total	**1,983**	Vans	18
		Total	**2,430**

Sources: DPKO Contingent Owned Equipment and Property Management Section; DPKO Surface Transport Section.

UNMIS Aircraft: 30 September 2007

	Transport Fixed Wing	Transport Helicopter	Attack Helicopter
Commercial	16	15	—
Contingent Owned	—	16 (6 India, 6 Pakistan, 4 Russia)	—
Total	**16**	**31**	—

Source: DPKO Air Transport Section.

UNMIS Budget and Expenditures (in thousands of US dollars)

Category	Budgeted Jul 06–Jun 07	Expenditures Jul 06–Jun 07	Budgeted Jul 07–Jun 08
Military Observers	36,224.3	29,911.4	21,607.3
Military Contingents	246,752.7	220,727.8	222,075.7
Civilian Police	34,512.3	30,326.9	24,080.8
Formed Police Units	—	—	—
International Staff	149,206.1	113,594.4	108,833.0
Local Staff	34,773.0	32,181.1	33,348.9
United Nations Volunteers	6,262.7	7,160.7	7,495.7
General Temporary Assistance	2,994.4	7,339.4	1,438.2
Government-provided Personnel	—	—	—
Civilian Electoral Observers	—	—	—
Consultants	638.5	731.6	622.8
Official Travel	2,542.1	10,671.3	6,028.8
Facilities and Infrastructure	156,047.7	162,335.0	107,336.2
Ground Transportation	44,562.2	49,073.8	24,647.1
Air Transportation	177,023.8	179,364.5	166,973.6
Naval Transportation	7,424.2	6.1	1,101.4
Communications and Information Technology	54,412.4	59,096.7	29,424.0
Supplies, Services and Equipment	124,158.0	85,755.5	90,263.7
Quick-impact Projects	2,000.0	2,000.0	1,000.0
Gross Requirements	**1,079,534.4**	**1,037,022.7**	**887,332.0**
Staff Assessment Income	20,255.7	—	18,050.4
Net Requirements	**1,059,278.7**	**1,037,022.7**	**869,281.6**
Voluntary Contributions in Kind (budgeted)	—	—	—
Total Requirements	**1,079,534.4**	**1,037,022.7**	**887,332.0**

Sources: UN Documents A/61/852/Add.13 and A/C.5/61/24; DPKO FMSS.
Notes: Financial figures are preliminary and subject to change. Gross requirements for July 2006–June 2007 expenditures include pro-rated costs of $46,746.5 thousand. Gross requirements for July 2007–June 2008 budgeted include pro-rated costs of $41,094.8 thousand.

UNMIS Expenditures on Contingent Owned Equipment: July 2006–June 2007 (in thousands of US dollars)

Major Equipment	39,188.7
Self-sustainment	38,883.8

Source: DPKO FMSS.

UNMIS Mission Expenditures: March 2005–June 2006 (in thousands of US dollars)

Category	Mar 05–Jun 05	July 05–Jun 06
Military and Police Personnel	15,168.6	231,665.0
Civilian Personnel	17,353.4	91,086.9
Operational Requirements	186,343.7	478,372.5
Other	—	—
Gross Requirements	**218,865.7**	**801,124.4**
Staff Assessment Income	2,090.2	10,968.4
Net Requirements	**216,775.5**	**790,156.0**
Voluntary Contributions in Kind (budgeted)	—	—
Total Requirements	**218,865.7**	**801,124.4**

Sources: UN Documents A/60/626 and A/61/689.

7.16 UNMIT (UN Integrated Mission in Timor-Leste)

UNMIT Key Facts	
Latest Key Resolution	22 February 2007 (date of issue and effect) UNSC Res. 1745 (four day and twelve month duration and increase in strength)
First Mandate	25 August 2006 (date of issue and effect) UNSC Res. 1704 (six month duration)
SRSG and Head of Mission	Atul Khare (India) SG letter of appointment 30 October 2006
First SRSG	Sukehiro Hasegawa (Japan)
Chief Military Liaison Officer	Colonel Graeme Roger Williams (New Zealand) Entry on duty 16 October 2006
Police Commissioner	Rodolfo Aser Tor (Philippines) Entry on duty 3 December 2006

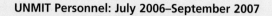

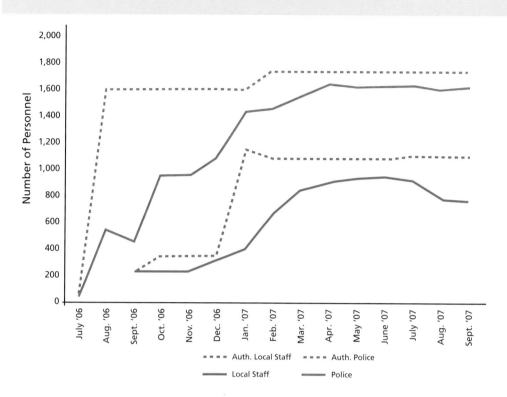

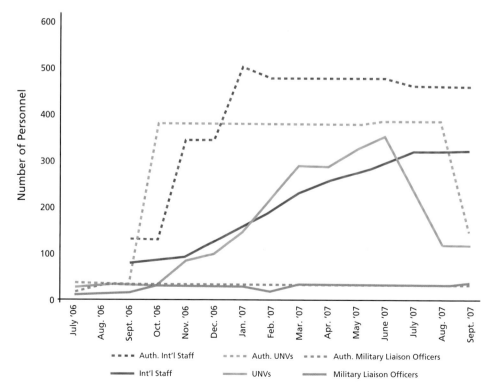

Sources: UN Document S/RES/1704; DPKO FGS; DPKO PD; DPKO PMSS; UNV Programme.
Note: Military Liaison Officer figures include 12 Staff Officers.

UNMIT Military and Police Contributors: 30 September 2007

Contributing Country	Troops	Military Observers	Police	Total	Contributing Country	Troops	Military Observers	Police	Total
Portugal	—	4	279	283	Brazil	—	5	6	11
Malaysia	—	2	205	207	Romania	—	—	10	10
Pakistan	—	4	195	199	Vanuatu	—	—	10	10
Bangladesh	—	4	192	196	Zambia	—	—	10	10
Philippines	—	3	145	148	Spain	—	—	9	9
Nepal	—	—	93	93	Yemen	—	—	9	9
Sri Lanka	—	—	63	63	Turkey	—	—	7	7
Australia	—	4	50	54	Canada	—	—	6	6
Nigeria	—	—	53	53	Uruguay	—	—	6	6
Thailand	—	—	38	38	India	—	—	5	5
Zimbabwe	—	—	38	38	Republic of Korea	—	—	5	5
Gambia	—	—	31	31	Sweden	—	—	5	5
New Zealand	—	1	25	26	Russia	—	—	4	4
Singapore	—	4	21	25	Jamaica	—	—	3	3
Egypt	—	—	17	17	Ukraine	—	—	3	3
Senegal	—	—	17	17	Croatia	—	—	2	2
Uganda	—	—	16	16	Fiji	—	2	—	2
China	—	3	10	13	Japan	—	—	2	2
Namibia	—	—	13	13	Kyrgyzstan	—	—	2	2
Samoa	—	—	13	13	Palau	—	—	1	1
El Salvador	—	—	12	12	Sierra Leone	—	1	—	1
					Total	—	37	1,631	1,668

Sources: DPKO FGS; DPKO PD.
Note: Police figures include formed police units provided by Bangladesh (142), Malaysia (140), Pakistan (140) and Portugal (216).

UNMIT International Civilian Personnel Occupations: 30 September 2007

Occupation	International Staff	Percentage International Staff
Administration	57	17.5%
Aviation	5	1.5%
Civil Affairs	2	0.6%
Economic Affairs	—	—
Engineering	17	5.2%
Finance	15	4.6%
Human Resources	14	4.3%
Human Rights	11	3.4%
Humanitarian Affairs	2	0.6%
Information Management	1	0.3%
Information Systems and Technology	23	7.1%
Legal Affairs	4	1.2%
Logistics	36	11.1%
Medical Services	4	1.2%
Political Affairs	21	6.5%
Procurement	7	2.2%
Programme Management	13	4.0%
Public Information	16	4.9%
Rule of Law	13	4.0%
Security	52	16.0%
Social Affairs	2	0.6%
Transport	10	3.1%
Total	**325**	

Source: DPKO PMSS.

UNMIT Personnel Gender Statistics: 30 September 2007

Personnel Type	Male	Female	Percentage Male	Percentage Female
Troops	—	—	—	—
Military Observers	36	1	97.3%	2.7%
Police	1,537	94	94.2%	5.8%
International Civilian Staff	208	117	64.0%	36.0%
Local Civilian Staff	637	128	83.3%	16.7%
Total	**2,418**	**340**	**87.7%**	**12.3%**

Sources: DPKO FGS; DPKO PD; DPKO PMSS.

UNMIT Fatalities: Inception–September 2007

Personnel Type

Time Period	Troop	MilOb	Police	Intl Staff	Local Staff	Other[a]	Total
2006	—	—	—	—	1	—	1
August-September	—	—	—	—	—	—	—
October-December	—	—	—	—	1	—	1
2007 (Jan-Sep)	—	—	1	—	—	—	1
January-March	—	—	—	—	—	—	—
April-June	—	—	1	—	—	—	1
July-September	—	—	—	—	—	—	—
Total Fatalilties	—	—	**1**	—	**1**	—	**2**

Incident Type

Time Period	Malicious Act	Illness	Accident	Other[b]	Total
2006	1	—	—	—	1
August-September	—	—	—	—	—
October-December	1	—	—	—	1
2007 (Jan-Sep)	—	—	—	1	1
January-March	—	—	—	—	—
April-June	—	—	—	1	1
July-September	—	—	—	—	—
Total Fatalilties	**1**	—	—	**1**	**2**

Source: DPKO Situation Centre.
Notes: a. Other refers to consultants, UNVs, etc.
b. Incident type is unknown, uncertain or under investigation. Other includes what were previously qualified as self-inflicted.

UNMIT Vehicles: 30 September 2007

Contingent Owned Vehicles		UN Owned Vehicles	
Vehicle Type	Quantity	Vehicle Type	Quantity
Combat Vehicles	16	4x4 Vehicles	854
Communications Vehicle	1	Ambulances	5
Material Handling Equipment	3	Automobiles	3
Support Vehicles (Commercial Pattern)	91	Boat	1
Support Vehicles (Military Pattern)	41	Buses	73
Trailers	15	Material Handling Equipment	23
Total	**167**	Trucks	23
		Vans	10
		Total	**992**

Sources: DPKO Contingent Owned Equipment and Property Management Section; DPKO Surface Transport Section.

UNMIT Aircraft: 30 September 2007

	Transport Fixed Wing	Transport Helicopter	Attack Helicopter
Commercial	1	4	—
Contingent Owned	—	—	—
Total	**1**	**4**	—

Source: DPKO Air Transport Section.

UNMIT Budget and Expenditures (in thousands of US dollars)

Category	Budgeted Jul 06–Jun 07	Expenditures Jul 06–Jun 07	Budgeted Jul 07–Jun 08
Military Observers	1,106.7	1,047.5	1,389.4
Military Contingents	—	—	—
Civilian Police	21,321.5	25,559.8	24,209.0
Formed Police Units	12,892.7	12,302.5	16,536.0
International Staff	26,570.6	21,477.8	43,566.1
Local Staff	3,252.1	2,719.2	4,281.4
United Nations Volunteers	7,605.4	6,783.9	4,417.9
General Temporary Assistance	670.3	74.1	316.8
Government-provided Personnel	—	—	—
Civilian Electoral Observers	—	—	—
Consultants	612.2	503.8	143.4
Official Travel	1,781.5	1,633.2	1,799.5
Facilities and Infrastructure	34,782.1	16,983.5	16,015.1
Ground Transportation	23,154.9	22,315.3	2,311.5
Air Transportation	9,220.1	7,093.1	12,348.7
Naval Transportation	—	—	—
Communications and Information Technology	31,306.5	23,022.8	11,202.7
Supplies, Services and Equipment	10,443.3	5,332.3	14,372.3
Quick-impact Projects	100.0	—	250.0
Gross Requirements	**184,819.9**	**146,848.8**	**160,589.9**
Staff Assessment Income	3,836.8	1,606.0	—
Net Requirements	**180,983.1**	**145,242.8**	**160,589.9**
Voluntary Contributions in Kind (budgeted)	—	—	—
Total Requirements	**184,819.9**	**146,848.8**	**160,589.9**

Sources: UN Documents A/61/802, A/61/852/Add.17, A/C.5/61/22 and A/C.5/61/24; DPKO FMSS.
Notes: Financial figures are preliminary and subject to change. Gross requirements for July 2007–June 2008 budgeted include pro-rated costs of $7,430.1 thousand.

UNMIT Expenditures on Contingent Owned Equipment: July 2006–June 2007 (in thousands of US dollars)

Major Equipment	1,901.8
Self-sustainment	1,324.6

Source: DPKO FMSS.

UNMIT Voluntary Contributions: July 2006–June 2007 (in thousands of US dollars)

Contributor	Contributions in Kind (budgeted)	Contributions in Kind (non-budgeted)	Contributions in Cash (budgeted)	Total
Australia	—	51.0	—	51.0
Total	**—**	**51.0**	**—**	**51.0**

Source: DM OPPBA.

7.17 UNMOGIP (UN Military Observer Group in India and Pakistan)

UNMOGIP Key Facts	
Latest Key Resolution	21 December 1971 (date of issue and effect) UNSC Res. 307 (to continue thereafter, until the Security Council decides otherwise)
First Mandate	21 April 1948, effective 1 January 1949 UNSC Res. 47 (no determined duration)
Acting Chief Military Observer	Colonel Jarmo Helenius (Finland)
First Chief Military Observer	Brigadier H.H. Angle (Canada)

UNMOGIP Personnel: July 2006–June 2007

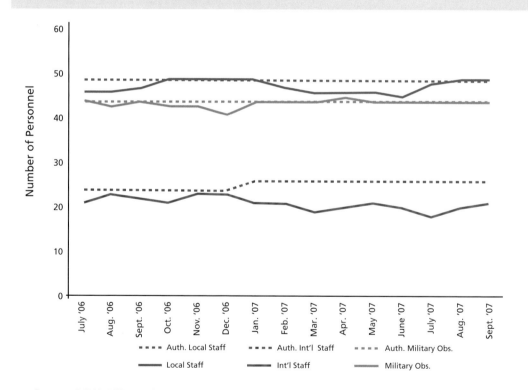

Sources: DPKO FGS; DPKO PMSS.

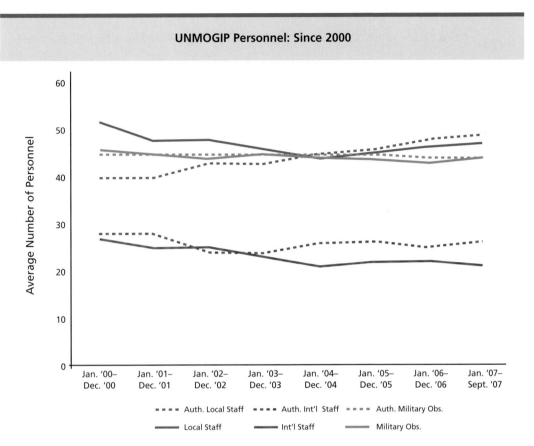

UNMOGIP Personnel: Since 2000

Sources: UN Documents: A/56/6 (Sect.5), A/58/6 (Sect.5) and A/60/6 (Sect.5); DPKO FGS; DPKO PMSS.

UNMOGIP Military and Police Contributors: 30 September 2007

Contributing Country	Troops	Military Observers	Police	Total
Republic of Korea	—	9	—	9
Croatia	—	8	—	8
Italy	—	7	—	7
Finland	—	6	—	6
Sweden	—	6	—	6
Denmark	—	4	—	4
Chile	—	2	—	2
Uruguay	—	2	—	2
Total	—	**44**	—	**44**

Source: DPKO FGS.

UNMOGIP International Civilian Personnel Occupations: 30 September 2007

Occupation	International Staff	Percentage International Staff
Administration	2	9.5%
Aviation	—	—
Civil Affairs	—	—
Economic Affairs	—	—
Engineering	2	9.5%
Finance	1	4.8%
Human Resources	2	9.5%
Human Rights	—	—
Humanitarian Affairs	—	—
Information Management	1	4.8%
Information Systems and Technology	8	38.1%
Legal Affairs	—	—
Logistics	—	—
Medical Services	—	—
Political Affairs	—	—
Procurement	2	9.5%
Programme Management	—	—
Public Information	—	—
Rule of Law	1	4.8%
Security	—	—
Social Affairs	—	—
Transport	2	9.5%
Total	**21**	

Source: DPKO PMSS.

UNMOGIP Personnel Gender Statistics: 30 September 2007

Personnel Type	Male	Female	Percentage Male	Percentage Female
Troops	—	—	—	—
Military Observers	43	1	97.7%	2.3%
Police	—	—	—	—
International Civilian Staff	16	5	76.2%	23.8%
Local Civilian Staff	47	2	95.9%	4.1%
Total	**106**	**8**	**93.0%**	**7.0%**

Sources: DPKO FGS; DPKO PMSS.

UNMOGIP Fatalities: Inception–September 2007

Personnel Type

Time Period	Troop	MilOb	Police	Intl Staff	Local Staff	Other[a]	Total
1949–1999	5	1	—	1	2	—	9
2000	—	—	—	—	—	—	—
2001	—	—	—	—	—	—	—
2002	—	—	—	—	1	—	1
2003	—	—	—	—	—	—	—
2004	—	—	—	—	—	—	—
2005	—	—	—	1	—	—	1
2006	—	—	—	—	—	—	—
January-March	—	—	—	—	—	—	—
April-June	—	—	—	—	—	—	—
July-September	—	—	—	—	—	—	—
October-December	—	—	—	—	—	—	—
2007 (Jan-Sep)	—	—	—	—	—	—	—
January-March	—	—	—	—	—	—	—
April-June	—	—	—	—	—	—	—
July-September	—	—	—	—	—	—	—
Total Fatalities	**5**	**1**	**—**	**2**	**3**	**—**	**11**

Incident Type

Time Period	Malicious Act	Illness	Accident	Other[b]	Total
1949–1999	—	1	8	—	9
2000	—	—	—	—	—
2001	—	—	—	—	—
2002	—	1	—	—	1
2003	—	—	—	—	—
2004	—	—	—	—	—
2005	—	—	1	—	1
2006	—	—	—	—	—
January-March	—	—	—	—	—
April-June	—	—	—	—	—
July-September	—	—	—	—	—
October-December	—	—	1	—	1
2007 (Jan-Sep)	—	—	—	—	—
January-March	—	—	—	—	—
April-June	—	—	—	—	—
July-September	—	—	—	—	—
Total Fatalities	**—**	**2**	**9**	**—**	**11**

Source: DPKO Situation Centre.
Notes: a. Other refers to consultants, UNVs, etc.
 b. Incident type is unknown, uncertain, or under investigation. Other includes what were previously qualified as self-inflicted.

UNMOGIP Vehicles: 30 September 2007

UN Owned Vehicles

Vehicle Type	Quantity
4x4 Vehicles	42
Ambulance	1
Automobiles	3
Buses	12
Trailers	5
Trucks	3
Total	**66**

Source: DPKO Surface Transport Section.

UNMOGIP Budget and Expenditures (in thousands of US dollars)

Category	Allotment Jan 06–Dec 07	Estimated Expenditures Jan 06–Dec 07
Posts	7,934.5	5,778.0
Other Staff Costs	2,691.4	2,146.0
Hospitality	2.5	0.7
Operational Requirement	5,167.6	4,517.0
Total	**15,796.0**	**12,441.7**

Source: DPKO FMSS.
Note: Financial figures are preliminary and subject to change.

UNMOGIP Mission Expenditures: January 2000 to December 2005 (in thousands of US dollars)

Category	Jan 00–Dec 01	Jan 02–Dec 03	Jan 04–Dec 05
Posts	5,574.1	6,370.9	6,482.6
Other Staff Costs	1,593.5	1,983.8	2,038.7
Official Travel	865.9	1,247.5	1,309.6
Contractual Services	—	38.9	21.5
General Operating Expenses	1,772.6	1,174.3	1,995.9
Hospitality	2.3	2.5	2.3
Supplies and Materials	1,022.4	800.1	355.7
Furniture and Equipment	1,332.0	1,107.6	2,527.5
Total Requirements	**12,162.8**	**12,725.6**	**14,733.8**

Source: DPKO FMSS.

7.18 UNOCI (UN Operation in Côte d'Ivoire)

UNOCI Key Facts	

Latest Key Resolutions	16 July 2007 (date of issue and effect)
	  UNSC Res. 1765 (six month duration)
	29 June 2007 (date of issue); 1 July 2007 (date of effect)
	  UNSC Res. 1763 (sixteen day duration)
	10 January 2007 (date of issue and effect)
	  UNSC Res. 1739 (twenty-one day and five month duration
	  and temporary authorization to redeploy troops between
	  UNMIL and UNOCI)
	15 December 2006 (date of issue and effect)
	  UNSC Res. 1726 (twenty-six day duration)

First Mandate	27 February 2004 (date of issue); 4 April 2004 (date of effect) UNSC Res. 1528 (twelve month duration)
SRSG and Head of Mission	Choi Young-jin (Republic of Korea) SG letter of appointment 22 October 2007
First SRSG	Albert Tevoedjre (Benin)

Force Commander	Major-General Fernand Marcel Amoussou (Benin)
	  SG letter of appointment 30 August 2006
	  Entry on duty 24 August 2005

First Force Commander	Major-General Abdoulaye Fall (Senegal)
Police Commissioner	Major-General Gerardo Cristian Chaumont (Argentina) Date of appointment 4 April 2006

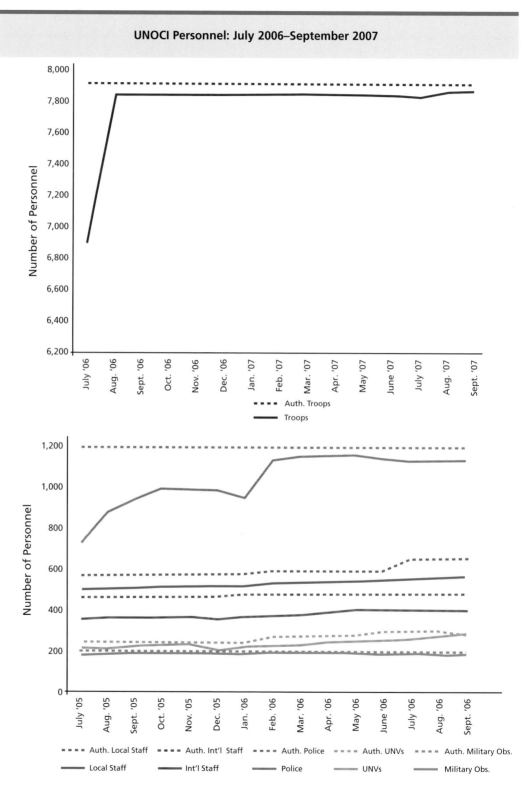

UNOCI Personnel: July 2006–September 2007

Sources: UN Documents S/RES/1609, S/RES/1682 and S/RES/1739; DPKO FGS; DPKO PD; DPKO PMSS; UNV Programme.

Note: Figures do not include government-provided personnel.

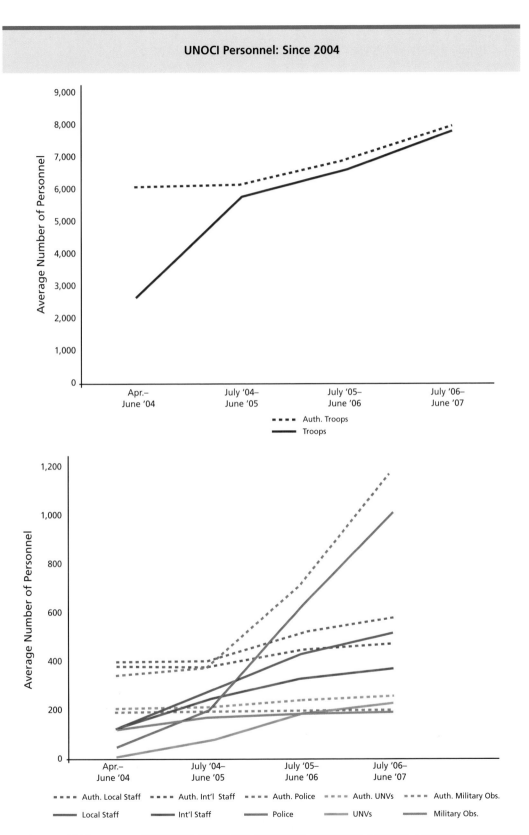

Sources: UN Documents S/RES/1528, S/RES/1609, S/RES/1682, S/RES/1739, A/59/750, A/60/630 and A/61/673; DPKO FGS; DPKO PD; DPKO PMSS; UNV Programme.

UNOCI Military and Police Contributors: 30 September 2007

Contributing Country	Troops	Military Observers	Police	Total	Contributing Country	Troops	Military Observers	Police	Total
Bangladesh	2,757	12	250	3,019	Romania	—	7	—	7
Jordan	1,058	7	382	1,447	Turkey	—	—	6	6
Pakistan	1,123	11	127	1,261	Guatemala	—	5	—	5
Morocco	724	—	—	724	Tunisia	1	4	—	5
Ghana	542	6	6	554	Canada	—	—	4	4
Benin	428	8	48	484	Central African Republic	—	—	4	4
Niger	384	6	56	446	Dominican Republic	—	4	—	4
Senegal	333	10	77	420	Republic of Guinea	—	4	—	4
Togo	319	6	1	326	Argentina	—	—	3	3
France	186	2	10	198	Bolivia	—	3	—	3
Cameroon	—	—	57	57	El Salvador	—	3	—	3
Djibouti	—	—	25	25	Gambia	—	3	—	3
Burundi	—	—	18	18	Nepal	—	3	—	3
Nigeria	—	5	11	16	Peru	—	3	—	3
Rwanda	—	—	14	14	Serbia	—	3	—	3
Madagascar	—	—	13	13	Tanzania	2	1	—	3
Chad	—	3	9	12	Uganda	2	1	—	3
Russia	—	11	—	11	Croatia	—	2	—	2
Yemen	—	6	4	10	Ethiopia	—	2	—	2
India	—	7	2	9	Ireland	—	2	—	2
Kenya	4	5	—	9	Moldova	—	2	—	2
Paraguay	2	7	—	9	Poland	—	2	—	2
Philippines	3	2	4	9	Switzerland	—	—	2	2
Uruguay	—	4	4	8	Zambia	—	2	—	2
Brazil	3	4	—	7	Zimbabwe	—	2	—	2
China	—	7	—	7	Ecuador	—	1	—	1
					Total	**7,871**	**188**	**1,137**	**9,196**

Sources: DPKO FGS; DPKO PD; DPKO PMSS.
Note: Police figures include formed police units provided by Bangladesh (249), Jordan (375) and Pakistan (125).

UNOCI Military Units: 30 September 2007

Number	Unit Type	Countries
1	Aviation Unit	Ghana
1	Communications Company	Bangladesh
3	Engineering Companies	Bangladesh, France, Pakistan
1	Guard and Administration Company	Bangladesh
1	Gendarme Security Company	Benin-Ghana-Niger-Senegal-Togo Composite
9	Infantry Battalions	Bangladesh (3), Benin, Ghana, Jordan, Morocco, Niger, Pakistan
2	Infantry Companies	Senegal, Togo
2	Level II Hospitals	Bangladesh, Ghana
1	Special Forces Company	Jordan
1	Transport Company	Pakistan

Source: DPKO FGS.
Note: Military headquarters staff and military observers not included.

UNOCI International Civilian Personnel Occupations: 30 September 2007

Occupation	International Staff	Percentage International Staff
Administration	53	13.1%
Aviation	10	2.5%
Civil Affairs	6	1.5%
Economic Affairs	—	—
Engineering	16	4.0%
Finance	14	3.5%
Human Resources	12	3.0%
Human Rights	11	2.7%
Humanitarian Affairs	—	—
Information Management	2	0.5%
Information Systems and Technology	39	9.6%
Legal Affairs	1	0.2%
Logistics	75	18.5%
Medical Services	3	0.7%
Political Affairs	43	10.6%
Procurement	8	2.0%
Programme Management	11	2.7%
Public Information	18	4.4%
Rule of Law	14	3.5%
Security	46	11.4%
Social Affairs	5	1.2%
Transport	18	4.4%
Total	**405**	

Source: DPKO PMSS.

UNOCI Personnel Gender Statistics: 30 September 2007

Personnel Type	Male	Female	Percentage Male	Percentage Female
Troops	7,808	63	99.2%	0.8%
Military Observers	178	10	94.7%	5.3%
Police	1,107	30	97.4%	2.6%
International Civilian Staff	283	122	69.9%	30.1%
Local Civilian Staff	432	136	76.1%	23.9%
Total	**9,808**	**361**	**96.4%**	**3.6%**

Sources: DPKO FGS; DPKO PD; DPKO PMSS.

UNOCI Fatalities: Inception–September 2007

Personnel Type

Time Period	Troop	MilOb	Police	Intl Staff	Local Staff	Other[a]	Total
2004	—	—	—	—	—	—	—
2005	10	1	1	1	2	—	15
2006	11	—	1	—	1	—	13
January-March	—	—	1	—	—	—	1
April-June	3	—	—	—	—	—	3
July-September	6	—	—	—	1	—	7
October-December	2	—	—	—	—	—	2
2007 (Jan-Sep)	4	—	2	2	—	—	8
January-March	1	—	1	2	—	—	4
April-June	2	—	1	—	—	—	3
July-September	1	—	—	—	—	—	1
Total Fatalities	**25**	**1**	**4**	**3**	**3**	**—**	**36**

Incident Type

Time Period	Malicious Act	Illness	Accident	Other[b]	Total
2004	—	—	—	—	—
2005	1	8	3	3	15
2006	—	4	8	1	13
January-March	—	1	—	—	1
April-June	—	2	1	—	3
July-September	—	—	6	1	7
October-December	—	1	1	—	2
2007 (Jan-Sep)	—	1	3	4	8
January-March	—	1	1	2	4
April-June	—	—	2	1	3
July-September	—	—	—	1	1
Total Fatalities	**1**	**13**	**14**	**8**	**36**

Source: DPKO Situation Centre.
Notes: a. Other refers to consultants, UNVs, etc.
b. Incident type is unknown, uncertain or under investigation. Other includes what were previously qualified as self-inflicted.

UNOCI Vehicles: 30 September 2007

Contingent Owned Vehicles		UN Owned Vehicles	
Vehicle Type	Quantity	Vehicle Type	Quantity
Aircraft/Airfield Support Equipment	4	4x4 Vehicles	829
Combat Vehicles	173	Aircraft/Airfield Support Equipment	5
Communications Vehicles	5	Ambulances	8
Engineering Vehicles	90	Automobiles	7
Material Handling Equipment	18	Buses	75
Naval Vessels	2	Engineering Vehicles	2
Support Vehicles (Commercial Pattern)	355	Material Handling Equipment	36
Support Vehicles (Military Pattern)	967	Trailers	12
Trailers	361	Trucks	98
Total	**1,975**	Vans	9
		Total	**1,081**

Sources: DPKO Contingent Owned Equipment and Property Management Section; DPKO Surface Transport Section.

UNOCI Aircraft: 30 September 2007

	Transport Fixed Wing	Transport Helicopter	Attack Helicopter
Commercial	3	4	—
Contingent Owned	—	3 (Ghana)	—
Total	**3**	**7**	**—**

Source: DPKO Air Transport Section.

UNOCI Budget and Expenditures (in thousands of US dollars)

Category	Budgeted Jul 06–Jun 07	Expenditures Jul 06–Jun 07	Budgeted Jul 07–Jun 08
Military Observers	9,777.3	10,006.2	9,943.6
Military Contingents	182,845.4	185,688.7	192,574.6
Civilian Police	19,922.5	18,548.9	20,205.4
Formed Police Units	18,708.0	17,613.3	19,715.9
International Staff	63,109.8	58,210.6	68,003.7
Local Staff	12,097.0	12,161.0	15,015.1
United Nations Volunteers	8,480.6	9,953.4	8,135.3
General Temporary Assistance	1,062.5	656.2	316.9
Government-provided Personnel	424.6	216.0	404.6
Civilian Electoral Observers	—	—	—
Consultants	189.9	163.0	301.9
Official Travel	1,647.6	3,527.2	2,742.6
Facilities and Infrastructure	58,016.1	50,646.0	46,925.1
Ground Transportation	19,615.0	16,367.1	10,645.0
Air Transportation	37,388.4	31,869.0	38,499.8
Naval Transportation	79.2	4.9	72.4
Communications and Information Technology	21,757.3	19,397.8	20,097.3
Supplies, Services and Equipment	16,768.1	14,744.9	16,256.9
Quick-impact Projects	1,000.0	995.4	1,000.0
Gross Requirements	**472,889.3**	**468,955.4**	**493,698.4**
Staff Assessment Income	8,020.1	—	9,379.3
Net Requirements	**464,869.2**	**468,955.4**	**484,319.1**
Voluntary Contributions in Kind (budgeted)	—	—	—
Total Requirements	**472,889.3**	**468,955.4**	**493,698.4**

Sources: UN Documents A/61/468 and A/61/852/Add.12; DPKO FMSS.
Notes: Financial figures are preliminary and subject to change. Gross requirements for July 2006–June 2007 expenditures include pro-rated costs of $18,185.8 thousand. Gross requirements for July 2007–June 2008 budgeted include pro-rated costs of $22,842.3 thousand.

UNOCI Expenditures on Contingent Owned Equipment: July 2006–June 2007 (in thousands of US dollars)

Major Equipment	38,967.1
Self-sustainment	30,628.4

Source: DPKO FMSS.

UNOCI Mission Expenditures: April 2004–June 2006 (in thousands of US dollars)

Category	Apr 04–Jun 04	Jul 04–Jun 05	Jul 05–Jun 06
Military and Police Personnel	29,354.7	152,773.2	185,684.0
Civilian Personnel	5,000.1	45,790.7	66,985.2
Operational Requirements	48,708.4	138,326.6	129,599.7
Other	—	—	—
Gross Requirements	**83,063.2**	**336,890.5**	**382,268.9**
Staff Assessment Income	547.3	4,906.3	6,878.8
Net Requirements	**82,515.9**	**331,984.2**	**375,390.1**
Voluntary Contributions in Kind (budgeted)	—	—	—
Total Requirements	**83,063.2**	**336,890.5**	**382,268.9**

Sources: UN Documents A/59/750, A/60/643 and A/61/673.

UNOMIG (UN Observer Mission in Georgia)

UNOMIG Key Facts	
Latest Key Resolutions	15 October 2007 (date of issue and effect)
	UNSC Res. 1781 (six month duration)
	13 April 2007 (date of issue and effect)
	UNSC Res. 1752 (six month duration)
	13 October 2006 (date of issue and effect)
	UNSC Res. 1716 (six month duration)
First Mandate	24 August 1993 (date of issue and effect)
	UNSC Res. 858 (six month duration)
SRSG and Head of Mission	Jean Arnault (France)
	SG letter of appointment 14 July 2006
First Special Envoy	Edouard Brunner (Switzerland)
Chief Military Observer	Major-General Niaz Muhammad Khan Khattak (Pakistan)
	Entry on duty 8 August 2005
First Chief Military Observer	Brigadier-General John Hviedergaard (Denmark)
Senior Police Advisor	Oleksiy Telychkin (Ukraine)
	Date of appointment 23 October 2006

UNOMIG Personnel: July 2006–September 2007

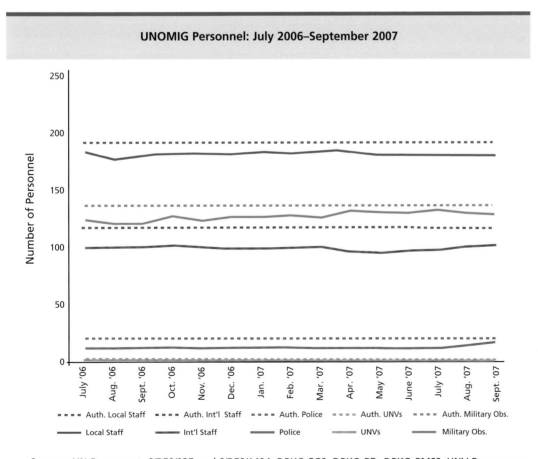

Sources: UN Documents S/RES/937 and S/RES/1494; DPKO FGS; DPKO PD; DPKO PMSS; UNV Programme.

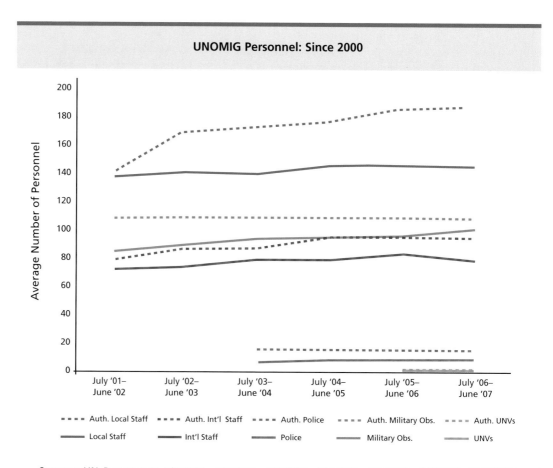

UNOMIG Personnel: Since 2000

Sources: UN Documents A/56/721, A/57/676, A/58/639, A/59/622, A/60/643, A/61/700, S/RES/937 and S/RES/1494; DPKO FGS; DPKO PD; DPKO PMSS; UNV Programme.

UNOMIG Military and Police Contributors: 30 September 2007

Contributing Country	Troops	Military Observers	Police	Total	Contributing Country	Troops	Military Observers	Police	Total
Germany	—	12	2	14	Indonesia	—	4	—	4
Pakistan	—	11	—	11	Albania	—	3	—	3
Bangladesh	—	8	—	8	France	—	3	—	3
Czech Republic	—	5	2	7	Uruguay	—	3	—	3
Hungary	—	7	—	7	Austria	—	2	—	2
Jordan	—	7	—	7	Croatia	—	2	—	2
Poland	—	5	2	7	Lithuania	—	2	—	2
Republic of Korea	—	7	—	7	Philippines	—	—	2	2
Ukraine	—	5	2	7	Romania	—	2	—	2
Russia	—	4	2	6	United States	—	2	—	2
Switzerland	—	4	2	6	Bolivia	—	1	—	1
Denmark	—	5	—	5	Ghana	—	—	1	1
Greece	—	5	—	5	Moldova	—	1	—	1
Sweden	—	3	2	5	Mongolia	—	1	—	1
Turkey	—	5	—	5	Nepal	—	1	—	1
United Kingdom	—	5	—	5	Yemen	—	1	—	1
Egypt	—	4	—	4	**Total**	—	130	17	147

Sources: DPKO FGS; DPKO PD.

UNOMIG Military Units: 30 September 2007

Number	Unit Type	Country
1	Level 1 Medical Unit	Germany

Source: DPKO FGS.
Note: Military observers not included.

UNOMIG International Civilian Personnel Occupations: 30 September 2007

Occupation	International Staff	Percentage International Staff
Administration	12	11.8%
Aviation	2	2.0%
Civil Affairs	3	2.9%
Economic Affairs	—	—
Engineering	5	4.9%
Finance	5	4.9%
Human Resources	2	2.0%
Human Rights	3	2.9%
Humanitarian Affairs	—	—
Information Management	—	—
Information Systems and Technology	8	7.8%
Legal Affairs	1	1.0%
Logistics	7	6.9%
Medical Services	—	—
Political Affairs	7	6.9%
Procurement	4	3.9%
Programme Management	1	1.0%
Public Information	1	1.0%
Rule of Law	2	2.0%
Security	31	30.4%
Social Affairs	—	—
Transport	8	7.8%
Total	**102**	

Source: DPKO PMSS.

UNOMIG Personnel Gender Statistics: 30 September 2007

Personnel Type	Male	Female	Percentage Male	Percentage Female
Troops	—	—	—	—
Military Observers	125	5	96.2%	3.8%
Police	14	3	82.4%	17.6%
International Civilian Staff	79	23	77.5%	22.5%
Local Civilian Staff	122	59	67.4%	32.6%
Total	**340**	**90**	**79.1%**	**20.9%**

Sources: DPKO FGS; DPKO PD; DPKO PMSS.

UNOMIG Fatalities: Inception–September 2007

Personnel Type

Time Period	Troop	MilOb	Police	Intl Staff	Local Staff	Other[a]	Total
1995–1999	1	2	—	1	—	—	4
2000	—	—	—	—	—	—	—
2001	4	—	—	—	—	—	4
2002	—	—	—	—	—	—	—
2003	1	—	—	—	—	—	1
2004	—	—	—	—	—	—	—
2005	—	—	—	—	1	—	1
2006	—	—	—	—	1	—	1
January-March	—	—	—	—	—	—	—
April-June	—	—	—	—	—	—	—
July-September	—	—	—	—	1	—	1
October-December	—	—	—	—	—	—	—
2007 (Jan-Sep)	—	—	—	—	—	—	—
January-March	—	—	—	—	—	—	—
April-June	—	—	—	—	—	—	—
July-September	—	—	—	—	—	—	—
Total Fatalities	**6**	**2**	**—**	**1**	**2**	**—**	**11**

Incident Type

Time Period	Malicious Act	Illness	Accident	Other[b]	Total
1995–1999	3	—	1	—	4
2000	—	—	—	—	—
2001	4	—	—	—	4
2002	—	—	—	—	—
2003	—	1	—	—	1
2004	—	—	—	—	—
2005	1	—	—	—	1
2006	—	—	1	—	1
January-March	—	—	—	—	—
April-June	—	—	—	—	—
July-September	—	—	1	—	1
October-December	—	—	—	—	—
2007 (Jan-Sep)	—	—	—	—	—
January-March	—	—	—	—	—
April-June	—	—	—	—	—
July-September	—	—	—	—	—
Total Fatalities	**8**	**1**	**2**	**—**	**11**

Source: DPKO Situation Centre.
Notes: a. Other refers to consultants, UNVs, etc.
b. Incident type is unknown, uncertain or under investigation. Other includes what were previously qualified as self-inflicted.

UNOMIG Vehicles: 30 September 2007

Contingent Owned Vehicles		UN Owned Vehicles	
Vehicle Type	Quantity	Vehicle Type	Quantity
Support Vehicles (Commercial Pattern)	2	4x4 Vehicles	151
Total	**2**	Ambulances	3
		Automobiles	7
		Buses	13
		Material Handling Equipment	7
		Trailer	1
		Trucks	12
		Vans	5
		Total	**199**

Sources: DPKO Contingent Owned Equipment and Property Management Section; DPKO Surface Transport Section.

UNOMIG Aircraft: 30 September 2007

	Transport Fixed Wing	Transport Helicopter	Attack Helicopter
Commercial	1	1	—
Contingent Owned	—	—	—
Total	**1**	**1**	—

Source: DPKO Air Transport Section.

UNOMIG Budget and Expenditures (in thousands of US dollars)

Category	Budgeted Jul 06–Jun 07	Expenditures Jul 06–Jun 07	Budgeted Jul 07–Jun 08
Military Observers	3,647.4	3,665.4	4,066.0
Military Contingents	64.7	62.5	64.7
Civilian Police	498.6	409.1	644.8
Formed Police Units	—	—	—
International Staff	15,080.7	14,553.7	16,219.3
Local Staff	3,173.5	3,291.8	3,790.2
United Nations Volunteers	33.2	31.4	43.4
General Temporary Assistance	214.5	7.9	49.3
Government-provided Personnel	—	—	—
Civilian Electoral Observers	—	—	—
Consultants	—	46.0	—
Official Travel	525.0	406.2	518.2
Facilities and Infrastructure	2,575.4	2,657.8	2,462.2
Ground Transportation	1,434.3	1,424.7	1,674.7
Air Transportation	2,903.1	2,570.8	2,687.0
Naval Transportation	—	—	—
Communications and Information Technology	2,616.1	2,312.2	2,265.4
Supplies, Services and Equipment	611.4	858.4	524.6
Quick-impact Projects	—	—	—
Gross Requirements	**33,377.9**	**33,746.5**	**36,708.2**
Staff Assessment Income	2,226.6	—	2,372.9
Net Requirements	**31,151.3**	**33,746.5**	**34,335.3**
Voluntary Contributions in Kind (budgeted)	—	—	—
Total Requirements	**33,377.9**	**33,746.5**	**36,708.2**

Sources: UN Documents A/C.5/61/22 and A/C.5/61/24; DPKO FMSS.
Notes: Financial figures are preliminary and subject to change. Gross requirements for July 2006–June 2007 expenditures include pro-rated costs of $1,448.6 thousand. Gross requirements for July 2007–June 2008 budgeted include pro-rated costs of $1,698.4 thousand.

UNOMIG Expenditures on Contingent Owned Equipment: July 2006–June 2007 (in thousands of US dollars)

Major Equipment	62.5
Self-sustainment	25.2

Source: DPKO FMSS.

UNOMIG Mission Expenditures: July 2000–June 2006 (in thousands of US dollars)

Category	Jul 00–Jun 01	Jul 01–Jun 02	Jul 02–Jun 03	Jul 03–Jun 04	Jul 04–Jun 05	Jul 05–Jun 06
Military and Police Personnel	3,701.8	3,466.6	3,345.0	3,670.6	3,887.7	3,953.6
Civilian Personnel	10,770.0	13,581.4	14,595.1	15,941.0	16,653.1	17,601.0
Operational Requirements	8,285.7	8,236.6	10,881.6	10,866.3	10,529.8	9,595.4
Other	1,491.5	—	—	—	—	—
Gross Requirements	**24,249.0**	**25,284.6**	**28,821.7**	**30,477.9**	**31,070.6**	**31,150.0**
Staff Assessment Income	1,752.0	1,749.1	1,920.3	2,139.8	2,161.6	2,191.3
Net Requirements	**22,497.0**	**23,535.5**	**26,901.4**	**28,338.1**	**28,909.0**	**28,958.7**
Voluntary Contributions in Kind (budgeted)	—	—	—	—	—	—
Total Requirements	**24,249.0**	**25,284.6**	**28,821.7**	**30,477.9**	**31,070.6**	**31,150.0**

Sources: UN Documents A/56/721, A/57/676, A/58/639, A/59/622, A/60/643 and A/61/700.

7.20 UNTSO (UN Truce Supervision Organization)

UNTSO Key Facts

Latest Key Resolution	23 October 1973 (date of issue and effect) UNSC Res. 339 (to continue thereafter, until the Security Council decides otherwise)
First Mandate	29 May 1948 (date of issue and effect) UNSC Res. 50 (no duration determined)
Chief of Staff	Major-General Ian Campbell Gordon (Australia) SG letter of appointment 10 November 2006 Entry on duty 1 December 2007
First Chief of Staff	Colonel Count Thord Bonde (Sweden)

UNTSO Personnel: July 2006–September 2007

Sources: DPKO FGS; DPKO PMSS.

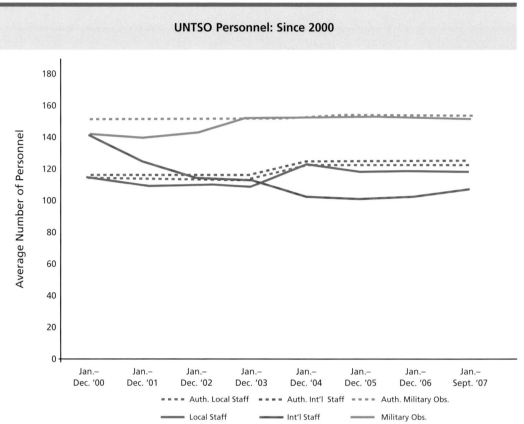

UNTSO Personnel: Since 2000

Sources: UN Documents A/54/6 (Sect.5), A/56/6 (Sect.5), A/58/6 (Sect.5), A/60/6 (Sect.5) and A/60/9 (Sect.5); DPKO FGS; DPKO PMSS.

UNTSO Military and Police Contributors: 30 September 2007

Contributing Country	Troops	Military Observers	Police	Total	Contributing Country	Troops	Military Observers	Police	Total
Finland	—	15	—	15	Argentina	—	5	—	5
Ireland	—	14	—	14	Russia	—	4	—	4
Australia	—	12	—	12	Chile	—	3	—	3
Denmark	—	12	—	12	China	—	3	—	3
Norway	—	12	—	12	Nepal	—	3	—	3
Netherlands	—	11	—	11	United States	—	3	—	3
Switzerland	—	9	—	9	Belgium	—	2	—	2
Canada	—	8	—	8	Estonia	—	2	—	2
New Zealand	—	8	—	8	France	—	2	—	2
Sweden	—	7	—	7	Slovakia	—	2	—	2
Austria	—	6	—	6	Slovenia	—	2	—	2
Italy	—	6	—	6	**Total**	—	**151**	—	**151**

Source: DPKO FGS.

UNTSO International Civilian Personnel Occupations: 30 September 2007

Occupation	International Staff	Percentage International Staff
Administration	28	26.7%
Aviation	—	—
Civil Affairs	—	—
Economic Affairs	—	—
Engineering	3	2.9%
Finance	5	4.8%
Human Resources	5	4.8%
Human Rights	—	—
Humanitarian Affairs	—	—
Information Management	3	2.9%
Information Systems and Technology	10	9.5%
Legal Affairs	1	1.0%
Logistics	5	4.8%
Medical Services	2	1.9%
Political Affairs	2	1.9%
Procurement	2	1.9%
Programme Management	—	—
Public Information	—	—
Rule of Law	2	1.9%
Security	24	22.9%
Social Affairs	—	—
Transport	13	12.4%
Total	**105**	

Source: DPKO PMSS.

UNTSO Personnel Gender Statistics: 30 September 2007

Personnel Type	Male	Female	Percentage Male	Percentage Female
Troops	—	—	—	—
Military Observers	143	8	94.7%	5.3%
Police	—	—	—	—
International Civilian Staff	86	19	81.9%	18.1%
Local Civilian Staff	105	17	86.1%	13.9%
Total	**334**	**44**	**88.4%**	**11.6%**

Sources: DPKO FGS; DPKO PMSS.

UNTSO Fatalities: Inception–September 2007

Personnel Type

Time Period	Troop	MilOb	Police	Intl Staff	Local Staff	Other[a]	Total
1948–1999	18	12	—	6	3	—	39
2000	—	—	—	—	—	—	—
2001	—	—	—	—	—	—	—
2002	—	—	—	—	—	—	—
2003	—	—	—	—	1	—	1
2004	—	1	—	1	—	—	2
2005	—	1	—	1	—	—	2
2006	—	4	—	—	—	—	4
January-March	—	—	—	—	—	—	—
April-June	—	—	—	—	—	—	—
July-September	—	4	—	—	—	—	4
October-December	—	—	—	—	—	—	—
2007 (Jan-Sep)	—	—	—	—	—	—	—
January-March	—	—	—	—	—	—	—
April-June	—	—	—	—	—	—	—
July-September	—	—	—	—	—	—	—
Total Fatalities	**18**	**18**	**—**	**8**	**4**	**—**	**48**

Incident Type

Time Period	Malicious Act	Illness	Accident	Other[b]	Total
1948–1999	25	5	8	1	39
2000	—	—	—	—	—
2001	—	—	—	—	—
2002	—	—	—	—	—
2003	—	1	—	—	1
2004	—	1	1	—	2
2005	1	1	—	—	2
2006	—	—	4	—	4
January-March	—	—	—	—	—
April-June	—	—	—	—	—
July-September	—	—	4	—	4
October-December	—	—	—	—	—
2007 (Jan-Sep)	—	—	—	—	—
January-March	—	—	—	—	—
April-June	—	—	—	—	—
July-September	—	—	—	—	—
Total Fatalities	**26**	**8**	**13**	**1**	**48**

Source: DPKO Situation Centre.
Notes: a. Other refers to consultants, UNVs, etc.
  b. Incident type is unknown, uncertain or under investigation. Other includes what were previously qualified as self-inflicted.

UNTSO Vehicles: 30 September 2007

UN Owned Vehicles

Vehicle Type	Quantity
4x4 Vehicles	143
Automobiles	22
Buses	22
Material Handling Equipment	3
Trailers	5
Trucks	17
Vans	5
Total	**217**

Source: DPKO Surface Transport Section.

UNTSO Budget and Expenditures (in thousands of US dollars)

Category	Allotment Jan 06–Dec 07	Estimated Expenditures Jan 06–Dec 07
Posts	43,179.4	12,390.1
Other Staff Costs	10,230.1	36,678.6
Official Travel	2,221.4	—
Contractual Services	—	—
General Operating Expenses	3,428.6	—
Hospitality	10.1	9.2
Supplies and Materials	1,078.9	—
Furniture and Equipment	2,397.4	—
Grants and Contributions	—	—
Other Expenditures	—	7,094.9
Total	**62,545.9**	**56,172.8**

Sources: UN Document A/60/9(Sect.5); DPKO FMSS.
Notes: Financial figures are preliminary and subject to change. Expenditures 2006–2007 are as of 30 November 2007.

UNTSO Mission Expenditures: January 2000–December 2005 (in thousands of US dollars)

Category	Jan 00–Dec 01	Jan 02–Dec 03	Jan 04–Dec 05
Posts	30,532.2	31,679.1	33,215.7
Other Staff Costs	8,547.1	9,588.0	10,443.2
Hospitality	—	7.8	7.6
Official Travel	1,793.3	2,658.2	2,763.5
Contractual Services	—	49.5	39.7
General Operating Expenses	2,538.2	3,422.8	5,010.0
Supplies and Materials	1,117.1	982.0	1,035.3
Furniture and Equipment	1,614.5	1,498.4	3,214.7
Total Requirements	**46,142.4**	**49,885.8**	**55,729.7**

Sources: UN Documents A/58/6 (Sect.5) and A/60/6(Sect.5); DPKO FMSS.

8 Statistics on The African Union Mission in Sudan

This chapter contains data on the African Union Mission in Sudan (AMIS). Military, police and civilian personnel data was provided by the Darfur Integrated Task Force (DITF) in Addis Ababa. Information on the military, including military observers and civilian police, covers the period from May 2004 to October 2007. Additional data on the status of the mission in September are provided in Chapter 6. Financial data was provided by the Finance Unit of the AU's Peace and Security Department and shows the budget for the period from January–June 2007 but does include expenditures. Notes are included to explain any discrepancies and/or omissions.

AMIS Key Facts

Latest Key Decisions	22 June 2007 (date of issue); 1 July 2007 (date of effect) PSC/RR/Comm(LXXIX) (six month duration pending AU-UN hybrid deployment) 27 December 2006 (date of issue) UNSC press statement welcoming letter of 23 December 2006 from President Al-Bashir on deployment of a hybrid AU-UN force in Darfur
First Decision	25 May 2004 (establishment of AMIS)
Head of Mission	Rodolphe Adada (Congo-Brazzaville)
First Head of Mission	Ambassador Babagana Kingibe (Nigeria)
Force Commander	General Martin Luther Agwai (Nigeria)
First Force Commander	General Festus Okonkwo (Nigeria)
Civilian Police Commissioner	Mohase Elias Tsiloane (South Africa)
First Civilian Police Commissioner	Anand Pillay (South Africa)

Note: The Head of Mission and the Force Commander continued as heads of the hybird AU-UN Mission.

AMIS Personnel: July 2004–October 2007

Date	Troops		AU Military Observers		Police		Support Staff	
	Actual	Authorized	Actual	Authorized	Actual	Authorized	Actual	Authorized
May-04	—	300	—	60	—	—	—	—
Jun-07	—	300	—	60	—	—	—	—
Jul-04	—	300	22	80	—	—	—	—
Oct-04	310	300	66	450	—	815	—	—
Jan-05	790	1,703	285	450	7	815	12	132
Apr-05	1,647	5,398	376	773	245	1,560	26	132
May-05	1,735	5,398	458	773	413	1,560	26	132
Nov-05	4,878	5,398	559	773	1,175	1,560	27	173
Apr-06	4,863	5,398	567	773	1,400	1,560	32	173
Aug-06	5,228	5,398	646	773	1,456	1,560	45	173
Aug-07	5,222	5,398	611	773	1,416	1,560	75	173
Oct-07	5,222	6,788	549	613	1,416	1,560	75	173

Source: AU DITF.

AMIS Personnel: July 2004–October 2007

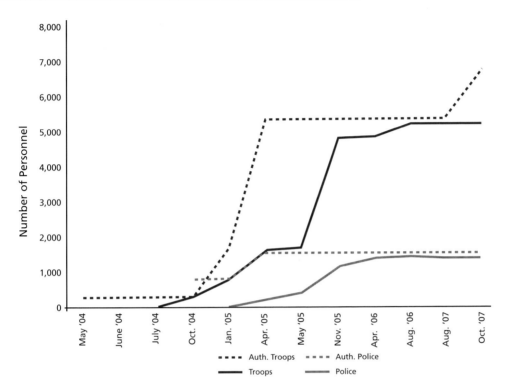

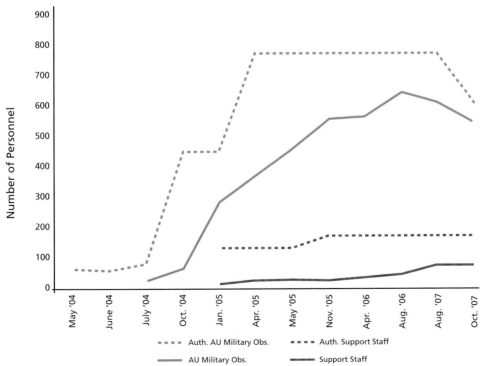

Source: AU DITF.

AMIS Military and Police Contributors: 31 August 2007

Country	Troops	Military Observers	Police	Total
Nigeria	2040	63	201	2304
Rwanda	1756	34	72	1862
South Africa	592	39	126	757
Senegal	538	36	54	628
Ghana	—	23	427	450
Gambia	196	20	94	310
Zambia	—	46	64	110
Kenya	60	45	—	105
Mali	—	45	40	85
Egypt	—	34	50	84
Cameroon	—	30	51	81
Uganda	—	5	76	81
Burundi	—	10	39	49
Niger	—	—	43	43
Burkina Faso	—	4	36	40
Chad	40	—	—	40
Mauritania	—	20	15	35
Malawi	—	25	—	25
Gabon	—	24	—	24
Namibia	—	24	—	24
Madagascar	—	9	9	18
Lesotho	—	5	12	17
Congo (Brazz)	—	15	—	15
Mozambique	—	15	—	15
Algeria	—	13	—	13
Botswana	—	10	2	12
Libya	—	9	—	9
Togo	—	8	—	8
Mauritius	—	—	5	5
Total	**5,222**	**611**	**1,416**	**7,249**

Source: AU DITF.
Notes: Parties' representatives not included. Refer to Chapter 6 for principal contributors as of 30 September 2007.

AMIS Military Units: 31 August 2007

Number	Unit Type	Countries
1	Engineering Company	South Africa
1	Explosive Ordinance Disposal Section	South Africa
1	Headquarters Company	Gambia
8	Infantry Battalions	Nigeria (3), Rwanda (3), Senegal, South Africa
1	Infantry Platoon	Chad
2	Military Police Platoons	Kenya
1	Platoon	Chad

Source: AU DITF.

MILITARY CONTRIBUTIONS
TO THE AFRICAN UNION MISSION IN SUDAN (AMIS)

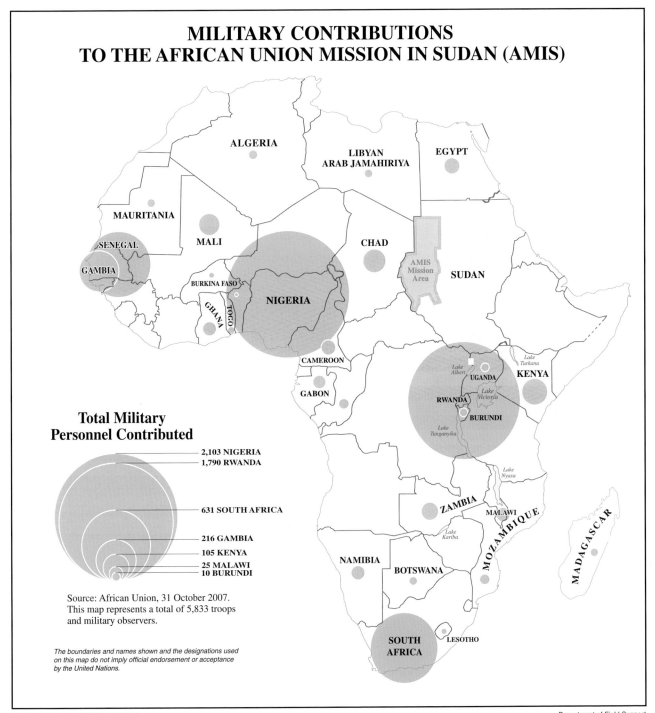

ALGERIA

LIBYAN
ARAB JAMAHIRIYA

EGYPT

MAURITANIA

SENEGAL

GAMBIA

MALI

BURKINA FASO

GHANA

TOGO

NIGERIA

CHAD

AMIS
Mission
Area

SUDAN

CAMEROON

GABON

Lake
Albert

UGANDA

Lake
Turkana

KENYA

RWANDA

Lake
Victoria

BURUNDI

Lake
Tanganyika

Lake
Nyasa

ZAMBIA

MALAWI

MOZAMBIQUE

MADAGASCAR

Lake
Kariba

NAMIBIA

BOTSWANA

SOUTH
AFRICA

LESOTHO

Total Military
Personnel Contributed

2,103 NIGERIA
1,790 RWANDA

631 SOUTH AFRICA

216 GAMBIA
105 KENYA
25 MALAWI
10 BURUNDI

Source: African Union, 31 October 2007.
This map represents a total of 5,833 troops
and military observers.

*The boundaries and names shown and the designations used
on this map do not imply official endorsement or acceptance
by the United Nations.*

Map No. 4291 Rev. 1   UNITED NATIONS
November 2007

Department of Field Support
Cartographic Section

AMIS International Civilian Personnel Nationality: 31 August 2007

Nationality	International Staff	Percentage of International Staff
Ethiopia	15	20.0%
Benin	8	10.7%
Nigeria	6	8.0%
Ghana	5	6.7%
Rwanda	5	6.7%
Cameroon	4	5.3%
Tanzania	4	5.3%
Botswana	2	2.7%
Burundi	2	2.7%
Gambia	2	2.7%
Senegal	2	2.7%
South Africa	2	2.7%
Uganda	2	2.7%
Zambia	2	2.7%
Zimbabwe	2	2.7%
Algeria	1	1.3%
Chad	1	1.3%
DR Congo	1	1.3%
Djibouti	1	1.3%
Malawi	1	1.3%
Mali	1	1.3%
Mauritania	1	1.3%
Niger	1	1.3%
Sierra Leone	1	1.3%
Tunisia	1	1.3%
N/A	2	2.7%
Total	**75**	

Source: AU DITF.
Notes: Includes military staff officers. Two international staff personnel nationalities are unaccounted for as of the date of publication.

AMIS International Civilian Personnel Occupations: 31 August 2007

Occupation	International Staff	Percentage International Staff
Administration	4	5.3%
Communications and Information Technology	1	1.3%
Economic Affairs	—	—
Financial Management	18	24.0%
Gender Advisory	—	—
Human Resources	—	—
Human Rights	3	4.0%
Humanitarian Affairs	3	4.0%
Information	1	1.3%
Legal Affairs	1	1.3%
Logistics	4	5.3%
Medical	19	25.3%
Military Advisory	1	1.3%
Mission Management	8	10.7%
Political Affairs	7	9.3%
Procurement	3	4.0%
Public Information/Affairs	2	2.7%
Total	**75**	

Source: AU DITF.

AMIS International Civilian Personnel Occupations: 31 August 2007

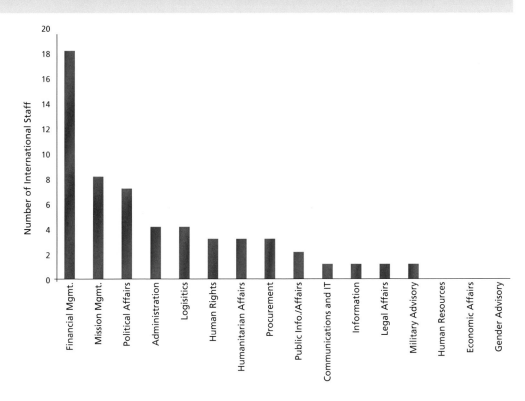

Source: AU DITF.

AMIS Fatalities: Inception–August 2006

	Appointment Type			
Time Period	Military	Police	Civilian	Total
2004	—	—	—	—
2005	7	1	2	10
2006	8	4	3	15
January-March	1	—	—	1
April-June	3	1	1	5
July-September	2	3	1	6
October-December	2	—	1	3
2007 (Jan-Sep)	22	2	3	27
January-March	5	1	2	8
April-June	7	1	1	9
July-September	10	—	—	10
Total Fatalities	**37**	**7**	**8**	**52**

	Incident Type				
Time Period	Malicious Act	Illness	Accident	Other/Unknown	Total
2004	—	—	—	—	—
2005	4	4	2	—	10
2006	6	5	2	2	15
January-March	1	—	—	—	1
April-June	2	1	1	1	5
July-September	3	3	—	—	6
October-December	—	1	1	1	3
2007 (Jan-Sep)	22	2	—	3	27
January-March	5	1	—	2	8
April-June	7	1	—	1	9
July-September	10	—	—	—	10
Total Fatalities	**32**	**11**	**4**	**5**	**52**

Source: AU DITF.

AMIS Vehicles: 31 October 2007

UN Owned Vehicles

Vehicle Type	Quantity
4X4 Vehicles	877
Armored Personnel Carriers	103
Automobiles	2
Buses	4
Material Handling Equipment	2
Trucks	173
Total	**1,161**

Source: AU DITF.
Note: Figures do not include 62 vehicles that have been hijacked or destroyed.

AMIS Aircraft: 31 August 2007

	Transport Fixed Wing	Transport Helicopter	Attack Helicopter
Commercial	4	—	—
Contingent Owned	—	—	—
Other	—	25 (Canada)	—
Total	**4**	**25**	**—**

Source: AU DITF.

AMIS Budget Estimate: January-June 2007 (in thousands of US dollars)

Category	Budget
Salaries and Allowances	50,021.6
Ration Expenses	18,301.5
Troop Reimbursement	18,846.0
Pre-deployment Expenses	14,217.0
Travel and Transportation	49,549.9
Life Insurance	7,000.0
Medical Expenses	4,996.0
Procurement and Supplies	1,208.5
Other Operating Costs	408.0
Rental Utilities and Services	5,003.1
Fixed Assets	37,355.5
Facilities and Infrastructure	70,622.0
Related Activities	20,110.5
Total Requirements	**297,639.5**

Source: AU PSD Finance Unit.

Index

Abdul Wahid Mohammed al-Nur, 74
Abdullahi Yusuf Ahmed, 121
Abkhazia-Georgia, 90–91
Adada, Rodolphe, 77
Afghanistan: Afghanistan Compact, 33;
    Afghanistan National Development
    Strategy, 37, 38; Afghan National
    Army, 32, 34; background, 32–33;
    Bonn Agreement, 32, 33; Comprehen-
    sive Approach Team, 39; coordination,
    strategic, 37–39; corruption within, 32,
    35; counterinsurgency, 32, 34; drug
    economy, 32, 35; EU Police Mission
    in Afghanistan, 181; governmental
    institutions, few effective, 35; hybrid
    operations creating confusion, 11;
    International Security Assistance
    Force, 2, 4, 24, 26, 32–39, 175; Joint
    Coordination and Monitoring Board,
    37, 38; Operation Enduring Freedom,
    24, 32–34; partnerships, peace opera-
    tion, 24, 26, 37–39; police reforms,
    32, 35; Policy Action Group, 38–39;
    provincial reconstruction teams, 33,
    35–38; reconstruction activities, 33,
    35–38; security and political develop-
    ments, 32, 33–34; September 11th
    terrorist attacks in US, 16; summary
    (strategic 2007) and conclusions, 2,
    6, 7, 39; UN Assistance Mission, 24,
    32–39, 230–238
Africa in 2007, strategic summary for,
    2–8. See also individual countries
African Peace Facility, 4, 27
African Standby Force (ASF), 75
African Union (AU): African Standby
    Force, 75; Comoros, 103–105; Côte
    d'Ivoire, 106; deployment, patterns of,
    4; funding mechanisms, predictable,
    26–27; overview, 2; partnerships,
    peace operation, 22–27; Somalia, 3,
    95, 129–130. See also AU listings
Agwai, Martin L., 77
Ahtisaari, Martti, 49–53
al-Bashir, Omar, 102
Algiers Agreement of 2000 (Ethiopia
    and Eritrea), 110

Ali Mohamed Gedi, 129
Alkatiri, Mari, 84, 85
al-Maliki, Nouri, 119
Al-Qaida, 64, 65, 67, 114
AMIS. See AU Mission in Sudan
AMISEC. See AU Mission in Support of
    Elections in Comoros
AMISOM. See AU Mission in Somalia
An Agenda for Peace, 36
Angola, 10, 45
Annan, Kofi, 110
Architect Engineers, 59
Argentina, 70
Aristide, Jean-Bertrand, 112
Arrogance and the mediation process,
    13–14
Arroyo, Gloria M., 119
Arusha Accords in 2000 (Burundi), 96
ASF. See African Standby Force
Ashdown, Paddy, 93
AU. See African Union
AU Electoral and Security Assistance
    Mission in Comoros (MAES), 103,
    180
AU Mission in Somalia (AMISOM), 96,
    129–130, 180
AU Mission in Sudan (AMIS), 24,
    73–77, 101, 180, 357–365
AU Mission in Support of Elections in
    Comoros (AMISEC), 103
Australia: Iraq, 112; partnerships, peace
    operation, 23, 25, 26; Solomon Islands,
    127–128; summary (strategic 2007), 4;
    Timor-Leste, 82, 84, 85, 88

Bacar, Mohamed, 103
Bai Koroma, Ernest, 117
Ban Ki-Moon, 7, 49, 54, 73, 80, 118, 130
Bangladesh, 4
Bangui Peace Agreement in 1997
    (Central African Republic), 99
al-Bashir, Omar, 102
Bedie, Konan, 106
Belgium, 45
Bemba, Jean P., 43
BINUB. See UN Integrated Office
    in Burundi

Bonn Agreement (Afghanistan), 32, 33
BONUCA. See UN Peacebuilding Support
    Office in the Central African Republic
Bosnia and Herzegovina, 23–26, 93–95,
    182, 186, 190
Bozizé, Francois, 99
Brahimi Report, 36, 85
Bryant, Gyude, 60
Burundi, 23, 96–98, 130, 200–203
Bush, George W., 117

Campaoré, Blaise, 105–107
Capstone Doctrine, 36
Carter, Jimmy, 73
Ceku, Agim, 52
Central African Republic (CAR), 2, 7,
    24, 99–100, 180, 182
Chad: Central African Republic, relations
    with, 101, 102; Darfur, relations with,
    101–102; displaced people, internally,
    101; EU Force in the Republic of Chad
    and the Central African Republic, 99,
    182; legitimacy and ownership,
    questions of, 26; partnerships, peace
    operation, 24; rebel groups based
    in Darfur, 101–102; refugees from
    Sudan and Central African Republic,
    101–102; Sudan, relations with, 76;
    summary (strategic 2007), 2, 4, 7; UN
    Mission in the Central African
    Republic and Chad, 101
Child protection advisers (CPAs), 47
CIS Peacekeeping Force (CISPKF) in
    Abkhazia-Georgia, 90, 180
CIS-South Ossetia Joint Peacekeeping
    Forces (JPKF), 131, 181
Civilian personnel, maintaining a supply
    of, 7. See also Statistics listings
Columbia, 115
Commonwealth of Independent States
    (CIS), 4, 23, 90, 131, 180–181
Comoros, 103–104
Complexity/breadth, peace operations
    growing in, 12
Compromise and dialogue. See Mediation
Congo. See Democratic Republic
    of Congo

Côte d'Ivoire: background, 105; citizenship identification process, 106; elections, 106; Forces Nouvelles, 105–106; Liberia, relations with, 58, 63; mediation process, 10; Operation Licorne, 4, 23, 105–106, 184; Ouagadougou Agreement, 106; overview, 101; partnerships, peace operation, 23; progress in peace process, lack of, 107; sexual scandal involving UN military personnel, 104; state authority, reestablishing, 107; summary (strategic 2007), 4; UN Operation in Côte d'Ivoire, 105–107; zone of confidence, dismantling of the, 106

Country Assistance Strategy (CAS), World Bank's, 43–44

Cyprus, 108–109, 254–262

Darfur: Chad, relations with, 101–102; mediation, 10; partnerships, peace operation, 22, 24–25, 27; summary (strategic 2007), 2–4. *See also* Sudan

Dayton Accords in 1995 (Bosnia and Herzegovina), 93

de Soto, Alvaro, 7

Déby, Idriss, 101, 102

Democratic Republic of Congo (DRC): background, 41–43; brassage process, 44–45, 47; Central African Republic, relations with, 97; Commission Nationale de Désarmenent Demobilsation et Réinsertion, 45, 46; Congrès National pour la Défense du Peuple, 46; Country Assistance Framework, 43; disarming/demobilization/reintegration, 41, 43, 44–45, 47; economic reconstruction, 43–44; EU Advisory and Assistance Mission for DRC Security Reform, 186; EU Force Democratic Republic of Congo, 23; EU Police Mission in Kinshasa, 186; EU Police Mission in the Democratic Republic of Congo, 42, 188; EU Security Sector Reform Mission in the Democratic Republic of Congo, 42; Forces Armées du République Démocratique du Congo, 43, 45, 48; Forces Armées Rwandaises, 45; Forces Démocratiques de la Libération du Rwanda, 43, 45; Forces de Résistance Patriotique d'Ituri, 47; human rights violations, 47–48; Interhamwe, 45; Lusaka Cease-Fire Agreement, 42; mixage process and renewed violence in the East, 45–46; Movement for Liberation of the Congo, 42; Operation Artemis, 23, 25, 42; overview, 41; partnerships, peace operation, 23–25; People's Party for Reconstruction and Development, 42; police reforms, 41, 44; political and security developments, 43; Rassemblement Congolais pour la Démocratie, 42; security sector reform, 41, 44–45;

summary/conclusions, 46–48; summary (strategic 2007), 3; Union des Patriotes Congolais, 47; UN Organization Mission in the Democratic Republic of Congo, 25, 41–48, 220–229

Denmark, 117, 133

Dialogue and compromise. *See* Mediation

Dnestr River, 121

Dorbor, Andrew, 58

Dyilo, Thomas L., 47

DynCorp, 59

East Timor. *See* Timor-Leste

ECOMICI. *See* ECOWAS Mission in Côte d'Ivoire

ECOMIL. *See* ECOWAS Mission in Liberia

Economic Community of West African States (ECOWAS): Côte d'Ivoire, 106; Liberia, 58; partnerships, peace operation, 22–23, 25, 26; Sierra Leone, 125

Economic reconstruction, 7. *See also individual countries/Missions*

ECOWAS Mission in Côte d'Ivoire (ECOMICI), 106

ECOWAS Mission in Liberia (ECOMIL), 58

ECOWAS. *See* Economic Community of West African States

Egypt, 69, 71–72

Eido, Walid, 67

El Salvador, 6

Eliasson, Jan, 74

Eritrea, 4, 23, 24, 110–111, 279–287

Ernest Bai Koroma, 125

Ethiopia, 4, 23, 24, 110–11, 129–130, 279–287

EU Advisory and Assistance Mission for DRC Security Reform (EUSEC DR CONGO), 186

EU BAM Rafah. *See* EU Border Assistance Mission at Rafah

EU Border Assistance Mission at Rafah (EU BAM Rafah), 24, 69, 71, 187

EUFOR Althea. *See* EU Force in Bosnia and Herzegovina

EU Force Democratic Republic of Congo (EUFOR RD Congo), 23

EU Force in Bosnia and Herzegovina (EUFOR Althea), 92, 182

EU Force in the Republic of Chad and the Central African Republic (EUFOR TCHAD/RCA), 101, 182

EUFOR RD Congo. *See* EU Force Democratic Republic of Congo

EUFOR TCHAD/RCA. *See* EU Force in the Republic of Chad and the Central African Republic

EUMM. *See* EU Monitoring Mission

EU Monitoring Mission (EUMM), 181

EUPM. *See* EU Police Mission in Bosnia and Herzegovina

EUPOL Afghanistan. *See* EU Police Mission in Afghanistan

EUPOL COPPS. *See* EU Police Mission for the Palestinian Territories

EU Police Mission for the Palestinian Territories (EUPOL COPPS), 69, 187

EU Police Mission in Afghanistan (EUPOL Afghanistan), 188

EU Police Mission in Bosnia and Herzegovina (EUPM), 93, 186

EU Police Mission in Kinshasa (EUPOL Kinshasa), 180

EU Police Mission in the Democratic Republic of Congo (EUPOL RD Congo), 42, 188

EUPOL Kinshasa. *See* EU Police Mission in Kinshasa

EUPOL RD Congo. See EU Police Mission in the Democratic Republic of Congo

EU Security Sector Reform Mission in the Democratic Republic of Congo (EUSEC Congo), 42

European Security and Defense Policy (ESDP), 49

European Union (EU): Afghanistan, 35; African Peace Facility, 4; Bosnia and Herzegovina, 93–96; Chad, 101; Côte d'Ivoire, 106; Democratic Republic of Congo, 42, 43; deployment, patterns of, 4; European Security and Defense Policy, 27; Kosovo, 49–53; Lebanon, 66; Liberia, 60, 62; Moldova-Transdniestria, 121–122; overview, 2; Palestinian territories, 69, 71; partnerships, peace operation, 22–26; Sri Lanka, 124. *See also* EU *listings*

EUSEC DR CONGO. *See* EU Advisory and Assistance Mission for DRC Security Reform

False promises and the mediation process, 17

FARDC. *See* Forces Armées du République Démocratique du Congo

Fatah al-Islam, 64, 67

Fatah, 69, 71

Fatalities, an analysis of UN peacekeeping, 70, 160–161

FDLR. *See* Forces Démocratiques de la Libération du Rwanda

Feith, Peter, 54

Finland, 131

Fomboni Accords (Comoros), 103

FOMUC. *See* Force Multinational de la Communauté Économique et Monétaire de l'Afrique Centrale

Force Multinational de la Communauté Économique et Monétaire de l'Afrique Centrale (FOMUC), 99–100, 180

Forces Armées du République Démocratique du Congo (FARDC), 43, 45, 48

Forces Démocratiques de la Libération du Rwanda (FDLR), 43, 45
France: Abkhazia-Georgia, 90; Côte d'Ivoire, 105; Middle East, 72; partnerships, peace operation, 23, 26; summary (strategic 2007), 4
Frente Popular para la Liberación de Saguia el-Hamra y de Río de Oro (POLISARIO) in Western Sahara, 134–135
Frente Revolucionária do Timor-Leste Independente (FRETILIN), 83, 86, 88
FRETILIN. See Frente Revolucionária do Timor-Leste Independente
Funding mechanisms and peace operation partnerships, 26–27

Gabon, 90
Gaye, Babacar, 46
Gaza Strip, 24, 64, 69, 71–72, 187
Gbagbo, Laurent, 105–107
Gedi, Ali Mohamed, 129
Gemayel, Pierre, 67
Gender and policing in UN peace operations, 61, 85
Georgia, 23, 90–91, 117, 131–132
Germany, 90
Ghana, 130
Ghanem, Antoine, 67
Global Peace Operations Initiative, 4
Graziano, Claudio, 65
Guéhenno, Jean-Marie, 36
Guinea, 58
Gulf War in 1991, 16
Gusmão, Xanana, 83, 84

Haiti: background, 112–113; border control and building state institutions, 114; deployment in, patterns of, 4; elections, 113, 114; gangs in Port-au-Prince slums, 113; gender and policing in UN peace operations, 61; HIV/AIDS, 87; International Civilian Mission in Haiti, 23; judicial system, reforming the, 114; overview, 112; partnerships, peace operation, 23–25; policing issues, 61, 85, 114; political processes, situations mitigating against legitimate, 112–113; proving ground for broader approach by UN, 2; root causes of persistent conflict, need to address, 114; security and political issues, interplay of, 6; sexual scandal involving peacekeepers, 115; stabilization but a tenuous peace, 114–115; UN Civilian Police Mission in Haiti, 112; UN Mission in Haiti, 85; UN Stabilization Mission in Haiti, 61, 112–15, 211–219; UN Support Mission in Haiti, 112; UN Transition Mission in Haiti, 112
Hamas, 64, 69, 71
Haradinaj, Ramush, 52

Hariri, Rafiq, 64
Haroun, Ahmed, 80
Hassan, Ishaya I., 75
Haste and the mediation process, 15–16
Hebron, 71, 176
Hezbollah, 64, 66, 68
HIV/AIDS, 87
Human Development Report (2002), 83
Human Development Report (2006), 88
Human rights, violations of, 47–48, 126
Hussein, Saddam, 117
Hybrid operations creating confusion, 11. See also Partnerships, peace operation

Iceland, 133
IGAD. See Inter-Governmental Authority on Development
Ignorance and the mediation process, 12–13
Impotence and the mediation process, 15
India, 4, 116
Indonesia, 82
Inflexibility and the mediation process, 16–17
Insulza, José M., 110
Integrated operations and peace operation partnerships, 24, 25
INTERFET. See International Force for East Timor
Inter-Governmental Authority on Development (IGAD), 129
Inter-institutional arrangements, 8. See also Partnerships, peace operation
International Civilian Mission in Haiti (MICIVIH), 24
International Compact with Iraq in 2007, 117
International Criminal Court (ICC), 47, 48
International Criminal Tribunal for the former Yugoslavia, 95
International Force for East Timor (INTERFET), 23
International Labor Organization (ILO), 60
International Monetary Fund (IMF), 6, 102
International Monitoring Team (IMT), 119–120, 184
International Organization for Migration, 78
International Police Task Force (IPTF) in Bosnia and Herzegovina, 93
International Security Assistance Force (ISAF) in Afghanistan, 4, 24, 26, 32–39, 182
International Security Forces (ISF), 185
Iraq, 16, 117–118, 183, 185, 238–245
Israel, 64–69, 71–72

Jemaah Islamiah network, 119
Johnson-Sirleaf, Ellen, 57, 58, 62
Joint Control Commission (JCC) Peacekeeping Force, 121–122, 131, 180
Julu, Charles, 58

Kabila, Joseph, 41–43, 45, 47
Kadege, Alphonse-Marie, 97

Kantanga, Germain, 47, 48
Karachi Agreement of 1949 (India and Pakistan), 116
Karadzic, Radovan, 95
Karzai, Hamid, 6, 34
Kayembe, Dieudonné, 46
Kemakeza, Alan, 127
Kiir, Slava, 79
Kokoity, Eduard, 132
Konare, Alpha O., 130
Korea, South, 117
Kosovo: Ahtisaari Plan, 49–56; elections, 54; Kosovo Force, 49, 52, 55–56, 182; limits of the peace operation, 54; OSCE Mission in Kosovo, 52, 191; overview, 2, 49, 51; partnerships, peace operation, 23–26; policing issues, 55–56; political and security issues, interplay of, 5; political environment, local, 10, 53–54; Preparation Team for the International Civilian Office, 54; reconfiguration process, 54; security situation, 5, 54–56; status negotiations, 51–53; summary/conclusions, 56; UN Interim Administration Mission in Kosovo, 24, 26, 49, 51–56, 288–295; UN Office of the Special Envoy for Kosovo, 52
Koukou, George, 58

Lahoud, Emile, 67
Lajcák, Miroslav, 94
Latin America, 4
Lebanon: Al-Qaida, 65; arms trafficking across Syrian-Lebanese border, 68; deployments into, increased troop, 65–66; elections, 67; European participation in, 66; Gemayel, assassination of Pierre, 67; Islamist groups, rise to prominence of extremist, 67; Israel, relations with, 64–68; landmines, clearing of, 66; local communities and peacekeepers, relations between, 65, 66; mediation process, 16; overview, 64–65; partnerships, peace operation, 26; Security Council Resolution 1701, 64–68, 72; security situation, deterioration of the, 67–68; summary (strategic 2007), 4–7; Taif Accords, 16, 65; UN Interim Force in Lebanon, 4–7, 64–68, 263–272
Liberation Tigers of Tamil Elam (LTTE), 133
Liberia: Armed Forces of Liberia, 58; background, 58; Comprehensive Peace Agreement, 58; corruption within, 62; Côte d'Ivoire, relations with, 58, 63; diamonds/timber, UN sanctions against, 60–61; disarmament/demobilization/reintegration, 58; drawdown of UN forces in, 57; economic reconstruction, 60–63; gender and policing in UN peace operations, 61; governance and

economic management assistance program, 61–63; governance and resource management, 60–61; HIV/AIDS, 87; justice sector, revamping the, 59; Liberia Emergency Employment Program-Liberia Employment Action Program, 60; Liberians United for Reconciliation and Democracy, 58; Movement for Democracy in Liberia, 58; National Patriotic Front of Liberia, 58; Operation Calm Down Fear, 58; overview, 57; partnerships, peace operation, 22–23, 25; policing issues, 59; security issues/reform, 58–59; Sierra Leone, relations with, 58, 63; summary (strategic 2007) and conclusions, 4, 7, 63; UN Mission in Liberia, 6, 23, 57–63, 296–305
Linked military-observer operations and peace operation partnerships, 23–24
Lobato, Rogério, 85
Longevity of peace operations, 11–12
LTTE. See Liberation Tigers of Tamil Elam
Lusaka Cease-Fire Agreement (Democratic Republic of Congo), 42

MAES. See AU Electoral and Security Assistance Mission in Comoros
Malaitia, 127
Malaysia, 84, 119–120
al-Maliki, Nouri, 117
Martin, Ian, 84, 123
MDJT. See Mouvement pour la Démocratie et la Justice au TCHAD
Mediation: arrogance, 13–14; challenges to effective exercise of mediator's role, 11–12; false promises, 17; haste, 15–16; ignorance, 12–13; impotence, 15; inflexibility, 16–17; overview, 10–11; partiality, 14–15; summary/conclusions, 17–18
MFO Sinai. See Multinational Force and Observers in Sinai
MICIVIH. See International Civilian Mission in Haiti
Middle East: deployment in, patterns of, 4; EU Border Assistance Mission at Rafah, 24, 69, 71; Multinational Force and Observers in Sinai, 24, 71–72, 183; overview, 64; partnerships, peace operation, 24; summary/conclusions, 72; Temporary International Presence in Hebron, 71, 184; UN Disengagement Observer Force, 68–69; UN Interim Force in Lebanon, 3–5, 64–68; UN Truce Supervision Organization, 69
MILF. See Moro Islamic Liberation Front
Minawi, Minni, 74
Mindanao, Philippines, 19–120
MINURCAT. See UN Mission in the Central African Republic and Chad
MINURSO. See UN Mission for the Referendum in Western Sahara

MINUSTAH. See UN Stabilization Mission in Haiti , 61, 112–115, 211–219
MIPONUH. See UN Civilian Police Mission in Haiti
Mission to Monitor the Implementation of the Bangui Agreements (MISAB), 97
Mladic, Ratko, 94
MNF-I. See Multinational Force in Iraq
Moldova-Transdniestria, 121–122, 180
MONUC. See UN Organization Mission in the Democratic Republic of Congo
Moro Islamic Liberation Front (MILF), 119–120
Morocco, 107, 134–135
Mouvement pour la Démocratie et la Justice au TCHAD (MDJT), 99
Multidimensional operations, 6–7
Multinational Force and Observers in Sinai (MFO Sinai), 24, 71–72, 176
Multinational Force in Iraq (MNF-I), 117, 185
Musharraf, Pervez, 38, 116

Ndayizeye, Domitien, 97
Nepal, 7, 123–124, 306–310
New Zealand, 3, 82, 85, 88
Nigeria, 130
Nkumbi, John, 45
Nkunda, Laurent, 42, 43, 45–46
Nkurunz, Pierre, 95
North Atlantic Council, 33, 38
North Atlantic Treaty Organization (NATO): Bosnia and Herzegovina, 93–95; deployment, patterns of, 4; International Security Assistance Force in Afghanistan, 3, 4, 24, 26, 32–39, 182; Iraq, 112; Kosovo, 49–52, 55–56, 182; North Atlantic Council, 33, 38; partnerships, peace operation, 22–28; political and security issues, interplay of, 5
Norway, 133

OAS Special Mission for Strengthening Democracy in Haiti, 188
OMIK. See OSCE Mission in Kosovo
ONUB. See UN Operation in Burundi
Operation Artemis (Democratic Republic of Congo), 23, 25, 42
Operation Enduring Freedom (OEF) (Afghanistan), 24, 32–34
Operation Licorne (Côte d'Ivoire), 4, 23, 105–107, 184
Organization for Security and Cooperation in Europe (OSCE): Bosnia and Herzegovina, 93, 94; Kosovo, 49, 52; Moldova-Transdniestria, 121; partnerships, peace operation, 22, 24, 25; South Ossetia-Georgia, 131; summary (strategic 2007), 4; Tajikistan, 91. See also OSCE listings
Organization of African Unity (OAU), 103
Organization of American States (OAS), 24, 25, 115, 188

Organization of the Islamic Conference, 119
OSCE Centre in Dushanbe, 91, 190
OSCE Mission in Kosovo (OMIK), 52, 191
OSCE Mission to Bosnia and Herzegovina, 93, 190–191
OSCE Mission to Georgia, 189
OSCE Mission to Moldova, 190
OSCE Spillover Monitor Mission to Skopje, 188
Ouattara, Alassane, 106

Pacific Islands Forum, 26, 127
Pakistan, 4, 34, 116
Palestinian territories, 24, 64, 69, 71–72, 187
Parallel operations and peace operation partnerships, 23–26
Partiality and the mediation process, 14–15
Partnerships, peace operation: Afghanistan, 24, 26, 37–39; benefits and costs, 25–26; Darfur, 24–25; evolving partnerships, background on, 22–23; funding mechanisms, 26–27; integrated operations, 24, 25; legitimacy and ownership, questions of, 26; lessons learned, 26–27; overview, 22; parallel operations, 23–26; personnel issues, 26; planning mechanisms, use of joint, 26; political framework for action, 26; sequential operations, 23, 25, 26; summary/conclusions, 28; trends and policy options, 27–28
Patassé, Ange-Félix, 97
Peace Operations 2010, 36
Pellegrini, Alain, 65
Petreaus, David, 117
Phako, M. E., 97
Philippines, 119–120
Poland, 117
Police institutions, 7, 85. See also individual countries/Missions
POLISARIO. See Frente Popular para la Liberación de Saguia el-Hamra y de Río de Oro
Political and security issues, interplay of, 4–5. See also Mediation; individual countries/Missions
Political framework for action and peace operation partnerships, 26
Portfolio of Police and Law Enforcement Projects 2007, 85
Portugal, 82, 84
Préval, René, 6, 103, 114
Pronk, Jan, 78
Putin, Vladimir, 121

Al-Qaida, 64, 65, 67, 114
Qazi, Ashraf, 79

Rajapakse, Mahinda, 133
Rakhmon, Imomali, 91
Ramos-Horta, José, 85, 86

RAMSI. *See* Regional Assistance Mission in the Solomon Islands

Regional action, 23. *See also* Partnerships, peace operation

Regional Assistance Mission in the Solomon Islands (RAMSI), 127–128, 185

Resolutions, Security Council. *See* Security Council Resolutions

Richards, David, 37

Romania, 17, 121

Royal Solomon Island Police (RSIP), 127

Ruberwa, Azarias, 43

Rugova, Ibrahim, 52

Russia, 3, 53, 90, 121–122, 131–132

Saakashvili, Mikhail, 131

Salim, Salim A., 74

Sanakoyev, Dmitri, 131

Sawyer, Amos, 62

Schwarz-Schilling, Christian, 93–94

Security and political issues, interplay of, 5–6. *See also individual countries/ Missions*

Security Council Resolutions: 937 (Abkhazia-Georgia), 90; 1386 Afghanistan, 32; 1401 (Afghanistan), 32; 1778 (Chad), 101; 1261 (child protection advisers), 47; 1765 (Côte d'Ivoire), 105, 106; 1769 (Darfur), 25, 74, 77; 1279 (Democratic Republic of Congo), 42; 1493 (Democratic Republic of Congo), 42; 1756 (Democratic Republic of Congo), 44; 1325 (gender and policing in UN peace operations), 61; 1608 (Haiti), 108; 1780 (Haiti), 115; 1546 (Iraq), 117; 1770 (Iraq), 116; 1244 (Kosovo), 24, 51–52, 54; 425 (Lebanon), 64; 426 (Lebanon), 64; 1559 (Lebanon), 64; 1701 (Lebanon), 64–68, 72; 1773 (Lebanon), 67; 1626 (Liberia), 62; 1777 (Liberia), 57; 1740 (Nepal), 123; 1725 (Somalia), 129; 1704 (Timor-Leste), 84; 1754 (Western Sahara), 134

Security independence and peace operation partnerships, 27

Senegal, 130

September 11th terrorist attacks in US, 16, 32

Sequential operations and peace operation partnerships, 23, 25, 26

Serbia, 52, 94. *See also* Kosovo

Sexual scandals involving peacekeepers, 107, 115

Sharia, Islamic, 130

Short-term military support and peace operation partnerships, 23, 25

Sierra Leone: background, 125; child protection advisers, 47; elections, 125–126; human rights commission, 126; Liberia, relations with, 58, 63; mediation process, 10; overview, 125; partnerships, peace operation, 22–23;

peacekeeping, contributions to international, 126; UN Assistance Mission in Sierra Leone, 23, 47, 125; UN Integrated Office in Sierra Leone, 125–126, 273–278; UN Peacebuilding Commission, 126

Sigua, David, 91

Simla Agreement of 1972 (India and Pakistan), 116

Sochi Accords in 1992 (South Ossetia-Georgia), 131

Sogavare, Manasseh, 128

Solomon Islands, 4, 26, 127–128, 185

Somalia, 3, 23, 96, 129–130, 180

Soro, Guillaume, 105, 106, 107

South Africa, 45

South Ossetia-Georgia, 131–132

Spain, 67

Special Representative of the Secretary-General (SRSG), 11–12. *See also* Mediation

Spiric, Nicola, 94

Sri Lanka, 133

Statistics on non-UN Missions, global: Africa by organization, deployment of police in, 179; Africa by organization, deployment of troops in, 177; civilian police/Missions, 186–191; cost of military/observer/civilian police and Missions, 192; Europe by organization, deployment of troops in, 178; heads of observer/civilian police and Missions, 193–194; military personnel, contributions of, 173; military personnel to regions, deployment of, 174; observer missions, military and, 180–185; overview, 167–169; police by organization, deployment of, 175; police contributors, top twenty, 170, 172; police to regions, deployment of, 176; troop contributors, top twenty, 170, 171

Statistics on UN Missions, global: Africa by region, origin of military personnel in, 151; Africa by region, origin of police personnel in, 152; budgets, 162–163; civilian personnel, total, 154; civilian staff by occupation, 155–156; fatalities, 160–161; financial contributors, top twenty, 163; gender statistics, 159; mandate renewals, 165; Middle East by region, origin of military personnel in, 153; Mission, troops deployed by UN, 138; observer contributors, top twenty, 141–142; observers, total military, 141; observers deployed by UN Mission, military, 143; personnel, total, 159; police, total, 143; police by UN Mission, formed, 146 police contributors, top twenty, 144, 145; police deployed by UN Mission, 144; police personnel by region, deployment of, 150; police personnel by region, origin of, 149; region, deployment/origin

of military personnel by, 147–148; representation, highest national, 157–158; timeline, operations, 166; troop contributions, top twenty, 139, 140; troops, total, 138

Statistics, UN Mission-by-Mission: overview, 1996; UN Assistance Mission in Afghanistan, 230–237; UN Assistance Mission in Iraq, 238–245; UN Disengagement Observer Force, 246–253; UN Integrated Office in Burundi, 200–203; UN Integrated Office in Sierra Leone, 273–278; UN Interim Administration Mission in Kosovo288–296; UN Interim Force in Lebanon, 263–272; UN Mission for the Referendum in Western Sahara, 204–210; UN Mission in Ethiopia and Eritrea, 279–287; UN Mission in Liberia, 296–305; UN Mission in Nepal, 306–310; UN Mission in Sudan, 311–320; UN Organization Mission in the Democratic Republic of Congo, 220–228; UN Peacekeeping Forced in Cyprus, 254–262; UN Stabilization Mission in Haiti, 211–219

Stockholm International Peace Research Institute (SIPRI), 168

Sudan: AU Mission in Sudan, 24, 73–77, 101, 180; Cease-Fire Commission, 76; Chad, relations with, 76; child protection advisers, 47; civilian staff vacancy rate, 53; Comprehensive Peace Agreement, 6, 73, 81; Darfur-Darfur Dialogue and Consultation, 75; Darfur Peace Agreement, 74–76; disarmament/ demobilization/reintegration, 80; humanitarian situation, 76–77; hybrid operations creating confusion, 11; interethnic and intraethnic fighting, 76; joint integrated units, 80; legitimacy and ownership, questions of, 26; National Petroleum Commission, 79; overview, 73; political and security issues, interplay of, 5; power and wealth sharing, 74–75, 79; security arrangements, 76, 79–80; Sudan Armed Forces, 80; Sudan Liberation Army, 75; Sudan People's Liberation Movement, 73, 80; summary/ conclusions, 80–81; Transitional Darfur Regional Authority, 74; Tripoli peace talks, 74; UN-AU Mission in Darfur, 6, 24–25, 77–78, 101; UN Mission in Sudan, 47, 53, 78–80, 311–320

Summary 2007, strategic: deployment, patterns of, 4–5; multiple dimensions of peace operations, 6–7; numbers, the year in, 2–4; organizational challenges, 7–8; political and security issues, interplay of, 5–6; summary/conclusions, 8; troubled year, 2. *See also* Statistics *listings*

Sweden, 133

Swing, William, 43
Syria, 64, 68–69

Taif Accords (Lebanon), 16, 65
Tajikistan, 23, 91
Taliban fighters, 34, 38
Tanzania, 67
Taylor, Charles, 58, 125
Temporary International Presence in
   Hebron (TIPH), 71, 184
Thaci, Hashim, 54
Timor-Leste: Australian/New Zealand
   troops, 82, 84, 85, 88; background,
   82–83; challenges for new government,
   profound, 86–88; civilian staff vacancy
   rate, 53; Conselho Nacional da Resistencia Timorense, 83; deployment in,
   patterns of, 4; economic reconstruction,
   88; FALINTIL-Forcas Armadas de
   Defesa de Timor-Leste, 83, 84, 88;
   Forcas Armadas da Libertacão Nacional
   de Timor-Leste, 83; Frente Revolucionária do Timor-Leste Independente,
   83, 86, 88; International Force for East
   Timor, 23; multidimensional operations
   in, 6; partnerships, peace operation, 23,
   25; Policia Nacional de Timor-Leste,
   83–86; political tensions, latent, 10;
   security sector reform, 88; summary/
   conclusions, 88; 2006, crisis in, 83–85;
   UN Integrated Mission in Timor-Leste,
   7, 53, 82–88; UN Mission of Support in
   East Timor, 83; UN Office in Timor-
   Leste, 83; UN Transitional Administra-
   tion in East Timor, 23, 82–83
TIPH. *See* Temporary International
   Presence in Hebron
Transdniestria, 121–122, 180
Turkey, 35
Tutu, Desmond, 73

Uganda, 42, 130
Ukraine, 121
UNAMA. *See* UN Assistance Mission in
   Afghanistan
UNAMI. *See* UN Assistance Mission in Iraq
UNAMID. *See* UN-AU Mission in Darfur
UNAMSIL. *See* UN Assistance Mission in
   Sierra Leone
UN Assistance Mission in Afghanistan
   (UNAMA), 24, 32–39, 230–237
UN Assistance Mission in Iraq (UNAMI),
   117–118, 238–245
UN Assistance Mission in Sierra Leone
   (UNAMSIL), 23, 47, 125
UN-AU Mission in Darfur (UNAMID), 6,
   24–25, 77–78, 101
UN Civilian Police Mission in Haiti
   (MIPONUH), 112
UN Department of Peacekeeping Opera-
   tions (DPKO): Capstone Doctrine, 36;
   child protection advisers, 47; HIV/AIDS,

87; Lebanon, 66; partnerships, peace
   operation, 25; summary (strategic 2007),
   7–8
UN Development Assistance Framework
   (UNDAF), 43
UN Disengagement Observer Force
   (UNDOF), 68–69, 246–253
UNDOF. *See* UN Disengagement Observer
   Force
UNFICYP. *See* UN Peacekeeping Forced
   in Cyprus
UN High Commissioner for Refugees
   (UNHCR), 24, 25
UNIFIL. *See* UN Interim Force in
   Lebanon
UN Integrated Mission in Timor-Leste
   (UNMIT), 7, 53, 82–88, 321–327
UN Integrated Office in Burundi (BINUB),
   200–203
UN Integrated Office in Sierra Leone
   (UNIOSIL), 125–126, 273–278
UN Interim Administration Mission in
   Kosovo (UNMIK), 24, 26, 49, 51–56,
   288–296
UN Interim Force in Lebanon (UNIFIL), 4,
   5–6, 64–68, 263–272
Union of Islamic Courts (UIC) in Somalia,
   129–130
UNIOSIL. *See* UN Integrated Office in
   Sierra Leone
United Kingdom (UK), 23, 26, 90
United Nations Development Programme
   (UNDP): Democratic Republic of
   Congo, 44; Liberia, 60; Sierra Leone,
   125; Sudan, 79; summary (strategic
   2007), 6
United Nations: Capstone Doctrine, 36;
   child protection advisers, 47; divisions
   within Security Council and between
   the regional players, 11–12; fatalities,
   an analysis of peacekeeping, 70; gender
   and policing in peace operations, 61,
   85; HIV/AIDS, 87; law enforcement
   projects, portfolio of, 85; September
   11th terrorist attacks in US, 16, 32;
   Special Representative of the Secretary-
   General, 11–12. *See also* Partnerships,
   peace operation; Security Council
   Resolutions; Statistics *listings;* Summary
   2007, strategic; UN *listings*
United States: Abkhazia-Georgia, 90;
   Democratic Republic of Congo, 45;
   fatalities, an analysis of UN peacekeeping, 70; Iraq, 16, 117–118;
   Kosovo, 53; Liberia, 59, 60; part-
   nerships, peace operation, 24, 26;
   September 11th terrorist attacks in US,
   16, 32; US Agency for International
   Development, 60
UNMEE. *See* UN Mission in Ethiopia
   and Eritrea
UNMIH. *See* UN Mission in Haiti

UNMIK. *See* UN Interim Administration
   Mission in Kosovo
UNMIL. *See* UN Mission in Liberia
UN Military Observer Group in India
   land Pakistan (UNMOGIP), 116,
   328–332
UNMIN. *See* UN Mission in Nepal
UNMIS. *See* UN Mission in Sudan
UNMISET. *See* UN Mission of Support
   in East Timor
UN Mission for the Referendum in
   Western Sahara (MINURSO), 134–135,
   296–305
UN Mission in Ethiopia and Eritrea
   (UNMEE), 110–111, 279–287
UN Mission in Haiti (UNMIH), 85
UN Mission in Liberia (UNMIL), 7, 23,
   57–63, 296–305
UN Mission in Nepal (UNMIN), 116–117,
   123–124, 306–310
UN Mission in Sudan (UNMIS), 47, 53,
   78–80, 311–320
UN Mission in the Central African
   Republic and Chad (MINURCAT),
   101
UN Mission of Observers to Tajikistan
   (UNMOT), 23
UN Mission of Support in East Timor
   (UNMISET), 83
UNMIT. *See* UN Integrated Mission in
   Timor-Leste
UNMOGIP. *See* UN Military Observer
   Group in India and Pakistan
UNMOT. *See* UN Mission of Observers
   to Tajikistan
UN Observer Mission in Georgia
   (UNOMIG), 23, 90–91, 343–350
UNOCI. *See* UN Operation in Côte
   d'Ivoire
UN Office in Timor-Leste (UNOTIL), 83
UN Office of the Special Envoy for
   Kosovo (UNOSEK), 52
UNOMIG. *See* UN Observer Mission in
   Georgia
UN Operation in Burundi (ONUB),
   96–97
UN Operation in Côte d'Ivoire (UNOCI),
   105–107, 333–342
UN Organization Mission in the
   Democratic Republic of Congo
   (MONUC), 25, 41–48
UNOSEK. *See* UN Office of the Special
   Envoy for Kosovo
UNOTIL. *See* UN Office in Timor-Leste
UN Peacebuilding Commission, 125
UN Peacebuilding Support Office in the
   Central African Republic (BONUCA),
   99–100
UN Peacekeeping Forced in Cyprus
   (UNFICYP), 108–109, 254–262
UN Secretariat, 24
UNSMIH. *See* UN Support Mission in Haiti

UN Stabilization Mission in Haiti (MINUSTAH), 61, 106–110, 205–213
UN Support Mission in Haiti (UNSMIH), 112
UNTAET. *See* UN Transitional Administration in East Timor
UN Tajikistan Office of Peacebuilding (UNTOP), 91
UNTMIH. *See* UN Transition Mission in Haiti

UNTOP. *See* UN Tajikistan Office of Peacebuilding
UN Transition Mission in Haiti (UNTMIH), 107
UN Transitional Administration in East Timor (UNTAET), 23, 82–83
UN Truce Supervision Organization (UNTSO), 69, 351–365
UNTSO. *See* UN Truce Supervision Organization

US Agency for International Development (USAID), 60

Vieira de Mello, Sergio, 117

West Bank, 64
Western Sahara, 134–135, 204–210
Women in peacekeeping operations, 61, 85
World Bank, 6, 7, 43–44, 60, 79, 106
World Food Programme, 78

About the Book

Unique in its breadth of coverage, the *Annual Review of Global Peace Operations* presents the most detailed collection of data on peace operations—those launched by the UN, by regional organizations, by coalitions, and by individual nations—that is available. Features of the 2008 volume include:

- a summary analysis of the trends and developments in peace operations through 2007
- a discussion of the nature and implications of "peacekeeping partnerships" among institutions involved in field operations
- incisive analyses of all peacekeeping missions on the ground in 2007
- in-depth explorations of key missions, focusing on those that faced significant challenges or underwent major developments during the year
- extensive, full-color maps, figures, and photographs

The editorially independent *Review* is a project of the **Center on International Cooperation** at New York University, with the support of the Peacekeeping Best Practices Section of the UN's Department of Peacekeeping Operations.